HISPANIC CONFEDERATES

Third Edition

By
John O'Donnell-Rosales

CLEARFIELD

All Rights Reserved by John O'Donnell-Rosales.

The text of this publication, or any part thereof, may not be reproduced in any manner whatsoever without written permission from the author.

The artwork and design of the front cover of this publication are the property of John O'Donnell-Rosales, all rights reserved by the author.

The flags on top of the front cover are from left to right:
3rd Confederate National, Spain, and the Confederate Naval Jack.
The flags on the bottom of the front cover are from left to right:
Cuba, Mexico, and Israel.

Copyright © 2006 by John O'Donnell-Rosales
All Rights Reserved.

First Edition
originally published 1997
Reprinted 1998, 2000

Second Edition
originally published 2002

Third Edition printed for
Clearfield Company, Inc., by
Genealogical Publishing Co., Inc.
Baltimore, Maryland
2006

International Standard Book Number: 0-8063-5230-2

Made in the United States of America

DEDICATION

This book is dedicated to my family: Rosa, Florentino, Susie, and Tania; to all my ancestors; and to all the men and women listed in this book. I would like to thank GOD for his blessings and guidance all the days of my life as none of this would have been possible without his assistance.

I would like to thank the following individuals and their families for their encouragement and, in many cases, assistance and advice during the writing of this book. There are others listed who helped me, at other times in my life, and offered me their friendship and counsel. The names follow alphabetically:

Russ Adams (Bienville Books, Mobile, ALA.), Gavin Almeida, Marcia Biggs, Gustavo Carmona, Charlotte Chamberlain, Christina Coxe, Antonio De La Cova, Rachael Dudley, Steven Fishbach, Mr. Foy, Denise Collins Garcia, Andrew Gold, Miriam Cera Gold, Julito Granda, Arthur E. Green, Victoria Griffin, Pat Guy, Eddie Hickman, Joseph Hickman, Chris Hobden, Abe Jardines, Tommy Jardines, Ivette Bastarrechea Jones, Charles Kargleder, Mike Kelly, Alexander Landi, Sara Lee, Gary Lima, Farris Long, Odalys Lopez, David Mader, Larry McAdams, Frank McCloskey, Holly Morales, Darrell Neese, Richard (Buck) Norred, Perry Outlaw, Linda Paulson, Raegan Peacock, Irvan Perez, John Rather, Joseph Ringhoffer, Jan Rojas, Wilma Jo Spanyer, Kenneth Stanton, Victor Stanton, Kathryn Still, Rheba Talbert, Tammy Timms, David Toifel, Johanna Tolpi, Patricia Tolpi, Nikki Tominac, Roy Tucker, Alalazu Ugoji, Daniel Walton, Gregory Waselkov, Bruce Willis, J.R. (Shelly) Wilson, and Ralph Woss.

I would like specifically to thank Mr. John Ellis—who, in my opinion, is one of the South's premier Confederate Naval Historians—for his assistance in locating information on Hispanics in both the Confederate Navy and the Marine Corps and on the Blockade Runners.

I would like to thank the many members of the Jewish Community in Mobile, Alabama, for their patience and kindness in answering the "thousands" of questions I seemed to ask of them.

I would also like to thank the management and staff at Clearfield Company for their patience and kindness during the writing of the various editions of this book, with a specific and direct thank you to Ms. Lorie Szarek.

PREFACE

My name is John O'Donnell-Rosales; I am a Cuban exile. My family's history is heavily intertwined with that of Louisiana, Florida, and the Gulf Coast dating to the colonial period. Our history in the United States did not begin when fleeing the Communist regime of Cuba; we arrived here in 1971. You see, we and others had been here before as explorers, colonists, missionaries, and soldiers in war. The proximity of Cuba and Mexico to the United States as well as the Spanish settlements in the Gulf Coast, the Southwest, and the Atlantic made commerce, immigration and intermarriage commonplace. There were whole regiments of Spanish Militia stationed in what became the Southern States; since these were in their majority, single bachelors intermarried with the diverse peoples of the area. When Spain sold Florida to the young United States in 1819, an era came to an end although Hispanic influence continued first as Spanish, then Mexican, in the Southwest and Texas up until the Mexican War of 1846–1848.

Links with Spain and her former colonies were not broken off. There was a brisk and steady business between the Spanish colonies of Cuba, Puerto Rico, and new Central and South American nations with New Orleans, Mobile, St. Augustine, Charleston, Pensacola, and other southern port cities. The business between the border of the United States and Mexico led an additional number of Hispanics to settle in Texas, Arizona, and New Mexico. This settlement and shipping business led to a strengthening and retention of the Spanish language and culture in the coastal Gulf, Atlantic, and Southwestern states.

The War for Southern Independence saw thousands of these men flock to the Confederate cause. Whole companies were raised, composed fully or partially of Spanish/Hispanic men. This history has been largely forgotten in this era of political correctness. The vogue term for us lately in the American media has been Latinos/Latinas. I personally do not speak Latin, nor was I born in ancient Latium; but I respect those who choose to identify themselves as Latinos/Latinas as I am sure they have their reasons to do so, just as I have mine against referring to myself as anything but Spanish, Hispanic, or Cuban. I am Hispanic, of Spain, by majority ancestry and speak Spanish proudly. I am olived skinned and proud of the racial and ethnic mixture that runs in my veins, which reflect the genes of the Spanish Canary Islanders, the Basque people of the mountains dividing Spain and France, and the Cuban Taino/Ciboney vestigial Native American "blood" of my direct lineal ancestors. I know the history of our people and can talk down racists because they can't refute facts without looking more ignorant than they already are, although lord knows they try.

The United States, like many other nations, has a very small minority of people who are racist, segregationist, and bigoted; yet for every racist, segregationist, and bigot, we have thousands of righteous men and women who combat their madness and ignorance. America is great because of righteous people like these; no other nation will ever be able to have its armies drink from our rivers or streams, for a united America can never be defeated. This lesson was learned by all our enemies and is a lesson racists and segregationists have also learned, for the betterment of our nation and its many diverse peoples. America is great because of its diversity, not in spite of it.

Hispanic Confederates

Hispanics can be of any race or religion. We run the color spectrum from "white," "brown," "red," "yellow," or "black" to a mixture of these. We have fought in every war the United States has been in, but we seem to have been forgotten and ignored by historians when it comes to the War of Southern Independence. The time has come to speak of these silent men who, like the Black American Confederates, have been almost forgotten. History is the study of facts, regardless of which group they bother or annoy. We can only learn from the past if it is studied, or we are doomed to repeat its mistakes again and again.

I have heard it said by real racists that we cannot assimilate, that we aren't part of Western Civilization, and other stupidities. They seem to forget that Spain is in Europe and that even in the most remote village in the Hispanic areas of the Philippines, Equatorial Guinea in Africa, Caribbean, Central, and South America, Spanish is the language of education and culture, even if the ethnic group is non-white Hispanic.

The purveyors of hate and disunity on all spectrums of the color line are the real enemies of America. I must honestly admit that, although I love the United States, I have never felt American; instead I feel Southern and Spanish. I love the swamps of Florida and Louisiana, the Blue Ridge of Virginia, and the red soil of Alabama. The South will only rise again when "white," "black," "red," "yellow," and "brown" realize that this is OUR land and that we have to live and work together not only to help the South, but also to help America flourish for countless generations to come.

This land is our sacred birthright; each group earned it by their blood and toil. When my Confederate ancestors (the Rosales and Larramendi) heard the call to arms, they went. Our family oral history, which was later researched and documented, states that one was wounded, one disappeared, and the rest returned to Cuba or surrendered—with the last Confederate units still active in the Army of the Trans-Mississippi—in June of 1865. You see, my friends, my entry into the United States in 1971 was paid a long, long time ago with their blood and sacrifices. The bravest sons of the South, of every color and tongue, went bravely to their duty. Their memories and sacrifices will be remembered as long as honest and truthful men walk the Southern soil.

Our ancestors were brave men and women who were not afraid or ashamed to fight for their proclaimed independence. We have no reason to let them look down from Heaven and be ashamed of us for not preserving their memories, history, and Confederate symbols. These symbols must be kept clean from those who in their absolute ignorance, racism, and segregationist hatred deem to use them to divide America and for other nefarious purposes and deeds.

Their spirits linger here in every valley and in every glen, on every hill and on every mountaintop, in every swamp and in every forest. They linger in places like Gettysburg and in fields known but to them and God. Thus let the Battle Flags fly! Let them once again catch the wind! It is the least we can do for our valiant dead. Deo Vindice.

John O'Donnell-Rosales, M.A.

INTRODUCTION TO THE THIRD EDITION

The South Central Gulf States of Louisiana, Mississippi, and Alabama are famous for their French heritage and are not usually considered to be a part of the Hispanic world culturally or linguistically. The three states all fell under Spanish rule in segments from 1763 through 1780. It was during this period that Spanish-speaking colonists came into this area, principally from the Canary Islands, but also from other parts of Spain. These settlers inhabited the coastal plain and two pockets of settlement inland. The coastal settlements were New Orleans and St. Bernard Parish, Louisiana; Biloxi/Pascagoula, Mississippi; and Mobile, Alabama. The interior settlements were Natchitoches, Louisiana; Natchez, Mississippi; St. Louis, Missouri; and the Bruli settlements of Ascension, Assumption, and Iberville Parishes, all in Louisiana. These settlers, with exceptions, were generally illiterate in the Spanish language during the Spanish Colonial Period. This situation worsened after the young United States took over the areas; the little education that was available was given in French, and eventually English, to the detriment of the Spanish language.

The linguistic similarities between the Spanish/French languages and the Roman Catholic faith led to intermarriage and borrowing from Louisiana French and later English into the Spanish language. Americanization has led to the almost complete extinction of Colonial era Spanish as a viable language with the exception of three small enclaves, all in Louisiana, where it still exists. The first type of Colonial Spanish still in existence is the Bruli version of the Spanish Canarian Dialect of the Canary Islands known as Isleno Spanish. It has approximately 7 to 14 speakers and semi-speakers all over the age of 65. It is undergoing irreversible language death and should become completely extinct in the next two decades.

The second form of the Isleno Spanish Dialect is still spoken and understood by approximately 500 speakers and semi-speakers in Saint Bernard Parish, Louisiana, all over 35 years of age, as of 2006. These 500 have been reinforced by new Hispanic immigrants from Central America and the Caribbean who have settled in the Parish in the last 20 years. There are also radio and television stations which transmit in Spanish from New Orleans and whose signals are easily heard in St. Bernard. There has been a lot of interest by the Spanish Government and local Isleno organizations in introducing usage of contemporary Spanish, and Isleno culture and history are being preserved by the recent erection and introduction, in the last two decades, of Isleno Museums and yearly festivals. The Saint Bernard Parish School system and Nunez Community College in St. Bernard are also teaching courses in Spanish, with the hope that Spanish will survive as a viable language into this century and beyond.

The third form of Colonial era Spanish still in existence in Louisiana is that of the Adaesenos. This Spanish Dialect is found in the area of the present-day Parishes of Sabine and Natchitoches. The dialect has also been referred to as Sabine River Spanish and is only remembered by approximately 30 to 50 semi-speakers, all over the age of 65. The majority of these colonial settlers were from Mexico, and a large percentage were of mixed Native American and Spanish extraction, with a handful who settled during the Spanish Louisiana period. This dialect is undergoing irreversible language death and should become completely extinct in the next two decades.

The Spanish colonies of Florida and Texas, plus the territory of Arizona (Confederate Territory of Arizona) that encompasses modern-day Arizona/New Mexico, saw Spanish exploration early. The state of Florida was the first to have a permanent European settlement when the city of St. Augustine was founded in 1565. This was followed in 1566 by a settlement at Saint Elena, South Carolina, which survived until 1587 (modern day Parris Island, which is now used as a Marine Corps Recruit Training Center and where the archaeological remains of the Spanish settlement can be toured). There was continuous Spanish exploration and settlement in what eventually became the United States up until the Mexican revolt against Spanish imperial rule.

The War for Southern Independence caught these settlers and many others in a decisive situation. Should they support their respective states and the newly founded Confederate Government or, as some foreigners did, exempt themselves from military obligation due to foreign nationality and sit out the war? The answer was to fight for their new-found homes. One then gets into the question of slavery. The answer is simple: less than ten percent of Southerners owned slaves. The Hispanic community generally did not own slaves due to poverty and social position. The few who did in any number were the "old" Creoles and the businessmen of Mobile, New Orleans, and other southern ports. The concept of slavery was abhorrent to many (but not all) Hispanics in Central and South America where it had been outlawed in all of those nations by the outbreak of war, but it was still practiced in the Spanish overseas colonies of Cuba and Puerto Rico. The Hispanic Confederate was not fighting for the right to keep ten percent of Southerners as slave owners. The question, then, is why fight? The answer, I believe, is that they fought to maintain their way of life and, afterwards, when the South was invaded, to protect their families and homes.

The concept of community and familial obligations runs deep in the Spanish tradition. That a perceived sociological responsibility was the reason these men joined the Confederate military is a possibility that should be further researched. The last reason returns us to the subject of social class. The best way to move upward socially (or downward) is during a general war. A war meant that an average man could become a hero, earn money, and rest on military laurels permitting him access to upper echelon social contacts that were undreamt of prior to the outbreak of hostilities. This situation combined with the educational opportunities (such as having to learn English out of dire necessity) gave these men a new outlook on the world and their perceived place in it. It is true that many soldiers returned to their original areas after the war, where their descendants still live, but these were not the same men who left home in 1861. They had a new world view and had seen literally by foot parts of the United States that they would have never visited unless the war had occurred.

This book also lists many men of the Jewish faith (Sephardics), whose ancestors were expelled from Spain in 1492 and then from Portugal. These valiant people continue to speak a dialect of Spanish written in Hebrew letters known as Ladino and hold onto other Spanish cultural traits. The Spanish and Portuguese Jews, once expelled, intermarried; in many cases they formed their own separate cultural and linguistic identity; due to the predominance of the more numerous Spanish Jews, a new "Sephardic" identity came into being in the Diaspora, with the Spanish strain predominating. The Sephardics were among some of the earliest settlers to colonial North America and have since been an integral part of all aspects of America society and history. The Spanish Dialect of Ladino is still spoken or understood by an estimated 70,000 people in Israel and thousands more in other nations. There are programs that are transmitted via short-wave radio in the Ladino Dialect by the governments of Israel and Spain. The Spanish Government also grants residency and citizenship to those who wish to resettle in Spain. The Sephardics who immigrated to the South concentrated in New Orleans, Louisiana; Savannah, Georgia; Charleston, South Carolina; Mobile, Alabama; and other southern ports before moving inland. The problem I faced when trying to list them was finding them by surname, as some were intermarried with non-Sephardic Jews, some were married to Christians, and some were non-practicing Jews by 1860. It was difficult to "place" them as being Sephardic or even to find if they were Sephardic; but I was able to find many of them, and I have included all those found in the book. It is important to remember their participation in the southern cause and to honor their birthright of Spanish descent and, most importantly, their contributions to American history.

There are five other specific groups represented in the listings. The first are the Mulattos of Spanish/African ancestry who had acculturated as Hispanics and in many cases were slave owners themselves or tied to the southern cultural and social "status quo" by business, land ownership, or other ties. These were mostly to be found in Louisiana, with the exception of very small pockets in Pensacola, Florida; St. Augustine, Florida; and Mobile County, Alabama. Other small pockets developed anywhere interracial marriage or interracial sexual relations occurred, and their descendants can be found all over the South. They considered themselves Creoles of Color, and many of the Louisiana men joined the companies of the Louisiana Native Guard. A few dozen also joined units with membership composed partially or fully of white Hispanics and Americans. Their descendants still refer to themselves as Creoles of Color and many live in the New Orleans area, but they can be found in many areas of Louisiana. The Alabama pocket, through intermarriage with the French Creoles of Color, eventually lost their ethnic identity and in almost all cases their Hispanic surnames. A few joined the Creole Guard, which before the war was known as the Creole Company of the Fire Department of Mobile, and served the Creoles of Color and the Black community, both free and slave. They served during the war as a Home Guard Unit and were active until late April 1865 (their name was changed to the Native Guards in the last weeks of the war). The descendants of these Alabama Creoles of Color can still be found in such areas as Mon Louis Island, Coden, Bayou La Batre, and in the northern part of Mobile County, Alabama.

The second group were the Mestizos of Spanish/Native American ancestry who joined many of the Texas regular and militia units. These units were composed of white and mestizo Hispanics (almost all of Mexican descent), white Americans, or a combination. These men were almost all from Texas, and most were born in Mexico or Texas when the area was Mexican territory or when Texas was an independent nation prior to joining the United States, with a few from the Confederate Territory of Arizona. These Mestizo men made up the majority of the men with Hispanic surnames who served in units and companies of both the regular Confederate Army and Militia from Texas. There are many photographs of them which have survived that can be found among both private and public collections that clearly show their ethnic mixture.

The third group included Asian men from the Philippines (a Spanish colony until 1898), who had settled in the New Orleans, Louisiana, area and then spread to other Gulf Coast states. There were a handful of them in the Confederate forces. The surviving documentation shows that they used Spanish in their correspondence and almost all had Spanish surnames. There are also a few photographs that survive which show them to be of Filipino or Filipino/Spanish mixture and not white Hispanic ancestry. These few men might be the reason that "Chinese" are mentioned as being part of the Louisiana Zouaves. There are still many descendants of these Filipino settlers in the New Orleans area who married into the local Hispanic communities or to newer immigrants from the Philippines.

The fourth group, the Minorcans of Florida, were composed of Minorcans (from the Balearic Islands in the Mediterranean Sea) who spoke a dialect of Catalan as well as, in many cases, Spanish. They intermarried with many of the Italians, Corsicans and Greeks (e.g., the Pacetti, Papy surnames, among others), who accompanied the colony to Florida during the British Period. The Minorcans and other Spanish settlers gradually absorbed the other nationalities during the second Spanish Florida Period and were then themselves later absorbed into American society. The Minorcan Dialect is now extinct, as is Colonial era Spanish, with only older members of the community having any vestigial knowledge of words or phrases. The concept of being part of the "Minorcan" community is something that has been passed down and is proudly mentioned by many inhabitants of St. Augustine, Florida, and its surrounding counties. There are now societies and historical groups that honor the Minorcan settlers and their history in Florida which have given new life to this long ignored Hispanic group and their descendants.

The fifth group—the white Spaniards (other than the Sephardics, Islenos and Minorcans)—could be broken down into three sub groups. The first were the old Creole settlers who had lived in any of the previous Spanish possessions in the southern United States and had stayed on after Spain lost these areas. The second sub group were immigrants from the former Spanish Colonies—among them Mexican revolutionaries and those fleeing the upheavals in Mexico, who settled in New Orleans, Louisiana—as well as from the then Spanish Colonies of Cuba and Puerto Rico.

In this second sub group were many Cubans who immigrated into Louisiana and Florida and many on the island who had strong business ties with one or all of the Gulf states. There was a vibrant Cuban Independence movement mostly headquartered in New Orleans, Louisiana, which plotted and in a few cases actually tried to invade

Cuba prior to 1860. There were Cuban immigrants in almost all of the larger southern port cities; the majority volunteered to fight for the Confederacy or assisted in blockade runner activities. Their business and social connections assisted the Confederacy both economically and politically. A good example of the mutual affection that existed between Cubans and the Confederacy can be shown by the gesture of the ladies of Matanzas, Cuba, who presented a First National Confederate Flag made of silk and colored red and gold (colors of the Spanish National Flag) to the Captain of the blockade runner Steamer *Gordon*, later renamed the *Theodora*, which ran the blockade from Charleston, South Carolina, into Cuba. The original flag survived the war and is presently in the Confederate Museum of Charleston, South Carolina. The last sub grouping were newer immigrants escaping the harsh economic and political conditions found in Spain once the Bourbon Dynasty was restored. These newer immigrants were reinforced by Basques and Catalonians fleeing from Spain during the 1st Carlist War (1833–1840) and its subsequent social and economic disruption.

The exact number of Hispanics in the Confederate military will never be definitely known as many Hispanic women married into other ethnic groups "daughtering" out their Hispanic surnames. The book lists over 6,175 men; if you estimate the "daughtered out" surnames, the total number who actually served could lie between a low of 8,000 to 10,000 men to a high of approximately 10,000 to 12,000 men. I have based my listing on those men I was able to find to be of Hispanic descent. My definition and the one used for the book is based on the concept of who qualifies as "Hispanic." I use the term "Hispanic" to refer to someone who has at least one parent of Hispanic descent and/or someone acculturated to Hispanic culture via intermarriage and/or religious beliefs and traditions. The exception to this rule are the hundreds of women who married French or American men in Louisiana. I did not include their children in this book except for some notable situations, such as when a Spanish colonial surname became extinct; but the Spanish "bloodline" continued via the French or American surname. The same was done with the Sephardic women who married out of their community.

This study of the contribution of Hispanics to the total Confederate military effort will, I hope, open the way for researchers, historians, genealogists, and anthropologists to one day truly present the forgotten history of the Hispanic Confederate soldiers, sailors, medical, and other designated personnel. There is a wealth of information contained in the following pages. I hope it adds to the rich history of our nation.

Hispanic Confederates xi

INTERPRETING THE LISTINGS

Readers should take note, before beginning the listings of soldiers, of a problem most researchers encounter when dealing with the French/Spanish Colonial records and subsequent nineteenth-century records from Louisiana and other Southern states. This problem is the language dilemma. French and Spanish are freely employed in both dialectical and standardized forms and, after the United States took power, by the Anglicization of Romance language names. Examples of letters changed include, but are not limited, to the following:

Letters changed (or vice versa)
C for S   X for J
B for V   Y for LL
S for Z   H for J
E for I   C for Q

Another change would be the lack of the letter H when followed by a vowel. The reader should be aware that many Hispanic names are sometimes preceded by De or Del (of). If you cannot find the name under the correct letter, it might have been written down with the De Los, De La, De Las, De, or Del preceding it. These names would all be found listed under the letter D instead of the actual letter of the surname.

I studied the dialectical forms of Spanish spoken in the South Central Gulf States prior to this manuscript's publication. This dialect can be divided into three surviving forms, which can now be found only in Louisiana. They are Adaeseno, Bruli Isleno, and Saint Bernard Isleno; the two former are virtually extinct, with the third having approximately 500 speakers and semi-speakers. In all of these forms is a tendency to omit consonant sounds when the name ended with a vowel. This tendency is a common practice in many languages but led to some fantastic spellings when the Spanish names were written in French or English. The other problem consists of given names. Surnames or given names were written by the person who took down the name and were usually Gallicized in Louisiana if the writer was French. The same thing happened in other states to names written down by those not familiar with Spanish, except in those cases the names were Anglicized.

There is also the problem of specific Spanish ethnic surnames (groups) which immigrated to America. Many Catalonian names are easily confused with French and Italian surnames. The Galician names are very close to Portuguese surnames, and Basque names exist on both sides of the French/Spanish border. These specific ethnic groups were perceived by their new American hosts not as Canary Islanders, Galicians, Basques or Catalonians, but as Spanish citizens. The differentiation existed between the immigrants, but they were perceived by others to be all "Spaniards" or "Spanish."

This perception has existed to this day, except the concept now is that we are a new "race" called "Hispanics" (or the term Latinos/Latinas) regardless of which nation or racial/ethnic group we individually consider ourselves to be members. The government of the United States and some American political "pressure" groups would like you to believe that a Black Cuban, a Mestizo from Mexico, or a White Spaniard are a new "ethnic" group requiring a completely new "racial" designation once we arrive in the United States. It has also led to some injustices such as "racial profiling," but a reverse form of discrimination also exists. A white Spaniard with blond hair and blue eyes (or white, in any form) can arrive today from Spain or another Spanish-speaking nation and automatically qualify for all types of "racial" protections and preferences that native-born American whites cannot obtain. These protections and preferences do not die with them but are passed down to their children, all because they now fall into the status of a "protected minority." The question no one is asking is what is going to happen when the Hispanic minority becomes the American majority? The Census Bureau estimates that the Hispanic minority will eventually become the American majority in a few decades. We are growing faster (by the day) than any other ethnic group via immigration (both legal and illegal) and birth rate and have now surpassed African-Americans as the largest "protected" class.

It is possible that a few mistakes and (many) omissions may be found in this listing. I had a very difficult time compiling this work; regardless, any omissions or mistakes are mine. There are a few men listed with non-Hispanic surnames. These men were either found to be Sephardic Jews, of Minorcan mixed ancestry, or their mothers were confirmed to be of Hispanic descent. I have also listed Hispanics who were politicians and government employees in their respective states during the war or who assisted in the Confederate military effort.

There is the possibility that a handful of Italians and Portuguese men with surnames similar to Hispanic surnames find themselves in the book. If any reader can identify a soldier who was of Portuguese, French, or Italian ancestry, please feel free to write me with your citation to their ethnicity, and I will gladly delete them from the subsequent editions of the book. If you have any information on any men who were of Hispanic descent and served but were not listed or if you know of the first name of any men listed with just initials, please feel free to contact me. I will gladly include them in subsequent editions of the book and give you credit for the citation.

If any reader desires to learn more information on any of the listed men, please feel free to write me. If you have any questions, suggestions and/or comments, send your letter (please include a self-addressed stamped envelope and a phone number at which I may reach you) to the following address:

John O'Donnell-Rosales, Author of *Hispanic Confederates*
c/o Clearfield Company
3600 Clipper Mill Road, Suite 260
Baltimore, Maryland 21211

ABBREVIATIONS USED IN BOOK

1st Cpl.—First Corporal
1st Lt.—First Lieutenant
1st Sgt.—First Sergeant
2nd Lt.—Second Lieutenant
ALA—Alabama
ARIZ—Arizona
ARK—Arkansas
Arty.—Artillery
Battn.—Battalion
Batty.—Battery
Brig.—Brigade
C.S.A.—Confederate States Army
Capt.—Captain
Cav.—Cavalry
Co._Company
Cons.—Consolidated
Cpl.—Corporal
FLA—Florida
GA—Georgia
Grd. / Grds.—Guard / Guards
Inf.—Infantry
Jr.—Junior

LA—Louisiana
Lt.—Lieutenant
Lt. Arty.—Light Artillery
KY—Kentucky
MD—Maryland
Mil.—Militia
MISS—Mississippi
MO—Missouri
N.C.—North Carolina
Pvt.—Private
QMaster—Quarter Master
Regt.—Regiment
S.C.—South Carolina
Sgt.—Sergeant
Sr.—Senior
St.—State
TENN—Tennessee
Tr.—Troops
TX—Texas
Vol.—Volunteer
Vols—Volunteer
VIR—Virginia

CONSULS REPRESENTING SPAIN AND MEXICO WHO SERVED IN THE CONFEDERACY BETWEEN 1861–1865

Callejon, Juan-Spanish Consul New Orleans, Louisiana

Le Baron, Charles-Mexican Consul Mobile, Alabama

Miranda, Joaquin G.-Spanish Consul Mobile, Alabama

Moreno, Francisco-Spanish Consul Pensacola, Florida

Nunez De Moncada, (No 1st name found)-Spanish Consul Charleston, S.C.

Peres, A.-Spanish Vice Consul Mobile, Alabama

Theron, B.-Mexican Vice Consul Galveston, Texas

HISPANIC NAVAL AND MARINE CORP PERSONNEL

CSN. = Confederate States Navy
CSS. = Confederate States Ship

Alvarez, Lucio-Captain Blockade Runner COMET, captured off of Mobile, ALA on May 15th, 1863.
Antonio, Charles-Masters Mate Pensacola Naval Yard, FLA
Antonio, Frank-Seaman CSS. MORGAN, ALA
Arbela, Ramon-Spanish Citizen forcibly taken off of the Steamer BLANCHE, off of Mariano, Cuba, on Oct. 7th, 1862 and held as a Union prisoner.
Avalado, Louis-Seaman CSS. MORGAN, ALA
Barco, Caleb-Seaman CSS. NORTH CAROLINA
Baya, William-Lt. of Marines, Privateer JEFF DAVIS, he later served as a Lt. Colonel in the 8th FLA Infantry (see listing in main roster).
Blanco, Bartholomew-Seaman Blockade Runner HANCOCK
Castillo, Emanuel-3rd Class Boy CSS. SPRAY, FLA
Cavas, (no 1st name)-Captain Blockade Runner MINNIE out of Aucilla River FLA, bound for Matanzas, Cuba, was captured on April 6th, 1863.
***For Cervantes see Serbantes
Costa, E.J.-Paymasters Clerk Charleston Station, S.C.
Costa, Thomas-Seaman CSS. CHATTAHOOCHEE, FLA
Del Cano, Jose Cruz-Seaman CSS. PETREL
De Leon, Perry Moses-Assistant Paymaster (he also held the rank of Captain) CSS. ALBEMARLE, S.C.
De Leon, Thomas Cooper-Chief Clerk Office of Pay, Provision and Clothing, CSN. Department, S.C. He is very well known for his many post war books including *Four Years in Rebel Capitals*.
De Oca, Manuel Montes-Seaman CSN.
Diaz, Fernando-Captain Blockade Runner TERESITA out of Havana; Cuba captured on Jan. 30th, 1862.
Diaz, Francis-Seaman CSS. FLORIDA
Domingo, Manuel-Seaman CSS. BRADFORD, FLA
Fernandi, John-Seaman captured on the Blockade Runner LINNET from Havana, Cuba, on May 14th, 1863.
Fernandez, Joseph-Seaman captured on the Blockade Runner STINGAREE off of the Brazos River, TX, on May 23rd, 1864. He is listed by the Union officer writing the report as a "Negro Seaman."
Florez, Antonio-Killed aboard CSS. ARKANSAS, he also served in the 28th LA Infantry.
Francisco, Antonio-Seaman CSS. CASWELL, N.C.
Francisco, Columbus-Landsman CSS. McRAE, LA
Francisco, Domingo-Seaman CSS. MORGAN, ALA
Francisco, Peter-Seaman CSS. MORGAN, ALA
Garcia, Anthony P.-Seaman CSS. HUNTSVILLE, ALA

Garcia, Antonio Manuel-Pvt. Confederate States Marine Corps
Garcia, Jose-His son (no 1st name given) and he were captured aboard the YOUNG GUSTAVE on Nov. 21st, 1862.
Garo, Abram-Seaman CSS. SPRAY, FLA
Gomez, John-2nd Class Fireman CSS. FLORIDA
Gonzales, Samuel Zacharias-Major Confederate States Marine Corps, FLA. He later served Naval Storekeeper at Pensacola, FLA, Montgomery, ALA, and Mobile, ALA
Gonzalez, Celestin-2nd Clerk Naval Storekeeper, Pensacola, FLA
Gonzalez Brent, Daniel-2nd Lt. Confederate States Marine Corps, Savannah, GA
Gonzalez, Jasper S.-Agent Confederate States Navy Pensacola, FLA
Gonzales, John-Seaman CSS. DIXIE
Gonzales, Joseph-Seaman CSS. DIXIE
Hernandez, Francis-Pilot Savannah Squadron, GA
Hernandez, Thomas L.-Pilot Savannah Station, GA / CSS. ATLANTA
Juan, Pedro-Seaman CSS. VIRGINIA
Larramendi, Jose Comas > see listing in main section
Larramendi, Manolito Comas > see listing in main section
Leon, Antonio-Seaman Blockade Runner BELLE captured April 29th, 1862.
Lopez, Jose-Passenger Blockade Runner JUANITA captured off of Galveston, TX on April 11th, 1864.
Llambias, J.F.-Landsman CSS. SPRAY, FLA
Malga, Victor-Spanish Citizen held as a prisoner of war aboard the USS. ARIES
Mallory, Stephen Russell Jr.-MidShipman CSS PATRICK HENRY (see main listing for details).
Malpaso, Henry-Seaman CSS. RALEIGH, N.C.
Manuel, John-Seaman CSS. FLORIDA
Marco, Samuel-Seaman CSS. ARTIC / Cook CSS. RALEIGH, N.C.
Marquez, Antonio-Captain Blockade Runner MARCELITA which was sunk off MISS (date unknown).
Martinez, Francisco-Captain / Owner Blockade Runner CAPTAIN SPEDDEN out of New Orleans captured off of Deer Island, MISS on Dec. 31st, 1861.
Menendez, Francisco-Captain Blockade Runner M.S. PERRY a.k.a. SALVOR
Menendez, Francois-Captain Blockade Runner CARMITA captured off of Marquesas Keys, FLA Dec. 27th, 1862.
Moses, Raphael J. Jr.-Master CSS. SAVANNAH / CSS. GEORGIA and also, Battery Semmes, James River, VIR
Ochoa, Ivan-Seaman CSS. ALABAMA
Oliva, Joseph-Pvt. Confederate States Marine Corps
Oliva, S.C.-Pvt. Confederate States Marine Corps
Olivera, W.D.-Masters Mate, promoted to Commander of CSS. RESOLUTE, GA
Pacetti, Adolphus N.-Master CSS. ALERT
Pacetti, Thomas A.-He was a Confederate Spy in Baltimore from 1861-1862. He was able to escape to Europe where he joined the crew of the CSS. RAPPAHANNOCK as a Hospital Steward.

Peres, (no 1st name listed)-Captain of the Blockade Runner RATTLER, captured off the Cedar Keys, FLA, on Jan. 16th, 1862.
Perez, A.-Stockholder in the Blockade Runner YORKTOWN out of Mobile, ALA 1862.
Peso, Piento-Captain of the Blockade Runner PHANTOM out of Mariel, Cuba captured off of the Suwanee River, FLA, March 2nd, 1865.
Pol, Miguel Leon-Captain of a small Blockade Runner out of Bayou La Batre, ALA
Puiz, Emilio-Spanish Citizen aboard the NUESTRA SENORA DE REGLA who was seized on Dec. 1st,1861, and held as a prisoner for violation of the blockade on the USS ARIES.
Ramires, Pedro-Mate Blockade Runner JUANITA captured off of Galveston, TX, on April 11th, 1864.
Riancho, Francisco-Captured while running mail into Mobile, ALA, on the YOUNG GUSTAVE on Nov. 21st, 1862.
Rivas, Charles-Pvt. Confederate States Marine Corps CSS. MCRAE, LA
Rodrigues, John-Seaman on the Blockade Runner DEER ISLAND, captured May 13th, 1862.
Rodrigues, M.-Seaman captured on the Blockade Runner SYLPHIDE off St. Luis Pass, TX on March 10th, 1864.
Rodriguez, Castro-2nd Class Fireman CSS. FLORIDA
Romero, Manuel-Seaman CSS. SPRAY, FLA
Salcedo, Antonio-Spanish Citizen of Havana, Cuba, captured on the Blockade Runner LA CRIOLLA on May 28th, 1862, and held on the USS. ARIES. He was the owner of the Blockade Runner.
Sanchez, B.-Applied in Savannah, GA for a Letter of Marque and Reprisal in 1861.
Sanchez, Ramon S.-Commanders Clerk CSS. JACKSON, LA
Santos, Don-Crewman Blockade Runner M.S. PERRY a.k.a. SALVOR
Serbantes, Antonio-Seaman CSS. WINSLOW
Silva, Antonio-Seaman CSS. SEA BIRD, N.C.
Silva, Antonio-Captain of the YOUNG GUSTAVE captured while running mail into Mobile, ALA, on Nov. 21st, 1862.
Silva, James-Seaman CSN.
Silva, Peter-Seaman CSS. FLORIDA
Slado, Francis-Owner of Cargo and passenger of the Blockade Runner DEER ISLAND, captured off Petit Bois Island, ALA, on May 13th, 1862.
Slado, Paul-Captain of the DEER ISLAND, (see above)
Slado, Ramon-Seaman on the DEER ISLAND, (see above)
Sylvia, Manuel-Seaman CSS. SPRAY, FLA
Swaroz, Henry-Pvt. Confederate States Marine Corps CSS. VIRGINIA
Trias, Jose Maria-Fireman CSS. VIRGINIA
Usina, Michael Philip-Pilot Savannah Squadron, GA / CSS. TALOMICO

INFANTRY, ARTILLERY, CAVALRY AND OTHER DESIGNATED MILITARY PERSONNEL

A

Abal, Jose-Pvt. Company D, 30th LA Infantry
Abeares, Narcisco-Pvt. Company 5, Cazadores Espanoles Regiment, LA Militia
Abito, Luciano-Pvt. Company C, 8th TX Infantry
Abolos, Juan-Pvt. TX Militia
Abraano, Francisco-Pvt. Co. A, 5th (Spanish) Regiment, European Brig., LA Mil.
Abrigo, Jinio-Pvt. 1st Company C, Ragsdale's Battalion, TX Cavalry
Abrigos, A.-Pvt. Company H, 4th TX Cavalry
Accosta, John-Pvt. Company D, 18th LA Infantry
Acebo, J.Y.-Pvt. Co. 1, 5th (Spanish) Regiment, European Brigade, LA Militia
***See Asevedo for Acevedo
Acosta, A.I.-Pvt. Finegan's Fernandina Volunteers, FLA Militia
Acosta, Andrew J.-1st. Sgt. Company I, 8th FLA Infantry
Acosta, Antoine-Pvt. Company E, 28th Thomas' LA Infantry
Acosta, Arcedio-Pvt. Company I, 8th FLA Infantry
Acosta, Atanacio-Pvt. Company C, Ragsdale's Battalion, TX Cavalry
Acosta, Augustin-Pvt. Company H, 28th LA Thomas' Infantry
Acosta, Bill-Pvt. TX Militia
Acosta, D.-Pvt. Company D, 20th TX Infantry
Acosta, Desire-Sgt. Company A, Squire's Battalion, LA Artillery
Acosta, Domingo-Pvt. Company G, 3rd TX Infantry
Acosta, E.J.-Pvt. 4th GA Cav., was possibly the same E.J. Acosta who was State Auctioneer for Nassau County, FLA, in 1861.
Acosta, Francisco-Pvt. Company A, 17th TX Cavalry
Acosta, George C.-Capt. Acosta's Milton Artillery, FLA Militia
Acosta, George W.-State Auctioneer, Duval County, FLA 1861
Acosta, Hypolite-Cpl. Landry's Company, Donaldsonville Artillery, LA
Acosta, John-Pvt. Company B, 1st LA Heavy Artillery
Acosta, John-Pvt. Company A, 17th Consolidated Dismounted, TX Cavalry
Acosta, Joseph-Pvt. Company H, 16th TX Infantry
Acosta, Joseph E.-Pvt. Company I, 8th FLA Infantry
Acosta, Juan Feliciano-Pvt. Company A, 17th TX Cavalry
Acosta, Julian E.-Commissioner of Pilotage, Nassau County, FLA 1861
Acosta, Julian J.-2nd Lt. Company I, 8th FLA Infantry
Acosta, Miguel-4th Cpl. Company E, 28th LA Thoams' Infantry
Acosta, N.-Pvt. Company I, 18th LA Infantry
Acosta, N.B.-Pvt. Company H, 28th LA Thomas' Infantry
Acosta, Paul-Arsenal Department, LA (unknown rank or position).
Acosta, Valentine-Pvt. Company E, 28th LA Infantry
Acoste, A.-Pvt. Company E, Lafourche Militia, LA
Acosto, T.-Pvt. Company C, 2nd TX State Troops

Adex, Jesus-Pvt. Company A, Ragsdale's Battalion, TX Cavalry
Agapito, Aquilon-Pvt. Company C, Benavides' Regiment, TX Cavalry
Agiluar, Elijio-Pvt. Company E, 8th TX Infantry
Agostin, Ramon-1st Sgt. Co. A, 5th (Spanish) Regt., European Brigade, LA Mil.
Agostine, F.M. Jr.-Pvt. Company D, 3rd Junior Reserve, N.C.
Agostine, Pascual P.-2nd Lt. Company C, 7th N.C. Infantry
Aguas, Vicente-Pvt. Company G, 21st ALA Infantry
Aguiar, L.-Pvt. Co. I, 5th (Spanish) Regiment, European Brigade, LA Militia
Aguienna, Librado-1st Cpl. Company I, Benavides' Regiment, TX Cavalry
***See also Aquilar
Aguilar, Agapito-Pvt. Company C, 8th Hobby's TX Infantry
Aguilar, Alejo-Pvt. Zapata's Company, Nueces County, TX State Troops
Aguilar, Antonio-Pvt. Co. 3, 5th (Spanish) Regt., European Brigade, LA Militia
Aguilar, Doroteo-Pvt. 8th TX Field Battery
Aguilar, Elijio-Pvt. Company E, 8th TX Infantry
Aguilar, Guadalupe-Pvt. Company A, Benavides' Regiment, TX Cavalry
Aguilar, J.A.-2nd Sgt. Company B, 5th TENN Infantry (also served from KY).
Aguilar, Jesus-Pvt. 1st Company A, Ragsdale's Battalion, TX Cavalry
Aguilar, Librado-Pvt. 1st Company I, 33rd TX Cavalry
Aguilar, Luciano-Pvt. Company C, 8th TX Infantry
Aguilar, Nepomiceno-Pvt. Trevinio's Company, TX Cavalry
Aguilar, Pedro-Pvt. Company 2, Cazadores Espanoles Regiment, LA Militia
Aguilar, Ramon-Pvt. 14th Field Battery, TX Artillery
*** This is the Louisiana French version of the surname Aguilar
Aguillard, A.-Pvt. Orleans Guards Regiment, LA Militia
Aguillard, Francois-Pvt. Company B, 2nd LA Reserve Corps
Aguillard, J.-Pvt. Company I, Chalmette Regiment, LA Militia
Aguillard, Joseph-Pvt. Pointe Coupee Artillery, LA
Aguillard, Jules-Pvt. Company H, Miles' Legion, LA
Aguillard, Leon-Pvt. Company K, 2nd LA Cavalry
Aguillard, Marceline-Pvt. Company K, 2nd LA Cavalry
Aguillard, Paul-Pvt. Company K, 2nd LA Cavalry
Aguillard, Omer-Pvt. Company D, Miles' Legion, LA
Aguillard, Oze-Pvt. Company B, 2nd LA Reserve Corps
Aguirre, Juan-Pvt. Company F, 3rd TX Infantry
Agusto, Antonio-Pvt. LA Militia
Ajuara, Jose-Pvt. Dunn's Company, Waller's Regiment, TX Cavalry
Alabado, Juan-Pvt. Co. 3, 5th (Spanish) Regiment, European Brigade, LA Mil.
Alabau, Jose-Sgt. Co. 2, 5th (Spanish) Regiment, European Brigade, LA Militia
Alafila > see Baco De Alafila
***See also Alleman, Allemand
Alaman, R.-Pvt. Company G, 3rd LA Infantry
Alanez, M.-Pvt. Company B, 22nd LA Infantry
Alanis, Edwardo-Pvt. 1st Company A, 3rd TX Infantry
Alanis, Esteban-Pvt. Company B, Benavides' Regiment, TX Cavalry

Alanis, George-Pvt. Company F, 1st TX Cavalry
Alanses, Domingo-Pvt. McNeel's Coast Guard, TX Local Defense
Alba, Charles-Pvt. Company B, Donaldsonville Artillery, LA
Alba, H.-Pvt. Company B, 1st Regiment, 2nd Brigade, 1st Division, LA Militia
Alba, Peter Francis-Sgt. Company D, Murphy's Battalion, ALA Cavalry
Alba, Rudolph E.-Pvt. Company H, 28th LA Infantry
Alba, S.P.-Pvt. Company H, 38th ALA Infantry
Alba, Thomas-Pvt. Company F, 59th ALA Infantry
Albane, August-Pvt. Company B, 1st LA Artillery
Albanes, F.-Pvt. Company H, Crescent Regiment, LA Infantry
Albanio, Eugene-Pvt. Company K, 22nd Consolidated LA Infantry
***See also Alvarado
Albarado, Auguste-Pvt. Company D, 18th LA Infantry
Albarado, Emanuel-Pvt. Company A, 26th LA Infantry
Albarado, Manuel-Pvt. Company A, 26th LA Infantry
Albarado, Sebastian-Pvt. Company A, 26th LA Infantry
Albare, C.-Pvt. Miles' Legion, LA
Albare, D.-Pvt. Miles' Legion, LA
Albare, Joseph-Pvt. Miles' Legion, LA
Albare, Jules- Pvt. Miles' Legion, LA
Albare, Julian-Pvt. Miles' Legion, LA
Albares, Augustin-Pvt. Landry's Company, Donaldsonville Artillery, LA
Albarez, Airaeleto-Cpl. Co. 4, 5th (Spanish) Regt., European Brigade, LA Militia
Albarez, Feliciano-Pvt. Co. 1, 5th (Spanish) Regt., European Brigade, LA Militia
Albarez, J.-Pvt. Company 8, 1st Chasseurs a pied, LA Militia
Albarez, Jose-1st Lt. Co. 1, 5th (Spanish) Regt., European Brigade, LA Militia
Albemasa, Miguel-Pvt. Company B, 1st LA Heavy Artillery.
Albero, Francisco-Pvt. Co. 9, 5th (Spanish) Regt., European Brigade, LA Militia
Alberti, Joseph-Pvt. Company B, Castellanos' Battery, LA Artillery
Alberty, Lawrence-Pvt. Co. 5, 5th (Spanish) Regt., European Brigade, LA Militia
Albiar, Juan-Pvt. Company C, Ragsdale's Battalion, TX Cavalry
Alcala, Francisco-Pvt. Co. 2, Cazadores Espanoles Regiment, LA Militia
Alcala, John A.-Pvt. Company B, 13th LA Infantry
Alcala, Ramon-Pvt. Company B, 22nd LA Infantry
Alcalan, Teodora-Pvt. Company C, 8th TX Infantry
Alcantar, Pedro-Pvt. Company A, 8th TX Infantry
Alcantara, Estaven-Pvt. Co. A, 5th (Spanish) Regt., European Brigade, LA Mil.
Alcante, Antonio-Bugler Company C, Benavides' Regiment, TX Cavalry
Alcante, Jesus-1st Sgt. Minute Men (Scouts), Starr County, TX Militia
Aldama, Demas-Pvt. Company G, 3rd TX Infantry
Aldon, Carlos-Pvt. Company F, 3rd TX Infantry
Alderete, Acencio-2nd Lt. Wilson County, TX Militia
Alderete, Jesus-1st Lt. Wilson County, TX Militia
Alderete, Pablo B.-Capt. 1st Company C, Ragsdale's Battalion, TX Cavalry
Alderete, Rafael-Capt. Jeff Davis Home Guard, Refugio County, TX Militia

Hispanic Confederates

Alderete, Trinidad-1st Lt. Jeff Davis Home Guard, Refugio County, TX Mil.
Aldon, Carlos-Pvt. Company F, 3rd TX Infantry
Alecandro, Miguel-Pvt. Co. A, 5th (Spanish) Regt., European Brigade, LA Mil.
Alego, Joseph-Pvt. Company I, 20th LA Infantry
Alegria, Lucas-Pvt. Company B, Benavides' Regiment, TX Cavalry
Alegria, Ponciano-Pvt. Company B, Benavides' Regiment, TX Cavalry
Aleix, Edouard-2nd Sgt. Company 8, 1st Chasseurs a pied, LA Militia
Aleix, J.-Capt. Co. 2, 5th (Spanish) Regiment, European Brigade, LA Militia
Aleix, L.-1st Lt. Company 2, 1st Chasseurs a pied, LA Militia
Aleix, Oscar-Capt. Company 8, 1st Chasseurs a pied, LA Militia
Aleix, P.O.-Capt. C.S.A.
***See also surname Protim Alfaro, Manuel
Alfaro, Guadalupe-Pvt. Company C, 2nd State Troops, TX Infantry
Alfaro, Manuel-Pvt. Gray's Company, Bexar County, TX Militia
Alfonso, Carlos-Pvt. Co. 1, 5th (Spanish) Regt., European Brigade, LA Militia
Alguante, Luis N.-Pvt. Rhodes' Company, 3rd Battalion, TX Cavalry
Allamarino, M.-Pvt. Company A, Confederate States Zouave Battalion, LA
***See also Alaman
Alleman, Alfred-Pvt. Lafourche Militia, LA
Alleman, Antoine-Pvt. Company C, 28th LA Infantry
Alleman, Emanuel-Pvt. Company E, 28th LA Infantry
Alleman, Francis-Pvt. Company E, 28th LA Infantry
Alleman, Joseph-Pvt. Company C, 18th Consolidated LA Infantry
Alleman, Luis-Pvt. Rhodes' Company, 3rd Battalion, Yager's TX Cavalry
Alleman, Pierre-Pvt. / Nurse Co. C, Consolidated Crescent Regt., LA Infantry
Allemand, Louis H.-Pvt. Company K, 28th LA Infantry
Allemand, Onezine-Pvt. Company I, 10th Battalion, LA Infantry
Allemond, Narcisse-Pvt. Company I, 18th LA Infantry
Allemond, Thelespore-Pvt. Company I, 18th LA Infantry
Allica, M.-Pvt. Spanish Guards, Mobile Home Guard, ALA Militia
Almaida, Antonio-Pvt. Co. 8, 5th (Spanish) Regt., European Brigade, LA Militia
Almanza, Juan-Pvt. Company F, 3rd TX Infantry
Almedo, J.-Pvt. Co. I, 5th (Spanish) Regiment, European Brigade, LA Militia
Almendar, Roquie-Pvt. 8th Field Battery, TX Artillery
Almendares, Ambrosio-Pvt. Company F, 3rd TX Infantry
Almiral, Francisco-Pvt. Co. 3, 5th (Spanish) Regt., European Brigade, LA Mil.
Almirral, Pedro-Pvt. Co. 4, 5th (Spanish) Regt., European Brigade, LA Militia
Alonzo, Andre-Pvt. Company H, 22nd LA Infantry
Alonzo, Andre B.-Pvt. Company E, 18th Consolidated LA Infantry
Alonzo, Antoine-Pvt. Company H, 18th LA Infantry
Alonzo, Peter-Pvt. Company K, 15th TX Infantry
Alonzo, T.M.-Capt. Co. D, 4th Regiment, 1st Brigade, 1st Division, LA Militia
Alpuent, Florian-Pvt. 1st Native Guards, LA Militia
Alsena, J.-Pvt. Company G, 1st Regiment, Charleston Guard, S.C.
Alsena, M.-Pvt. 1st Regiment, Charleston Guard, S.C.

Alsina, Eusebio-Pvt. Co. 9, 5th (Spanish) Regt., European Brigade, LA Militia
Alsina, Juan-Pvt. Co. 3, 5th (Spanish) Regiment, European Brigade, LA Militia
Altamirano, Miguel-Pvt. Co. B, Confederate States Zouave Battalion, LA Militia
Alunas, Edmond D.-1st Sgt Company I, 1st LA Heavy Artillery
Alvado, Ramon-Pvt. Company B, 22nd LA Infantry
Alvado, Raymond-Pvt. Company G, 1st LA Heavy Artillery
***See Also Albarado
Alvarado, Antonio-Musician Company G, 1st LA Heavy Artillery
Alvarado, Antoine-Pvt. Company K, 2nd LA Reserve Corps
Alvarado, Bacilio-Bugler Benavides' Regiment, TX Cavalry
Alvarado, Francis-Pvt. Company E, 26th LA Infantry
Alvarado, Frank-Pvt. Company D, 2nd TX Mounted Rifles
Alvarado, Nicolas-4th Sgt. Jeff Davis Home Guard, Refugio County, TX Militia
Alvardo, J.-Pvt. Company 8, 1st Chasseurs a pied, LA Militia
***See also Albare, Albares, Albarez and Villa y Alvarez
Alvarez, Alexander King-Sgt. Company B, 3rd ALA Infantry
Alvarez, Aniceto-Pvt. Co. 5, 5th (Spanish) Regt., European Brigade, LA Militia
Alvarez, David Uler-Pvt. Company B, 2nd FLA Cavalry
Alvarez, Emanuel-Pvt. Mobile Home Guard, ALA. He was also a Constable for the
    4th Ward City of Mobile ALA, in 1861.
Alvarez, F.A.-Pvt. Von Phul's Company, MO Light Artillery
Alvarez, Ferdinand-Pvt. Company G, 9th MO Infantry (possibly same as above).
Alvarez, Henry-Pvt. Mobile City Troop, ALA Militia
Alvarez, James-Justice of the Peace, Bradford County, FLA 1863.
Alvarez, Joachin-Pvt. Co. 6, 5th (Spanish) Regt., European Brigade, LA Militia
Alvarez, John R.-Pvt. Company B, 2nd FLA Cavalry
Alvarez, Joseph-Pvt. Company B, 2nd FLA Cavalry
Alvarez, Joseph F.-Pvt. Mobile City Troop, ALA Militia
Alvarez, Juaquin-Pvt. Cazadores Espanoles Regiment, LA Militia
Alvarez, Louis-Pvt. 2nd Field Battery, TX Artillery
Alvarez, M.R.-Pvt. Co. 5, 5th (Spanish) Regiment, European Brigade, LA Mil.
Alvarez, Osias M.-Pvt. Company I, 1st FLA Infantry Reserve
Alvarez, P.-Pvt. Co. 1, 5th (Spanish) Regiment, European Brigade, LA Militia
Alvarez, Pedro- Pvt. 15th Field Battery, TX Artillery
Alvarez, T.U.-Sgt. 5th Battery, ARK Light Artillery
Alvarez, Teodoro-Pvt. 1st Company A, Ragsdale's Battalion, TX Cavalry
Alvarez, Thomas V.-Sgt. Company C, 2nd Battalion, ALA Light Artillery
Alvarez, Vicente-Pvt. Co. 3, 5th (Spanish) Regt., European Brigade, LA Militia
Alvarez, William Henry-Pvt. Company G, 4th ALA Reserve
Alverado, Frank-Pvt. Davis' Company, Confederate Light Artillery
Alveras, Ponoseno-Pvt. Davis' Company, Confederate Light Artillery
Alverez, Nicholas-Pvt. Company I, 16th TX Infantry
Alverez, Roman-Pvt. Company I, 1st FLA Reserve
Alvino, Phenix-Pvt. Company G, 2nd LA Infantry
Amado, Domingo-Pvt. Company B, Refugio County, TX Militia

Amado, Rios-Pvt. Company K, 2nd TX Cavalry
Amador, Antonio-Pvt. Co. 1, 5th (Spanish) Regt., European Brigade, LA Militia
Amador, Enemencior-Pvt. Company E, 36th TX Cavalry
Amador, Jesus-Pvt. Company E, 8th TX Infantry
Amador, Jose Maria-Pvt. Company C, Baird's Regiment, TX Cavalry
Amador, Juan-Pvt. Company E, 8th TX Infantry
Amador, Ruiz-Pvt. Company B, 2nd TX Mounted Rifles
Amadore, Joseph-Pvt. Company A, 30th LA Infantry
Amalla, Anastacio-Bugler Company D, Benavides' Regiment, TX Cavalry
Amasio, Franco-Pvt. Co. 3, 5th (Spanish) Regt., European Brigade, LA Militia
Amedore, Jesus-Pvt. Company E, 8th TX Infantry
Amedore, Juan-Pvt. Company E, 8th TX Infantry
Amelio, Peter-Pvt. Company K, 33rd TX Cavalry
Anaya, J.-Pvt. 14th Field Battery, TX Artillery
Ancira, G.-Pvt. Teel's Company, TX State Troops
Andana, Pablo-Pvt. Company D, 28th Thomas' LA Infantry
Andrada, Andres-Pvt. Company C, 8th TX Infantry
Andre, Leo-Sgt. Company E, Ragsdales' Battalion, TX Cavalry
Andres, Jacob-Pvt. Company I, 21st LA Infantry
Andres, Marcelino-Pvt. Co. A, 5th (Spanish) Regt., European Brigade, LA Mil.
Andres, P.-Pvt. Spanish Guards, Mobile Home Guard, ALA Militia
Andres, Thomas J.-Pvt. Company F, Ogden's LA Cavalry
Andreu, Francis P.-5th Sgt. Company B, 3rd FLA Infantry
Andreu, Jerome C.-Pvt. Company F, 2nd FLA Infantry Battalion
***Andrew is the Floridian version of the surname Andreu
Andrew, Antonio-Pvt. Company D, 8th FLA Infantry
Andrew, Emanuel P.-Pvt. Company B, 3rd FLA Infantry
Andrew, Ignatio-Pvt. Company A, 3rd FLA Infantry
Andrew, Joseph M.-Pvt. Company B, 3rd FLA Infantry
Andrew, Laboris B.-Cpl. Company B, 3rd FLA Infantry
Andrew, Lawrence M.-1st Lt. Company B, 3rd FLA Infantry
Andrew, Manuel-Pvt. Co. C, 5th (Spanish) Regt., European Brigade, LA Mil.
Andrew, Nicholas-Pvt. Company B, 3rd FLA Infantry
Andrew, Thomas-Sgt. Company I, 8th FLA Infantry
Anduval, Benino-Pvt. Company G, 3rd TX Infantry
Anesta, Manuel-Pvt. Company H, 24th TX Cavalry
Anglada, Pedro-Pvt. Co. 10, 5th (Spanish) Regt., European Brigade, LA Militia
Anglada, Simeon-Pvt. Co. 10, 5th (Spanish) Regt., European Brigade, LA Militia
Angolo, John B.- Pvt. Company I, 22nd Consolidated LA Infantry
Angui, Henry-Pvt. Company K, 7th FLA Infantry
Anguera, Jose M.-Lt. Colonel Cazadores Espanoles Regiment, LA Militia
Ania, Jesus-Pvt. Company B, Ragsdales' Battalion, TX Cavalry
Ansia, Rufino-Pvt. Pointe Coupee Artillery, LA
Antonio, Angel-Pvt. Johnson Station Rangers, Tarrant County, TX Militia
Antonio, Emanuel-Pvt. Bligh's Company, ALA Militia

Antonio, J.F.-Pvt. Company B, 3rd Palmetto Battalion, S.C. Light Artillery
Antonio, John-Pvt. Company B, 4th Regiment, 1st Division, LA Militia
Antonio, John-Pvt. Company A, Wheat's 1st TX State Troops.
Antonio, Jose-Pvt. Company I, 10th LA Infantry
Antonio, Juan-Cpl. Co. A, 5th (Spanish) Regiment, European Brigade, LA Militia
Antonio, L.W.-Pvt. Company C, 7th S.C. Infantry
Antonio, M.-Pvt. Mobile Home Guard, ALA Militia
Antonio, Manuel-Pvt. LA Militia
Antonio, Mariano-Pvt. Co. A, 5th (Spanish) Regt., European Brigade, LA Mil.
Antonio, Mateo-Pvt. Co. 8, 5th (Spanish) Regt., European Brigade, LA Militia
Antonio, S.W.-Pvt. Company C, 7th S.C. Infantry
Antonio, Usleo-Pvt. Company 5, 5th Regiment, European Brigade, LA Militia
Antony, E.L.-Pvt. ALA Militia
Apolonio, Nestor-Pvt. Co. 9, 5th (Spanish) Regt., European Brigade, LA Militia
Apolonio, Nicolas-Pvt. Co. 7, 5th (Spanish) Regt., European Brigade, LA Mil.
Apostal, Andres-Pvt. Co. 9, 5th (Spanish) Regt., European Brigade, LA Militia
***See also Aguilar
Aquila, Dorotheo-Pvt. 8th Field Battery, TX Artillery
Aquilar, Jesus-Pvt. Company D, Benavides' Regiment, TX Cavalry
Aquino, Torbiode-Pvt. Company C, Benavides' Regiment, TX Cavalry
Aragon, Juan-Pvt. Company C, Baird's Regiment, TX Cavalry
Arais, Lorenzo-Pvt. 3rd TX Infantry
Arales, Juan-Pvt. 1st Company C, Ragsdale's Battalion, TX Cavalry
Arambola, Faustino-Pvt. Company F, 1st Yager's TX Cavalry
Arambula, Fernando-Pvt. 1st Company A, Ragsdale's Battalion, TX Cavalry
Arambula, Lorenzo-Pvt. Company C, 8th TX Infantry
Arambula, Luis-Pvt. Company C, 8th TX Infantry
Aramburo, John- Pvt. Company F, Orleans Fire Regiment, LA Militia
Arango, James-Pvt. Company G, 8th FLA Infantry
Arango, Manuel Perez-Pvt. Co. 4, 5th (Spanish) Regt., European Brig., LA Mil.
Aranter, Jose Tejera-Pvt. Co. 4, 5th (Spanish) Regt., European Brigade, LA Mil.
Arbala, Antonio-Pvt. LA Militia
Arbanez, Vicente-Pvt. Company 2, Cazadores Espanoles Regiment, LA Militia
Arcaute, Jesus-1st Sgt. Minute Men (Scouts), TX Militia
Arce, Pascual-Pvt. Watkin's Company, Uvalde County, TX Troops
Archolle, Gregorio-Pvt. Co. 10, 5th (Spanish) Regt., European Brigade, LA Mil.
Archuleta, Ignacio-Pvt. Gray's Company, Bexar County, TX Militia
Arciaga, Juan-Pvt. Company F, 3rd TX Infantry
Arciniega, Gregorio-Pvt. Company B, 33rd TX Cavalry
Ardoyno, Bartolome F.-Pvt. Company C, ALA State Artillery
Areda, D.-Pvt. Company B, 2nd TX Cavalry
Arellano, Cristobal-Pvt. Company F, 3rd TX Infantry
Arevallo > see Wallet
Arena, Vincent-Pvt. Company F, Cazadores Espanoles Regiment, LA Militia
Arenas, Martin-Pvt. Company I, 8th TX Infantry

Hispanic Confederates 11

Arero, Jose-Pvt. Company G, 37th TX Cavalry
Aresola, Dario-Pvt. Benavides' Regiment, TX Cavalry
Areuejo, Manuel-Pvt. Company 5, Cazadores Espanoles Regiment, LA Militia
Arguelles, Juan-Pvt. Co. 3, 5th (Spanish) Regt., European Brigade, LA Militia
Ariola, Eli-Pvt. Company C, 12th TX Cavalry
Ariola, J.E.-Pvt. Company C, 16th TX Infantry
Ariola, John-Pvt. Pedernales Cavalry, Blanco County, TX Militia
Ariola, Juan Guadalupe-Pvt. Company A, 17th TX Cavalry
Ariola, Lewis-Pvt. Company B, 2nd TX Cavalry
Ariola, Louis-Pvt. Company I, Benavides' Regiment, TX Cavalry
Ariola, M.-Pvt. Company K, 16th TX Infantry
Ariola, Thomas-Pvt. Company B, 2nd TX Cavalry
Ariolo, Andres-Pvt. 2nd Company F, 2nd TX Cavalry
Arispe, Jesus-Pvt. Bustillo's Company, Bexar County, TX Militia
Arispe, Ygnacio-Pvt. Bustillo's Company, Bexar County, TX Militia
Arista, Manuel-Pvt. Company C, 16th TX Infantry
Arlino, John-Pvt. Company B, 1st Battalion, FLA Cavalry
Arman, Ferdinan-Pvt. / Gunsmith Dunham's Co., Milton Light Artillery, FLA
Arman, Ferdinand-Pvt. Company I, 24th TX Cavalry
Arme, Mariano-Pvt. Co. A, 5th (Spanish) Regt., European Brigade, LA Militia
Armendariz, Sabino-Pvt. Gray's Company, Bexar County, TX Militia
Armijo, Manuel and Rafael Armijo-They were wealthy merchants who assisted the Confederacy in Alberqueque, New Mexico, by placing their storehouses containing $200,000 in goods at the disposal of Confederate forces. They had to evacuate New Mexico with their families when the Confederacy withdrew.
***See also Arnow
Arnau, Francis M.-Musician / 2nd Sgt. Company B, 28th GA Infantry
Arnau, James M.-Pvt. Company E, 1st Ramsey's GA Infantry
Arnau, M.-Pvt. Co. 5, 5th (Spanish) Regiment, European Brigade, LA Militia
Arnau, M.V.-Pvt. Company E, 25th S.C. Infantry
Arnau, Paul-Capt. Arnau's Coast Guard, FLA Militia. He had served until March 1st, 1862, as Mayor of St. Augustine, FLA
Arnau, Robert M.-Pvt. Company A, Hampton Legion, S.C.
Arnica, A.-Pvt. Company C, 4th TX Cavalry
Arnnedo, A.-Pvt. Company A, 30th LA Infantry
Arnol, L.-Pvt. FLA Militia Reserve
Arnow, Benjamin J.-Pvt. Perry's Company, FLA Light Artillery
Arnow, George Joseph-QuarterMaster 7th FLA Cavalry
Arnow, Henry H.-Sgt. Major Company F, 8th FLA Infantry
Arnow, Peter D.-Pvt. Company B, 5th FLA Infantry
Arnow, Peter R.-Musician Company C, 7th FLA Infantry
Arocha, A.-Pvt. Company E, 33rd TX Cavalry
Arocha, B.-Pvt. Company E, 33rd TX Cavalry
Arocha, John N.-Pvt. TX Militia
Arocha, Jose Antonio-Pvt. Gray's Company, Bexar County, TX Militia

Arocha, Lino-Pvt. Gray's Company, Bexar County, TX Militia
Arocha, Nepomuceno-Pvt. Bustillo's Company, Bexar County, TX Militia
Arocha, Periosino-Pvt. Company B, 2nd TX Cavalry
Arocho, Alexandre-Pvt. Trevinio's Company, TX Cavalry
Aromi, Juan-Drummer Co. 3, 5th (Spanish) Regt., European Brigade, LA Militia
Arosteguy, Jean-Cpl. Company 4, 3rd Regiment, European Brigade, LA Militia
Arrami, A.-Pvt. Spanish Guards, Mobile Home Guard, ALA Militia
Arredondo, Canuto-Pvt. Company B, Benavides' Regiment, TX Cavalry
Arredondo, Cristobal-Sgt. Company F, 3rd TX Infantry
Arredondo, Joaquin-Pvt. Company D, Benavides' Regiment, TX Cavalry
Arredondo, Juan-Pvt. Company A, Benavides' Regiment, TX Cavalry
Arroyo, Arthur-Pvt. Company 5, Washington Artillery Battalion, LA
Arroyo, Charles-Cpl. Company 5, Washington Artillery Battalion, LA
Arroyo, Charles-1st Lt. Company B, Confederate States Zouave Battalion, LA
Arroyo, Felix-1st Lt. Company G, Orleans Guard Regiment, LA Militia
Arroyo, Franco-Pvt. Co. 5, 5th (Spanish) Regt., European Brigade, LA Militia
Arroyo, Oscar-Asst. Secretary of State to the LA State Senate; he also served in the QuarterMaster Department of LA.
Arsuaga, Juan-Pvt. Company F, 3rd TX Infantry
Artacho / Artache > see Jeanmard
Artiaga, Florencio-Pvt. 1st Company C, 3rd TX Infantry
Artigas, C.-1st Sgt. 5th (Spanish) Regiment, European Brigade, LA Militia
Artigue, J.-Pvt. Co. 7, 3rd Regiment French Brigade, LA Militia
Artigue, Pierre-1st Lt. Company 7, French Volunteer Battalion, LA Militia
Artigues, Louis-Capt. Company 9, French Volunteer Battalion, LA Militia
Artimas, Joseph-Pvt. Company B, 28th Gray's LA Infantry
Ascarraga, Ramon-Pvt. Co. 6, 5th (Spanish) Regt., European Brigade, LA Militia
Ascencion, Joseph-Pvt. 1st Native Guards, LA Militia
Asevedo, Geraldo-Pvt. 1st Company C, 3rd TX Infantry
Assevedo, Joseph-Pvt. Company G, 28th Thomas' LA Infantry
Astredo, Antonio-Sgt. Company F, Cazadores Espanoles Regiment, LA Militia
Astredo, J.-Pvt. Company E, Orleans Guard Regiment, LA Militia
Atilano, Carlos-Pvt. Co. A, 5th (Spanish) Regt., European Brigade, LA Militia
Augustin, Gregorio-Pvt. Co. A, 5th (Spanish) Regt., European Brigade, LA Mil.
Auliva, Juan-Pvt. Company D, Confederate States Zouave Battalion., LA
Avalos, Gavino-Pvt. Company H, 3rd TX Infantry
Avalos, Juan-Pvt. Company C, Baird's Regiment, TX Cavalry
Avendano, T.-Capt. Co. 1, 5th (Spanish) Regiment, European Brigade, LA Mil.
Avey, Octavio-Pvt. Company B, Ragsdale's Battalion, TX Cavalry
Avice, Alexander F.-Pvt. Company D, 8th FLA Infantry
Avila, Juan-Pvt. Company F, 3rd TX Infantry
Avila, Luciano-Pvt. Company C, 8th TX Infantry
Aviles, Benigno-Pvt. Company D, 2nd TX Mounted Rifles
Ayala, Ygnasio-Pvt. Co. 2, 5th (Spanish) Regiment, European Brigade, LA Mil.
Azcona, Mateo-Pvt. Co. 3, 5th (Spanish) Regt., European Brigade, LA Militia

Azmenaga, Domingo-Pvt. Co. 2, 5th (Spanish) Regt., European Brigade, LA Mil.

B

Baca, Loretto-Pvt. 1st Company H, 33rd TX Cavalry
Baca, Pedro-Prominent Citizen of Socorro, New Mexico, who defied Union Military Authorities in his support for the Confederacy.
Baca, Proxidos-4th Cpl. Company I, Benavides' Regiment, TX Cavalry
Baca, Rafael-Pvt. Hyne's Company, Bee County, TX Militia
Baca, Ygnacio-Pvt. Zapata's Company, Nueces County, TX State Troops
Baca, Ylario-Pvt. 1st Company I, Benavides' Regiment, TX Cavalry
Bacas, Bernardin-Pvt. Company E, 18th LA Infantry
Bacas, Joseph-Pvt. Company E, 18th LA Infantry
Bachelo, Ygnacio-Pvt. Co. 9, 5th (Spanish) Regt., European Brigade, LA Militia
Bachin, G.A.-Pvt. Company F, Benavides' Regiment, TX Cavalry
Bacilia, Alvarado-Bugler Company I, Benavides' Regiment, TX Cavalry
Baco De Alafila, Francisco-Pvt. TX Militia
Balades, Francisco-Pvt. Tevinio's Company, TX Cavalry
Balades, Juan Amio-Pvt. Trevinio's Company, TX Cavalry
Balades, Mariano-Pvt. Minute Men (Scouts), Starr County, TX Militia
Balaguer, E.A.-Medical Department, C.S.A
Balboa, J.F.-Pvt. Co. 1, 5th (Spanish) Regiment, European Brigade, LA Militia
Baldas, Jose M.-Cpl. Trevinio's Company, TX Cavalry
Baldeas, Manuel-Pvt. Company B, Ragsdale's Battalion, TX Cavalry
Balengo, Santo-Pvt. Company E, 2nd LA Cavalry
***See also Valdez
Baldes, A.-Pvt. Spanish Guards, Mobile Home Guard, ALA Militia
Baldez, Frances-Pvt. Company C, Benavides' Regiment, TX Cavalry
Baldez, Jenis-Pvt. Company C, 8th TX Infantry
Baldez, Juan-Pvt. Company E, 8th TX Infantry
Baldez, Manuel-Pvt. 1st Company H, 33rd TX Cavalry
Baldez, Santos-Pvt. Company E, 8th TX Infantry
Baldor, Jose-Pvt. Company D, 30th LA Infantry
Baldor, Pedro Y.-Pvt. Company 1, Cazadores Espanoles Regiment, LA Militia
Ballego, Trinidad-Pvt. 1st Company A, 3rd TX Infantry
Balles, Locario-Pvt. 1st Company H, 33rd TX Cavalry
Ballester, Joaquin-2nd Lt. Co. 6, 5th (Spanish) Regt., European Brigade, LA Mil.
Balli, Juan-Pvt. Thomas' Company, TX Partisan Rangers
Balsamo, Francisco-Pvt. Company E, Cazadores Espanoles Regt., LA Militia
Baltar, Dario-Pvt. Co. 8, 5th (Spanish) Regiment, European Brigade, LA Militia
Baltar, Jacinto-Pvt. Co. 8, 5th (Spanish) Regiment, European Brigade, LA Militia
Baltazar, Carlos-Pvt. Bustillo's Company, Bexar County, TX Militia
Baltazar, Domingo-Pvt. 1st Company H, 33rd TX Cavalry
Balu, Eugenio-Pvt. Company D, 8th TX Infantry
***See also Valverde

Balverde, Francisco-Pvt. Company I, 33rd TX Cavalry
Ban, Eduardo-Pvt. Benavides' Regiment, TX Cavalry
Ban, John-Pvt. Company F, Martin's Regiment, TX Cavalry
Banda, Anacleto-Pvt. Company G, 3rd TX Infantry
Banda, Magdaleno-Pvt. Bustillo's Company, Bexar County, TX Militia
Bando, Juan-Pvt. Trevinio's Company, TX Cavalry
Bantista, Manuel R.-Pvt. Co. 4, 5th (Spanish) Regt., European Brigade, LA Mil.
Bantu, Narcisco-Pvt. Cameron County Coast Guard, TX Militia
Bara, Aristide-Pvt. Company D, 18th Consolidated LA Infantry
Barajas, Claudio-Pvt. Company C, 8th TX Infantry
Barajas, Juan-Pvt. Engledow's Company, Nueces County, TX Militia
Barau, Pedro-Pvt. Company F, 10th LA Infantry
Barba, Fernando-Pvt. Co. 5, 5th (Spanish) Regt., European Brigade, LA Militia
Barba, J.-1st Lt. Co. 1, 5th (Spanish) Regiment, European Brigade, LA Militia
Barbara, Emanuel-Sgt. Kean's Battery, LA Artillery
Barbaras, G.-Pvt. Company D, 1st Strawbridge's LA Infantry
***See also E'Barbo, Ibarbo, Ybarbo and Yebarbo
Barbo, G.-Pvt. Company E, 28th TX Cavalry
Barbo, Hassey-Pvt. Company L, 28th TX Cavalry
Barbo, J.-Pvt. Company G, 3rd LA Infantry
Barbo, Laano-Pvt. Company A, 2nd Battalion, LA Heavy Artillery
Barbo, Pentalliou-Pvt. Company A, 2nd Battalion, LA Heavy Artillery
Barbo, Pierre-Pvt. Company A, 2nd Battalion, LA Heavy Artillery
Barcelo, M.-Pvt. Co. 5, 5th (Spanish) Regiment, European Brigade, LA Militia
Barcello, Jean-Pvt. Co. G, 4th Regiment, 1st Brigade, 1st Division, LA Militia
Barco, John A.-Pvt. Wakulla Militia, FLA
Barco, Joseph P.-1st. Lt. Company G, 9th FLA Infantry
Barco, Nickabud-Pvt. Agnew's Company, 1st FLA Cavalry
Barco, P.J.-Pvt. Company D, 2nd FLA Cavalry
Barco, Thomas-Pvt. Company G, 2nd FLA Cavalry
Barco, William E.-2nd Cpl. Company G, 7th FLA Infantry
***See also Varela
Barela, Alfonzo-Pvt. Company C, 8th Hobby's TX Infantry
Barela, Antonio-Pvt. Victoria County, TX Militia
Barela, Manuel-Pvt. Co. 7, 5th (Spanish) Regt., European Brigade, LA Militia
Barela, Marselino-Pvt. Company C, Ragsdales' Battalion, TX Cavalry
Barela, Timoteo-Pvt. Company C, 8th TX Infantry
Bareno, Jeff-Pvt. LA Militia
Barera, J.-Pvt. Company K, 33rd TX Cavalry
Bargus, Antonio-Pvt. 1st Company I, 33rd TX Cavalry
Bargus, Polonio-Pvt. 1st Company I, 33rd TX Cavalry
Bario, Rafael-Pvt. Cameron County Coast Guard, TX Militia
Baron, George-Pvt. Co. 5, 5th (Spanish) Regiment, European Brigade, LA Militia
Barquez, Fernando-Pvt. Co. 4, 5th (Spanish) Regt., European Brigade, LA Militia
Barquin, John F.-Pvt. Company D, Confederate Engineer Troops

Barra, Julian-Pvt. Gray's Company, Bexar County, TX Militia
Barrada, Sylvester-Pvt. Company C, 2nd MO Infantry
Barragan, H.-Pvt. Medina Guards, Bexar County, TX Militia
Barrales, (No 1st Name listed)-Pvt. Company C, 3rd TX Infantry
Barras, Adolphe-Pvt. Company A, 30th LA Infantry
Barras, Aristide-Pvt. Company B, 18th LA Infantry
Barras, Arthur-Pvt. Company H, 7th LA Cavalry
Barras, Emile-Pvt. Donaldsonville Artillery, LA
Barras, George-Pvt. LA Militia
Barras, J.-Pvt. Lafourche Regiment, LA Militia
Barras, Jean Baptiste-Pvt. Company A, Pointe Coupee Artillery, LA
Barras, Julian-Pvt. Company D, 7th LA Cavalry
Barras, Vincent-Pvt. Company A, 13th LA Infantry
Barrera, A.M.-Capt. Bexar County, TX Militia
Barrera, Antonio-Pvt. Watkin's Company, Uvalde County, TX Troops
Barrera, Antonio-3rd Lt. Co. 5, 5th (Spanish) Regt., European Brigade, LA Mil.
Barrera, Carlos-Pvt. Company F, 3rd TX Infantry
Barrera, Inocencio-Pvt. Co. A, 5th (Spanish) Regt., European Brigade, LA Militia
Barrera, Jacinto-Pvt. Thomas' Company, TX Partisan Rangers
Barrera, Jesus(1st)-Pvt. 1st Company A, 3rd TX Infantry.
Barrera, Jesus-(2nd)-Pvt. Company C, 8th TX Infantry
Barrera, John-Pvt. Duff's Company, Bexar County, TX Militia
Barrera, Jose Maria-Pvt. Company A, Benavides' Regiment, TX Cavalry
Barrera, Jose Rios-Pvt. Company I, 8th TX Infantry
Barrera, Juan E.-1st Sgt. Company H, 8th TX Infantry
Barrera, Juan G.-Sgt. Company F, 3rd TX Infantry
Barrera, M.-Pvt. Company K, 33rd TX Cavalry
Barrera, Melchior-Pvt. Company D, 30th LA Infantry
Barretos, Pedro-Pvt. Co. A, 5th (Spanish) Regt., European Brigade, LA Militia
Barria, Emile-Pvt. LA Militia
Barria, Joseph-Pvt. LA Militia
Barriente, Francis-Pvt. Company E, 28th Thomas' LA Infantry
Barriente, Gabino-Pvt. Company C, 3rd TX Infantry
Barriente, Joseph-Pvt. Company E, 28th Thomas' LA Infantry
Barrientos, L.-Pvt. Company C, 8th TX Infantry
Barrientos, Salvador-Pvt. Rhode's Company, 3rd Battalion, TX Cavalry
Barrio, Jose-Pvt. Georges' Company, Herbert's Battalion, ARIZ Cavalry
Barrios, Alexandre-Pvt. Company H, Orleans Guard Battery, LA Light Artillery
Barrios, Andrew-Pvt. Plaquemine Mounted Rangers, LA Militia
Barrios, Cornelio-Sgt. Company A, Ragsdale's Battalion, TX Cavalry
Barrios, Firmin-Pvt. Company E, 18th LA Infantry
Barrios, G.D.-Pvt. He served under General Smith, LA Infantry
Barrios, Octave-Sgt. Lafourche Regiment, LA Militia
Barrios, Prosper-Pvt. Company G, 18th LA Infantry
Barro, Buenaventura-Pvt. Co. 6, 5th (Spanish) Regt., European Brigade, LA Mil.

Barro, Emanuel-1st Sapper, Gallimard's Company, Sappers / Miners, C.S.A
Barron, Carlos-Pvt. Company C, 8th TX Cavalry
Barros, Nagin-Pvt. Co. 7, 5th (Spanish) Regt., European Brigade, LA Militia
Baruch, A.W.-Surgeon Army of Northern Virginia
Baruch, Abram-Pvt. Company C, 4th Regiment, European Brigade, LA Militia
Baruch, Benjamin S.-Sgt. Company B, 17th Battalion, S.C. Infantry
Baruch, Herman-Courier Staff of General Beauregard and a member of Company K, 7th S.C. Infantry
Baruch, Simon-Asst. Surgeon 3rd Battalion, S.C. Inf., also 13th MISS Infantry
Basan, Alejo-Cpl. Thomas' Company, TX Partisan Rangers
Basan, Bernardino-Pvt. Minute Men (Scouts), Starr County, TX Militia
Basan, Desiderio-Pvt. Minute Men (Scouts), Starr County, TX Militia
Basan, Francisco-Pvt. Zapata's Company, Nueces County, TX State Troops
Basan, Juan-Pvt. Company I, 33rd TX Cavalry
Basco, C.-Pvt. Company K, 27th LA Infantry
Basco, Denis-Pvt. Company A, 26th LA Infantry
Basco, F.-Pvt. Company K, 27th LA Infantry
Basco, Jean Baptiste-Pvt. Company G, Consolidated Crescent Regiment, LA Inf.
Basco, Michel Adout- Pvt. Company F, Consolidated Crescent Regiment, LA Inf.
Basco, Lorant Noel-Pvt. Company A, 26th LA Infantry
Basco, Phanor-Pvt. Company C, 2nd LA Cavalry
Basco, Thomas-Pvt. Company A, 26th LA Infantry
***See also Vasques, Vasquez
Bascos, Julio-Pvt. Company B, Ragsdale's Battalion, TX Cavalry
Bascus, Decedra-Pvt. Company A, 11th TX Infantry
Bascus, Hose-Pvt. Company A, 2nd LA Cavalry
Bascus, Matteas-Pvt. Company A, 11th TX Infantry
Bascus, William-Pvt. Company C, Consolidated Crescent Regiment, LA Infantry
Basque, L.-Pvt. 1st Regiment, C.S.A.
Basque, Jose-Pvt. Company I, Benavides' Regiment, TX Cavalry
Basque, Juan-Pvt. Company G, 10th LA Infantry
Basques, Cerraino-Pvt. Company A, 3rd Yager's Battalion, TX Cavalry
Basques, Jose-Pvt. Company A, 2nd LA Infantry
Basques, Juan-Pvt. 1st Company C, 3rd TX Infantry
Basquez, Ferdinand-Pvt. 2nd Regiment, 2nd Brigade, 1st Division, LA Militia
Basquez, Thomas-Pvt. Company I, 3rd TX Infantry
Bassan, Alejo-Cpl. Thomas' Company, TX Partisan Rangers
Bateo, Gabino-Pvt. Company G, 3rd TX Infantry
Battala, Diego-Pvt. Company 5, Cazadores Espanoles Regiment, LA Militia
Battilo, George-Pvt. Company A, 1st Battalion, ALA Light Artillery
Battistella, Antonio-Pvt. Co. 3, 5th (Spanish) Regt., European Brigade, LA Mil.
Baul, Lorenzo-Pvt. Co. 6, 5th (Spanish) Regiment, European Brigade, LA Militia
Bautista, Juan-Pvt. Teel's Company, TX State Troops
Bautista, Juan-Pvt. Co. 8, 5th (Spanish) Regiment, European Brigade, LA Militia
Bautista, Miguel-Pvt. Co. 8, 5th (Spanish) Regt., European Brigade, LA Militia

Bauxes, Domingo-Pvt. Co. 2, 5th (Spanish) Regt., European Brigade, LA Militia
Bauza, Sancho-Pvt. LA Militia
Baya, Eleuterio Faustino-Pvt. Company G, 10th FLA Infantry
Baya, Francis Jose-2nd Lt. Company H, 2nd FLA Infantry
Baya, H.T.-Capt. Chief Clerk, Confederate Subsistence Department, S.C.
Baya, Joseph-Cpl. Company B, 2nd FLA Cavalry
Baya, Joseph Fecundus-Pvt. Company D, 8th FLA Infantry
Baya, Tayo-Pvt. Company B, 2nd FLA Infantry
Baya, William-Lt. Colonel 8th FLA Infantry
Bayhi, Anselme-Pvt. Company F, 30th LA Infantry
Bayhi, E.-Pvt. Company K, Chalemtte Regiment, LA Militia
Bayhi, Gustave V.-Pvt. Company F, 30th LA Infantry
Bayhi, Jules-Pvt. Company F, 30th LA Infantry
Bayhi, Leo-Pvt. Company K, Chalmette Regiment, LA Militia
Bayhi, Th.-Pvt. Company 4, Chasseurs a Pied, LA Militia
Bayhi, V.S.-Pvt. Company C, Orleans Guard Regiment, LA Militia
Baza, Antonio-Civilian taken prisoner by Union Forces near Palatka, FLA, on March 3rd, 1863, for his support of the Confederacy. He had his personal property confiscated but was able to escape and elude his captors.
Becerra, Francisco-2nd Lt. 1st Company C, 3rd TX Infantry
Beharahal, F.-Pvt. Company G, 8th TX Infantry
Beharahal, M.-Pvt. Company G, 8th TX Infantry
Bella, Vitur-Pvt. Medina Guards, Bexar County, TX Militia
***See also Velasco
Belasco, Francisco-Pvt. Co. 9, 5th (Spanish) Regt., European Brigade, LA Militia
Belisano, Moses-Pvt. Company A/B, 18th GA Infantry
Bello, P.-Cpl. Company D, 1st TX Heavy Artillery
Bello, Charles-Pvt. LA Infantry (unit unknown).
Bello, Valery-Pvt. Company B, 18th LA Infantry
Bellory, Pedro-Pvt. Company G, 10th LA Infantry
Beltran, Andres-Pvt. Company D, 30th LA Infantry
Beltran, Aniceto-Pvt. Company C, 8th TX Infantry
Beltran, Jesus-Pvt. 1st Company C, Ragsdale's Battalion, TX Cavalry
Beltran, Jose-Pvt. 1st Company C, 3rd TX Infantry
Beltran, Manuel-Pvt. 1st Company C, Ragsdale's Battalion, TX Cavalry
Beltran, R.-Pvt. Orleans Guard Battery, LA Light Artillery
Beltran, R.-Capt. LA Legion Brigade
Beltran, Stephen-Pvt. 4th Field Battery, TX Artillery
Ben, Manuel-Pvt. Co. 5, 5th (Spanish) Regiment, European Brigade, LA Militia
Bena, A.-Pvt. Mobile City Troop, ALA Militia
Benavides, Atilano-Pvt. 1st Company H, 33rd TX Cavalry
Benavides, Basilio-Pvt. Benavides' Regiment, TX Cavalry
Benavides, Cristobal-Capt. 1st Company H, 33rd TX Cavalry
Benavides, D.-Pvt. Company I, Border's Regiment, TX Cavalry
Benavides, David-Pvt. Weisigers' Company, Giddings' Battalion, TX Cavalry

Benavides, Lorenzo-Pvt. 1st Company H, 33rd TX Cavalry
Benavides, Luis-Pvt. 1st Company H, 33rd TX Cavalry
Benavides, Pablo-Pvt. / Musician Company C, 8th TX Infantry
Benavides, Pedro-Pvt. Company D, 30th LA Infantry
Benavides, Pedro-Pvt. Company F, 3rd TX Infantry
Benavides, Refugio-Capt. 1st Company I, 33rd TX Cavalry
Benavides, Jose De Los Santos-Colonel 33rd TX Cavalry
Benavidis, John-Pvt. Mullany's Company, Mobile Fire Battalion, ALA Militia
Beneridos, Pedro-Pvt. Company D, 30th LA Infantry
Benet, Casimiro-Pvt. Company D, 8th FLA Infantry
Benet, Hypolite-Pvt. Company C, 16th LA Infantry
Benet, J.R.-2nd Lt. Independent Rangers Iberville, LA Militia Cavalry
Benet, Peter L.-1st Lt. Company D, 8th FLA Infantry
Benet, Stephan A.-Pvt. Company B, 3rd FLA Infantry
Benet, Thomas-Musician Company D, 8th FLA Infantry
Benitez, Angel-Pvt. Co. 1, 5th (Spanish) Regt., European Brigade, LA Militia
Benjamin, Judah P.-Attorney General of the Confederacy Feb.- Sept., 1861. He was later acting Confederate Secretary of War from Sept.-Nov. 1861, after which he was confirmed. He served as Confederate Secretary of State from March 1863, until the end of the War.
Benjamin, Joseph-Capt. HQ's Escort Co., Major General Richard Taylor, LA
Bentoza, Joachin-Pvt. Company B, Milton Light Artillery, FLA
Bensadon, J.-Surgeon LA C.S.A.
Berara, Jose M.-Pvt. Company K, 6th LA Infantry
Beras, Phillipe-Pvt. 4th Field Battery, TX Artillery
Berban, Jose Maria-Pvt. Medina Guards, Bexar County, TX Militia
Berban, Pascual-Pvt. Medina Guards, Bexar County, TX Militia
Berenguer, J.-Cpl. Co. 1, 5th (Spanish) Regiment, European Brigade, LA Militia
Berientes, L.-Pvt. Company C, 8th TX Infantry
Bermudez, B.-Pvt. Company E, Orleans Guard Regiment, LA Militia
Bermudez, Edward Edmond-1st Lt. / Adjt. Orleans Guard Regt., LA Militia
Bermudez, J.-Pvt. Company A, Orleans Guard Regiment, LA Militia
Bermudez, Phillipe-Assistant Indian Translator State of Florida, 1863.
***Unknown if this surname below was Hernandez or Fernandez
Bernandez, Daniel-Pvt. Company D, Confederate States Zouave Battalion, LA
Bernal, Jesus-Pvt. Company D, Ragsdale's Battalion, TX Cavalry
Bernal, Jose-3rd Lt. Co. 3, 5th (Spanish) Regiment, European Brigade, LA Mil.
Bernal, J.V.-Pvt. Cattles' Company, Nashville Battalion, TENN Infantry
Bernal, Leandro-1st Sgt. Company F, 3rd TX Infantry
Bernal, Refugio-Sgt. Rhodes' Company, 3rd Yager's Battalion, TX Cavalry
Bernales, Eulogis-Pvt. Company C, 3rd TX Infantry
Bernardine, Hector-Pvt. Company H, 1st Strawbridge's LA Infantry
Bernardo, Antonio-Pvt. Company D, 30th LA Infantry
Bernaza, G.-Pvt. Co. 1, 5th (Spanish) Regiment, European Brigade, LA Militia
Berral, Jesus-Pvt. Company D, Ragsdale's Battalion, TX Cavalry

Berrera, C.-Pvt. Company F, 3rd TX Infantry
Berrera, Juan E.-1st Sgt. Company H, 8th Hobby's TX Infantry
Berrio, T.-Pvt. Company C, McCord's Frontier Regiment, TX Cavalry
Berthancourt, Alexandra-Pvt. Company F, 10th LA Infantry
Betancur, Fairstino-Pvt. Co. 4, 5th (Spanish) Regt., European Brigade, LA Militia
Betancur, Manuel-Pvt. Co. 10, 5th (Spanish) Regt., European Brigade, LA Militia
Beya, Vincent-Pvt. Company F, Cazadores Espanoles Regiment, LA Militia
Bianel, Leopoldo-Pvt. Co. 4, 5th (Spanish) Regt., European Brigade, LA Militia
Billera, W.-Pvt. Lafourche Regiment, LA Militia
Bins, Juan-Pvt. Co. 2, 5th (Spanish) Regiment, European Brigade, LA Militia
Bitanco, Manuel-Pvt. Company C, 1st Strawbridge's LA Infantry
Blanco, Manuel-Pvt. Co. 3, 5th (Spanish) Regt., European Brigade, LA Militia
Blanco, Santos-Pvt. Company B, 2nd TX Cavalry
Blasco, Amedee-Pvt. 1st Native Guards, LA Militia
Blasco, Eugenio J.-Capt. Company E/I, 13th LA Infantry
Blasco, Henry-Pvt. Company D, 5th LA Infantry
Blasco, Oscar-Pvt. Company D, 13th LA Infantry
Bloy, Julio-Pvt. Co. 5, 5th (Spanish) Regiment, European Brigade, LA Militia
Bloy, P.-Pvt. Co. D, 5th (Spanish) Regiment, European Brigade, LA Militia
Bo, Antonio Juan-Pvt. Co. 10, 5th (Spanish) Regt., European Brigade, LA Mil.
Boadas, James-Pvt. Co. 2, 5th (Spanish) Regiment, European Brigade, LA Mil.
Bobe, Ignatius V.-Pvt. 3rd Battalion, FLA Cavalry
Bobe, Ferdinand-Pvt. Company E, 2nd Battalion, ALA Light Artillery
Bobe, John V.-Pvt. 2nd FLA Cavalry
Boca, Miguel J.M.-Pvt. Company I, Benavides' Regiment, TX Cavalry
Boca Negra, Longino-Pvt. Company F, 3rd TX Infantry
Bocas, J.-Pvt. Company B, 18th Consolidated LA Infantry
Bonet, Juan-Pvt. Co. 9, 5th (Spanish) Regiment, European Brigade, LA Militia
Bonet, Vicente-Pvt. Co. 9, 5th (Spanish) Regiment, European Brigade, LA Mil.
Bonifacio, Martin-Pvt. Co. A, 5th (Spanish) Regt., European Brigade, LA Mil.
Bonilla, Charles L.-Sgt. Littleton's Company, Ford's Regiment, TX Cavalry
Bonito, F.A.-Pvt. Orleans Fire Regiment, LA Militia
Boraga, Ignacio-Pvt. Dunn's Company, Waller's Regiment, TX Cavalry
Borata, Agustin-Pvt. Co. 3, 5th (Spanish) Regt., European Brigade, LA Militia
Borego, Secundino-Pvt. Company 8, 8th TX Cavalry
Borgas, Jeronimo-Pvt. Company B, Ragsdale's Battalion, TX Cavalry
Bornagera, F.-Cpl. Company 1, Cazadores Espanoles Regiment, LA Militia
***See also Garcia y Borras, Jose
Borras, John-Pvt. Co. 5, 5th (Spanish) Regiment, European Brigade, LA Militia
Borrell, Jose M.-Pvt. Co. 5, 5th (Spanish) Regt., European Brigade, LA Militia
Bosne, Pablo-Pvt. Company 2, Cazadores Espanoles Regiment, LA Militia
Bosque, A.-Pvt. 1st Native Guards, LA Militia
Bosque, Lorenzo-Pvt. Company H, 10th LA Infantry
Bosque, Lorenzo-Pvt. 2nd Company C, 1st TENN Heavy Artillery
Bosque, Theophile-Pvt. 1st Native Guards, LA Militia

Bosques, Saturnino-Pvt. 1st Company H, 33rd TX Cavalry
Botario, John-Pvt. 1st LA Infantry
Botello, Antonio-Pvt. Company H, 33rd TX Cavalry
Botello, Concepcion-Pvt. 1st Company H, 33rd TX Cavalry
Botello, Gavino-Pvt. 1st Company H, 33rd TX Cavalry
Botello, Marco-Pvt. 1st Company H, 33rd TX Cavalry
Botello, Matilde-Pvt. 1st Company H, 33rd TX Cavalry
Botello, Victor Sr.-Pvt. 1st Company H, 33rd TX Cavalry
Botello, Victor Jr.-Pvt. 1st Company H, 33rd TX Cavalry
Botello, Viviano-Pvt. 1st Company H, 33rd TX Cavalry
Boteo, Gabina-Pvt. Company G, 3rd TX Infantry
Boter, Sebastian-Pvt. Company A, 5th TX Cavalry
Botero, Joseph-Pvt. 2nd Field Battery, TX Artillery
Bouligny, Charles-Pvt. Company D, 10th Battalion, LA Infantry
Bouligny, Dominique-Pvt. Company D, Orleans Guard Regiment, LA Militia
Bouligny, Edmond-Pvt. Pointe Coupee Artillery, LA
Bouligny, Gustave Jr.-2nd Lt. Co. A, 2nd Regt., 2nd Brig., 1st Division, LA Mil. He later served as a Recruiting Officer.
Bouligny, Louis-Board of City Assessors, New Orleans, LA from 1859 to 1861.
Bouligny, Ursin Victor-Pvt. Company H, Orleans Guard Regiment, LA Militia
Boustillos, Antoin-Pvt. 1st Native Guards, LA Militia
Boy, Antonio-Pvt. Company G, 21st ALA Infantry
Bragel, Antonio-Pvt. Company 2, Cazadores Espanoles Regiment, LA Militia
Braje, Antonio-Pvt. Co. 9, 5th (Spanish) Regiment, European Brigade, LA Militia
Brand, Manuel-Pvt. Company H, 1st LA Cavalry
Brandao, Edward A.-Pvt. Fenner's Battery, LA Artillery
Brasano, Encarnacion-Pvt. 1st Company A, Ragsdale's Battalion, TX Cavalry
Bravo, Alonzo Anastacio-3rd Lt. Company D, 8th FLA Infantry
Bravo, Christobal-Mayor St. Augustine, FLA, surrendered city to Union forces on March 12, 1862. His son is the man listed below.
Bravo, Christobal M.-4th Cpl. Company B, 3rd FLA Infantry
Bravo, John-Pvt. Gillis's Company, FLA Militia
***Also Listed as Briseno
Bresino, Margarito-Pvt. Company B, Ragsdale's Battalion, TX Cavalry
Brisen, Incarnacion-Pvt. Medina Guards, Bexar County, TX Militia
Brito, Gabino-Bugler 1st Company A, Ragsdale's Battalion, TX Cavalry
Brito, Nepomuceno-Pvt. Company C, 3rd TX Infantry
Bronat, Marselino-Cpl. Co. A, 5th (Spanish) Regt., European Brigade, LA Mil.
Bruna, Juan-Pvt. Company B, 18th VIR Infantry
Brunaso, Juan-Capt. Co. 8, 5th (Spanish) Regiment, European Brigade, LA Mil.
Bua, Francis-Pvt. Company I, 7th LA Infantry
Bua, Francisco-Pvt. Company D, 3rd Palmetto Battalion, S.C. Light Artillery
Buela, R.-Pvt. Company 1, Cazadores Espanoles Regiment, LA Militia
Bueno, Juan-Pvt. TX Militia
Buit, Pedro-Pvt. Co. 3, 5th (Spanish) Regiment, European Brigade, LA Militia

Bujol, J. Edmond-Pvt. Company K, 8th LA Infantry
Bulnez, Raymond-Pvt. Co. A, 8th LA Infantry (see also De Bulnez, Alphonso)
Bunol, Jacinto-Pvt. Co. 9, 5th (Spanish) Regiment, European Brigade, LA Militia
Bunol, Pedro-Pvt. Co. 9, 5th (Spanish) Regiment, European Brigade, LA Militia
Burges, F. Fernandez-Pvt. Avis' Company, 129th VIR Militia
Burguera, Antonio-Pvt. Co. 4, 5th (Spanish) Regt., European Brigade, LA Militia
Burlesta, Ramon-Pvt. Company B, 7th FLA Infantry
Busas, Jacinto-Pvt. Co. 6, 5th (Spanish) Regiment, European Brigade, LA Militia
Bustamante, Bensualdo-Pvt. Littleton's Company, Ford's Regiment, TX Cavalry
Bustamante, Manuel-Pvt. Bustillo's Company, Bexar County, TX Militia
Bustamente, G.D.-Capt. / Asst. Commissary, Staff of General Moore; he served with the 40th MISS Infantry.
Bustamente, Lucas-Pvt. Rhodes' Company, 3rd Yager's Battalion, TX Cavalry
Bustamente, Toribio-Cpl. Company C, Benavides' Regiment, TX Cavalry
Bustamente, Ylario-Pvt. Company C, 8th TX Infantry
***See also Boustillos
Bustillo, Clemente-Capt. Bustillo's Company, Bexar County, TX Militia
Bustillo, F.-Pvt. Teel's Company, TX State Troops
Bustillos, Antonio-Pvt. Company K, 6th TX Infantry

C

Caballer, Jose Torres-Pvt. Co. 2, 5th (Spanish) Regt., European Brigade, LA Mil.
Caballero, Andres-Pvt. Company E, Benavide's Regiment, TX Cavalry
Caballero, Fernando-Pvt. Co. 7, 5th (Spanish) Regt., European Brigade, LA Mil.
Cabello, Emilio-Pvt. Company A, Ragsdale's Battalion, TX Cavalry
Cabezas, Edward-Pvt. Co. B, 3rd Regiment, 2nd Brigade, 1st Division, LA Mil.
Cabiro, Antonio-1st Sgt. Company E, 1st FLA Cavalry
Cabos, Frailan-Pvt. Company C, 3rd TX Infantry
Cabos, John-Pvt. Company H, 1st LA Artillery
***Also listed as Cabrera, Magado
Cabraro, Magado-Pvt. Company E, 8th TX Infantry
Cabrillo, Antonio-Pvt. Company D, 8th TX Infantry
Cacais, Santiago-Pvt. Company B, 2nd TX Cavalry
Cachot, Antonio-Pvt. Co. 2, 5th (Spanish) Regt., European Brigade, LA Militia
Cachot, Bernardo-Pvt. Co. 2, 5th (Spanish) Regt., European Brigade, LA Militia
Cachot, Jose-Pvt. Co. 2, 5th (Spanish) Regiment, European Brigade, LA Militia
Cacias, Santos-Pvt. Company C, Benavides' Regiment, TX Cavalry
Cadena, Antonio-Pvt. Jeff Davis Home Guards, Refugio County, TX Militia
Cadenas, Rafael-Pvt. Company H, 8th TX Infantry
Cadenas, Syrildo-Pvt. Company D, Benavides' Regiment, TX Cavalry
Cadenas, Syvillo-Pvt. 1st Company A, Ragsdale's Battalion, TX Cavalry
Cadis, Henry A.-Pvt. Company A, 7th LA Infantry
Cadis, John-Pvt. Company C/H, Crescent Regiment, LA Infantry
Cadiz, Edward-Pvt. Company F, 1st Nelligan's LA Infantry

Cadiz, J.-Pvt. Company I, 18th LA Infantry
Caenasso, Bartolo-Pvt. Co. 6, 5th (Spanish) Regt., European Brigade, LA Militia
Cainniro, Juan Jose-Pvt. Co. 4, 5th (Spanish) Regt., European Brigade, LA Mil.
Cajigas, Teodoro-Pvt. Co. 9, 5th (Spanish) Regt., European Brigade, LA Militia
Calafell, J.-Sgt. Co. 1, 5th (Spanish) Regiment, European Brigade, LA Militia
Caldeira > see Silveira y Caldeira, I.
Calderon, Anselino-Pvt. Company A, Ragsdale's Battalion, TX Cavalry
Calderon, Augustin-Pvt. Company C, 2nd MO Cavalry
Calderon, Beninquas-Pvt. Creole Fire Company, Mobile, ALA Militia
Calderon, C.-Pvt. Teel's Company, TX State Troops
Calderon, J.-Pvt. Creole Fire Company, Mobile, ALA Militia
Calderon, J.G.-Pvt. Company B, 1st TX Cavalry
Calderon, Lewis-Pvt. Rhodes' Company, 3rd Yager's Battalion, TX Cavalry
Calderon, N.-Pvt. Teel's Company, TX State Troops
Calderon, Ramon-Sgt. Company F, 3rd TX Infantry
Calderon, Rafael-Cpl. Bustillos' Company, Bexar County, TX Militia
Caldue, Vicente-Pvt. Co. 4, 5th (Spanish) Regt., European Brigade, LA Militia
Callego, M.-Pvt. Company H, Orleans Guard Regiment, LA Militia.
Calleja, Manuel-Sgt. Major Company F/I, 10th LA Infantry
Calletano, Manuel-Pvt. Company D, 4th Regt., 1st Brig., 1st Division, LA Mil.
Calvet, Antonio-Pvt. Co. 6, 5th (Spanish) Regt., European Brigade, LA Militia
Calvet, Dominique-Pvt. Company 6, 2nd Regiment, French Brigade, LA Militia
Calvillo, Francisco-Pvt. Company H, 8th TX Infantry
Calvino, Jose-Pvt. Co. 3, 5th (Spanish) Regiment, European Brigade, LA Militia
Calvo, C.A.-Sgt. Company E, 1st Charleston Battalion, S.C. Infantry
Calvo, J.P.M.-Pvt. Company H, 3rd Battalion, GA State Guards
Calzado, Toruvio-Pvt. 1st Company C, 3rd TX Infantry
Camacho, Candelario-Pvt. Rhode's Company, 3rd Yager's Battalion, TX Cavalry
Camacho, John-Pvt. Company E, 8th LA Infantry
Camargo, Pedro-Bugler Company I, Benavides' Regiment, TX Cavalry
Camargo, Yues-Pvt. Company I, Benavides' Regiment, TX Cavalry
Camos, A.-Pvt. Company H, Chalmette Regiment, LA Militia
Camos, L.-Pvt. Company H, Chalmette Regiment, LA Militia
Campana, Joseph-Pvt. Borge's Company, Garnet Rangers, LA Militia
Campas, Antonio-Pvt. Company G, 10th LA Infantry
Campo, Albert-Capt. Quartermaster Department, C.S.A.
Campo, Dormian-2nd Lt. 5th (Spanish) Regt., European Brigade, LA Militia
Campo, Honore-Pvt. Company H, 2nd LA Cavalry
Campo, John-Pvt. Madison's Company, Mounted Spies and Guides, C.S.A
Campo, Julian-Pvt. Company B, Ragsdale's Battalion, TX Cavalry
Campo, S.-Pvt. Company H, Chalmette Regiment, LA Militia
Campo, Thomas-Pvt. Tucker's Regiment, Confederate Infantry
Campora, Pedro-Pvt. Co. 10, 5th (Spanish) Regt., European Brigade, LA Militia
Campos, Antonio-Pvt. Company D, 9th TX Cavalry
Campos, Emile-Pvt. Company G, Beauregard Battalion, LA Militia

Campos, J.-Pvt. Company G, 10th LA Infantry
Campos, Joseph E.-Sgt. Company F, 8th FLA Infantry
Campos, Julian-1st Sgt. Co. 4, 5th (Spanish) Regt., European Brigade, LA Militia
Campos, Justo-Pvt. Company D, 17th TX Infantry
Camps, Antonio-Pvt. Brander's Company, VIR Light Artillery
Camps, Damian-2nd Lt. Co. A, 5th (Spanish) Regt., European Brigade, LA Mil.
Camps, Francisco-Pvt. Co. 8, 5th (Spanish) Regt., European Brigade, LA Militia
Camps, J. Jr.-Pvt. 1st Native Guards, LA Militia
Camps, Manuel-Pvt. 1st Native Guards, LA Militia
Camulgy, Vicente-Sgt. Co. 5, 5th (Spanish) Regt., European Brigade, LA Militia
Canales, Alcario-Pvt. Company F, Waul's Legion, TX
Canales, J.M.-Pvt. Zapata's Company, Nueces County, TX State Troops
Canales, Mateo-Pvt. Company H, 8th TX Infantry
Canales, Santiago-Pvt. Zapata's Company, Nueces County, TX State Troops
***Also listed as Canavero
Canavara, Antonio-Pvt. Company D, 8th TX Infantry
Candida, Jose Antonio-Pvt. Company F, 10th LA Infantry
Candido, Juan-Pvt. Company B, 30th LA Infantry
Caneda, C.-Pvt. Company H, 29th TX Cavalry
Canet, Antonio-Pvt. Co. 9, 5th (Spanish) Regt., European Brigade, LA Militia
Canet, F.-Pvt. Co. 1, 5th (Spanish) Regiment, European Brigade, LA Militia
Cano, Andres-Pvt. 1st Company C, 3rd TX Infantry
Cano, Encarnacion-Pvt. 1st Company I, 33rd TX Cavalry
Cano, Jose Maria-Pvt. Rhodes' Company, 3rd Yager's Battalion, TX Cavalry
Cano, P.-Pvt. Company H, 4th TX Infantry
***See also Conova
Canova, Andreas B.-2nd Lt. Company D, 1st FLA Cavalry
Canova, Andrew P.-Pvt. Company B, 3rd FLA Infantry
Canova, Antonio A.-Major / Chief of Subsistence, Staff of Gen. J. Finegan, FLA. He
    was also a member of the FLA State Legislature during the war.
Canova, Antonio L.-Pvt. Co. B, 3rd FLA Inf., detailed as a Telegraph Operator.
Canova, Bartolo-Pvt. Company D, 1st FLA Cavalry
Canova, Bartolo Casamana-Pvt. Company F, 2nd FLA Infantry
Canova, George P.-Pvt. Company G, 2nd FLA Infantry
Canova, Isadore-Musician Company E, 6th FLA Infantry
Canova, Mattias-Mayor of St. Augustine, FLA 1861.
Canova, Paul-Sub Agent Commissary of Subsistence, FLA
Canova, Paul B.-2nd Lt. Company G, 1st FLA Infantry Reserve
Canova, Ramon-1st Sgt. Company F, 2nd FLA Infantry
Canta, D.-Pvt. Company G, 8th TX Infantry
Canta, M.-Pvt. Company G, 8th TX Infantry
Canta, Ociana-Pvt. Company C, Benavides' Regiment, TX Cavalry
Cantallops, Jamie-Cpl. Co. 4, 5th (Spanish) Regt., European Brigade, LA Militia
Cante, Agustin-Pvt. Company F, 3rd TX Infantry
Cante, Narcisso-Pvt. Thomas' Company, TX Partisan Rangers

Canter, Leonardo-Pvt. Rhodes' Company, 3rd Yager's Battalion, TX Cavalry
Canter, Pedro Tomas-Pvt. Rhodes' Company, 3rd Yager's Battalion, TX Cavalry
Cantilla, Bernard-Pvt. Company A, 1st Wheat's LA Infantry
Cantitrice, Pedro-Pvt. Co. 5, 5th (Spanish) Regt., European Brigade, LA Militia
Canto, Francisco-Pvt. Co. 9, 5th (Spanish) Regt., European Brigade, LA Militia
Cantu, Aciano-Pvt. Company C, 8th TX Infantry
Cantu, Agustin-Pvt. Company F, 3rd TX Infantry
Cantu, Felix-Pvt. Jeff Davis Home Guard, Refugio County, TX Militia
Capeans, Miguel-Pvt. Co. 4, 5th (Spanish) Regt., European Brigade, LA Militia
Capella, Bernardo-Pvt. Co. 5, 5th (Spanish) Regt., European Brigade, LA Militia
Capella, Francisco-Pvt. Co. 9, 5th (Spanish) Regt., European Brigade, LA Militia
Capella, Guillermo-Pvt. Co. 1, 5th (Spanish) Regt., European Brigade, LA Mil.
Capella, Laurence-Pvt. Acosta's Milton Artillery, FLA
Capella, Martas-Pvt. Co. 7, 5th (Spanish) Regt., European Brigade, LA Militia
Capella, Miguel-Pvt. Co. 5, 5th (Spanish) Regt., European Brigade, LA Militia
Capella, Severena-Pvt. Company D, 8th FLA Infantry
Capo, H.-Pvt. Company I, 15th TX Cavalry
Capo, Jose-Pvt. Co. 9, 5th (Spanish) Regiment, European Brigade, LA Militia
Capo, Joseph-Pvt. Company B, 3rd FLA Infantry
Capo, Lewis-1st Sgt. Company D, 8th FLA Infantry
Capo, Philip V.-Pvt. Company B, 3rd FLA Infantry
Capo, Rafael-Pvt. Co. 7, 5th (Spanish) Regiment, European Brigade, LA Militia
Capo, William Sr.-Pvt. Company D, 8th FLA Infantry
Capo, William Jr.-Pvt. Company D, 8th FLA Infantry
Capo, Ygnacio-Pvt. Co. 1, 5th (Spanish) Regiment, European Brigade, LA Militia
Caraillo, J.S.-Pvt. Company B, 8th LA Infantry
Cararas, A.-Cpl. 30th LA Infantry
Carasco, C.G.-Pvt. Company C, 18th LA Infantry
Carasco, Felix-Pvt. 1st Company A, Ragsdale's Battalion, TX Cavalry
Carasco, Frinquilino-Pvt. 1st Company A, Ragsdale's Battalion, TX Cavalry
Carasco, Hilaire-Pvt. Company C, 18th LA Infantry
Carasco, Juan-Pvt. Company H, Mann's Regiment, TX Cavalry
***See also Carvahal, Carbyjal
Carbajal, A.-Pvt. Company E, Waller's TX Cavalry
Carbajal, A. Gonzales-Pvt. Co. 1, 5th (Spanish) Regt., European Brig., LA Mil.
Carbajal, F. Garcia-Pvt. Co. 1, 5th (Spanish) Regt., European Brigade, LA Militia
Carbajal, Francisco-Pvt. Company E, 8th TX Infantry
Carbajal, Luis-Pvt. Company B, 2nd TX Mounted Rifles
Carbajal, Mesindo-Pvt. Company H, 33rd TX Cavalry
Carbajal, Vicente-Pvt. Co. 3, 5th (Spanish) Regt., European Brigade, LA Militia
Carbello, J. Alvin-Pvt. Calcasieu Parish Home Guard, LA Militia
Carbo, Antonio-Pvt. Co. 8, 5th (Spanish) Regt., European Brigade, LA Militia
Carbo, Agustin-Pvt. 8th LA Infantry
Carbo, Francis-Pvt. Company B, 8th ARK Infantry
Carbo, John-Pvt. Company A, 18th VIR Infantry

Carbo, Jose-Cpl. Co. 5, 5th (Spanish) Regiment, European Brigade, LA Militia
Carbo, Lorenzo-2nd Lt. Co. 8, 5th (Spanish) Regt., European Brigade, LA Militia
Carbyjal, Antonio-Sgt. Thomas' Company, TX Partisan Rangers
Cardena, Euluterio-Pvt. 1st Company C, 3rd TX Infantry
Cardena, F.-Musician Company G, 10th LA Infantry
Cardenas, Antonio-Pvt. Company G, 10th LA Infantry
Cardenas, Ceballos-Pvt. Company A, Ragsdale's Battalion, TX Cavalry
Cardenas, Gabriel-Pvt. 1st Company I, 33rd TX Cavalry
Cardenas, Ignacio-Pvt. Company I, 8th LA Infantry
Cardenas, Jose-Pvt. Duran / Tom's Company, Atascosa County, TX Troops
Cardenas, Joseph-Pvt. Medina Guards, Bexar County, TX Militia
Cardenas, Juan-1st Sgt. Company E, Benavides' Regiment, TX Cavalry
Cardenas, Nicanor-Pvt. Company C, 8th TX Infantry
Cardenas, Olegarde-Cpl. Company G, 37th TX Cavalry
Cardenas, Pablo-Pvt. Company D, Ragsdale's Battalion, TX Cavalry
Cardenas, Rafael-Pvt. Company B, 2nd TX Cavalry
Cardenas, Silvio-Pvt. Company A, Ragsdale's Battalion, TX Cavalry
Cardenas, V.-Pvt. Company D, 30th LA Infantry
Cardina, George-Pvt. Company C, Mobile Home Guard, ALA Militia
Cardona, Angel-Pvt. Co. 3, 5th (Spanish) Regiment, European Brigade, LA Mil.
Cardona, Antonio-Pvt. Co. 2, 5th (Spanish) Regt., European Brigade, LA Militia
Cardona, John-Pvt. Company B, 12th Battalion, VIR Light Artillery
Cardona, M.-Musician Company D, 25th VIR Infantry
Cardona, Miguis-Pvt. Co. 4, 5th (Spanish) Regt., European Brigade, LA Militia
Cardoza, Abraham J.-Pvt. Company E, 4th VIR Cavalry
Cardoza, C.P.-Pvt. Company C, 2nd VIR State Reserve
Cardoza, Charles E.-Pvt. Company D, 1st VIR Artillery
Cardoza Levy, David Jr.-2nd Lt. Company G/H, 13th LA Infantry
Cardoza, Edward S.-Pvt. Smith's Company, VIR Artillery
Cardoza, Julian C.-Pvt. Company D, 1st VIR Infantry
Cardoza, Julian H.-Pvt. Company A, 13th Battalion, VIR Light Artillery
Cardoza, William H.-Pvt. Company F, 4th Battalion, VIR Local Defense
Cardozo, M.C.-1st Sgt. Company K, 1st Farinholt's VIR Reserve
Caredo, Louis D.-Ordnance Sgt. Company F, 8th FLA Infantry
Cargol, P.-Pvt. Co. 1, 5th (Spanish) Regiment, European Brigade, LA Militia
Cargol, Thomas-Cpl. Company K, 2nd ALA Cavalry
Cario, Antonio-Pvt. Company D, 11th Volunteer Infantry Battalion, TX
Carion, Joaquin-Pvt. Company C, Benavides' Regiment, TX Cavalry
Carion, Segundo-Pvt. Zapata's Company, Nueces County, TX State Troops
Carmona, Hosea Leroy-1st Sgt. Company A/F, 8th LA Infantry
***See also Carro
Caro, A.-Pvt. Company H, Chalmette Regiment, LA Militia
Caro, Albert V.-Pvt. FLA Militia
Caro, Antonio-Pvt. Company C, 11th TX Infantry
Caro, Incarnacion-Pvt. Company 3, 3rd LA Infantry

Caro, J.C.-Capt. QuarterMaster Corps, C.S.A.
Caro, James W.-Sgt. Company A, 1st FLA Infantry
Caro, John B.-Assistant Surgeon, C.S.A.
Caro, Thomas-Pvt. Company B, 37th TX Cavalry
Carreno, F.-Cpl. Co. 2, 5th (Spanish) Regiment, European Brigade, LA Militia
Carrera, Francis-1st Lt. Steele's 16th Regiment, FLA Militia
Carreras, Antonio-Pvt. Co. 8, 5th (Spanish) Regt., European Brigade, LA Militia
Carreras, Bartolome-Pvt. Co. 2, 5th (Spanish) Regt., European Brigade, LA Mil.
Carreras, Gaspar-Pvt. Company A, 2nd FLA Infantry
Carreras, Juan-Pvt. Co. 6, 5th (Spanish) Regiment, European Brigade, LA Militia
Carreras, Pedro-1st Sgt. Company 5, Cazadores Espanoles Regiment, LA Militia
Carreras, Stephen-Pvt. Company B, 3rd FLA Infantry
Carretero, Alejo-Pvt. Co. 5, 5th (Spanish) Regiment, European Brigade, LA Mil.
Carriga, J.-Pvt. TX Infantry
Carillo, A.-Pvt. Company F, 5th TX Infantry
Carrillo, A.P.-Cpl. Company 3, 1st Chasseurs a pied, LA Militia
Carrillo, Antonio-Pvt. 1st Company I, 33rd TX Cavalry
Carrillo, B.-Cpl. Company 3, 1st Chasseurs a pied, LA Militia
Carrillo, Joseph-Pvt. Company B, 2nd TX Cavalry
Carrillo, Joseph A.-Pvt. Company I, 10th LA Infantry
Carrillo, Pancho-Pvt. Company B, 2nd TX Cavalry
Carro, Jose M.-Pvt. Company K, 2nd TX Cavalry
Carvahal, Vincent F.-Pvt. TX Militia
Carvas, J.-Pvt. Company E, 13th S.C. Infantry
Carvedo, Antonio-Pvt. Company H, 25th VIR Infantry
Casals, Joaquin-Cpl. Co. 7, 5th (Spanish) Regiment, European Brigade, LA Mil.
Casandra, G.-Pvt. Company C, 8th TX Infantry
Casanova, Cristiano-Pvt. Tom's Company, Atascosa County, TX Militia
Casanova, E.P.-Pvt. Coast Guard Battalion, GA Militia
Casanova, Juan Gomila-Pvt. Co. 2, 5th (Span.) Regt., European Brigade, LA Mil.
Casanova, Juan Antonio-Pvt. Company H, 8th TX Infantry
Casanova, Ventura-Pvt. Medina Guards, Bexar County, TX Militia
Casaras, Cecelia-Pvt. Company D, 36th TX Cavalry
Casares, Antonio-Pvt. Company A, 3rd Battalion, TX Cavalry
Casares, Francisco-Pvt. Company A, 3rd Battalion, TX Cavalry
Casas, Estaniola-Pvt. 1st Company A, 3rd TX Infantry
Casas, Joaquin-Pvt. TX Militia
Casas, Miguel-Pvt. 1st Company C, 3rd TX Infantry
Casia, P.-Pvt. Company B, 2nd TX Cavalry
Cassanova, John B.-Pvt. Barret's Company, MO Light Artillery
Cassanovas, A.-Pvt. Company 3, 1st Chasseurs a pied, LA Militia
Cassiano, Fermin-Pvt. Duff's Company, Bexar County, TX Militia
Cassiano, Ignacio J.-Pvt. Company A, 33rd TX Cavalry
Cassiano, Simon-Pvt. 1st Company I, 33rd TX Cavalry
Cassillas, Santiago-Pvt. Medina Guards, Bexar County, TX Militia

Cassillas, Santos-Pvt. Company C, Benavides' Regiment, TX Cavalry
Cassillos, Jose-Pvt. Duff's Regiment, TX Cavalry
Cassiris, Antonio-Pvt. Company A, 3rd Yager's Battalion, TX Cavalry
Cassiris, Francisco-Pvt. Company A, 3rd Yager's Battalion, TX Cavalry
Castaneda, Carlos-Pvt. Rhodes' Company, 3rd Yager's Battalion, TX Cavalry
Castaneda, Juan-Pvt. Rhodes' Company, 3rd Yager's Battalion, TX Cavalry
Castanedo, A.-Pvt. Company F, 30th LA Infantry
Castanedo, Arthur A.-2nd Lt. Co. K, 3rd Regt., 2nd Brig., 1st Division, LA Mil.
Castanedo, Desiderio-Pvt. Rhodes' Company, 3rd Yager's Battn., TX Cavalry
Castanedo, Julio-Cpl. Company E, 22nd Consolidated LA Infantry
Castanedo, John A.-2nd Lt. Company E, Orleans Guard Regiment, LA Militia
Castanedo, T.-Pvt. Trevinio's Company, TX Cavalry
Castanera, Eusebio-Pvt. Co. 9, 5th (Spanish) Regt., European Brigade, LA Mil.
Castanio, Manuel-Pvt. Company G, 10th LA Infantry
Castano, Severo-Pvt. 1st Company A, 3rd TX Infantry
Castanol, Juan-Pvt. Company C, Benavides' Regiment, TX Cavalry
Castanon, Luis-2nd Sgt. Duran's Company, Atascosa County, TX Troops
Castanon, Simon-Pvt. Medina Guards, Bexar County, TX Militia
Castella, B.-Pvt. Company G, 5th LA Infantry
Castellaneo, T.-Pvt. Trevinio's Company, TX Cavalry
Castellano, Thomas-Pvt. Company F, 3rd TX Infantry
Castellanos, Henry Charles-Capt. Castellanos' Battery, LA Artillery
Castello, Antonio-Pvt. Co. 2, 5th (Spanish) Regt., European Brigade, LA Militia
Castello, Nicolas-Pvt. Company B, 2nd TX Infantry
Castellon, G.W. Sr.-Pvt. Macon Local Defense, GA Militia
Castanens, J.W.-Pvt. Company H, 21st N.C. Infantry
Castenon, J.-Pvt. Trevinio's Company, TX Cavalry
Castera, L.-3rd Lt. Company 2, 1st Chasseurs a pied, LA Militia
Castillan, J.D.-Cpl. Company B, 9th TENN Infantry
***Castile, Castille is the Louisiana French version of the surname Castillo, which was originally Castel.
Castile, Adolphe-Pvt. Company H, 7th LA Cavalry
Castile, Coronacion-Pvt. Company H, 19th LA Infantry
Castile, D.-Pvt. Company G, Crescent Regiment, LA Infantry
Castile, H. Jr.-Pvt. Company F, 3rd Wingfield's LA Cavalry
Castile, Michael-Pvt. Company K, 18th LA Infantry
Castile, Jose-Pvt. Company B, 28th Thomas' LA Infantry
Castille, A.H.-Pvt. Company H, Mile's Legion, LA
Castille, Alexander-1st Lt. Company A, 18th Consolidated LA Infantry
Castille, Anatole-Cpl. Company D, 18th Consolidated LA Infantry
Castille, Cezaire-Pvt. Company D, 18th Consolidated LA Infantry
Castille, Cezene E.-Pvt. Company D, 18th Consolidated LA Infantry
Castille, Dermas-Pvt. Company A, 7th LA Cavalry
Castille, Derneville-Pvt. Company D, 18th Consolidated LA Infantry
Castille, Don Louis-Pvt. Company C, 8th LA Infantry

Castille, Doucere-Pvt. Company D, 18th Consolidated LA Infantry
Castille, Elphige-Pvt. Company K, 28th Thomas' LA Infantry
Castille, Francisco-Pvt. Company B, 18th LA Infantry
Castille, J.A.-Capt. Company K, 18th LA Infantry
Castille, Jean-Cpl. Company K, 28th Thomas' LA Infantry
Castille, Raymond-Pvt. 1st Native Guards, LA Militia
Castille, Theogene-1st Lt. Company G, 10th Battalion, LA Infantry
Castille, Valmont-Pvt. LA Militia
Castille, Valsain-Pvt. Company C, 8th LA Infantry
Castilliro, B.-Pvt. Trevinio's Company, TX Cavalry
Castillo, Alcario-Cpl. Company B, Ragsdale's Battalion, TX Cavalry
Castillo, Basilia-Pvt. Company A, 24th LA Infantry
Castillo, C.A.-1st Lt. Company H, Orleans Guard Regiment, LA Militia
Castillo, Charles A.-QuarterMaster LA Legion Brigade
Castillo, Cicilio-Pvt. Medina Guards, Bexar County, TX Militia
Castillo, Cristobal-Pvt. 1st Company H, 33rd TX Cavalry
Castillo, David C.-Pvt. Company B, 8th FLA Infantry
Castillo, Faustino-Pvt. Jeff Davis Home Guard, Refugio County, TX Militia
Castillo, Henry-2nd Lt. Company 3, 13th LA Infantry
Castillo, John-Musician Company B, 8th FLA Infantry
Castillo, John-Pvt. Company H, Miles' Legion, LA
Castillo, John-Pvt. 15th Field Battery, TX Artillery
Castillo, Jose-Pvt. Company I, 8th TX Infantry
Castillo, Juan-Pvt. Co. 6, 5th (Spanish) Regiment, European Brigade, LA Militia
Castillo, Lewis D.-County Commissioner, Escambia County, FLA 1861.
Castillo, Nicomedes-Pvt. Thomas' Company, TX Partisan Rangers
Castillo, Ozemi-Pvt. Company K, 7th LA Cavalry
Castillo, Precilano-Pvt. 1st Company C, 3rd TX Infantry
Castillo, Refugio-Pvt. Company D, 3rd TX Infantry
Castillo, Serapio-Pvt. 1st Company H, 33rd TX Cavalry
Castillo, Serveriano-Pvt. Company C, 8th TX Infantry
Castillon, Estevan-Pvt. Dunn's Company, Waller's Regiment, TX Cavalry
Castillon, Hipolito-Pvt. Dunn's Company, Waller's Regiment, TX Cavalry
Castillon, Severo-Pvt. Company I, 8th TX Infantry
Castio, F.-Pvt. Teel's Company, TX State Troops
Castio, Jose Maria-Pvt. Company E, 8th TX Infantry
Castrillon, C.-Cpl. Co. 2, 5th (Spanish) Regiment, European Brigade, LA Militia
Castro, A.A.-Pvt. Company D, 1st ALA Cavalry
Castro, Amedio-Pvt. 8th Field Battery, TX Artillery
Castro, C.-Pvt. Company F, 2nd TX Infantry
Castro, C.-Pvt. Company 2, Cazadores Espanoles Regiment, LA Militia
Castro, Cuiton-Pvt. 4th LA Cavalry
Castro, F.-Cpl. Co. 2, 5th (Spanish) Regiment, European Brigade, LA Militia
Castro, J.F.-1st Lt. Company H, Baird's Regiment, TX Cavalry
Castro, Jacob-Pvt. Company B, 18th TX Cavalry

Castro, Jesus P.-Pvt. Company C, 8th TX Infantry
Castro, Jesus T.-2nd Lt. 1st Company C, Ragsdale's Battalion, TX Cavalry
Castro, Joseph T.-2nd Lt. Company F, Benavides' Regiment, TX Cavalry
Castro, Manuel-Cpl. Company 1, Cazadores Espanoles Regiment, LA Militia
Castro, Michel-Pvt. Company K, 18th Consolidated LA Infantry
Castro, Miguel-Pvt. Company F, 3rd TX Infantry
Castro, Narcissus-Pvt. Company A, 16th LA Infantry
Castro, Savano-Pvt. / Teamster ARIZ Battalion
Castro, Serafin-Pvt. Company C, 1st Regiment Mobile Volunteers, ALA
Castro, V.-Pvt. Trevinio's Company, TX Cavalry
Castro, Vicente-Pvt. Company D, 8th TX Infantry
Cataneo, Leonardo-Pvt. Company F, Cazadores Espanoles Regiment, LA Militia
Cavada, J.H.-Pvt. Company I, 61st ALA Infantry
Cavallier, D.-Pvt. Company I, 19th LA Infantry
Cavasas, Lucas-Pvt. 1st Company C, 3rd TX Infantry
Cavassos, Antonio-Pvt. 4th Field Battery, TX Artillery
Cavazos, Dimas-Pvt. Company F, 3rd TX Infantry
Cavazos, Nepanuceno-Sgt. Rhodes' Company, 3rd Yager's Battalion, TX Cavalry
***This is the Floridian version of the surname Quevedo
Cavedo, Adolphus G.-1st Cpl. Company C, 2nd FLA Cavalry
Cavedo, John S.-Major Camden City Mounted Militia, GA
Cavedo, Louis D.-Pvt. Company G, 10th FLA Infantry
Cayetano, Juan-Pvt. Company 1, Cazadores Espanoles Regiment, LA Militia
Cayigas, Feodoro-Pvt. Company 5, Cazadores Espanoles Regiment, LA Militia
Cazares, Michel-2nd Lt. Donaldsonville Artillery, LA
***Also Listed as Ceballos, Antonio
Cebelio, Antonio-Pvt. Company F, 3rd TX Cavalry
***See also Seferia
Ceferia, Jose-Pvt. Company D, 30th LA Infantry
Celestin, Charles D.-Sgt. Company D, 2nd TX Infantry
Celis, Jayme-Pvt. Co. 2, 5th (Spanish) Regiment, European Brigade, LA Militia
Cendon, Manuel-Pvt. Co. 2, 5th (Spanish) Regt., European Brigade, LA Militia
Cendra, Agustin-Pvt. Co. 10, 5th (Spanish) Regt., European Brigade, LA Militia
Centeno, Alcee-Pvt. Company C, 22nd Consolidated LA Infantry
Centeno, Alex-Pvt. Company C, 22nd Consolidated LA Infantry
Centeno, E.-Pvt. Company C, 22nd Consolidated LA Infantry
Centeno, Emile-Pvt. Company D, 30th LA Infantry
Centeno, Henry-Pvt. Company H, 28th Thomas' LA Infantry
Cerbera, Antonio-Pvt. Co. 4, 5th (Spanish) Regt., European Brigade, LA Militia
***Cerda also appears as Cerdo
Cerda, Antonio-Pvt. Rhode's Company, 3rd Battalion, TX Cavalry
Cerda, Blas-Pvt. Company B, 33rd TX Cavalry
Cerda, Eugenio-Pvt. Company H, 33rd TX Cavalry
Cerda, Gregorio-Pvt. Cameron County Coast Guard, TX Militia
Cerda, Jesus-Pvt. Zapata's Company, Nueces County, TX State Troops

Cerda, Jose-Pvt. Bustillo's Company, Bexar County, TX Militia
Cerda, Pedro-Pvt. Co. 10, 5th (Spanish) Regiment, European Brigade, LA Militia
Cerda, Ramon-Pvt. Trevino's Company, TX Partisan Rangers
Cerilo, G.-Pvt. Company B, 8th LA Infantry
Cerilo, Serapio-Pvt. Company B, 8th LA Infantry
Cerquera, Manuel-Pvt. Co. 10, 5th (Spanish) Regt., European Brigade, LA Militia
Certinas, Jose M.-Pvt. Company D, Ragsdale's Battalion, TX Cavalry
***See also Servantez
Cervantes, Casanio-Pvt. Company I, 8th TX Infantry
Cervantes, Juan-Pvt. Company H, 8th TX Infantry
Cervantes, Manuel-Pvt. TX Militia
Cervera, Gaston-Pvt. Company I, 8th TX Infantry
Cervera, Juan-Pvt. Jeff Davis Home Guard, Refugio County, TX Militia
Cervera, Manuel-Pvt. Company H, 8th TX Infantry
Cesar, M.-Drummer Company I, 13th LA Infantry
Cevallos, Pedro-Capt. Company F, 3rd TX Infantry
Chacon, Carlos-Pvt. Gray's Company, Bexar County, TX Militia
Chamar, T.-Pvt. Company F, 9th LA Infantry
Chapa, Bernardo-Pvt. Company B, Benavides' Regiment, TX Cavalry
Chapa, Francisco-Pvt. Company H, 8th TX Infantry
Charres, C.-Pvt. Trevinio's Company, TX Cavalry
Charri, Charles P.-Pvt. Company H, 3rd FLA Infantry
Charria, Augustin-Pvt. Company H, 8th LA Infantry
Charo, Nicolas-Cpl. 1st Company H, 33rd TX Cavalry
Charo, Refugio-Pvt. TX Militia
Chavana, Alvino-Pvt. Company C, Benavides' Regiment, TX Cavalry
Chavaria, Bonifacio-Pvt. Dunn's Company, Waller's Regiment, TX Cavalry
Chavaria, Jose M.-Pvt. Company I, Benavides' Regiment, TX Cavalry
Chaves, Bernardino-Pvt. Company I, Benavides' Regiment, TX Cavalry
Chaves, Erasmo J.-2nd Lt. Company H, 8th TX Infantry
Chaves, Francisco-Pvt. Company C, 8th TX Infantry
Chaves, Isidoro-Pvt. Jeff Davis Home Guard, Refugio County, TX Militia
Chaves, Jose M.-Pvt. Mitchell's Minute Men, Bexar County, TX Militia
Chaves, Jesus-Pvt. Company A, Ragsdale's Battalion, TX Cavalry
Chaves, Martin-Pvt. Company F, 3rd TX Infantry
Chavez, Irineo-Pvt. 1st Company C, Ragsdale's Battalion, TX Cavalry
Chavez, Mariano-Pvt. 1st Company C, Ragsdale's Battalion, TX Cavalry
Chavez, Pedro-Pvt. 8th Field Battery, TX Artillery
Chavire, Manuel-Pvt. 8th Field Battery, TX Artillery
Cherino, Jose M.-Pvt. Company A, 17th TX Cavalry
Cherino, Louis-Pvt. Company A, 1st Cavalry Battalion, TX State Troops
Cheysan, Fernando-Pvt. Hughes' Company, TX Light Artillery
Chico, Francis-Pvt. LA Militia
Chincho > see Rivas y Chincho, J.
Chivano, Stephan-Pvt. Company A, 11th TX Infantry

Hispanic Confederates 31

Chulian, Manuel-Pvt. Co. 10, 5th (Spanish) Regt., European Brigade, LA Militia
Cientos, Sabeo-Pvt. Company A, 2nd FLA Infantry
Cimbre, Rosario-Pvt. Company G, 21st ALA Infantry
Ciprian, Cecilio-Pvt. Company I, Benavides' Regiment, TX Cavalry
Cipriano, Benigno-Pvt. Company C, 8th TX Infantry
Cipriano, Pablo-Pvt. Company H, 33rd TX Cavalry
Cintes, Christopher-Pvt. Co. 5, 5th (Spanish) Regt., European Brigade, LA Mil.
Cisnero, John-Pvt. Lamar Home Guards, Refugio County, TX Militia
Cisneros, Santos-Pvt. 15th Field Battery, TX Artillery
Cobelo, Miguel-Pvt. Co. 9, 5th (Spanish) Regiment, European Brigade, LA Mil.
Cobos, Jose Maria-Capt. Brownsville Home Guard, TX Militia
Codina, Simeon-Pvt. Co. 5, 5th (Spanish) Regiment, European Brigade, LA Mil.
Cohen, Lawrence L.-Pvt. Palmetto Battn., SC Lt. Arty. (son of Miriam De Leon)
Colas, Rafael-Pvt. 1st Native Guards, LA Militia
Colchado, Ylario-Pvt. Company B, Benavides' Regiment, TX Cavalry
Coll, Antonio-Pvt. Co. 4, 5th (Spanish) Regiment, European Brigade, LA Militia
Coll, Jayme-Pvt. Co. 7, 5th (Spanish) Regiment, European Brigade, LA Militia
Coll, Manuel-Pvt. Company G, Orleans Guard Regiment, LA Militia
Coll, Moses-Pvt. Company A, 13th LA Infantry
Colomines, Vicente-Pvt. Company 1, Cazadores Espanoles Regiment, LA Mil.
Colon, E.-Sgt. Company A, 7th LA Infantry
Colon, Robert-Tax Assesor, LA
Colona, A.-Pvt. Company G, 8th ALA Infantry
Columbo > see Villa y Columbo, J.
***See also Manolito Comas Larramendi and Jose Comas Larramendi
Comas, Joseph Henry-Pvt. Company F, 47th GA Infantry
Comas, P.-Pvt. Co. 1, 5th (Spanish) Regiment, European Brigade, LA Militia
Comas, S.-Pvt. Co. 5, 5th (Spanish) Regiment, European Brigade, LA Militia
Comerchi, John-Pvt. Company E, 8th LA Infantry
Comero, Michael-Pvt. Company A, Squire's Battalion, LA Artillery
Concha, J.B.-3rd Lt. Company A, 24th ALA Infantry
Concha, J.D.-Pvt. Company G, 6th VIR Cavalry
Concha, R.-Pvt. Spanish Guards, Mobile Home Guard, ALA Militia
Conda, Elcardio-Pvt. Company 3, 3rd TX Infantry
Conda, John-Pvt. Company I, 17th VIR Infantry
Conde, Frederick-Pvt. Company E, 3rd TX Infantry
Condi, Pablo-Pvt. Thomas' Company, TX Partisan Rangers
Condie, Bernardo-Pvt. Company G, 8th TX Infantry
Condie, R.G.-Pvt. Company A, 8th MISS Infantry
Condis, J.R.-Pvt. Company A, 9th ALA Infantry
Conova, Joseph-Pvt. Company G, 26th S.C. Infantry
Constancia, Simon-Pvt. Medina Guards, Bexar County, TX Militia
Constantia, Anastasia-Pvt. Company G, 10th LA Infantry
Constantino, Juan-Pvt. Company H, 10th LA Infantry
*** Contario is the Louisiana Adaeseno version of the surname Quintero. This name

was also found as Kintano.
Contario, Raymond-Pvt. Company D, 27th LA Infantry
Contrarus, Becelio-Pvt. Company C, 8th TX Infantry
Contrarus, Jose-Pvt. Company C, 8th TX Infantry
Contreras, John-Pvt. Company C, Chalmette Regiment, LA Militia
Contreras, Manuel-Cpl. Company C, 3rd TX Infantry
Contreras, N.-Pvt. Company E, 8th TX Cavalry
Contreras, Peter-Pvt. Hampton Legion, S.C.
Cordero, John W.-Sgt. Company C, 1st McCreary's S.C. Infantry
Cordonia, Paul-Pvt. Graham's Company, VIR Horse Artillery
Cordova, J.D.-Pvt. Eubank's Company, Nacogdoches County, TX Militia
Cordova, M.-Pvt. Company D, S.C. Militia Reserve
Cordova, Mercal-Pvt. Company B, 2nd TX Cavalry
Cordova, Peter-Pvt. Company E, 2nd LA Cavalry
Cordova, Ramon-Pvt. Eubank's Company, Nacogdoches County, TX Militia
Corona, Anastacio-Pvt. 1st Company I, 33rd TX Cavalry
Corona, Antonio-Pvt. Company I, 33rd TX Cavalry
Corona, Ilario-Pvt. 1st Company H, 33rd TX Cavalry
Corona, Mario-Pvt. 33rd TX Cavalry
Corona, Paz-Pvt. 1st Company H, 33rd TX Cavalry
Coronado, Nester-Pvt. Company F, 3rd TX Infantry
Coronado, Reyes-Pvt. Company B, Benavides' Regiment, TX Cavalry
Corre, Jean-Pvt. Company H, 21st ALA Infantry
Corrales, Susano-Pvt. Gray's Company, Bexar County, TX Militia
Correges, J. Jr.-Pvt. Company G, Saint James Regiment, LA Militia
Correjolles, L.P.-Pvt. Guyol's Company, Orleans Artillery, LA
Correjolles, Octave-Pvt. Company D, Manigault's Battalion, S.C. Artillery
Corrillo, Raphael-Pvt. Company C, 30th TX Cavalry
Cortes, Ferdinand-Pvt. 9th MO Infantry
Cortes, John-Pvt. 30th TENN Infantry
Cortes, Joseph-Pvt. Company C, Crescent Regiment, LA Infantry
Cortes, Paul-Pvt. Company B, Confederate States Zouave Battalion, LA
Cortes, Peter-Pvt. Company H, 3rd MISS Infantry
Cortes, Rene E.-2nd Lt. Tobin's Company, TENN Light Artillery
Cortez, Antonio-Pvt. 1st Company C, 3rd TX Infantry
Cortez, C.W.-Pvt. Company E, 13th VIR Cavalry
Cortez, Carlos Hernandez-Pvt. Company C, 3rd TX Infantry
Cortez, Eluardo-Pvt. Lafourche Regiment, LA Militia
Cortez, Emile-Pvt. 18th LA Infantry
Cortez, Felix-Pvt. Company 3, 3rd MISS Infantry
Cortez, H.-Pvt. Company F, 2nd TX Infantry
Cortez, Jesus-Pvt. Teel's Company, TX State Troops
Cortez, Joseph-Pvt. Company I, 10th LA Infantry
Cortez, Julian-Pvt. Company C, 8th TX Infantry
Cortez, Julio-Pvt. Rhodes' Company, 3rd Yager's Battalion., TX Cavalry

Hispanic Confederates 33

Cortez, Louis G.-Pvt. Company G, 7th LA Infantry
Cortez, Simon-Pvt. Company E, 8th TX Infantry
***See also Courtinez
Cortenas, Manuel-Pvt. Company E, 8th TX Infantry
Cortenus, Enus-Pvt. Company H, 19th LA Infantry
Cortina, Ramon-Pvt. Co. 4, 5th (Spanish) Regt., European Brigade, LA Militia
Cortinas, Benino-Pvt. Jeff Davis Home Guard, Refugio County, TX Militia
Cortinas, John N.-2nd Lt. Company F, 3rd TX Infantry
Cortinas, Jose-Pvt. Company B, 2nd TX Cavalry
Cortinez, Joseph-Pvt. Company B, 28th Gray's LA Infantry
Cortisso, Selos-Pvt. Estill's Company, Local Defense, S.C.
Costa, A.-Pvt. Company B, 18th LA Infantry
Costa, Adolphe M.-Pvt. LA Guard Battery
Costa, E.J.-Pvt. Jones' Company, 16th Regiment S.C. Infantry
Costa, J.-Pvt. Company D, Charleston Guard, S.C. Militia
Costa, Jose-Pvt. Company G, 21st ALA Infantry
Costa, Joseph A.-Sgt. Company G, 6th TX Infantry
Costa, Juan-Pvt. Co. 10, 5th (Spanish) Regiment, European Brigade, LA Militia
Costa, Martin-Pvt. Russell's Company, 5th Infantry GA State Guards
Costo, A.-Pvt. Crescent Regiment, LA Infantry
Costantino, Grano-Pvt. Company G, 21st ALA Infantry
Costello, John-Pvt. Company C, 7th LA Infantry
Courtinez, E.M.-Pvt. Company L, Consolidated Crescent Regt., LA Infantry
Covas, Frailan-Pvt. Company C, 3rd TX Infantry
Covas, Rafael-Pvt. Company D, 95th ALA Militia
Coy, Alex-Pvt. Company C, 2nd TX Infantry
Coy, Antonio-Pvt. Company C, 8th TX Infantry
Coy, Juan-Bugler Company H, 8th TX Infantry
Coyre, Manuel-Pvt. Co. 2, 5th (Spanish) Regiment, European Brigade, LA Mil.
Craguet, Jose-Pvt. Company 5, Cazadores Espanoles Regiment, LA Militia
Craxell, Vicente-Cpl. Co. A, 5th (Spanish) Regiment, European Brigade, LA Mil.
Cresos, John-Pvt. Company A, 1st State Troops, TX Infantry
***In some rosters Crespillo appears as Crespo; this might be 2 different individuals or the same person
Crespillo, Juan-Pvt. Co. 10, 5th (Spanish) Regiment, European Brigade, LA Mil.
Crespillo, Juan-Pvt. Company D, 30th LA Infantry
Cruanes, Agustin-Cpl. Co. 7, 5th (Spanish) Regt., European Brigade, LA Militia
Cruanes, F.D.-1st Lt. Co. K, 2nd Regiment, 2nd Brigade, 1st Division, LA Militia
Cruz, Apolonio-Pvt. Company D, 13th LA Infantry
Cruz, Higinio-Pvt. 2nd Field Battery, TX Artillery
Cruz, J.S.-Pvt. Company C, 33rd TX Cavalry
Cruz, Jenaro-Pvt. TX Militia
Cruz, Jose Maria-Pvt. 2nd Field Battery, TX Artillery
Cruz, Miguel-Pvt. Company E, 8th TX Infantry
Cruz, Peter-Pvt. Company B, Baylor's Regiment, TX Cavalry

Cruz, Thomas-Pvt. Company H, 12th KY Cavalry
Cruz, Tomas-Pvt. Company C, Cater's Battalion, TX Cavalry
Cruz, Tomas-Pvt. Trevinio's Company, TX Cavalry
Cruz, Vicente-Pvt. 2nd Field Battery, TX Artillery
Cruzat, Gustave-Capt. Company D, Orleans Guard Regiment, LA Militia
Cruzat, Henry-Pvt. Company D, Orleans Guard Regiment, LA Militia
Cruzat, William-Sgt. Company D, Orleans Guard Regiment, LA Militia
Cuadeas, Francisco-Pvt. Co. 3, 5th (Spanish) Regt., European Brigade, LA Mil.
Cubelo, Manuel-Pvt. Cazadores Espanoles Regiment, LA Militia
Cucullu, Gustave-Sgt. Assistant Enrolling Officer, LA
Cucullu, J. Ernest-1st Lt. Company F, 10th LA Infantry
Cucullu, Louis-Pvt. Company E, Orleans Guard Regiment, LA Militia
Cucullu, Paul-Pvt. Company F, 30th LA Infantry
Cucullu, Sainville-Capt. Company E, 10th LA Infantry
Cuebas, Marcial-Pvt. Co. 6, 5th (Spanish) Regt., European Brigade, LA Militia
Cuellar, Antonio-Lt. Bexar County, TX Militia
Cuellar, Cenobio-Pvt. Company F, 1st Yager's TX Cavalry
Cuellar, Conception J.-Pvt. Company F, 1st Yager's TX Cavalry
Cuellar, Matias-Lt. Wilson County, TX Militia
Cuellar, Milesio-Pvt. Company F, 1st Yager's TX Cavalry
Cuellar, Ramon-Pvt. Company F, 1st Yager's TX Cavalry
Cuellar, Santiago-Bugler 1st Company H, 33rd TX Cavalry
Cueto, Isidore-Pvt. Co. G, 4th Regiment, 1st Brigade, 1st Division, LA Militia
Cueto, M.-Cpl. Co. 2, 5th (Spanish) Regiment, European Brigade, LA Militia
Cueva, Marcelino-Pvt. Company D, 30th LA Infantry
***See also Quave for Cuevas
Cuevas, Charles J.-Pvt. Company F, 3rd MISS Infantry
Cuevas, James A.-Pvt. Company F, 3rd MISS Infantry
Cuevas, Juan-Pvt. Engledow's Company, Nueces County, TX Militia
Cuevas, Raymond-Pvt. Company F, 3rd MISS Infantry
Cuquet, Pedro-Pvt. Company 1, Cazadores Espanoles Regiment, LA Militia
Cuquet, S.-Pvt. Company 1, Cazadores Espanoles Regiment, LA Militia
Curi, Pablo-Pvt. Co. 4, 5th (Spanish) Regiment, European Brigade, LA Militia
Curra, Pedro-Pvt. Rhodes' Company, 3rd Yager's TX Cavalry
Curtes, Moses M.-Pvt. Company A, 1st Infantry Kings State Troops, MISS
Curvello, Pedro-2nd Sgt. Jeff Davis Home Guard, Refugio County, TX Militia
Curvillo, A.-Pvt. Company F, 5th TX Infantry
Cyprian, Benino-Pvt. Company E, 8th TX Infantry
Cyprian, Pablo-Pvt. 1st Company H, 33rd TX Cavalry

D

*** Please note that if the surname you are searching for under the letter D, starting with > D', Da, De, Del, De Las or De Los is not found, search under the surname only. Example > if you are looking for De Leon try only Leon under the letter L.

D'Angelo, Antonio-Pvt. Company H, 10th LA Infantry
D'Albenas, Edmond-1st Sgt. 1st LA Artillery
D'Alvarade, Julian-Pvt. Co. 2, 5th (Spanish) Regiment, European Brig., LA Mil.
Damaso, Vidal-Pvt. Co. A, 5th (Spanish) Regiment, European Brigade, LA Mil.
Da Cana, Samuel-Pvt. Company G, 15th LA Infantry
Da Costa, Aaron W.-Clerk of the Circuit Court, Duval County, FLA 1863.
Da Costa, B.A.-Sgt. Company G, 11th S.C. Infantry
Da Costa, F.J.-Pvt. Laughlin's Irish Regiment, LA Militia
Da Costa, John B.-Pvt. Company E, 7th FLA Infantry
Da Costa, Raymond-Pvt. Company I, 7th FLA Infantry
Da Costa, William H.-Cpl. Company B, 20th GA Infantry
Darien, Joaquin-Pvt. Gray's Company, Bexar County, TX Militia
Darien, Mariano-Pvt. Gray's Company, Bexar County, TX Militia
Darien, Vicente-Pvt. Gray's Company, Bexar County, TX Militia
Da Silva, Juan-Pvt. Co. 8, 5th (Spanish) Regiment, European Brigade, LA Mil.
Da Silva, David H.-Pvt. Company G, 1st LA Infantry
Da Silva, Manuel Francisco-Pvt. Co. 8, 5th (Spanish) Regt., Euro., Brig., LA Mil.
Da Vega, Columbus-Surgeon / Major 23rd S.C. Infantry
Daviline, Juan-4th Sgt. Company I, Benavides' Regiment, TX Cavalry
Davilla, Francisco-Pvt. Company K, 2nd TX Cavalry
Daya, M.-Pvt. Spanish Guards, Mobile Home Guard, ALA Militia
Dea, Antonio-Pvt. Co. 5, 5th (Spanish) Regiment, European Brigade, LA Militia
De Alafila > see Baco De Alafila
De Alcala, Manuel-Pvt. Thomas' Company, TX Partisan Rangers
De Allos, Valentin-Pvt. Company C, Benavides' Regiment, TX Cavalry
De Alren, Jose-Pvt. Co. 4, 5th (Spanish) Regiment, European Brigade, LA Mil.
De Andar, Tiburcio-Pvt. Jeff Davis Home Guards, Refugio County, TX Militia
De Angulo, Joachin S.-Pvt. Co. C, 5th (Spanish) Regt., European Brig., LA Mil.
De Aquino, Torebio-Pvt. Company C, 8th TX Infantry
De Aragon, Ramon T.-Surgeon 9th TX Infantry, also served out of Tennessee.
De Aresti, Julian-Pvt. Co. 4, 5th (Spanish) Regt., European Brigade, LA Militia
De Armas, Alfredo-Pvt. Company E, Orleans Guard Regiment, LA Militia
De Armas, Carlos-Pvt. Orleans Guard Battery, LA Light Artillery
De Armas, C.A.-Assistant Engineer, LA Militia
De Armas, E.-Pvt. Company A, Orleans Guard Regiment, LA Militia
De Armas, F.-Pvt. Company E, Orleans Guard Regiment, LA Miltia
De Armas, Leon A.-Capt. / Engineer C.S.A.
De Armas, Michel-Pvt. Company G, Orleans Guard Regiment, LA Militia
De Audrade, Antonio-Pvt. Co. 8, 5th (Spanish) Regt., European Brigade, LA Mil.
De Bard, Herrera-Pvt. Company G, 1st TX Infantry
De Ben, Antonio-Pvt. 5th (Spanish) Regiment, European Brigade, LA Militia
De Ben, Jose Maria-Pvt. 5th (Spanish) Regiment, European Brigade, LA Militia
De Ben, Manuel-Pvt. Company 2, Cazadores Espanoles Regiment, LA Militia
De Bolle, Manuel-2nd Lt. Company D, 8th LA Infantry

De Botello > see Gonzales De Botello, Antonio
De Bulnez, Alphonso-Pvt. Co. A, Miles' Legion, LA (see also Bulnez, Raymond).
De Carpio, Paul-Pvt. Company C, 5th TX Cavalry
De Casa, Philip-Pvt. 1st Battalion, ALA Artillery
De Cassares, E.G.-Pvt. LA Militia
De Castro, G.O.-Pvt. Company I, Orleans Guard Regiment, LA Militia
De Castro, Isaac-Pvt. Company A, 7th Battalion LA Infantry
De Castro, J.-Pvt. Company A, 1st Regiment Mobile Volunteers, ALA
De Cordova, H.M.-Pvt. Company D, Hardeman's Regiment, TX Cavalry
De Cordova, Jacob-District 60 Tax Collector, TX, also Deputy Clerk Bosque County, TX, 1864.
De Cordova, Joshua R.-Pvt. Company H, 10th TX Infantry
De Cordova, W.F.-Pvt. 1st Company C, 1st Confederate Cavalry
De Costa, A.-Pvt. Company H, Orleans Guard Regiment, LA Militia
De Costa, William H.-Pvt. Company H, Chalmette Regiment, LA Militia
Decrusses, J.-Pvt. Company H, Chalmette Regiment, LA Militia
De Cruz, Manuel Sola-Pvt. Co. 7, 5th (Spanish) Regt., European Brig., LA Mil.
De Cuenco, F.-Cpl. Co. 2, 5th (Spanish) Regiment, European Brig., LA Militia
De Dias Leon, Juan-Cpl. Company C, Benavides' Regiment, TX Cavalry
De Egano, Domingo-Cpl. Co. 4, 5th (Spanish) Regt., European Brigade, LA Mil.
De Faria, J.-Pvt. Spanish Guards, Mobile Home Guard, ALA Militia
De Ferias, Jose-Pvt. Company D, 30th LA Infantry
De Freitas, Francisco-Pvt. Co. 7, 5th (Spanish) Regt., European Brigade, LA Mil.
De Frentes, Manuel-Pvt. Company G, 21st ALA Infantry
De Fuentes, Charles L.-2nd Cpl. Company D, 22nd LA Infantry
De Fuentes, Fernando-Pvt. Co. 5, 5th (Spanish) Regt., European Brigade, LA Mil.
De Fuentes, J.-Sgt. Company B, Orleans Guard Regiment, LA Militia
De Galdo, Francisco-Pvt. Company 2, Cazadores Espanoles Regiment, LA Militia
De Gournay, Paul Francis-Lt. Colonel 12th LA Heavy Artillery
De Guterre, Benjamin-Pvt. Company G, Miles' Legion, LA
De Hoa > See Hoa
De Hoyos, Leonardo-Pvt. Company F, 2nd TX Mounted Rifles
De Hoyos, Pablo-Pvt. Company D, 3rd TX Infantry
De Hoyos, Valentin-Pvt. Company C, Benavides' Regiment, TX Cavalry
De La Barpa, Jose-Pvt. Company D, 5th TX Cavalry
De La Barrera, Jose-Pvt. Company H, 3rd TX Infantry
De La Carre, S.P.-Pvt. Company E, 22nd Consolidated LA Infantry
***See also De La Zerda
De La Cerda, G.-Pvt. Medina Guards, Bexar County, TX Militia
De La Cerda, Nemecio Jr.-2nd Lt. Company H, Benavides' Regiment, TX Cav.
De La Cerda, Pedro-Pvt. Company E, Benavides' Regiment, TX Cavalry
De La Cerra, Santiago-Pvt. Company D/G, 26th LA Infantry
De La Crus, Espirito-Pvt. Co. A, 5th (Spanish) Regt., European Brigade, LA Mil.
De La Crus, Felipe-Pvt. Co. A, 5th (Spanish) Regt., European Brigade, LA Mil.
De La Crus, Juan-Pvt. Co. A, 5th (Spanish) Regt., European Brigade, LA Militia

Hispanic Confederates 37

De La Crus, Macario-Sgt. Co. A, 5th (Spanish) Regt., European Brigade, LA Mil.
De La Crus, Romaldo-Pvt. Co. A, 5th (Spanish) Regt., European Brig., LA Mil.
De La Cruz, Bernardo-Pvt. Company C, 8th TX Infantry
De La Cruz, Genaro-Pvt. Company F, 3rd TX Infantry
De La Cruz, Jas.-Pvt. Medina Guards, Bexar County, TX Militia
De La Cruz, Martin-Pvt. Company C, 8th TX Infantry
De La Garcia, S.-Pvt. Company G, 8th TX Infantry
De La Garza, Cayetano-Scout 33rd TX Cavalry
De La Garza, Emanuel-Pvt. Davis Guards, Victoria County, TX Militia
De La Garza, Fernando-Pvt. Neal's Artillery Company, TX
De La Garza, Francisco-Pvt. Lamar Home Guards, Refugio County, TX Militia
De La Garza, Geraldo-Pvt. Davis Guards, Victoria County, TX Militia
De La Garza, H.-Pvt. Company A, Waller's Regiment, TX Cavalry
De La Garza, Ignacio-Pvt. Cameron County Coast Guards, TX Militia
De La Garza, Jose Antonio-Pvt. Medina Guards, Bexar County, TX Militia
De La Garza, Juan-Pvt. Davis Guards, Victoria County, TX Militia
De La Garza, Justo-Pvt. Company E, 8th TX Infantry
De La Garza, Miguel-Pvt. Medina Guards, Bexar County, TX Militia
De La Garza, Rafael-Pvt. Company A, Waller's Regiment, TX Cavalry
De La Garza, Salvador-Pvt. TX Militia
De La Grana, Rosendo-Pvt. Co. 3, 5th (Spanish) Regt., European Brig., LA Militia
De La Herrera Garcia, Francisco-Cpl. Co. 5, Cazadores Espanoles Regt., LA Mil.
De La Hoz Garcia, Francisco-2nd Sgt. Co. 6, 5th (Sp.) Regt., Euro., Brig., LA Mil.
De La Pena, Pablo-Pvt. Co. A, 5th (Spanish) Regt., European Brigade, LA Militia
De La Rosa, Beneslado-Pvt. Company C, 8th TX Infantry
De La Rosa, Francisco-Pvt. Co. 7, 5th (Spanish) Regt., European Brig., LA Mil.
De La Rosa, Ramon-Pvt. 1st Company C, 3rd TX Infantry
De La Rosa, Tibarico-Pvt. Co. 7, 5th (Spanish) Regt., European Brigade, LA Mil.
De La Rua, F.E.-Circuit Court Clerk, Escambia County, FLA 1861-1862. He was appointed Keeper of City Archives while the Confederate Municipal Government of Pensacola was in exile, in Alabama, from 1862-1865.
De La Rua, Filomeno-Pvt. Company B, 62nd ALA Infantry
De La Rua, John-Pvt. 15th Confederate Cavalry
De La Torre, Daniel-Pvt. Company G, 10th LA Infantry
De La Vega, S.J.-Pvt. Co. 1, 5th (Spanish) Regiment, European Brigade, LA Mil.
De La Venta, Jose-Cpl. Co. 6, 5th (Spanish) Regt., European Brigade, LA Militia
De La Zerda, Ramon-Pvt. TX Militia
Del Campo, Francisco-Cpl. Co. 3, 5th (Spanish) Regt., European Brig., LA Militia
Del Castillo, A.-Sgt. Gomez's Company, 22nd LA Infantry
Del Castillo, G.-1st Lt. Cuban Rifles, LA Legion Brigade
Del Collado, Pedro-Pvt. Co. 6, 5th (Spanish) Regt., European Brigade, LA Mil.
Del Corral, Ed-Pvt. Co. 8, 5th (Spanish) Regiment, European Brigade, LA Militia
Del Corral, Gabriel-1st Lt. Co. 8, 5th (Spanish) Regt., European Brigade, LA Mil.
*** See also De Lyon, D'Lyon, Cohen, Levy, Moses and Moise
De Leon, A.-Pvt. French Guards, Mobile Home Guard, ALA Militia

De Leon, Antonio-Pvt. Company G, 10th LA Infantry
De Leon, Antonio-Pvt. Company E, Benavides' Regiment, TX Cavalry
De Leon, Antonio-Pvt. Company H, 8th TX Infantry
De Leon, David Camden-Surgeon General of the Confederacy; Major / Chief of the Medical Staff of General Braxton Bragg. He was appointed to the Post of Surgeon General of the Confederacy where he served, from May- July 1861. He later served as Medical Director for the Army of Northern Virginia and under Magruder in TX.
De Leon, Edwin-Special Confederate Envoy to Europe, served from 1862 to 1864.
De Leon, Frank-Pvt. Ferguson's Cavalry Company, Victoria County, TX Militia
De Leon, Gervacia-2nd Sgt. Company I, Benavides' Regiment, TX Cavalry
De Leon, J.A.H.-Pvt. Crescent Artillery, LA
De Leon, Hampton H.-3rd Lt. Eason's Company, 16th S.C. Militia
De Leon, Harmon Hendricks-Rendered valuable aid to the Confederacy in purchasing supplies, as well as in donating large sums of his money in S.C.
De Leon, Jesus-Sgt. 8th Field Battery, TX Artillery
De Leon, Juan(1st)-Pvt. Gray's Company, Bexar County, TX Militia
De Leon, Juan(2nd)-Pvt. Gray's Company, Bexar County, TX Militia
De Leon, S.-4th Sgt. Ferguson's Cavalry Company, Victoria County, TX Militia
De Leon, Sylvester-Pvt. Company A, Waller's Regiment, TX Cavalry
De Leon, Thomas Cooper-Capt. Secretary to President Jefferson Davis. He was a well-known author after the war and wrote many notable books including "Four Years in Rebel Capitals" (see also his listing under Naval personnel).
De Leon, Valentine-Pvt. Gray's Company, Bexar County, TX Militia
De Leon Garza, Juan-Pvt. Lamar Home Guard, Refugio County, TX Militia
De Leon Moses, A.-Pvt. Company C, Hampton Legion, S.C.
Deleza, Clemente-Pvt. 1st Company I, 33rd TX Cavalry
Delgado, Alex-Pvt. Greenleaf's Company, Orleans Light Horse, LA
Delgado, Alexander-Pvt. Company B, Crescent Regiment, LA Infantry
Delgado, Bartolo-Pvt. Gray's Company, Bexar County, TX Militia
Delgado, Clemente-Interpreter / Pvt. 1st Company H, 33rd TX Cavalry
Delgado, Gorgonio-Pvt. Medina Guards, Bexar County, TX Militia
Delgado, J.M.-Pvt. Trevinio's Company, TX Cavalry
Delgado, Jose De Jesus-Pvt. TX Militia
Delgado, Leandro-Pvt. Company E, 8th TX Infantry
Delgado, Macedonio-Pvt. Tom's Company, Atascosa County, TX Militia
Delgado, Marcello-Pvt. Company E, 8th TX Infantry
Delgado, Nicholas-Pvt. Tom's Company, Atascosa County, TX Militia
Delgado, Pedro-Pvt. 1st Company H, 33rd TX Cavalry
Delgado, Pedro-Pvt. Bustillo's Company, Bexar County, TX Militia
Delgado, Rafael-Pvt. Company D, 30th LA Infantry
Delgado, S.-Pvt. Company G, Confederate Guards Regiment, LA Militia
Delgado, Severo-Pvt. Company D, 25th TX Cavalry
Delgado, Sisero-Pvt. Company E, 8th TX Infantry
Delgardo, Joseph-Pvt. LA Militia

Delgardo, Victor-Pvt. Company C, 1st Yager's TX Cavalry
De Jesus, Pedro-Pvt. Company I, Benavides' Regiment, TX Cavalry
De Ljano, Antonio-Pvt. Co. 3, 5th (Spanish) Regt., European Brigade, LA Militia
Del Nodal, Eduardo-3rd Lt. 1st Chasseurs a pied, LA Militia
Del Nodal, Esteban-2nd Lt. Jackson Rifle Battalion, LA Militia
Delores, E.-Pvt. Company B, 2nd TX Cavalry
Delos, Antonio-1st Sgt. Co. 10, 5th (Spanish) Regt., European Brigade, LA Mil.
Delos, John-Pvt. 2nd Regiment, 2nd Brigade, 1st Division, LA Militia
De Los Reyes, Antonio-Pvt. Trevinio's Company, TX Cavalry
De Los Reyes, Juan-Pvt. Company H, 8th TX Infantry
De Los Santos, Jose-Pvt. Co. A, 5th (Spanish) Regt., European Brigade, LA Mil.
De Los Santos, Juan-Pvt. Co. A, 5th (Spanish) Regt., European Brigade, LA Mil.
De Los Santos, Martin-Pvt. Company C, 8th TX Infantry
De Los Santos, Seperino-Pvt. Co. A, 5th (Span.) Regt., European Brig., LA Mil.
Del Rio, G.-Pvt. Company D, 8th LA Cavalry
Del Rio, Natalis-Cpl. Co. 10, 5th (Spanish) Regt., European Brigade, LA Militia
Del Toro, Ignacio-Pvt. Company F, 3rd TX Infantry
Del Valle, E.-Pvt. Trevinio's Company, TX Partisan Rangers
Del Valle, Pedro-Pvt. Co. 10, 5th (Spanish) Regt., European Brigade, LA Militia
*** See also De Leon and D'Lyon
De Lyon, Charles Henry-Musician Company A, 1st Olmstead's GA Infantry
De Lyon, James-Musician Company I, Olmstead's GA Infantry
De Mar, James J.-2nd Lt. Company A, 1st Nelligan's LA Infantry
De Martin, R.-Pvt. 1st Local Troops Cavalry Company, Augusta, GA
De Maza, Abraham R.-Cpl. Company 2, 2nd TX Infantry
Demelo, Juan-Pvt. Co. 8, 5th (Spanish) Regiment, European Brigade, LA Militia
De Meza, A.-Pvt. Company C, Orleans Guard Regiment, LA Militia
De Meza, George W.-Pvt. Company K, 15th LA Infantry
De Meza, Joseph-QMaster Sgt. Company 3, Washington Artillery Battalion, LA
De Meza, L.-Pvt. Company 5, 1st Chasseurs a pied, LA Militia
De Mina, F.-Pvt. Company H, Crescent Regiment, LA Militia
De Monesterio, Ceferino-Pvt. Co. 9, 5th (Spanish) Regt., Euro., Brigade, LA Mil.
De Moya, Diego-Pvt. Company D, 30th LA Infantry
De Moya, F.-Pvt. Company 7, 1st Chasseurs a pied, LA Militia
De Neyre, Pedro Fernandez-Pvt. Co. 2, Cazadores Espanoles Regt., LA Militia
De Oca, Charles Montes-Pvt. Company K, 8th FLA Infantry
De Oca, John Montes-State of Florida Indian Interpreter, 1863
Deogracias, Pierre Francis-Pvt. Co. B, Confederate States Zouave Battalion, LA
De Olemar, D.-Pvt. Company F, Baylor's Regiment, TX Cavalry
De Oliden, Pedro-Pvt. Co. 7, 5th (Spanish) Regt., European Brigade, LA Militia
De Olles, Pablo-Pvt. Company H, 8th TX Infantry
De Ollos, Leonardo-Pvt. Tobin's Company, TX
De Ornelas, J.A.-Pvt. Company B, 22nd Consolidated LA Infantry
De Oyes, Leonardo-Pvt. 2nd Company F, 2nd TX Cavalry
De Ozez, Pedro-Pvt. Company I, Benavides' Regiment, TX Cavalry

*** This Sephardic surname was originally De Paz
De Pass, E.-Sgt. Company G, 5th GA Reserves
De Pass, Jacob W.-Sgt. Co. E/G, 3rd Palmetto Battalion, SC Light Artillery
De Pass, James P.-Pvt. Company G, 3rd Palmetto Battalion, SC Light Artillery. He also served as Chaplain of Company F, 5th SC State Troops
De Pass, John-Pvt. Company H, Orleans Guards Regiment, LA
De Pass, Phoenix O.-Sgt. Company D, 21st Patton's LA Infantry
De Pass, Samuel C.-Lt. Colonel 16th Regiment, SC Militia
De Pass, William Lambert-Capt. Co. E/G, 3rd Palmetto Battn., SC Light Artillery
De Padua, Juan-Pvt. Co. A, 5th (Spanish) Regiment, European Brigade, LA Mil.
De Perez Parra, Francisco-Pvt. Co. 5, 5th (Span.) Regt., European Brig., LA Mil.
De Romero, L.-Sgt. Company D, 30th LA Infantry
De Rosa, Jose Ygnacio-Pvt. Company G, 21st ALA Infantry
De Rosa, Manuel-Pvt. Co. 4, 5th (Spanish) Regt., European Brigade, LA Militia
De Salles, P.-Pvt. 1st Native Guards, LA Militia
De Santos, Joaquin S.-Pvt. Co. 6, 5th (Spanish) Regt., European Brigade, LA Mil.
De Santos, S.O.-Pvt. Company A, 7th LA Infantry
De Saucedo > see Lerrin De Saucedo, Antonio
De Seta, Pablo-Capt. Benavides' Regiment, TX Cavalry
De Silva, Bernardo-Pvt. Co. 7, 5th (Spanish) Regt., European Brigade, LA Militia
De Sola, A.-Pvt. Company I, Orleans Guard Regiment, LA Militia
De Sola, Aaron-Cpl. Company A, 4th ALA Reserve
De Sola, B.H.-Pvt. Company I, Consolidated Crescent Regiment, LA Infantry
De Sosa Dios, Juan-Pvt. Company A, Ragsdale's Battalion, TX Cavalry
De Soto, Joseph-Pvt. Company B, 28th Gray's LA Infantry
De Soto, Joseph A.-Pvt. Co. B, Consolidated Crescent Regiment, LA Infantry
De Soto, Jules-Pvt. Company C, 12th LA Infantry
De Soto, Marcel S.-Pvt. Company A, 11th LA Infantry
De Soto, Saustin O.-Pvt. Company A, 11th LA Infantry
De Souza, P.-Pvt. Company H, Orleans Guard Regiment, LA Militia
De Souza, S.-Pvt. Company H, Orleans Guard Regiment, LA Militia
Deu, Eduardo-2nd Lt. Co. 6, 5th (Spanish) Regt., European Brigade, LA Militia
De Undido, Braulio-Pvt. Co. 4, 5th (Spanish) Regt., European Brigade, LA Militia
De Urriola, J.A.-Sgt. Co. 4, 5th (Spanish) Regt., European Brigade, LA Militia
De Ybarra, Justo R.-Pvt. Co. 5, 5th (Spanish) Regt., European Brigade, LA Mil.
De Zavalla, A.-Cpl. Company A, Madison's Regiment, TX Cavalry
De Zevallos, Hector D.-Pvt. Company E, 7th LA Infantry
Dias, Abraham-Pvt. Company B, 2nd GA Cavalry
Dias, Albino-Pvt. Minute Men (Scouts), Starr County, TX Militia
Dias, Antoine-Pvt. Company D/G, 7th LA Cavalry
Dias, B.-Pvt. Spanish Guards, Mobile Home Guard, ALA Militia
Dias, Benjamin-Pvt. Company E, 17th LA Infantry
Dias, Clement-Pvt. Company C, 25th Dismounted TX Cavalry
Dias, Clemente-Pvt. Company H, 9th Nicholas' TX Infantry
Dias, David-Pvt. Company A, 8th TENN Infantry

Dias, Desiderio-Pvt. Company I, Benavides' Regiment, TX Cavalry
Dias, E.-Pvt. Company G, 5th FLA Cavalry
Dias, G.K.-Pvt. Company F, 22nd TX Infantry
Dias, Florentino-Pvt. Company C, 3rd TX Infantry
Dias, George-Pvt. Company C, 9th FLA Infantry
Dias, Henry-Pvt. Company G, 2nd S.C. Artillery
Dias, J.-Pvt. Company C, 32nd GA Infantry
Dias, J.-Pvt. Company B, 9th LA Infantry
Dias, James-Pvt. Company C, 1st FLA Cavalry
Dias, Jesse-Pvt. Company G, 15th TENN Cavalry
Dias, Jesus-Pvt. 1st Company A, Ragsdale's Battalion, TX Cavalry
Dias, John-Pvt. Company G, 17th GA Infantry
Dias, John-Pvt. Company K, 8th MISS Infantry
Dias, Manuel-Pvt. TX Militia
Dias, Miguel-Pvt. Company G, Benavides' Regiment, TX Cavalry
Dias, Miguel-Pvt. Company C, 8th TX Infantry
Dias, Pedro-Pvt. Company F, 3rd TX Infantry
Dias, Reuben H.-Pvt. Company E, 57th ALA Infantry
Dias, Theodule-Pvt. Barnes' Battery, LA Artillery
Dias, Thomas S.-Pvt. Company E, 4th ALA Infantry
Dias, V.-Pvt. Company D, Benavides' Regiment, TX Cavalry
Dias, Victoriano-Pvt. 1st Company A, Ragsdale's Battalion, TX Cavalry
Dias, William-Pvt. Company C, 9th FLA Infantry
Dias, Zachariah-Pvt. Pritchard's Co., Washington Artillery, GA Light Artillery
Diaz, Cayetano-Cpl. Company 2, Cazadores Espanoles Regiment, LA Militia
Diaz, D.-Pvt. Old Company F, 6th ARK Infantry
Diaz, J.-Pvt. 1st Native Guards, LA Militia
Diaz, J.A.-Pvt. Montgomery County Home Guard, ALA Militia
Diaz, J.A. Fernandez-Pvt. Co. 2, 5th (Spanish) Regt., European Brigade, LA Mil.
Diaz, J. Alvarez-Cpl. Co. 2, 5th (Spanish) Regt., European Brigade, LA Militia
Diaz, Jesse-Pvt. Medina Guards, Bexar County, TX Militia
Diaz, Jose-Pvt. Company D, 30th LA Infantry
Diaz, Jose Antonio-Pvt. Co. 10, 5th (Spanish) Regt., European Brigade, LA Mil.
Diaz, Jose Maria-Pvt. Medina Guards, Bexar County, TX Militia
Diaz, Juan Cruz-Pvt. Co. 4, 5th (Spanish) Regt., European Brigade, LA Militia
Diaz, Manuel-Pvt. Co. 10, 5th (Spanish) Regiment, European Brigade, LA Militia
Diaz, Manuel-Sgt. Co. 3, 5th (Spanish) Regiment, European Brigade, LA Militia
Diaz, Manuel Francisco-Pvt. Co. K, 7th FLA Inf. (escaped Union held Key West, FLA
    and made it to Confederate lines where he enlisted).
Diaz, Pedro-Pvt. Bustillo's Company, Bexar County, TX Militia
Diaz, Pedro-Prominant Pro-Confederate Supporter in Zapata County, TX
Diaz, Ramon-Pvt. Company 5, Cazadores Espanoles Regiment, LA Militia
Diaz, Reducindo-Pvt. Engledow's Company, Nueces County, TX Militia
Diego, Nicolas-Pvt. Trevinio's Company, TX Cavalry
Dingman, B.S.-Sgt. Company B, 15th LA Infantry

Dios > see De Sosa Dios, Juan
Discampo, Fernando-Pvt. Co. A, 5th (Spanish) Regt., European Brigade, LA Mil.
D'Hamel, Enrique B.-1st Lt. Company G, 33rd TX Cavalry
*** See also De Leon and De Lyon
D'Lyon, Levi Sheftall-City Court Judge, Savannah, GA 1861-1862.
Dobo, M.-Pvt. Co. 1, 5th (Spanish) Regiment, European Brigade, LA Militia
*** The following Louisiana listed men all have French versions of the surnames Dominguez, Domingues, Domingo and Domingos
Domain, A.N.-Pvt. Company G, 18th LA Infantry
Domaine, Francis-Pvt. Company G, 7th LA Cavalry
Domaing, A.-Pvt. Company K, 18th LA Infantry
Domaing, Emanuel-Pvt. Company G, 28th Gray's LA Infantry
Domaing, J.B.-Pvt. Company F, 22nd LA Infantry
Domaing, J.P.-Pvt. Company A, 15th Battalion, LA Sharpshooters
Domaing, John-Pvt. Company A, 26th LA Infantry
Doman, Henry-Pvt. Saint Martin Rangers, LA Militia
Domangi, Joseph-Pvt. Company 8, 1st Chasseurs a pied, LA Militia
Domango, L.C.-Pvt. Company H, 7th LA Cavalry
Domeg, J.-Pvt. Co. 7, 1st Regiment French Brigade, LA Militia
Domengeau, L.-Pvt. Company A, 28th LA Infantry
Domengeaux, L. Pierre-Pvt. Company C, 8th LA Infantry
Domengi, Joseph-Pvt. Company E/G, 13th LA Infantry
Domengi, Louis-Pvt. Company E, 13th LA Infantry
Domig, C.-Pvt. French Company of Saint James, LA Militia
Domina, J.-Pvt. Company D, 13th LA Infantry
Doming, Lone-Pvt. Company G, 7th LA Cavalry
Domingeau, L.-Pvt. Company G, 10th LA Infantry
Domingeaux, Linval-Pvt. Company A, 28th Thomas' LA Infantry
Domingle, Clement-Pvt. Company B, 1st LA Heavy Artillery
Domingle, Yasinte-Pvt. Company B, 1st LA Heavy Artillery
Dominges, Juan-Pvt. Co. 7, 5th (Spanish) Regiment, European Brigade, LA Mil.
Domingo, C.-Pvt. / Scout Benavides' Regiment, TX Cavalry
Domingo, Falcon-Pvt. LA Militia
Domingo, Francis-Pvt. Company F, 11th LA Infantry
Domingo, J.P.-Pvt. Company G, Miles' Legion, LA
Domingo, Jose-Capt. Company C, LA Defenders Battalion
Domingo, Jose-Pvt. Co. 5, 5th (Spanish) Regiment, European Brigade, LA Mil.
Domingo, Lorenzo-Pvt. Young's Company, VIR Cavalry
Domingo, San-Pvt. Company H, 17th Moore's TX Cavalry
Domingoes, J.J.-Pvt. Company G, 27th LA Infantry
Domingon, Eugene-Pvt. Company H, Miles' Legion, LA
Domingon, Jules-Sgt. 1st Native Guards, LA Militia
Domingos, Isacc-Pvt. Company G, 51st GA Infantry
Domingue, Adonis-Pvt. Company A, 18th LA Infantry
Domingue, Alcide-Pvt. Company A/G, 7th LA Cavalry

Domingue, Alphonse-Pvt. Company H, 2nd LA Reserve Corps
Domingue, Antoine Pierre-Pvt. Company A, 26th LA Infantry
Domingue, Auguste-Pvt. Company K, 2nd LA Reserve Corps
Domingue, Donician-Pvt. Company I, 7th LA Cavalry
Domingue, Don Louis-Pvt. Company E, 18th Consolidated LA Infantry
Domingue, Felicien-Pvt Company D, 7th LA Infantry
Domingue, Francois-Pvt. Company D, 18th LA Infantry
Domingue, Jean-Pvt. Company F, 26th LA Infantry
Domingue, John Baptiste-Pvt. Company H, 26th LA Infantry
Domingue, Leon-Pvt. Company F, 10th LA Infantry
Domingue, M.D.-Pvt. Company K, 2nd LA Reserve Corps
Domingue, Manuel Sosthene-Pvt. Co. F, Wood's Regiment, Confederate Cavalry
Domingue, Paul-Pvt. Company A, 1st LA Cavalry
Domingue, Pierre-Pvt. Co. H, 4th Regiment, 1st Brigade, 1st Division, LA Militia
Domingues, Adrien-Pvt. Saint Martin Militia, LA
Domingues, Louis-Pvt. Saint Martin Militia, LA
Domingues, Manuel J.-Pvt. Company H, 18th LA Infantry
Domingues, Peter A.-Pvt Company H, 19th LA Infantry
Domingues, Sixto-Pvt. Thomas' Company, TX Partisan Rangers
Dominguez, Antonio-Pvt. Co. 8, 5th (Spanish) Regt., European Brigade, LA Mil.
Dominguez, B.-Pvt. Company 8, 1st Chasseurs a pied, LA Militia
Dominguez, Eduardo-Pvt. Company C, 2nd LA Cavalry
Dominguez, Hipolito-Pvt. Co. D, Confederate Guards Regiment, LA Militia
Dominguez, Jean William-Pvt. Company A, 26th LA Infantry
Dominguez, Joseph-Pvt. Company D, Confederate Guards Regiment, LA Militia
Dominguez, Santiago-Pvt. Co. 9, 5th (Spanish) Regt., European Brigade, LA Mil.
Domingus, J.J.-Pvt. Company A, 19th LA Infantry
Domingus, J.B.-Pvt. Company A, 19th LA Infantry
Doumenge, Ovid B.-Pvt. Company G, 13th LA Infantry
Dumeige, A.-Pvt. Watson Battery, LA Artillery
Donez, M.D.-QuarterMaster Sgt. 10th LA Infantry
Dovalina, Francisco-Pvt. 2nd TX Mounted Rifles
Dovalina, Juan-Pvt. Company I, Benavides' Regiment, TX Cavalry
Dromundo, Joaquin-Pvt. Co. 3, 5th (Spanish) Regt., European Brigade, LA Mil.
Duarte, Jose Garcia-Pvt. Co. 8, 5th (Spanish) Regt., European Brigade, LA Militia
Duarte, Joseph-Pvt. Company B, 18th GA Infantry
Duran, Antonio-Pvt. Trevinio's Company, TX Cavalry
Duran, B.F.-Pvt. Company D, 7th TX Cavalry
Duran, Bartolo-Sgt. Company H, Bairds Regiment, TX Cavalry
Duran, Joseph A.-1st Lt. Duran's Company, Atascosa County, TX Troops
Duran, Mateo-Pvt. Co. 5, 5th (Spanish) Regiment, European Brigade, LA Militia
Duran, L.J.-1st Sgt. 2nd TX Infantry
Duran, Polinario-Pvt. 1st Company C, Ragsdale's Battalion, TX Cavalry
Duran, Precente-Pvt. Company A, Benavides' Regiment, TX Cavalry
Duran, Simon-Pvt. Company 1, Cazadores Espanoles Regiment, LA Militia

Durau, Liborio-3rd Lt. Co. 7, 5th (Spanish) Regt., European Brigade, LA Militia

E

***See also Barbo, Ibarbo, Ybarbo and Yebarbo
E'Barbo, Antonio-Pvt. Company H, 19th LA Infantry
E'Barbo, Juan-Pvt. Company G, 37th TX Cavalry
Ecamiga, Miguel-Pvt. Company D, 30th LA Infantry
Echar, Juan-Pvt. Co. 2, 5th (Spanish) Regiment, European Brigade, LA Militia
Echevarria, Arthur-Cpl. Landry's Company, Donaldsonville Artillery, LA
Elerarez, Matias-Pvt. Medina Guards, Bexar County, TX Militia
Elenismo, Pedro-Pvt. Co. A, 5th (Spanish) Regt., European Brigade, LA Militia
Elisando, Doroteo-Pvt. Minute Men (Scouts), Starr County, TX Militia
Elizardi, Peter-Pvt. Company A, Dreux's Cavalry, LA
Elosegue, Francisco-Cadet Co. 5, Cazadores Espanoles Regiment, LA Militia
Elosegui, Fernando-Capt. Cazadores Espanoles Regiment, LA Militia
Eluterio, Mauricio-Pvt. Company B, Benavides' Regiment, TX Cavalry
Emilio, Amiguette-Pvt. Company D, 13th LA Infantry
Endardo, Pedro-Pvt. Company A, 3rd Yager's Battalion, TX Cavalry
***See also Henriques, Henriquez
Enriquez, Andres-Pvt. Bustillo's Company, Bexar County, TX Militia
Enriquez, Felipe-Pvt. Company G, 3rd TX Infantry
Enriquez, George-Musician / Pvt. Company C, 6th TX Cavalry
Enriquez, Jose Maria-Pvt. TX Militia
Erascar, Francisco-Pvt. 2nd Company F, 2nd TX Cavalry
Enselmo, Del Y.-Pvt. Weisiger's Company, Giddings' TX Cavalry
Eres, Lazaro-Pvt. Company D, 30th LA Infantry
Ernesto, J.-Pvt. Company B, 4th Oswald's TX Infantry
Erraro, Gregorio-Pvt. Oury's Company, Herbert's Battalion, ARIZ Cavalry
Esara, A.A.-Pvt. Culpepper's Battery, LA Artillery
Escalante, Juan G.-Pvt. 1st Company H, 33rd TX Cavalry
Escalara, J.-Pvt. Weisiger's Company, Giddings' Battalion, TX Cavalry
Escalera, Jose Maria-Pvt. 1st Company I, 33rd TX Cavalry
Escalero, Jose M.-2nd Lt. Mission Guards, Bexar County, TX Militia
Escamilla, Amalio-Pvt. Company H, 33rd TX Cavalry
Escamilla, Aneseto-Pvt. 1st Company H, 33rd TX Cavalry
Escamilla, Angel-Pvt. 1st Company I, 33rd TX Cavalry
Escamilla, Crispin-Pvt. 1st Company H, 33rd TX Cavalry
Escamilla, Estanislado-Pvt. 1st Company H, 33rd TX Cavalry
Escamilla, Inez-Sgt. 1st Company H, 33rd TX Cavalry
Escamilla, Pablo-Pvt. 1st Company H, 33rd TX Cavalry
Escamillo, Emilio-Pvt. Company C, 8th TX Infantry
Escandell, Jose-Pvt. Co. 3, 5th (Spanish) Regt., European Brigade, LA Militia
Escano, Andres-Cpl. Co. A, 5th (Spanish) Regt., European Brigade, LA Militia
Escano, Joseph-Pvt. Company H, 28th Thomas' LA Infantry

Escaraguell, Frank-Pvt. Guyol's Company, Orleans Artillery, LA
Escavedo, Cesario-Pvt. Rhodes' Company, 3rd Yager's Battalion, TX Cavalry
Escobal, Martin-Pvt. Co. 1, 5th (Spanish) Regt., European Brigade, LA Militia
Escobar, Felix-Pvt. Company H, 33rd TX Cavalry
Escobida, M.-Pvt. Company G, 3rd LA Infantry
Esconza, Francisco-Pvt. Company 1, Cazadores Espanoles Regiment, LA Mil.
Escobedo, Cesario-Pvt. 3rd Battalion, TX Cavalry
Escovado, Justo-Pvt. Company B, Baylor's Regiment, TX Cavalry
Escovedo, Simon-Pvt. Company C, 8th TX Infantry
Escubeda, Andres-Pvt. 1st Company C, Ragsdale's Battalion, TX Cavalry
Escudero, Gregorio-Drummer / Pvt. Co. D, Powell's Detachment, Infantry School of Practice
Eshandio, Domingo-Pvt. Co. 3, 5th (Spanish) Regt., European Brigade, LA Mil.
Eslava, A.-Pvt. Company G, 3rd ALA Militia
Eslava, Charles H.-Pvt. Company B, Murphy's Battalion, ALA Cavalry
Eslava, Jerome-2nd Lt. Mobile City Troop, ALA Militia. He was also a Deputy Sherrif, Mobile County, 1861.
Eslava, Mitchel S.-Pvt. Company I, 11th TX Infantry
Eslava, Oscar Denis-Pvt. Company E, 36th ALA Infantry
Espalla, John-2nd Lt. Company B, Mobile Fire Battalion, ALA Militia
Espanarza, Enriques-Pvt. TX Militia
Esparsa, Bernardo-Pvt. Company E, 8th TX Infantry
Esparsa, F.-Pvt. 1st Company A, Ragsdale's Battalion, TX Cavalry
Esparsa, Francisco-Pvt. Company D, Benavides' Regiment, TX Cavalry
Esparsa, J.-Pvt. Company C, 8th TX Infantry
Esparsa, Jesus-Pvt. Company E, 8th TX Infantry
Espero, Manuel-Pvt. Co. 6, 5th (Spanish) Regt., European Brigade, LA Militia
Espinosa, Elricus-Pvt. 1st Company A, 3rd TX Infantry
Espinosa, Manuel-Pvt. Company D, 30th LA Infantry
Espinosa, Santa Cruz-Pvt. Medina Guards, Bexar County, TX Militia
Espinosa, Valentin-Pvt. Bustillo's Company, Bexar County, TX Militia
Espinosa, Valentino-Pvt. Company G, 3rd TX Infantry
Espinoza, Candido-Pvt. Co. 3, 5th (Spanish) Regt., European Brigade, LA Militia
Espinoza, Jose Maria-Pvt. Company B, 33rd TX Cavalry
Espinoza, Lino-Pvt. Company C, 8th TX Infantry
Espontano, J.-Cpl. Company D, 1st Olmstead's GA Infantry
Esquela, Isidio-Pvt. Company F, 8th TX Infantry
Esqueval, Theodore-Pvt. TX Militia
Esquerre, A.-Pvt. Company 2, 1st Regiment, French Brigade, LA Militia
Esquerre, J.-Sgt. Company H, Crescent Regiment, LA Infantry
Esquianos, Francis-Pvt. 1st Native Guards, LA Militia
Esquival, John-Pvt. Alderete's Company, TX Militia
Esquivel, Alejo-Pvt. Company H, 8th TX Infantry
Esquivell, Luis-Pvt. Company D, 3rd TX Infantry
Esquivell, Ysidro-Pvt. Company D, 3rd TX Infantry

Estapa, Leon-Cpl. Thomas' Company, TX Partisan Rangers
Esteban, Paul-Pvt. Frois' Company, 3rd Regiment, European Brigade, LA Militia
Estella, M.-Pvt. Company I, Confederate Guards Regiment, LA Militia
Estepa, Antonio-Cpl. Co. 7, 5th (Spanish) Regt., European Brigade, LA Militia
***Esteve is the Louisiana French version of the surname Esteves
Esteve, Charles-Pvt. 1st Native Guards, LA Militia
Esteve, Francois-Pvt. Lafourche Militia, LA
Esteve, John-Pvt. Lafourche Militia, LA
Esteva, W.-Pvt. Co. 2, 5th (Spanish) Regiment, European Brigade, LA Militia
Esteves, Antoine Manuel-Pvt. LA Militia
Esteves, Francis-Cpl. Company G, 28th Thomas' LA Infantry
Estiven, Juan-Pvt. Company B, Benavides' Regiment, TX Cavalry
***Estopinal is the Louisiana version of the surnames Estopinan / Estupinan
Estopinal, F.-Capt. Guards de Saint Bernard, 2nd Brigade, 1st Division, LA Mil.
Estopinal, Martin Albert-Sgt. Company G, 22nd Consolidated, LA Infantry
Estrada, Antonio-Pvt. Ragsdale's Battalion, TX Cavalry
Estrada, Bonifacio-Pvt. Company B, 10th LA Infantry
Estrada, Gaberiano-Pvt. Ragsdale's Battalion, TX Cavalry
Estrada, Jacobo-Musician Company I, 8th LA Infantry
Estrada, Sebastino-Pvt. Company G, 10th LA Infantry
Estrada, Severiano-Pvt. Ragsdale's Battalion, TX Cavalry
Estrado, Francisco-Pvt. Company C, Cater's Battalion, TX Cavalry
Estrado, Natividad-Pvt. Davis' Company, Confederate Light Artillery
Estrella, J.-Musician Confederate Guards Regiment, LA Militia
Evangelista, M.-Pvt. Spanish Guards, Mobile Home Guard, ALA Militia
Ezekial, Ezekial M.-Pvt. Company G, 12th VIR Infantry
Ezekial, Jacob-Pvt. Company D, 1st VIR State Reserve
Ezekial, Joseph K.-Pvt. Company A, 1st VIR Infantry
Ezekial, Moses Jacob-Cadet/1st Sgt./1st Lt. Company C, VIR Military Institute
Ezekial, Napthole-Pvt. Company D, 1st VIR State Reserve
Ezekial, Walter-Drummer 19th VIR Militia

F

Fabiano, Mariano-Sgt. Co. A, 5th (Spanish) Regt., European Brigade, LA Militia
Fabreyas, Jayme-Pvt. Co. 5, 5th (Spanish) Regt., European Brigade, LA Militia
Faisa, Antonio-Pvt. Company 2, Cazadores Espanoles Regiment, LA Militia
Falana, Benjamin-Pvt. Company A, 3rd FLA Infantry
Falana, Fernando-Pvt. Company A, Pickett's Company, FLA Militia
Falana, George R.-Pvt. Company C, 1st FLA Cavalry
Falana, Houston-Pvt. Company B, 2nd FLA Cavalry
Falana, Joshua E.-Pvt. Company C, 1st FLA Infantry
Falana, Joshua H.-Pvt. 2nd FLA Cavalry
Falana, Roman-3rd Cpl. Company A, 3rd FLA Infantry
Falaney, Emanuel-Pvt. Company D, 11th FLA Infantry

Hispanic Confederates

Falaney, John-Musician Company D, 11th FLA Infantry
Falaney, Joseph-Pvt. Company D, 1st FLA Cavalry
Falaney, Thomas-Pvt. Company D, 1st FLA Cavalry
Falco, Antonio-Pvt. Co. 6, 5th (Spanish) Regiment, European Brigade, LA Mil.
Falco, J.-Pvt. Spanish Guards, Mobile Home Guard, ALA Militia
Falco, Rafael-Pvt. Co. 6, 5th (Spanish) Regiment, European Brigade, LA Militia
Falcon, John-Pvt. Saint Martin Parish Militia, LA
Falcon, Jose M.-3rd Cpl. Trevinio's Company, TX Cavalry
Falcon, Joseph-Pvt. Company H, 19th LA Infantry
Falcon, Juan J.-Cpl. 1st Company A, Ragsdale's Battalion, TX Cavalry
Falcon, Martin-Pvt. Saint Martin Parish Militia, LA
Falcon, Ramon-Jr. 2nd Lt. Wilson County, TX Militia
Falcon, Ramon-Pvt. 8th Field Battery, TX Artillery
Fane, M.-Pvt. Spanish Guards, Mobile Home Guard, ALA Militia
Faneca, Juan-Pvt. Company 1, Cazadores Espanoles Regiment, LA Militia
Fararo, Carlos-Pvt. Company G, 3rd S.C. Cavalry
Faria, Jose-Pvt. Co. 8, 5th (Spanish) Regiment, European Brigade, LA Militia
Farias, Antonio-Pvt. Gray's Company, Bexar County, TX Militia
Farias, Juan-Pvt. Company B, Ragsdale's Battalion, TX Cavalry
Farias, Leocadio-Pvt. Minute Men (Scouts), Starr County, TX Militia
Farias, Leonard-2nd Lt. Minute Men (Scouts), Starr County, TX Militia
Farias, Pablo-Pvt. Gray's Company, Bexar County, TX Militia
Farias, Trinidad-Sgt. Company H, 33rd TX Cavalry
Fatio, Lawrence J.-Pvt. Company A, 3rd FLA Infantry
Fatjo, Domingo-Capt. Co. 5, 5th (Spanish) Regt., European Brigade, LA Militia
Fatjo, Thomas-Pvt. Co. 5, 5th (Spanish) Regt., European Brigade, LA Militia
Fauria, Vicente-Pvt. Co. 2, 5th (Spanish) Regt., European Brigade, LA Militia
Faurie, Buenaventura-Pvt. Co. 7, 5th (Spanish) Regt., European Brigade, LA Mil.
Faustino, J.-Pvt. Spanish Guards, Mobile Home Guard, ALA Militia
Fecundo, Manuel Machado-Pvt. Co. 10, 5th (Span.) Regt., Euro., Brig., LA Mil.
Federico, A.-Pvt. Co. 1, 5th (Spanish) Regiment, European Brigade, LA Militia
Federico, Frank-Pvt. Co. 1, 5th (Spanish) Regiment, European Brigade, LA Militia
Fednanders, Ezekiel M.-Pvt. Company F, 2nd Battalion, ALA Light Artillery
Feerro, Pedro-Pvt. Company 5, Cazadores Espanoles Regiment, LA Militia
Felice, Antonio-Pvt. Company D, 30th LA Infantry
Felis, Sebastian-1st Lt. Company G, 21st ALA Infantry
***See also Fraig y Femenias, J.
Femenias, L.-Pvt. Co. 5, 5th (Spanish) Regiment, European Brigade, LA Militia
Ferales, Cresencio-Pvt. Hall's Company, TX
Ferdinando, O.-Musician Company E, 14th LA Infantry
Ferella, Manuel-Pvt. Crescent Regiment, LA Infantry
Ferera, H.-Pvt. Sigwalds Company, 16th S.C. Militia
Fermandes, Pierre-Pvt. 18th LA Infantry
Fernandes, George G.-Surgeon 3rd S.C. Infantry
Fernandes, Henry-Pvt. 2nd Company E, 5th S.C. Infantry

Fernandes, James G.-Pvt. 1st Company E, 5th S.C. Infantry
Fernandes, Joseph-Pvt. Company A, 54th VIR Militia
Fernandez, A.R.-Pvt. Company H, Orleans Guard Regiment, LA Militia
Fernandez, Adolphus-Pvt. Company H, 2nd FLA Infantry
Fernandez, Anselmo-4th Sgt. Company D, 30th LA Infantry
Fernandez, Antonio Sr.-Pvt. Co. 5, 5th (Span.) Regt., European Brigade, LA Mil.
Fernandez, Antonio Jr.-Pvt. Co. 5, 5th (Spanish) Regt., European Brig., LA Mil.
Fernandez, Augustin-Pvt. Co. 2, Cazadores Espanoles Regiment, LA Militia
Fernandez, Benito-Pvt. Co. 6, 5th (Spanish) Regt., European Brigade, LA Militia
Fernandez, D.-2nd Sgt. Orleans Guard Regiment, LA Militia
Fernandez, Denis-2nd Lt. Company A, Orleans Guard Regiment, LA Militia
Fernandez, E.A.-Capt. Fernandez's Mounted Company, FLA Militia
Fernandez, Edward A.-Pvt. Company K, 40th GA Infantry
Fernandez, Emile-Pvt. Knap's Company, Fausse River Guards, LA Militia
Fernandez, F.-Capt. Co. A, 1st Regiment, 2nd Brigade, 1st Division, LA Militia
Fernandez, F.F..-Pvt. Company E, Confederate States Zouave Battalion, LA
Fernandez, Faustino-Pvt. Co. A, 5th (Spanish) Regt., European Brigade, LA Mil.
Fernandez, Felipe-Pvt. Co. 5, 5th (Spanish) Regt., European Brigade, LA Militia
Fernandez, Francisco-Pvt. Company E, 13th LA Infantry
Fernandez, Gabriel-Pvt. Cameron County Coast Guard, TX Militia
Fernandez, Harry-Cpl. Company E, Hampton Legion, S.C.
Fernandez, Henry G.-1st Lt. Company G, 11th MISS Infantry
Fernandez, J.T.-Lt. Company 2, Cazadores Espanoles Regiment, LA Militia
Fernandez, J. Angel-Pvt. Co. 5, 5th (Spanish) Regt., European Brigade, LA Mil.
Fernandez, Joaquin-Cpl. Co. 3, 5th (Spanish) Regt., European Brigade, LA Mil.
Fernandez, John-Pvt. Stiles' Company, 1st Olmstead's GA Infantry
Fernandez, John-Pvt. Company A, 2nd LA Infantry
Fernandez, John-1st Lt. Co. 5, 5th (Spanish) Regt., European Brigade, LA Militia
Fernandez, John-Pvt. Company I, 6th VIR Infantry
Fernandez, Jose-Pvt. Co. 5, 5th (Spanish) Regt., European Brigade, LA Militia
Fernandez, Jose-Pvt. Co. 2, 5th (Spanish) Regt., European Brigade, LA Militia
Fernandez, Juan-Pvt. Company G, 10th LA Infantry
Fernandez, Juan-2nd Lt. Co. 5, 5th (Spanish) Regt., European Brigade, LA Mil.
Fernandez, Juan-Pvt. Co. 4, 5th (Spanish) Regt., European Brigade, LA Militia
Fernandez, Juan-Pvt. Company D, 3rd TX Infantry
Fernandez, Juan-Pvt. Company H, 8th TX Infantry
Fernandez, L.-Pvt. 1st Native Guards, LA Militia
Fernandez, Louis-Pvt. Company H, 21st ALA Infantry
Fernandez, M.-Pvt. Company A, Brooks' Battalion, Confederate Infantry
Fernandez, Macsimiano-Pvt. Co. A, 5th (Span.) Regt., European Brig., LA Mil.
Fernandez, Manuel-Pvt. Co. A, 5th (Spanish) Regt., European Brigade, LA Mil.
Fernandez, Manuel-Pvt. Company D, 30th LA Infantry
Fernandez, Manuel-Pvt. Company 1, Cazadores Espanoles Regt., LA Militia
Fernandez, Manuel Alvarez-Pvt. Co. 4, 5th (Span.) Regt., Euro., Brig., LA Mil.
Fernandez, Manuel Amancio-Pvt. Co. 9, 5th (Span.) Regt., Euro., Brig., LA Mil.

Fernandez, N.B.-Pvt. Company I, 13th LA Infantry
Fernandez, O.-Pvt. 1st Native Guards, LA Militia
Fernandez, Octave Victor-Pvt. / Commissary Clerk Miles' Legion, LA
Fernandez, P.-Pvt. 1st Native Guards, LA Militia
Fernandez, P.-Pvt. Company H, Crescent Regiment, LA Infantry
Fernandez, P.O.-Cpl. 1st Native Guards, LA Militia
Fernandez, Pablo-Pvt. Co. 10, 5th (Spanish) Regt., European Brigade, LA Militia
Fernandez, Paco-Pvt. Company G, 11th MISS Infantry
Fernandez, Phillip-Pvt. Company D, 30th LA Infantry
Fernandez, R.-4th Cpl. Company A, Orleans Guard Regiment, LA Militia
Fernandez, R. Menendez-Pvt. Co. 2, 5th (Span.) Regt., European Brig., LA Militia
Fernandez, Raphael-Pvt. Company F, 8th TX Infantry
Fernandez, Rosendo-Pvt. Co. 9, 5th (Spanish) Regt., European Brigade, LA Mil.
Fernandez, S. Jr.-Cannoneer Company 6, Washington Artillery Battalion, LA
Fernandez, Salvador-Pvt. Co. 5, 5th (Spanish) Regt., European Brigade, LA Mil.
Fernandez, Simplicio-Pvt. Co. A, 5th (Spanish) Regt., European Brigade, LA Mil.
Fernandez, Seves-Pvt. 5th Field Battery, TX Artillery
Fernandez, V.-Cpl. Co. 1, 5th (Spanish) Regiment, European Brigade, LA Militia
Fernandez, Vicente-Pvt. Co. 6, 5th (Spanish) Regt., European Brigade, LA Mil.
Fernandez, Victor-Pvt. Co. C, 2nd Regiment, 2nd Brigade, 1st Division, LA Mil.
Fernandez, Vincent-Pvt. Company H, 28th Thomas' LA Infantry
Fernandez y Henia, Manuel-Pvt. Co. 9, 5th (Span.) Regt., Euro., Brig., LA Mil.
Fernando, P.-Musician Company E, 14th LA Infantry
Fernando, O.L.-3rd Sgt. Company C, 2nd Battery, ALA Artillery
Fernando, S.C.-Pvt. Company K, 1st Kings Infantry, MISS State Troops
Ferreira, F.-Pvt. Fickling's Company, Brook's Light Artillery, S.C. Artillery
Ferreira, Francisco-Pvt. Co. 7, 5th (Spanish) Regt., European Brigade, LA Militia
Ferreira, Francis C.-Pvt. Company K, 2nd S.C. Infantry
Ferreira, Joseph V.-Cpl. Company B, 3rd FLA Infantry
Ferreiro, Antonio-Cpl. Co. 10, 5th (Spanish) Regt., European Brigade, LA Militia
Ferrer, A.M.-Pvt. Company G, 48th GA Infantry
Ferrer, Andres-Pvt. Co. 2, 5th (Spanish) Regiment, European Brigade, LA Militia
Ferrer, C.-Cpl. Company 1, Cazadores Espanoles Regiment, LA Militia
Ferrer, Camillus-Pvt. Jeff Davis Legion, MISS
Ferrer, Cayetano-Sgt. Co. 8, 5th (Spanish) Regt., European Brigade, LA Militia
Ferrer, F.-Pvt. Co. 1, 5th (Spanish) Regiment, European Brigade, LA Militia
Ferrer, Gabriel-Pvt. Co. 6, 5th (Spanish) Regiment, European Brigade, LA Militia
Ferrer, James H.-Cpl. Company B, 36th Villepigues' GA Infantry
Ferrer, Jayme-Pvt. Co. 7, 5th (Spanish) Regiment, European Brigade, LA Militia
Ferrer, Jeptha W.-Pvt. Company B, 57th ALA Infantry
Ferrer, Jose-Pvt. Co. 8, 5th (Spanish) Regiment, European Brigade, LA Militia
Ferrer y Ferrer, Jose-Sgt. Cazadores Espanoles Regiment, LA Militia
Ferrer, Juan-Pvt. Co. 9, 5th (Spanish) Regiment, European Brigade, LA Militia
Ferrer, Juan Salvador-Pvt. Co. 2, 5th (Spanish) Regt., European Brigade, LA Mil.
Ferrer, Leon-1st Cpl. Company D, 30th LA Infantry

Ferrer, Miguel-Pvt. Co. 9, 5th (Spanish) Regiment, European Brigade, LA Militia
Ferrer, Pedro-Sgt. Company 5, Cazadores Espanoles Regiment, LA Militia
Ferrer y Ferrer, Pedro-Pvt. Co. 5, Cazadores Espanoles Regiment, LA Militia
Ferrer, T.J.-Pvt. Co. 1, 5th (Spanish) Regiment, European Brigade, LA Militia
***See also Fararo and Forrara
Ferrera, Antonio-1st. Sgt. Co. G, 21st ALA Infantry. He was later detailed to Lt. Anderson and the Submarine Defenses.
Ferro > see Salvador, J. Ferro
Figaroa, Juan Domingo-Pvt. Co. 1, Cazadores Espanoles Regiment, LA Militia
Figueroa, Antonio-Pvt. Company E, 8th TX Infantry
Figueroa, Francisco-Pvt. Company E, 8th TX Infantry
Figueroa, Geronimo-Pvt. Company E, 8th TX Infantry
Figurie, Emanuel-Pvt. Company E, 16th LA Infantry
Fillippe, P.-Pvt. Company B, 4th ALA Militia Reserve
Fleijas, J.-Pvt. Co. 1, 5th (Spanish) Regiment, European Brigade, LA Militia
Fleitas, F.B.-Pvt. Greenleaf's Company, Orleans Light Horse, LA
Fleitas, J.B.-Capt. Company B, Confederate States Zouave Battalion, LA
Fleitas, William A.-Pvt. Company E, 20th MISS Infantry
Florentino, Jose-Pvt. Co. A, 5th (Spanish) Regt., European Brigade, LA Militia
Flores, Adiano-Pvt. Company E, Benavides' Regiment, TX Cavalry
Flores, Adolfo-Pvt. 1st Company H, 33rd TX Cavalry
Flores, Adolph-1st Sgt. Company A, 11th LA Infantry
Flores, Agustin-Pvt. Bustillo's Company, Bexar County, TX Militia
Flores, Andre-Pvt. Company H, 33rd TX Cavalry
Flores, Angelin-Pvt. Company I, 8th LA Infantry
Flores, Antonio-Pvt. Company G, 28th Thomas' LA Infantry
Flores, Antonio-Pvt. Company A, Benavides' Regiment, TX Cavalry
Flores, B.-Pvt. Company C, 8th TX Infantry
Flores, B.A.-Pvt. Benton's Company, Guadalupe County, TX Volunteers
Flores, Bartolo-Pvt. Zapata's Company, Nueces County, TX State Troops
Flores, Benjamin-Pvt. Company E, 1st LA Reserve
Flores, Brigido-4th Cpl. Zapata's Company, Nueces County, TX State Troops
Flores, Canute-Pvt. Bustillo's Company, Bexar County, TX Militia
Flores, Carlos-Pvt. Company F, 3rd TX Infantry
Flores, Casimero-Pvt. 1st Company I, 33rd TX Cavalry
Flores, Cecidro-Pvt. Gray's Company, Bexar County, TX Militia
Flores, Cenobio-Pvt. Gray's Company, Bexar County, TX Militia
Flores, Cerento-Lt. Benavides' Regiment, TX Cavalry
Flores, Corasmer-Sgt. Company H, 19th LA Infantry
Flores, Cosmo-Pvt. Trevenio's Company, TX Cavalry
Flores, Domingo-Cpl. Company C, 8th TX Infantry
Flores, Domingo-Sgt. Company C, Benavides' Regiment, TX Cavalry
Flores, Domingo-Pvt. Bustillo's Company, Bexar County, TX Militia
Flores, F.-Pvt. Company D, 3rd LA Infantry
Flores, Felipe-Pvt. Company D, 1st McCulloch's TX Cavalry

Hispanic Confederates 51

Flores, Felipe-Pvt. Company H, 36th TX Cavalry
Flores, Felix-Pvt. Company H, 36th TX Cavalry
Flores, Francis B.-Pvt. Company G, Beauregard Battalion, LA Militia
Flores, Georgio-Pvt. Company E, Madison's Regiment, TX Cavalry
Flores, Gertrudis-Pvt. Company C, Ragsdale's Battalion, TX Cavalry
Flores, H.-Sgt. Company B, 1st Battalion State Guards, LA
Flores, H.D.-Pvt. Company D, 4th TX Infantry
Flores, Henry-Pvt. Company H, 15th TX Infantry
Flores, Ignacio-Pvt. Company F, 3rd TX Infantry
Flores, J.F.-Pvt. Company I, 8th LA Infantry
Flores, Jacinto-Sgt. Company C, 3rd TX Cavalry
Flores, James P.-Pvt. Company G, 12th TX Infantry
Flores, James E.-Pvt. Company B, Consolidated Crescent Regiment, LA Infantry
Flores, Jesus-Pvt. Company D, 4th TX Cavalry
Flores, Jesus-Pvt. 24th Battalion, TX Infantry
Flores, John-Pvt. Company G, 1st TX Heavy Artillery
Flores, John-Pvt. Jones' Company, TX Light Artillery
Flores, Jose A.-Pvt. 2nd Company F, 2nd TX Cavalry
Flores, Jose Maria-Pvt. Medina Guards, Bexar County, TX Militia
Flores, Joseph A.-Pvt. Company A, 11th TX Infantry
Flores, Joseph E.-Pvt. Company A, 11th LA Infantry
Flores, Juan-Pvt. Company 1, Cazadores Espanoles Regiment, LA Militia
Flores, Juan-Pvt. Trevino's Squad, TX Partisan Mounted Volunteers
Flores, Juan B.-Pvt. Company 1, Cazadores Espanoles Regiment, LA Militia
Flores, Julian-Cpl. 1st Company C, 3rd TX Infantry
Flores, Justo-Pvt. Dunn's Company, Waller's Regiment, TX Cavalry
Flores, L.-Drummer 21st Patton's LA Infantry
Flores, L.B.-Pvt. Company D, Crescent Regiment, LA Infantry
Flores, Louis-Pvt. Company G, 3rd LA Infantry
Flores, M.-Pvt. Company D, Timmon's Regiment, TX Infantry
Flores, M.-Pvt. Victoria County, TX Militia
Flores, Manuel-Pvt. Co. 9, 5th (Spanish) Regt., European Brigade, LA Militia
Flores, Manuel-Cpl. Company E, Benavides' Regiment, TX Cavalry
Flores, Manuel-Pvt. Company H, 8th TX Infantry
Flores, Manuel-Pvt. Bustillo's Company, Bexar County, TX Militia
Flores, Marcos-Musician Company F, Waul's Legion, TX
Flores, Mariano-1st Lt. Wilson County, TX Militia
Flores, Merock-Pvt. Company A, 11th LA Infantry
Flores, Patricio-Pvt. 1st Company C, 3rd TX Infantry
Flores, Pedro-Pvt. Company B, 2nd TX Cavalry
Flores, Pedro-Pvt. Company G, 3rd TX Infantry
Flores, Pedro-3rd Lt. Bustillo's Company, Bexar County, TX Militia
Flores, R.-Pvt. Company C, 8th TX Infantry
Flores, Ramon-Pvt. Bustillo's Company, Bexar County, TX Militia
Flores, Refugio-Pvt. Company F, 3rd TX Infantry

Flores, Rain-Pvt. Company B, 3rd LA Infantry
Flores, Richard-Pvt. Company H, 19th LA Infantry
Flores, Salvadore-Pvt. Company F, 9th TX Cavalry
Flores, Victor-Pvt. Company F, 9th LA Infantry
Flores, Victor-Pvt. Company H, 7th TX Cavalry
Flores, Viviano-Pvt. Gray's Company, Bexar County, TX Militia
Flores, Ursin H.-Pvt. Company D, 2nd LA Cavalry
Floria, Domingo-Pvt. Co. 7, 5th (Spanish) Regt., European Brigade, LA Militia
Floris, A.-Pvt. Company I, 8th LA Infantry
Floris, Sylvester-Pvt. Company B, Gray's LA Infantry
Florit, Juan-Pvt. Co. 9, 5th (Spanish) Regiment, European Brigade, LA Militia
Folivar, Angel-Cpl. Company 5, Cazadores Espanoles Regiment, LA Militia
Fonentes, Manuel-Pvt. 1st Native Guards, LA Militia
Fonseca, John-Pvt. Lafourche Regiment, LA Militia
Font, Francisco-Pvt. Company G, 21st ALA Infantry
Font, S.J.-1st Lt. Co. 2, 5th (Spanish) Regiment, European Brigade, LA Militia
Foo, Rosendo-Pvt. Company 2, Cazadores Espanoles Regiment, LA Militia
Forell, Manuel-Pvt. Co. 9, 5th (Spanish) Regt., European Brigade, LA Militia
Fores, Antonio-Pvt. Cazadores Espanoles Regiment, LA Militia
Fornaris, A.-2nd Lt. Co. 1, 5th (Spanish) Regt., European Brigade, LA Militia
Fornaris, Jose-Pvt. Co. 9, 5th (Spanish) Regt., European Brigade, LA Militia
Fornell, Manuel-Pvt. Co. 9, 5th (Spanish) Regt., European Brigade, LA Militia
Fornes, Antonio-Pvt. Company 1, Cazadores Espanoles Regiment, LA Militia
Forney, Vicente-Pvt. Co. 6, 5th (Spanish) Regt., European Brigade, LA Militia
Foro, Francisco-Pvt. Company 2, Cazadores Espanoles Regiment, LA Militia
Forrara, Manuel-Pvt. Co. D, 4th Regiment, 1st Brigade, 1st Division, LA Militia
Forrara, Marsolan-Pvt. Company C, 26th LA Infantry
Fraetas, Canazio-2nd Lt. Company E, 3rd VIR Infantry
Fraig y Femenias, J.-Pvt. Co. 5, Cazadores Espanoles Regiment, LA Militia
Francansisco, Gloria-Pvt. Company D, 95th ALA Militia
Francisco, Augustus-Cpl. Company B, 45th VIR Infantry
Francisco, A.M.-Pvt. Spanish Guards, Mobile Home Guard, ALA Militia
Francisco, Antonio-Pvt. Co. 8, 5th (Spanish) Regt., European Brig., LA Militia
Francisco, James M.-Pvt. Company D, 2nd TX Mounted Rifles
Francisco, John-Pvt. Company H, Cobb's Legion, GA
Francisco, John H.-Pvt. TX Militia
Francisco, Jose-Musician Company F, 2nd TX Infantry
Francisco, Juan-Pvt. Company F, 6th TX Infantry
Francisco, L.-Pvt. Spanish Guards, Mobile Home Guard, ALA Militia
Francisco, M.-2nd Lt. Hert's Company, ALA Militia
Franco, Antonio-Pvt. Co. 2, 5th (Spanish) Regt., European Brigade, LA Militia
Franquez, Etienne-Pvt. Company K, 28th Thomas' LA Infantry
Franquez, Leonard Sr.-Pvt. Company D, 7th LA Cavalry
Fransisco, Agustin-Pvt. Co. A, 5th (Spanish) Regt., European Brigade, LA Mil.
Fransisco, Antonio-Pvt. Co. A, 5th (Spanish) Regt., European Brigade, LA Mil.

Hispanic Confederates

Fransisco, Flaro-Sgt. Co. A, 5th (Spanish) Regt., European Brigade, LA Militia
Fransisco, Nicolas-Cpl. Co. A, 5th (Spanish) Regt., European Brigade, LA Mil.
Fransisco, R.L.-Assistant QuarterMaster 4th VIR Infantry
Fransisco, Visente-Pvt. Co. A, 5th (Spanish) Regt., European Brigade, LA Mil.
Frausto, Jose Maria-Sgt. Company C, 3rd TX Infantry
Frausto, Ramon-Pvt. Company I, 33rd TX Cavalry
Frausto, Santiago-Pvt. Company B, Benavides' Regiment, TX Cavalry
Freigas, Antonio-Pvt. Company A, 1st Battalion, N.C. Heavy Artillery
Freitas, Francisco-Pvt. Co. 8, 5th (Spanish) Regt., European Brigade, LA Militia
Freitas, Jose-Pvt. Company 8, 5th (Spanish) Regt., European Brigade, LA Militia
Frietas, Jack-Pvt. Company D, 4th Regiment, 1st Brigade, 1st Division, LA Mil.
Frietass, Frank-Pvt. Company D, 2nd TX Infantry
Fruch, Manuel-Capt. Co. 10, 5th (Spanish) Regt., European Brigade, LA Militia
Fuentes, Charles-Pvt. Co. 1, 5th (Spanish) Regt., European Brigade, LA Militia
Fuentes, Hernandez-Pvt. Company G, 3rd TX Infantry
Fuentes, Homer-Sgt. 1st Native Guards, LA Militia
Fuentes, Luis-Pvt. Company C, 3rd TX Infantry
Fuentes, Paul-Cpl. Company D, 22nd Consolidated LA Infantry
Fuentes, Martin-Pvt. Company H, 8th TX Infantry
Funeya, Juan-Cpl. Co. 7, 5th (Spanish) Regiment, European Brigade, LA Militia

G

Gabino, J.-Pvt. Spanish Guards, Mobile Home Guard, ALA Militia
Gaeta, Emilio-Cpl. Co. 3, 5th (Spanish) Regiment, European Brigade, LA Militia
Gaetan, Charles-Pvt. 1st Native Guards, LA Militia
Gaete, Jacinto-Cpl. Co. 10, 5th (Spanish) Regiment, European Brigade, LA Mil.
Gahona > see Segui y Gahona, Gabriel
Galan, Francisco-Pvt. TX Militia
Galatas, G.-Pvt. Company K, Chalmette Regiment, LA Militia
Gali, Jose Claro-Pvt. Bustillo's Company, Bexar County, TX Militia
Gallatas, J.N.-Pvt. Company B, Miles' Legion, LA
Galau, Manuel-Sgt. Company H, 8th TX Infantry
Galceran, Denis-Pvt. Floyd's Legion, GA
Galceran, J. Pvt. Co. 1, 5th (Spanish) Regiment, European Brigade, LA Militia
Galceran, James-Pvt. Company A, Floyds' Legion, GA
Galceran, M.P.-Pvt. Company I, Floyds' Legion, GA
Galindo, Clemente-Pvt. Company E, Benavides' Regiment, TX Cavalry
Galindo, Josiano-Pvt. Medina Guards, Bexar County, TX Militia
Galindo, Urbano-Pvt. Company C, 8th TX Infantry
Gallard, Andres-Pvt. Co. 10, 5th (Spanish) Regt., European Brigade, LA Militia
Gallard, Juan-Pvt. Co. 10, 5th (Spanish) Regiment, European Brigade, LA Mil.
Gallard, Vicente-Pvt. Co. 10, 5th (Spanish) Regiment, European Brigade, LA Militia
Gallardo, Manuel-Pvt. 1st Company A, Ragsdale's Battalion, TX Cavalry
Gallego, Trinidad-Pvt. Company A, 3rd TX Infantry

Gallo, Stephan-Pvt. Company A, 11th LA Infantry
Galvan, Dolores-Pvt. Company F, 3rd TX Infantry
Galvan, Jesus-Pvt. Company C, 8th TX Infantry
Galvan, Ramon-Pvt. Company F, 3rd TX Infantry
Gamas, C.-Pvt. Company G, 26th LA Infantry
Gambo, James-Pvt. Company D, 23rd S.C. Infantry
Gambo, Nasario-Pvt. Company I, Benavides' Regiment, TX Cavalry
Gambo, William-Pvt. Company D, 4th S.C. Cavalry
Gamboa, Bartolo-Pvt. 1st Company I, 33rd TX Cavalry
Gamboa, Jacinto-Pvt. Company B, Benavides' Regiment, TX Cavalry
Gamboa, Prudencio-Pvt. 1st Company I, 33rd TX Cavalry
Gamboa, Ramon-Sgt. 1st Company I, 33rd TX Cavalry
Gamboa, Sorbines-Pvt. 1st Company I, 33rd TX Cavalry
Gambor, Antonio-Pvt. 1st Company H, 33rd TX Cavalry
Gambor, Pablo-Pvt. 2nd Field Battery, TX Artillery
Gana, A.-Pvt. Gomez's Company, 22nd LA Infantry
Gaona, Narciso-Pvt. Bustillo's Company, Bexar County, TX Militia
Gara, Manuel-Pvt. Teel's Company, TX State Troops
Garabia, F.-Pvt. Trevinio's Company, TX Cavalry
Garbri, Ysabel-Pvt. Company H, 8th TX Infantry
Garca, E.-Pvt. Company G, 3rd LA Infantry
Garcia, A.-Pvt. Spanish Guards, Mobile Home Guard, ALA Militia
Garcia, A.-Pvt. Company 8, 1st Chasseurs a pied, LA Militia
Garcia, A.-Pvt. Company G, 8th TX Infantry
Garcia, A.D.-1st Lt. Orleans Artillery Battalion, LA
Garcia, A.E.-Pvt. Company F, 30th LA Infantry
Garcia, A.M.-Pvt. Gomez's Company, 22nd LA Infantry
Garcia, Abelanio-Pvt. Zapata's Company, Nueces County, TX State Troops
Garcia, Amando-Pvt. Co. 3, 5th (Spanish) Regt., European Brigade, LA Militia
Garcia, Andres-Pvt. Cameron County Coast Guard, TX Militia
Garcia, Anesello-Pvt. 1st Company H, 33rd TX Cavalry
Garcia, Anicito-Pvt. Company A, Benavides' Regiment, TX Cavalry
Garcia, Antonio-Pvt. Co. 3, 5th (Spanish) Regt., European Brigade, LA Militia
Garcia, Antonio-Pvt. Company H, 3rd TX Infantry
Garcia, Antonio-Pvt. Company E, 8th TX Infantry
Garcia, Antonio-Pvt. 24th Battalion, TX Infantry
Garcia, Armando-Pvt. Company 5, Cazadores Espanoles Regiment, LA Militia
Garcia, B.-Pvt. Company A, 3rd State Guards Battalion, GA
Garcia, Balentin-Pvt. 1st. Company C, 3rd TX Infantry
Garcia, Benino-Pvt. Company E, 8th TX Infantry
Garcia, Benito-Pvt. Cameron County Coast Guard, TX Militia
Garcia, Bernabel-Pvt. 1st Company A, Ragsdale's Battalion, TX Cavalry
Garcia, Bernardo-Pvt. Company C, 8th TX Cavalry
Garcia, Bernardo-Cpl. Co. 6, 5th (Spanish) Regt., European Brigade, LA Militia
Garcia, Braulio-Pvt. Company C, Ragsdale's Battalion, TX Cavalry

Garcia, C.-Pvt. Company D, Crescent Regiment, LA Infantry
Garcia, C.-3rd Lt. Co. A, 1st Regiment, 2nd Brigade, 1st Division, LA Militia
Garcia, Carlos-Pvt. Company D, 3rd TX Infantry
Garcia, Cesario-Pvt. 1st Company H, 33rd TX Infantry
Garcia, Cresencio-Pvt. Skidmore's Company, San Patricio County, TX Militia
Garcia, D.J.-1st Sgt. Company 2, Cazadores Espanoles Regiment, LA Militia
Garcia, E.-Pvt. Co. 1, 5th (Spanish) Regiment, European Brigade, LA Militia
Garcia, E.-Pvt. Company 3, 8th TX Infantry
Garcia, Eduardo-Cpl. Company 1, Cazadores Espanoles Regiment, LA Militia
Garcia, Emanuel-Pvt. Sabine Reserve, LA Militia
Garcia, Emanuel-Pvt. Company D, 22nd TX Cavalry
Garcia, Estevan-Pvt. Thomas' Company, TX Partisan Rangers
Garcia, Eugenio-Sgt. 1st Company H, 33rd TX Cavalry
Garcia, Feliciano-Pvt. 1st Company A, Ragsdale's Battalion, TX Cavalry
Garcia, Felipe-Pvt. Co. 6, 5th (Spanish) Regiment, European Brigade, LA Militia
Garcia, Fernando-Pvt. Company I, 8th TX Infantry
Garcia, Fernando-Pvt. Tom's Company, Atascosa County, TX Militia
Garcia, Francisco-Pvt. Cox's Company, Mann's Battalion, TX Cavalry
Garcia, Francisco-Pvt. 1st Company C, Ragsdale's Battalion, TX Cavalry
Garcia, Francois-Pvt. Co. F, 4th Regiment, 2nd Brigade, 1st Division, LA Militia
Garcia, Gabriel-Pvt. Co. 5, 5th (Spanish) Regiment, European Brigade, LA Mil.
Garcia, George-1st Sgt. Company I, Benavides' Regiment, TX Cavalry
Garcia, Geraldo-Pvt. 24th Brigade, TX Militia
Garcia, Geronimo-Pvt. Company E, 3rd TX Infantry
Garcia, Gollo-3rd Sgt. Company I, Benavides' Regiment, TX Cavalry
Garcia, Guadalupe-5th Sgt. Trevinio's Company, TX Cavalry
Garcia, Guadalupe-Pvt. Company B, Baylor's Regiment, TX Cavalry
Garcia, Guiguno-3rd Sgt. Company I, Benavides' Regiment, TX Cavalry
Garcia, Henrique-Pvt. Company D, Miles' Legion, LA
Garcia, Heraldo-Pvt. 14th Field Battery, TX Artillery
Garcia, Hilario-Pvt. 8th Field Battery, TX Artillery
Garcia, Idelfonso-Pvt. Bustillo's Company, Bexar County, TX Militia
Garcia, Ignacio-Pvt. Medina Guards, Bexar County, TX Militia
Garcia, Inocente-Pvt. Company H, 8th TX Infantry
Garcia, Isadore-Pvt. TX Militia
Garcia, Incarnacion-Pvt. 1st Company H, 33rd TX Cavalry
Garcia, J.-Pvt. Company C, 8th TX Infantry
Garcia, J.B.-Pvt. 1st Native Guards, LA Militia
Garcia, J.E.-Pvt. Co. 1, 5th (Spanish) Regiment, European Brigade, LA Militia
Garcia, Jeronimo-Pvt. Company E, 2nd TX Infantry
Garcia, Jesus-Pvt. Company A, 33rd TX Cavalry
Garcia, Jesus-Pvt. Trevinio's Squad, TX Cavalry
Garcia, John-Pvt. Teel's Company, TX State Troops
Garcia, Jose-Pvt. 3rd Battalion, TX Cavalry
Garcia, Jose-Pvt. Co. 4, 5th (Spanish) Regiment, European Brigade, LA Militia

Garcia Hevia, Jose-Pvt. Co. 3, 5th (Spanish) Regt., European Brigade, LA Militia
Garcia, Jose Antonio-Pvt. Co. 2, 5th (Spanish) Regt., European Brigade, LA Mil.
Garcia, Jose Maria-Pvt. Thomas' Company, TX Partisan Rangers
Garcia, Jose Maria-1st Lt. 1st Company H, 33rd TX Cavalry
Garcia, Jose Maria-Pvt. Bustillo's Company, Bexar County, TX Militia
Garcia Gusman, Jose Maria-Pvt. Rhodes' Co., 3rd Yager's Battalion, TX Cavalry
Garcia, Joseph-Pvt. Company F, 19th LA Infantry
Garcia, Joseph-Pvt. Company K, 8th LA Infantry
Garcia, Juan-Pvt. 1st Company C, 3rd TX Infantry
Garcia, Juan-Pvt. Victoria County, TX Militia
Garcia, Juan-Pvt. Bustillo's Company, Bexar County, TX Militia
Garcia, Juan-Pvt. Company I, 8th LA Infantry
Garcia, Juan-Pvt. Co. 4, 5th (Spanish) Regiment, European Brigade, LA Militia
Garcia, Juan-Pvt. Thomas' Company, TX Partisan Rangers
Garcia, Julian-Pvt. Company F, 3rd TX Infantry
Garcia, Julian-Capt. Company H, Benavides' Regiment, TX Cavalry
Garcia, Justo-Pvt. Cameron County Coast Guard, TX Miltia
Garcia, Leonardo-Sgt. 1st Company H, 33rd TX Cavalry
Garcia, Librau-Pvt. Company D, Ragsdale's Battalion, TX Cavalry
Garcia, Lino-Pvt. 1st Company I, 33rd TX Cavalry
Garcia, Lionisio-Pvt. Lamar Home Guards, Refugio County, TX Militia
Garcia, Lucas-Pvt. 1st Company H, 33rd TX Cavalry
Garcia, Luis-Sgt. Company E, Benavides' Regiment, TX Cavalry
Garcia, Luis-Cpl. Company H, 8th TX Infantry
Garcia, M.-Pvt. Trevinio's Company, TX Cavalry
Garcia, M.-Pvt. Company E, 8th TX Infantry
Garcia Robes, M.-Pvt. Co. 2, 5th (Spanish) Regt., European Brigade, LA Militia
Garcia Soto, M.-Capt. Recruiting Officer, TX
Garcia, Marcelino-2nd Cpl. Company D , 30th LA Infantry
Garcia, Manuel-Pvt. Company C, 1st Nelligan's LA Infantry
Garcia, Manuel-Pvt. Company D, 13th LA Infantry
Garcia, Manuel-Pvt. Company F, Orleans Guard Regiment, LA Militia
Garcia, Manuel-Pvt. Company 2, Cazadores Espanoles Regiment, LA Militia
Garcia, Manuel-Pvt. Company F, 3rd MISS Infantry
Garcia, Manuel-Pvt. Company D, 3rd TX Infantry
Garcia, Manuel-Pvt. Company C, 8th TX Infantry
Garcia, Marcello-Cpl. 1st Company I, 33rd TX Cavalry
Garcia, Mariano-Pvt. Bustillo's Company, Bexar County, TX Militia
Garcia, Mariano-Pvt. Company E, Benavides' Regiment, TX Cavalry
Garcia, Mariano-Pvt. Company H, 8th TX Infantry
Garcia, Melcher-Pvt. Company I, Benavides' Regiment, TX Cavalry
Garcia, Michael-Pvt. Panaloosa's TX Cavalry
Garcia, Michel-Sgt. Company 8, 1st Chasseurs a pied, LA Militia
Garcia, Miguel-Pvt. Company C, 8th TX Infantry
Garcia, Nepomeceno-Sgt. Company C, 8th TX Infantry

Garcia, Nicanor-Pvt. Mitchell's Company, Bandera County, TX Militia
Garcia, Pablo-Pvt. Company D, 2nd TX Mounted Rifles
Garcia, Patricio-Pvt. Company 2, Cazadores Espanoles Regiment, LA Militia
Garcia, Pedro-Pvt. 5th (Spanish) Regiment, European Brigade, LA Militia
Garcia, Pierre-Pvt. 1st Native Guards, LA Militia
Garcia, Polinario-Pvt. Company G, 8th TX Infantry
Garcia, Prajedis-Pvt. Company E, Benavides' Regiment, TX Cavalry
Garcia, Presideo-Pvt. Company H, 8th TX Infantry
Garcia, Prudencio-Pvt. Engledow's Company, Nueces County, TX Militia
Garcia, R.N.-Pvt. Massenburg's Battery, Jackson Artillery, GA Light Artillery
Garcia, Rafael-Pvt. Company D, Benavides' Regiment, TX Cavalry
Garcia, Ramire-Cpl. Company B, 8th LA Infantry
Garcia, Ramon-Pvt. 1st Company H, 33rd TX Cavalry
Garcia, Raphael-Pvt. 8th Field Battery, TX Artillery
Garcia, Raymond-Pvt. Company B, 4th FLA Infantry
Garcia, Raymond-Sgt. Company E, 1st Strawbridge's LA Infantry
Garcia, Refugio-Pvt. Victoria County, TX Militia
Garcia, Robert-Pvt. Company I, 25th TX Cavalry
Garcia, Santiago-Pvt. Co. 3, 5th (Spanish) Regt., European Brigade, LA Militia
Garcia, Stephen-Pvt. 2nd TX Cavalry
Garcia, T.-Pvt. Company C, 8th TX Infantry
Garcia, Teodoro-Cpl. Rhodes' Company, 3rd Yager's Battalion, TX Cavalry
Garcia, Teodoro-Pvt. 8th Field Battery, TX Artillery
Garcia, Trinidad-Pvt. Company D, Benavides' Regiment, TX Cavalry
Garcia, Trinidad-Bugler 1st Company A, Ragsdale's Battalion, TX Cavalry
Garcia, Urban-Pvt. TX Militia
Garcia, Valerio-1st Lt. Co. 3, 5th (Spanish) Regt., European Brigade, LA Militia
Garcia, Vicente-Pvt. Company C, 8th TX Infantry
Garcia, Vicente-Pvt. Company C, Benavides' Regiment, TX Cavalry
Garcia, W.-Pvt. Company G, 8th TX Infantry
Garcia, Ylario-Pvt. Company C, 8th TX Infantry
Garcia, Ynoceuti-Pvt. Company H, 8th TX Infantry
Garcia y Borras, Jose-Sgt. Co. 8, 5th (Span.) Regt., European Brigade, LA Mil.
Garcia y Medina, Emilio-Pvt. Jackson Rifle Battalion, LA Militia
Garga, Luis-Pvt. Company C, 8th Hobby's TX Infantry
Garibay, F.-Pvt. Trevinio's Company, TX Partisan Rangers
Garibay, Ysabel-Pvt. Company H, 8th TX Infantry
Garnidena, John-Pvt. Company I, 3rd TX Infantry
Garnett, James Mercer-Son of Theodore Stanford Garnett Sr. and Florentina Moreno. He was a Capt. Divisional Ordnance Officer on the staff of General Robert Emmett Rodes, Army of Northern Virginia
Garnett, Theodore Stanford Jr.-Brother of the above, served as a Capt. Assistant Adjutant General on the staff of General William P. Roberts, Army of Northern Virginia.
Garrastago, Juan-Sgt. Co. 6, 5th (Spanish) Regt., European Brigade, LA Militia

Garriga, Francisco-Pvt. Co. 5, 5th (Spanish) Regt., European Brigade, LA Militia
Garriga, M.-Pvt. Co. 5, 5th (Spanish) Regt., European Brigade, LA Militia
Garriga, Simon-Pvt. Co. 5, 5th (Spanish) Regiment, European Brigade, LA Militia
Garriga, Teodoro-Pvt. Co. 7, 5th (Spanish) Regt., European Brigade, LA Militia
*** Garryo, Gario, Garyo and later Gary became the Louisiana version of the surname Garrido
Gario, Edward-Pvt. Company B, Miles' Legion, LA
Gario, Valante-Pvt. Company C, 10th Battalion, LA Infantry
Garyo, Jospeh Alcide-Pvt. Company D, 10th Battalion, LA Infantry
Garryo, Aristides-Pvt. LA Militia
Garryo, Lazincourt-Pvt. LA Militia
Gary, D.-Pvt. Dreux's LA Cavalry
Gary, Don Louis-Pvt. Company C, 10th Battalion, LA Infantry
Gary, Estache-Pvt. Company C, 10th Battalion, LA Infantry
Gary, G. (1st)-Pvt. Company D, 15th Battalion Sharpshooter's, LA
Gary, G.A. (2nd)-Pvt. Company A, 18th LA Infantry
Gary, Joseph-Cpl. Company G, 7th LA Cavalry
Gary, Joseph Homer-Pvt. Company G, Messenger's Regiment, LA Infantry
Gary, Jules-Pvt. Company I, 3rd LA Cavalry
Gary, Leon-Pvt. Company C, 18th LA Infantry
Gary, Philozin-Pvt. Company A, 18th Consolidated LA Infantry
Garsa, Juan-Pvt. Company A, 11th TX Infantry
Garsa, William-Pvt. Company G, 8th TX Infantry
Garza, Alejo-Pvt. Skidmore's Company, San Patricio County, TX Militia
Garza, Alex-Pvt. Company 3, 3rd LA Infantry
Garza, Andres-Pvt. Thomas' Company, TX Partisan Rangers
Garza, Antonio-Pvt. Medina Guards, Bexar County, TX Militia
Garza, Bisente-Pvt. Company I, 33rd TX Cavalry
Garza, Candelario-Pvt. 1st Company H, 33rd TX Cavalry
Garza, Cirinco-Pvt. Gray's Company, Bexar County, TX Militia
Garza, David-Pvt. Company D, 17th TX Infantry
Garza, E.-Pvt. / Nurse Company G, 3rd LA Infantry
Garza, Estanislado-Pvt. 1st Company H, 33rd TX Cavalry
Garza, Esteban-Pvt. Company B, 2nd TX Cavalry
Garza, Eugenio-2nd Lt. Company I, 33rd TX Cavalry
Garza, Felix-Pvt. Thomas' Company, TX Partisan Rangers
Garza, Francisco-Pvt. Company D, Benavides' Regiment, TX Cavalry
Garza, Francisco-Pvt. Company I, 8th TX Infantry
Garza, Geronimo-Pvt. Company A, Waul's Legion, TX
Garza, Ildefonzo-Pvt. 1st Company H, 33rd TX Cavalry
Garza, J.-Pvt. Company B, 2nd TX Cavalry
Garza, Jesus-Pvt. Company A, 33rd TX Cavalry
Garza, Jesus-2nd Lt. Bustillo's Company, Bexar County, TX Militia
Garza, Jesus-Pvt. 1st Company C, 3rd TX Infantry
Garza, Jesus-Pvt. Company A, 3rd TX Infantry

Garza, Jesus-Pvt. 2nd TX Mounted Infantry
Garza, John-Pvt. Victoria County, TX Militia
Garza, Jose-Pvt. Company E, 33rd TX Cavalry
Garza, Jose Maria-Pvt. Thomas' Company, TX Partisan Rangers
Garza, Joseph R.-1st Lt. Company H, 17th TX Dismounted Cavalry
Garza, Juan-Pvt. Company I, Benavides' Regiment, TX Cavalry
Garza, Juan De Leon-Pvt. Lamar Home Guard, Refugio County, TX Militia
Garza, Lazara-Musician Company C, 8th TX Infantry
Garza, Lazaro-Pvt. Company C, Benavides' Regiment, TX Cavalry
Garza, Leandro-Pvt. Company E, 8th TX Infantry
Garza, Luciano-2nd Lt. Thomas' Company, TX Partisan Rangers
Garza, Luis-Pvt. Company C, 8th TX Infantry
Garza, Madalene-Pvt. 1st Company C, 3rd TX Infantry
Garza, Manuel-Pvt. 14th Field Battery, TX Artillery
Garza, Manuel-Pvt. Company F, 3rd TX Infantry
Garza, Marcos-Pvt. Company F, 3rd TX Infantry
Garza, Michael-Pvt. Company G, 2nd TX Cavalry
Garza, Miguel-Cpl. 1st Company A, Ragsdale's Battalion, TX Cavalry
Garza, Nepomocino-Pvt. 1st Company H, 33rd TX Cavalry
Garza, Pablo-Pvt. Company D, Benavides' Regiment, TX Cavalry
Garza, Pablo-1st Sgt. 1st Company A, Ragsdale's Battalion, TX Cavalry
Garza, Perfecto-Pvt. 1st Company I, 33rd TX Cavalry
Garza, Presilliem-Pvt. TX Militia
Garza, Protacio-Pvt. 1st Company I, 33rd TX Cavalry
Garza, R.-Pvt. Trevinio's Company, TX Cavalry
Garza, Rafael-Pvt. Company A, 1st Yager's TX Cavalry
Garza, Rafael-Pvt. Company H, 33rd TX Cavalry
Garza, Rafael-Pvt. Company F, 3rd TX Infantry
Garza Rios, Rafael-Pvt. Minute Men (Scouts), Starr County, TX Militia
Garza, Rafael B.-Pvt. Company I, 3rd TX Infantry
Garza, Ramon-Pvt. Company B, 8th TX Cavalry
Garza, Ricardo-Pvt. Gray's Company, Bexar County, TX Militia
Garza, S.-Pvt. Company C, Cater's Battalion, TX Cavalry
Garza, Saveranio-Pvt. Company I, 8th TX Infantry
Garza, Serapio-Capt. Minute Men (Scouts), Starr County, TX Militia
Garza, Simon-Pvt. Company K, 6th TX Infantry
Garza, Stephan-Pvt. Company F, Benavides' Regiment, TX Cavalry
Garza, Telespero-Pvt. Trevinio's Company, TX Partisan Rangers
Garza, Tomas-Pvt. Company I, Benavides' Regiment, TX Cavalry
Garza, Victoriano-Pvt. Company D, 3rd TX Infantry
Garza, Wenceslaus-Pvt. Company K, 36th TX Cavalry
Garza, Ygnacio-Pvt. TX Militia
Gayardo, Joseph-Pvt. Co. K, 3rd Regiment, 1st Brigade, 1st Division, LA Militia
Gayardo, Julian-Pvt. Bexar County, TX Militia
Gayarre, Charles Etienne Arthur-Delegate to the Southern States Assoc., which voted

on 12/24/1860 for the delegates to the LA State Secession Convention. He was an ardent Confederate supporter and lost his fortune in the war. He remains one of Louisiana's most famous historians for his work on the early history of the state.
Gelpi, A.-Cpl. Company 1, Cazadores Espanoles Regiment, LA Militia
Gelpi, Gerome-Cpl. Co. 5, 5th (Spanish) Regiment, European Brigade, LA Mil.
Gelpi, Jose-Pvt. Co. 5, 5th (Spanish) Regiment, European Brigade, LA Militia
Gener, Antoine-Pvt. Pointe Coupee Artillery, LA
Gener, Bartolome-Pvt. Co. 4, 5th (Spanish) Regt., European Brigade, LA Militia
Gener, F.-Sgt. Company E, 22nd LA Infantry
Gener, Frank Francis-Pvt. Pointe Coupee Artillery, LA
Gener, Juan-Pvt. Co. 2, 5th (Spanish) Regiment, European Brigade, LA Militia
Gener, Ramon-Pvt. Co. 4, 5th (Spanish) Regiment, European Brigade, LA Militia
Genova, Sebastian-4th Cpl. Company D, 1st FLA Cavalry
Genovar, Bartolo-Pvt. Company B, 3rd FLA Infantry
Genovar, William-Pvt. Company B, 3rd FLA Infantry
Gerraro, Cladio-Cpl. Company B, Ragsdale's Battalion, TX Cavalry
Ghirrad, Jose-Pvt. Co. 6, 5th (Spanish) Regiment, European Brigade, LA Militia
Gigardo, Mariano-Pvt. Company B, Ragsdale's Battalion, TX Cavalry
*** See also Jil
Gil, Devates-Pvt. TX Militia
Gil, Jesus-Pvt. TX Militia
Gil, Luis-Cpl. 1st Company H, 33rd TX Cavalry
Gil, Manuel-Pvt. TX Militia
Gil, Miguel-Pvt. TX Militia
Gil, Polinario-Pvt. TX Militia
Gileta, Barthelemy-Pvt. Company D, 13th LA Infantry
Gillard, Armas-Sgt. Company D, 18th Consolidated LA Infantry
Gillard, William-Pvt. Company H, 1st ALA Reserve
***See Also Hemanus, Jimenez and Ximenez
Gimenez, Francisco-Cpl. Co. 4, 5th (Span.) Regt., European Brigade, LA Militia
Ginart, James-Cpl. Company C, Orleans Fire Regiment, LA Militia
Ginart, M.-Pvt. Company C, Orleans Fire Regiment, LA Militia
***Also found as Godines
Godina, Jesus-Pvt. Company F, 3rd TX Infantry
Godina, Julian-Pvt. 1st Company C, Ragsdale's Battalion, TX Cavalry
Gomas, Felician-Pvt. Company C, 2nd TX Cavalry
Gomas, I.-Pvt. TX Militia
Gomas, John-Pvt. Company G, 8th TX Infantry
Gomas, Levi-Pvt. Company E, 21st VIR Infantry
Gomes, Calisto-Pvt. Cameron County Coast Guard, TX Militia
Gomes, Domin-Pvt. ALA Militia
Gomes, John-Pvt. Company K, 8th LA Infantry
Gomes, Julian-Pvt. Jeff Davis Home Guards, Refugio County, TX Militia
Gomes, M.-Pvt. Company E, 2nd Battalion State Troops, MISS Infantry
Gomes, Magurisco-Pvt. Company E, 8th TX Infantry

Gomes, Mariano-Cpl. 1st Company C, 3rd TX Infantry
Gomes, Salome-Pvt. Thomas' Company, TX Partisan Rangers
Gomez, Andre-Pvt. Company F, 13th LA Infantry
Gomez, Atanacio-Pvt. Company F, 1st Yager's TX Cavalry
Gomez, B.G.-Pvt. Company A, Arsenal Battalion, Columbus, GA
Gomez, Charles L.-Pvt. 8th LA Infantry
Gomez, Dominique-Pvt. Pointe Coupee Artillery, LA
Gomez, Elario-Pvt. TX Militia
Gomez, Enocencia-Pvt. Company C, 8th TX Infantry
Gomez, F.-Pvt. Company A, 1st State Troops, TX Infantry
Gomez, F.-Capt. Company 1, Orleans Artillery Battalion, LA
Gomez, Francisco-Capt. Company A/C, 22nd LA Infantry
Gomez, J.-Cpl. Company G, 22nd Consolidated LA Infantry
Gomez, J.F.-Pvt. Company 3, Chasseurs a pied, LA Militia
Gomez, James-Pvt. Company 5, Washington Artillery Battalion, LA
Gomez, John-Pvt. Parsons' Company, FLA Militia
Gomez, Jose Maria-Pvt. Company D, 3rd TX Infantry
Gomez, Juan-Pvt. Co. 4, 5th (Spanish) Regiment, European Brigade, LA Militia
Gomez, Juan-Pvt. Co. 8, 5th (Spanish) Regiment, European Brigade, LA Militia
Gomez, Juan Jose-Pvt. 1st Company H, 33rd TX Cavalry
Gomez, Jules-Pvt. 1st Native Guards, LA Militia
Gomez, Luciano-Pvt. Gray's Company, Bexar County, TX Militia
Gomez, Luis-Pvt. / Teamster Company H, 8th TX Infantry
Gomez, Manuel-Pvt. Company G, 21st ALA Infantry
Gomez, Manuel-Pvt. Co. 3, 5th (Spanish) Regiment, European Brigade, LA Mil.
Gomez, Nicholas-Pvt. Company D, 8th FLA Infantry
Gomez, P.A.-Jr. 1st Lt. Company C, 22nd LA Infantry
Gomez, Phillip L.-1st Sgt. Company D, 8th FLA Infantry
Gomez, R.-Pvt. Company D, 13th LA Infantry
Gomez, Sabino-Sgt. Company 2, Cazadores Espanoles Regiment, LA Militia
Gomez, Silverio-Pvt. Gray's Company, Bexar County, TX Militia
Gomez, Tomas-Pvt. Co. 8, 5th (Spanish) Regt., European Brigade, LA Militia
Gomez, Tomas-Pvt. Bustillo's Company, Bexar County, TX Militia
Gomila > see J. Gomila Pons and Juan Gomila Casanova
Goncara, Gillino-Pvt. TX Militia
Gondelfo, Manuel-Pvt. Company 1, Cazadores Espanoles Regiment, LA Militia
Gongora, Agustin-Pvt. Company H, Baird's Regiment, TX Cavalry
Gongorra, E.-Pvt. Company C, 8th TX Infantry
Goni, Santiago-Pvt. Company H, 8th TX Infantry
Gonia, I.A.-Pvt. Company E, 39th MISS Infantry
Gonia, J.A.-Pvt. Company H, Power's Regiment, MISS Cavalry
Gonia, W.B.-Pvt. Company C, Hughes' Battalion, MISS Cavalry
***See also Gunsaulus
Gonsalas, Peter-Pvt. Smith's Ranger Company, TX State Troops
Gonsales, John-Pvt. Company D, 18th LA Infantry

Gonsales, Silver-Pvt. Company K, 61st VIR Infantry
Gonsales, Sirildo-Pvt. Jeff Davis Home Guards, Refugio County, TX Militia
Gonsalez, Joseph-Pvt. Company G, 28th Thomas' LA Infantry
Gonsallez, Trinidad-Pvt. Company B, 33rd TX Cavalry
Gonsava, Cristobal-Pvt. TX Militia
Gonsolas, J.J.-Pvt. Smith's Ranger Company, TX State Troops
Gonzales, A.-Pvt. Company K, 18th LA Infantry
Gonzales, A.-Cpl. Company E, 5th LA Infantry
Gonzales, A.-5th Sgt. Company C, Orleans Guard Regiment, LA Militia
Gonzales, A.- Pvt. 2nd Company C, 3rd TX Infantry
Gonzales, A.-Pvt. Spanish Guards, Mobile Home Guard, ALA Militia
Gonzales, Alberto-Pvt. Co. A, 5th (Spanish) Regt., European Brigade, LA Militia
Gonzales, Ambrosio Jose-Colonel Chief of Artillery / Generals Beauregard, Hardee, and Johnston.
Gonzales, Amotha-Pvt. Company E, 9th MISS Infantry
Gonzales, Andre-Pvt. Company C, 3rd TX Infantry
Gonzales, Anthony-Pvt. Company B, 8th LA Infantry
Gonzales, Antoine-Pvt. Company B, Lafourche Regiment, LA Militia
Gonzales, Antoine-Pvt. Company E, 28th Thomas' LA Infantry
Gonzales, Antonio-Pvt. Company G, 12th TX Infantry
Gonzales, Antonio-Pvt. Medina Guards, Bexar County, TX Militia
Gonzales, Antonio-Pvt. Company G, 10th LA Infantry
Gonzales De Botello, Antonio-Pvt. TX Militia
Gonzales, Apolonio-Pvt. 1st Company H, 33rd TX Cavalry
Gonzales, Armand-Pvt. 1st Native Guards, LA Militia
Gonzales, Atanacio-Pvt. Company C, 8th TX Infantry
Gonzales, Augustine-Pvt. Company D, 8th FLA Infantry
Gonzales, B.-Pvt. Trevinio's Company, TX Cavalry
Gonzales, Balentin-Pvt. 1st Company C, Ragsdale's Battalion, TX Cavalry
Gonzales, Benito-Pvt. Company F, 3rd TX Infantry
Gonzales, Bentura-Pvt. 1st Company H, 33rd TX Cavalry
Gonzales, Bonifacio-Pvt. 8th Field Battery, TX Artillery
Gonzales, Brigido-Pvt. Tom's Company, Atascosa County, TX Militia
Gonzales, Buck-Pvt. FLA Militia
Gonzales, Carlos-Pvt. 1st Company C, 3rd TX Infantry
Gonzales, Concepcion-Pvt. Dunn's Company, Waller's Regiment, TX Cavalry
Gonzales, Dario-2nd Lt. 1st Company H, 33rd TX Cavalry
Gonzales, Decidero-Sgt. 1st Company C, 3rd TX Infantry
Gonzales, Demas-Bugler Company H, 8th TX Infantry
Gonzales, Desire-Pvt. Company H, 28th Thomas' LA Infantry
Gonzales, Domingo-Pvt. Company B, Ragsdale's Battalion, TX Cavalry
Gonsales, E.-Pvt. Orleans Guard Regiment, LA Militia
Gonzales, Emanuel-Pvt. Company D, 25th TX Cavalry
Gonzales, Eugenio-Cpl. Company I, Benavides' Regiment, TX Cavalry
Gonzales, Eulalia-Pvt. Company F, 3rd TX Infantry

Gonzales, F.-Pvt. Company C, 2nd LA Cavalry
Gonzales, F.-Pvt. Orleans Guard Battery, LA Light Artillery
Gonzales, F.X.-Pvt. Company H, Chalmette Regiment, LA Militia
Gonzales, Felipe-Pvt. Company C, Benavides' Regiment, TX Cavalry
Gonzales, Firman-Pvt. Company C, 8th TX Infantry
Gonzales, Florence-Cpl. Company E, 26th LA Infantry
Gonzales, Florville-1st Sgt. 1st Native Guards, LA Militia
Gonzales, Francis-Pvt. Company E, 28th Thomas' LA Infantry
Gonzales, Francisco-Pvt. 1st Company C, 3rd TX Infantry
Gonzales, Francisco-Pvt. Company C, 8th TX Infantry
Gonzales, G.-Pvt. Johnson Station Rangers, Tarrant County, TX Militia
Gonzales, G.-Pvt. Chalmette Regiment, LA Militia
Gonzales, Gabriel-Pvt. Company 1, Cazadores Espanoles Regiment, LA Militia
Gonzales, Gomes-Pvt. Company H, 8th TX Infantry
Gonzales, Gregorio-Pvt. Company A, 3rd TX Infantry
Gonzales, Guadalupe-Pvt. Company H, 8th TX Infantry
Gonzales, Gustave-Pvt. 1st Native Guards, LA Militia
Gonzales, Hilario-Pvt. Davis' Company, Confederate Light Artillery
Gonzales, I.-Pvt. Company C, 18th Consolidated LA Infantry
Gonzales, Irinio-Pvt. Mitchell's Company, Bandera County, TX State Troops
Gonzales, J.-Pvt. Lewis' Company, Calhoun County, TX Militia
Gonzales, J.-Pvt. Johnson Station Rangers, Tarrant County, TX Militia
Gonzales, J.A.-Pvt. Company A, 9th LA Infantry
Gonzales, John Alfred-2nd Lt. Company A, Ogden's LA Cavalry
Gonzales, J.S.-Capt. Assistant Inspector General, C.S.A.
Gonzales, J.T.-Pvt. Company 3, 1st Chasseurs a pied, LA Militia
Gonzales, J.V.-Jr. 2nd Lt. Montgomery Fireman Guard, Montgomery, ALA
Gonzales, James-Pvt. Company G, 3rd ALA Reserve
Gonzales, James G.-Pvt. New Company K, 1st FLA Infantry
Gonzales, Jasper G.-Pvt. Company K, 1st FLA Infantry
Gonzales, Jesus-Pvt. Company A, Benavides' Regiment, TX Cavalry
Gonzales, Jesus-Pvt. Company B, Ragsdale's Battalion, TX Cavalry
Gonzales, Jesus-Pvt. Company H, 3rd TX Infantry
Gonzales, John-Pvt. Company D, 17th TX Infantry
Gonzales, John R.-Pvt. Company H, 28th Thomas' LA Infantry
Gonzales, Jose-Pvt. Company H, 24th ALA Infantry
Gonzales, Jose Maria-Pvt. Zapata's Company, Nueces County, TX State Troops
Gonzales, Joseph-Sgt. Company A, 12th ALA Infantry
Gonzales, Joseph Michael-Capt. Company A, Ogden's LA Cavalry
Gonzales, Juan-Pvt. Company 3, 1st Chasseurs a pied, LA Militia
Gonzales, Juan-Pvt. Company D, 3rd TX Infantry
Gonzales, Juan B.-Pvt. Zapata's Company, Nueces County, TX State Troops
Gonzales, Juan J.-Pvt. Company B, Cazadores Espanoles Regiment, LA Militia
Gonzales, Julian-Pvt. 1st Company C, Ragsdale's Battalion, TX Cavalry
Gonzales, Lino-Pvt. Minute Men (Scouts), Starr County, TX Militia

Gonzales, Lirado-Pvt. Company C, 8th TX Infantry
Gonzales, Luis-Pvt. 1st Company H, 33rd TX Cavalry
Gonzales, M.-Pvt. Company C, 8th TX Infantry
Gonzales, M.-Pvt. Co. A, 4th Regiment, 1st Brigade, 1st Division, LA Militia
Gonzales, M.-Cpl. Co. 1, 5th (Spanish) Regt., European Brigade, LA Militia
Gonzales, M.C.-Pvt. Company D, 22nd Consolidated LA Infantry
Gonzales, Manuel-Pvt. Trevinio's Squad, TX Partisan Mounted Rangers
Gonzales, Manuel-Cpl. 1st Company C, 3rd TX Infantry
Gonzales, Manuel-Pvt. Company E, 8th TX Infantry
Gonzales, Manuel F.-Pvt. Old Company K, 1st FLA Infantry
Gonzales, Mariano-Pvt. Co. A, 5th (Spanish) Regt., European Brigade, LA Mil.
Gonzales, Martin-2nd Lt. 1st Company H, 33rd TX Cavalry
Gonzales, Miguel-Cpl. Trevinio's Squad, TX Partisan Mounted Rangers
Gonzales, Monico-Pvt. 1st Company B, 33rd TX Cavalry
Gonzales, N.-Pvt. Company A, 4th TX Infantry
Gonzales, Nicholas C.-Pvt. Company B, Pointe Coupee Artillery, LA
Gonzales, P.-Pvt. Company A, Austin County, TX Militia
Gonzales, Pancho-Pvt. Company H, Benavides' Regiment, TX Cavalry
Gonzales, Pascual-Pvt. Company C, 8th TX Infantry
Gonzales, Paul-Pvt. 1st Native Guards, LA Militia
Gonzales, Polonio-Pvt. 1st Company H, 33rd TX Cavalry
Gonzales, Rafael-Pvt. Rhodes' Company, 3rd Yager's Battalion, TX Cavalry
Gonzales, Ramon-Pvt. Co. 10, 5th (Spanish) Regt., European Brigade, LA Militia
Gonzales, Raphel-Pvt. Company H, 24th TX Cavalry
Gonzales, Refolio-Pvt. Company A, 3rd Yager's Battalion, TX Cavalry
Gonzales, Ricardo-Pvt. Company I, 8th TX Infantry
Gonzales, Ricardo-Pvt. 1st Company H, 33rd TX Cavalry
Gonzales, S.-Pvt. Bridges' Battery, LA Light Artillery
Gonzales, S.-Pvt. 22nd LA Infantry
Gonzales, S.-Pvt. 1st Company B, Manigault's Battalion, S.C. Artillery
Gonzales, Santos-Pvt. Mitchell's Company, Bandera County, TX Militia
Gonzales, Thomas-Capt. Wilson, Gonzales', Hughes', TX Light Artillery
Gonzales, Trinidad-Pvt. Company B, 33rd TX Cavalry
Gonzales, V.-Pvt. Company H, Chalmette Regiment, LA Militia
Gonzales, Ventura-Pvt. Thomas' Company, TX Partisan Rangers
Gonzales, Vicente-Pvt. Company H, 8th TX Infantry
Gonzales, Vicente-Pvt. Company E, Benavides' Regiment, TX Cavalry
Gonzales, William-Pvt. Company H, 1st Strawbridge's LA Infantry
Gonzales, William-Pvt. Company H, 57th ALA Infantry
Gonzales, Yudelencio-Pvt. Thomas' Company, TX Partisan Rangers
Gonzalez, Bernardo-Pvt. Co. 2, 5th (Spanish) Regt., European Brigade, LA Mil.
Gonzalez, Celestino-Capt. New Company H, 1st FLA Infantry
Gonzalez, Charles B.-Pvt. Company B, 3rd FLA Infantry Battalion
Gonzalez, Francisco-Pvt. Co. 3, 5th (Spanish) Regt., European Brigade, LA Mil.
Gonzalez, Hipolite-Pvt. Company 2, Cazadores Espanoles Regiment, LA Militia

Hispanic Confederates 65

Gonzalez, J.-Pvt. Co. 5, 5th (Spanish) Regiment, European Brigade, LA Militia
Gonzalez, Jasper-Port Warden, Escambia County, FLA 1861.
Gonzalez, John B.-Pvt. Company B, 62nd ALA Infantry
Gonzalez, Jose-2nd Lt. Co. 3, 5th (Spanish) Regt., European Brigade, LA Militia
Gonzalez, Jose-Pvt. Co. 6, 5th (Spanish) Regiment, European Brigade, LA Mil.
Gonzalez, Juan-Pvt. Company 2, Cazadores Espanoles Regiment, LA Militia
Gonzalez, Miles F.-Capt. / Assistant QuarterMaster / Staff of General B. Bragg
Gonzalez, Tomas-Pvt. Co. 8, 5th (Spanish) Regt., European Brigade, LA Militia
Gonzalle, S.-Pvt. Company 6, 10th LA Infantry
Gora, Joseph-Pvt. Company B, 18th LA Infantry
Gorgullon, Tomas-Pvt. Co. 8, 5th (Spanish) Regt., European Brigade, LA Militia
Gorondona, Eugenio-Pvt. Co. 3, 5th (Spanish) Regt., European Brigade, LA Mil.
Gorondona, Marulino-Pvt. Co. 3, 5th (Spanish) Regt., European Brigade, LA Mil.
Gorrino, Gaetano-Pvt. Company F, Cazadores Espanoles Regiment, LA Militia
Gortaire, Manuel-Pvt. Company E, Benavides' Regiment, TX Cavalry
Gortari, Blas-Cpl. Company H, 8th TX Infantry
Gortari, Felix C.-1st Lt. Company C, Benavides' Regiment, TX Cavalry
Gortari, Nieves-Pvt. Company H, 8th TX Infantry
Gouralez, Buenaventura-Pvt. Co. 7, 5th (Spanish) Regt., European Brig., LA Mil.
Goutierez, Joseph-Pvt. Company D, 18th LA Infantry
Govante, Jose Gonzales-Pvt. Co. 3, 5th (Span.) Regt., European Brigade, LA Mil.
Goynochea, Juan B.-Pvt. Company 2, Cazadores Espanoles Regiment, LA Militia
Gram, Carlos-Pvt. Co. 1, 5th (Spanish) Regiment, European Brigade, LA Militia
Granado, Rafael-Pvt. Company D, 30th LA Infantry
Granzelis, Antonio-Pvt. Co. 10, 5th (Spanish) Regt., European Brigade, LA Mil.
Gras, Nicolas-Pvt. Co. 5, 5th (Spanish) Regiment, European Brigade, LA Militia
Gregoria, Emanuel-Pvt. Company C, Orleans Guard Regiment, LA Militia
Griego, Julio-Pvt. 1st Company C, Ragsdale's Battalion, TX Cavalry
Griego, N.-Pvt. Trevinio's Company, TX Cavalry
Griego, Sesario-Pvt. Company C, Ragsdale's Battalion, TX Cavalry
Grillo, Salvador-Pvt. Company A, 62nd Mounted VIR Infantry
Grillo, Samuel J.-Pvt. New Company B, 10th MISS Infantry
Guadalope, J.-Pvt. Teel's Company, TX State Troops
Guadiz, D.-2nd Lt. 1st Native Guards, LA Militia
Guairdo, Jose-Pvt. Teel's Company, TX State Troops
Guajardo, Aniceto-Pvt. Company A, Ragsdale's Battalion, TX Cavalry
Guajardo, Demetrio-Pvt. Company G, 3rd TX Infantry
Guajardo, J.-Pvt. Teel's Company, TX State Troops
Guajardo, Juan M.-Pvt. Company B, Ragsdale's Battalion, TX Cavalry
Guajardo, Louis J.-Pvt. Company B, Ragsdale's Battalion, TX Cavalry
Guajardo, Mariano-Cpl. Company B, Ragsdale's Battalion, TX Cavalry
Gual, Pablo-Pvt. Co. 9, 5th (Spanish) Regiment, European Brigade, LA Militia
Guana, Narciso-Sgt. Company C, 8th Hobby's TX Infantry
Guano, Damacio-Pvt. Company I, 28th TX Cavalry
Guardado, J.-Pvt. Co. 1, 5th (Spanish) Regiment, European Brigade, LA Militia

Guardia, P.N.-Pvt. Company F, 4th LA Infantry
Guardia, R.-Pvt. Company A, Miles' Legion, LA
Guardiola, J.-Pvt. Spanish Guards, Mobile Home Guard, ALA Militia
Gucardo, Louis J.-Pvt. Company B, Ragsdale's Battalion, TX Cavalry
Guerra, Francisco-Pvt. Cameron County Coast Guards, TX Militia
Guerra, Luis-Pvt. Co. 10, 5th (Spanish) Regiment, European Brigade, LA Militia
Guerra, M.-1st Lt. Company B, 36th TENN Infantry
Guerra, Manuel-Pvt. Company B, 2nd TX Cavalry
Guerra, Martin-Pvt. Company I, 8th Hobby's TX Infantry
Guerra, Sylvester-Pvt. Thomas' Company, TX Partisan Rangers
Guerrera, Antonio-Pvt. Company A, Mann's Regiment, TX Cavalry
Guerrera, Manuel-Pvt. Company C, 8th TX Infantry
Guerrero, Angel-Musician Trevinio's Squad, TX Partisan Mounted Rangers
Guerrero, Concepcion-Pvt. 1st Company I, 33rd TX Cavalry
Guerrero, Felipe-Pvt. Company B, 2nd TX Cavalry
Guerrero, Francisco-Pvt. Co. 5, 5th (Spanish) Regt., European Brigade, LA Mil.
Guerrero, Librado-Pvt. 1st Company I, 33rd TX Cavalry
Guerrero, Miguel-Pvt. Company K, 7th FLA Infantry
Guerrero, Narciso-Pvt. Company I, Benavides' Regiment, TX Cavalry
Guerrero, Thomas-Cpl. Company E, 10th Nelson's TX Infantry
Guiardo, M.-Cpl. 1st Company A, Ragsdale's Battalion, TX Cavalry
Guillermo, Francisco-Pvt. Co. 8, 5th (Span.) Regt., European Brigade, LA Militia
Guillermo, Juan-Pvt. Co. 8, 5th (Spanish) Regt., European Brigade, LA Militia
Guinard, Jayme-Pvt. Co. 3, 5th (Spanish) Regt., European Brigade, LA Militia
Guinard, Miguel-Pvt. Co. 3, 5th (Spanish) Regt., European Brigade, LA Militia
Guinart, L.P.-Pvt. Tobin's Company, TENN Light Artillery
Guitar, Antonio-Pvt. Co. 7, 5th (Spanish) Regt., European Brigade, LA Militia
Guitar, Francisco-Pvt. Co. 7, 5th (Spanish) Regt., European Brigade, LA Militia
Guitar, John-Pvt. Company C, Robertson's Regiment, MO State Guards
Guitar, Jose-Pvt. Co. 7, 5th (Spanish) Regiment, European Brigade, LA Militia
Guiteras, Juan-Pvt. Company B, Baylor's Regiment, TX Cavalry
Guiteras, Nepomenceno-Pvt. Company C, 3rd TX Infantry
Gunsaulus, J.-Pvt. Company D, 2nd Battalion, Dorch's KY Cavalry
Gurgura, Agustin-Pvt. Company H, Baird's Regiment, TX Cavalry
Gurna, A.-Pvt. Company 1, 5th (Spanish) Regiment, European Brigade, LA Mil.
Gurnes, Jose-Pvt. Co. 3, 5th (Spanish) Regiment, European Brigade, LA Militia
***See also Garcia Gusman, Jose Maria
Gusman, A.V.-Cpl. Company E, 5th LA Infantry
Gusman, Alejandro-Pvt. 1st Company I, 33rd TX Cavalry
Gusman, Antoine Louis-Capt. Company A, 8th LA Infantry
Gusman, Bartholomew-Sgt. Company F, 3rd MISS Infantry
Gusman, Benigno-Pvt. 1st Company I, 33rd TX Cavalry
Gusman, G.-Pvt. Company C, 12th ALA Infantry
Gusman, John C.-1st Sgt. Company F, 22nd Consolidated LA Infantry
Gusman, Juan-Pvt. 1st Company I, 33rd TX Cavalry

Hispanic Confederates 67

Gusman, Leon P.-4th Cpl. Company A, 8th LA Infantry
Gusman, Paul-Pvt. Company E, 5th LA Infantry
Gusman, Paul-2nd Lt. Company F, 10th LA Infantry
Gustias, Domingo-Pvt. Company B, Ragsdale's Battalion, TX Cavalry
Gustillo, F.-Pvt. Teel's Company, TX State Troops
***See also Goutierez and De Guterre
Guterres, Antonio-Pvt. Company H, 8th TX Infantry
Guterres, S.-Pvt. Tevinio's Company, TX Cavalry
Gutier, Alexandro-Pvt. Company 2, Cazadores Espanoles Regiment, LA Militia
Guiteres, Faustino-Pvt. 1st Company A, Ragsdale's Battalion, TX Cavalry
Gutierrez, Antonio-Pvt. Company E, Benavides' Regiment, TX Cavalry
Gutierrez, Celso-Pvt. Zapata's Company, Nueces County, TX State Troops
Gutierrez, Isidro-Pvt. Wood's Regiment, TX
Gutierrez, Sernano-Pvt. Benavides' Regiment, TX Cavalry
Guitierrez, H.-Pvt. Co. 2, 5th (Spanish) Regiment, European Brigade, LA Militia
Guitierrez, J. Fernandez-Pvt. Co. 2, 5th (Span.) Regt., European Brigade, LA Mil.
Gutierrez, Juan-Pvt. Company B, Baylor's Regiment, TX Cavalry
Guiterrez, Juan-Pvt. Company G, 10th LA Infantry
Gutterez, Thomas J.-Pvt. Company H, 43rd ALA Infantry
Guturies, Orofre-Pvt. 1st Company H, 33rd TX Cavalry
Guturies, Pedro-Pvt. 1st Company H, 33rd TX Cavalry
Guturies, Querino-Pvt. 1st Company H, 33rd TX Cavalry
Guzman, Agustin-Pvt. Company I, 2nd ALA Cavalry
Guzman, Eustachio-Pvt. Medina Guards, Bexar County, TX Militia
Guzman, Marino-Pvt. Rhode's Company, 3rd Yager's Battalion, TX Cavalry
Guzman, Martin J.-Pvt. Company A, 61st ALA Infantry
Guzman, Maximo-Pvt. Rhodes' Company, 3rd Yager's Battalion, TX Cavalry
Guzman, Santos-Pvt. Medina Guards, Bexar County, TX Militia
Guzman, Victor-Pvt. Rhodes' Company, 3rd Yager's Battalion, TX Cavalry

H

Harnas, Vicente-Pvt. Co. H, 5th (Spanish) Regt., European Brigade, LA Militia
Harreta, Jose-Pvt. Co. 10, 5th (Spanish) Regt., European Brigade, LA Militia
Hechar, Manuel-Pvt. Co. 9, 5th (Spanish) Regt., European Brigade, LA Militia
Helizo, Antonio-1st Lt. Co. A, 5th (Spanish) Regt., European Brigade, LA Mil.
***See also Jimenez, Gimenez, Ximenez
Hemanus, J.W.-Pvt. Company G, 2nd FLA Cavalry
Hence, Juan T.-Pvt. Co. 6, 5th (Spanish) Regiment, European Brigade, LA Militia
Henia > see Fernandez y Henia, Manuel
***See also Enriquez
Henriques, Albert David-Pvt. Company E, Crescent Regiment, LA Infantry
Henriques, J.L.-Pvt. Company E, Crescent Regiment, LA Infantry
Henriquez, Andreas-Pvt. Company G, 3rd TX Infantry
Henriquez, D.F.-Pvt. Burrowes' Company, British Guard Battalion, LA Militia

Henriquez, J.D.A.-Pvt. Company D, Orleans Guard Regiment, LA Militia
Herales, Crecencio-Pvt. 4th Field Battery, TX Artillery
***See also Herrera
Herera, Amado-Pvt. Benavides' Regiment, TX Cavalry
Herera, M.-Pvt. Company H, 2nd TX Infantry
Herera, Manuel-Pvt. LA Militia
Heres, Bernardo-3rd Lt. Co. 4, 5th (Spanish) Regt., European Brigade, LA Militia
Heres, F.-Drummer Co. 1, 5th (Spanish) Regiment, European Brigade, LA Militia
Heres, O.-Pvt. Company H, 2nd FLA Cavalry
Hernandes, Aniceto-Pvt. 1st Company C, 3rd TX Infantry
Hernandes, Antonio-Pvt. Johnson Station Rangers, Tarrant County, TX Militia
Hernandes, Antonio-Pvt. Company E, Benavides' Regiment, TX Cavalry
Hernandes, Antonio-Pvt. Company B, 3rd Yager's Battalion, TX Cavalry
Hernandes, B.T.-Sgt. Company G, 2nd N.C. Infantry
Hernandes, Benjamin Venancio-Master At Arms, Symons' Company, S.C. Militia
Hernandes, Gerardo-Pvt. Atascosa County, TX Militia
Hernandes, Juan-Pvt. Jeff Davis Home Guards, Starr County, TX Militia
Hernandes, M.-Pvt. Spanish Guards, Mobile Home Guard, ALA Militia
Hernandes, Mariano-Pvt. Trevinio's Squad, TX Partisan Mounted Rangers
Hernandes, Nicolas-Pvt. 1st Company C, 3rd TX Infantry
Hernandez, A.J.-Pvt. Company A, 3rd FLA Infantry
Hernandez, Alejos-Cpl. Company C, 8th TX Infantry
Hernandez, Alonzo-Sgt. Company D, 10th FLA Infantry
Hernandez, Ambrosio-Pvt. Medina Guards, Bexar County, TX Militia
Hernandez, Amos-Musician Company E, 6th TX Cavalry
Hernandez, Anastacio-Pvt. Zapata's Company, Nueces County, TX State Troops
Hernandez, Angel-Pvt. Company C, 8th TX Infantry
Hernandez, Antonio-Pvt. Co. 7, 5th (Span.) Regt., European Brigade, LA Militia
Hernandez, Antonio-Pvt. Company A, 3rd FLA Infantry
Hernandez, Antonio-Pvt. Co. 4, 5th (Span.) Regt., European Brigade, LA Militia
Hernandez, Antonio-Pvt. Company H, 8th TX Infantry
Hernandez, Augustin-Pvt. LA Militia
Hernandez, Baltazar-Pvt. Company E, 28th Thomas' LA Infantry
Hernandez, Bartolo-Pvt. Company H, 8th TX Infantry
Hernandez, Benjamin-Musician 27th S.C. Infantry
Hernandez, Benjamin-Pvt. Charleston Battalion, S.C., detached as a Cockswain on Charleston Harbor transport.
Hernandez, Benito-Pvt. Company E, 8th TX Infantry
Hernandez, Bicente-Pvt. 1st Company C, Ragsdale's Battalion, TX Cavalry
Hernandez, Bruno-Pvt. Company I, 33rd TX Cavalry
Hernandez, C.-Pvt. Company D, 1st FLA Infantry Reserve
Hernandez, C.P.-Sgt. Company I, Ogden's LA Cavalry
Hernandez, Carlos-Pvt. 1st Company C, 3rd TX Infantry
Hernandez, Cassimero-Pvt. 1st Company C, 3rd TX Infantry
Hernandez, Catarino-Pvt. Medina Guards, Bexar County, TX Militia

Hispanic Confederates

Hernandez, Christopher-Pvt. Company F, 5th GA Infantry
Hernandez, Crescencio-Cpl. Company D, Benavides' Regiment, TX Cavalry
Hernandez, Cortes-Pvt. Company C, 3rd TX Infantry
Hernandez, D.-1st Sgt. Company D, Benavides' Regiment, TX Cavalry
Hernandez, D.-Pvt. Company H, Chalmette Regiment, LA Militia
Hernandez, D.-Pvt. Co. I, 4th Regiment, 1st Brigade, 1st Division, LA Militia
Hernandez, Diego J.-Pvt. Company F, 63rd GA Infantry
Hernandez, Doroteo-Pvt. 1st Company A, Ragsdale's Battalion, TX Cavalry
Hernandez, Douglas H.-Ordnance Department, LA (unknown rank/position).
Hernandez, E.-Pvt. Company H, 2nd FLA Cavalry
Hernandez, Encarnacion-Pvt. Trevinio's Company, TX Cavalry
Hernandez, Eduardo-Cpl. Company B, Benavides' Regiment, TX Cavalry
Hernandez, Edward-Sgt. Company B, 3rd FLA Infantry
Hernandez, Edwardo-Pvt. Company A, Ragsdale's Battalion, TX Cavalry
Hernandez, Edwin Randolph-Pvt. Company F, 54th GA Infantry
Hernandez, Estevan-Pvt. Trevinio's Company, TX Cavalry
Hernandez, Esteve-Pvt. 6th Battery, LA Artillery
Hernandez, F.-Artificer LA Artillery (unknown unit).
Hernandez, F.B.-Pvt. Company E, Orleans Guard Regiment, LA Militia
Hernandez, Feliciano-Pvt. Company D, 3rd TX Infantry
Hernandez, Felipe-Pvt. Company G, 3rd TX Infantry
Hernandez, Fernando-Pvt. Duran's Company, Atascosa County, TX Militia
Hernandez, Fernando-1st Sgt. Company D, 33rd TX Cavalry
Hernandez, Fortunato-Sgt. Company A, Ragsdale's Battalion, TX Cavalry
Hernandez, Francis-Pvt. Company I, 10th FLA Infantry
Hernandez, Francis T.-Pvt. Company A, 3rd FLA Infantry
Hernandez, Francisco-Pvt. Company F, 3rd TX Infantry
Hernandez, G.-Pvt. Company D, 1st LA Heavy Artillery
Hernandez, G.-Pvt. Chalmette Regiment, LA Militia
Hernandez, Geraldo-Pvt. Tom's Company, Atascosa County, TX Militia
Hernandez, Gervacio-Pvt. Company D, Benavides' Regiment, TX Cavalry
Hernandez, Gilbert-Pvt. Company G, 26th LA Infantry
Hernandez, Gustavus-Pvt. Company G, 16th LA Infantry
Hernandez, H.-Pvt. Company K, 3rd LA Infantry
Hernandez, I.D.-Pvt. LA Militia
Hernandez, Ignacio-Pvt. Company B, Ragsdale's Regiment, TX Cavalry
Hernandez, J. Baptiste-Pvt. Company K, 2nd LA Reserve Corps
Hernandez, J.D.-Pvt. Confederate States Zouave Battalion, LA
Hernandez, J.H.-Pvt. Rhett's Company, S.C. Militia
Hernandez, J.M.-1st Lt. LA Defenders Battalion
Hernandez, Jesenty-Pvt. Company F, 1st TX Heavy Artillery
Hernandez, Jesse-Pvt. Company F, 3rd TX Infantry
Hernandez, Jesus(1st)-Pvt. Company E, 3rd TX Infantry
Hernandez, Jesus(2nd)-Cpl. Company F, 3rd TX Infantry
Hernandez, Jesus-Pvt. Company E, 8th TX Infantry

Hernandez, John-Pvt. Landry's Company, Donaldsonville Artillery, LA
Hernandez, John-Pvt. Company F, 3rd FLA Infantry
Hernandez, Jorge-Musician Company C, 6th TX Infantry
Hernandez, Jose-Pvt. Company F, 3rd TX Infantry
Hernandez, Jose-Pvt. Company F, Benavides' Regiment, TX Cavalry
Hernandez, Jose Antonio-Pvt. Company I, 8th LA Infantry
Hernandez, Jose Maria-Pvt. Company B, 2nd TX Cavalry
Hernandez, Jose Maria-Pvt. 1st Company A, 3rd TX Infantry
Hernandez, Jose Maria(1st)-Pvt. Company H, 8th TX Infantry
Hernandez, Jose Maria(2nd)-Pvt. Company C, 8th TX Infantry
Hernandez, Joseph-Pvt. Company K, 2nd LA Reserve Corps
Hernandez, Joseph-Pvt. Company A, 8th Battalion, LA Heavy Artillery
Hernandez, Joseph-Pvt. Company I, 8th FLA Infantry
Hernandez, Joseph-Pvt. Company I, 10th FLA Infantry
Hernandez, Joseph S.-2nd Lt. Company A, 26th GA Infantry
Hernandez, Joseph V.-Pvt. Company B, 3rd FLA Infantry
Hernandez, L.-Pvt. Company K, 3rd LA Infantry
Hernandez, Lanterio-Pvt. 1st Company C, Ragsdale's Battalion, TX Cavalry
Hernandez, M.E.-Pvt. Company A, Orleans Guard Regiment, LA Militia
Hernandez, Manuel-Pvt. Company G, 28th Thomas' LA Infantry
Hernandez, Manuel-Pvt. Company H, Chalmette Regiment, LA Militia
Hernandez, Manuel B.-Sgt. New Company A, 1st FLA Infantry
Hernandez, Marco S.-Pvt. Company F, 3rd TX Infantry
Hernandez, Mariano-Pvt. 1st Company A, 3rd TX Infantry
Hernandez, Mauricio-Pvt. Company B, 2nd TX Cavalry
Hernandez, Meliton-Pvt. 1st Company A, 3rd TX Infantry
Hernandez, Miguel-Pvt. Company B, Benavides' Regiment, TX Cavalry
Hernandez, Nicanor-Musician / Cpl. Co. C, Benavides' Regiment, TX Cavalry
Hernandez, Nicolas-Pvt. Company C, 3rd TX Infantry
Hernandez, P.-Pvt. Company H, 2nd LA Cavalry
Hernandez, P.M.-Pvt. Company K, 3rd Harrison's LA Cavalry
Hernandez, Pablo-Pvt. 1st Company A, Ragsdale's Battalion, TX Cavalry
Hernandez, Pedro-Pvt. Company C, 3rd TX Infantry
Hernandez, Peter M.-Pvt. Company I, 8th LA Infantry
Hernandez, Phillip-Pvt. Company E, 28th Thomas' LA Infantry
Hernandez, Pierre-Pvt. Company F, 18th LA Infantry
Hernandez, Polinario-Pvt. Company D, Ragsdale's Battalion, TX Cavalry
Hernandez, Randolph-2nd Lt. New Company A, 1st FLA Infantry
Hernandez, Robert-Pvt. Company K, 1st FLA Infantry
Hernandez, Rosario-Pvt. Victoria County, TX Militia
Hernandez, S.-Pvt. Company E, 33rd TX Cavalry
Hernandez, S.M.-Pvt. Company H, 2nd LA Cavalry
Hernandez, Silvere-Pvt. Company G, 3rd LA Infantry
Hernandez, Silvestre-Pvt. 1st Company C, 3rd TX Infantry
Hernandez, Sostines-Pvt. Company A, Benavides' Regiment, TX Cavalry

Hernandez, Teodoro-Pvt. Medina Guards, Bexar County, TX Militia
Hernandez, Thomas L.-Pvt. Company B/D, 63rd GA Infantry
Hernandez, Ursin-Pvt. Company F, 18th LA Infantry
Hernandez, V.-Pvt. Company E, 1st Regiment Mobile Volunteers, ALA
Hernandez, V.-Pvt. Company G, 3rd LA Infantry
Hernandez, V.-Pvt. Company E, 22nd Consolidated LA Infantry
Hernandez, V.-Pvt. 1st Company A, Ragsdale's Battalion, TX Cavalry
Hernandez, Valentin-Pvt. Company F, 7th LA Cavalry
Hernandez, Vicente-Pvt. Company F, 7th LA Cavalry
Hernandez, William-1st Sgt. Company D, 1st Olmstead's GA Infantry
Hernandez, Ynocencio-Pvt. 1st Company C, 3rd TX Cavalry
Hernandies, John-Pvt. Company G, 1st Butler's S.C. Infantry
***See also Herera
Herrera, Amada-Pvt. Company F, 3rd TX Infantry
Herrera, Ben-Pvt. Company E, Benavides' Regiment, TX Cavalry
Herrera, Benito-Pvt. Company H, 8th TX Infantry
Herrera, Blas Jr.-2nd Cpl. Medina Guards, Bexar County, TX Militia
Herrera, Elijio-Cpl. 1st Company I, 33rd TX Cavalry
Herrera, Esteban-Pvt. 1st Company I, 33rd TX Cavalry
Herrera, Gregorio-Pvt. Baird's Regiment, TX Cavalry
Herrera, J.-Sgt. Co. 2, 5th (Spanish) Regiment, European Brigade, LA Militia
Herrera, J.-Pvt. Company H, 33rd TX Cavalry
Herrera, Jesus-Pvt. 1st Company I, 33rd TX Cavalry
Herrera, Jose Maria-Pvt. Company I, 33rd TX Cavalry
Herrera, Juan-Pvt. Company B, Ragsdale's Battalion, TX Cavalry
Herrera, Juan Jose-Pvt. Company H, 8th TX Infantry
Herrera, Manuel C.-Capt. Wilson County, TX Militia
Herrera, Natividad-Cpl. 1st Company H, 33rd TX Infantry
Herrera, Pedro-Pvt. 1st Company I, 33rd TX Cavalry
Herrera, Prudencio-Pvt. 1st Company H, 33rd TX Cavalry
Herrere, Jean-Pvt. 1st Native Guards, LA Militia
Herrero, Francisco-Pvt. Company B, 2nd TX Cavalry
Herrero, Jose-Pvt. Co. 2, 5th (Spanish) Regiment, European Brigade, LA Militia
Herrero, Severin S.-2nd Lt. Company G, 10th LA Infantry
Hevia > see Garcia Hevia, Jose
Hidalgo, Adolphe-Pvt. Company A, Crescent Regiment, LA Infantry
Hidalgo, Ernest-Pvt. Donaldsonville Artillery, LA
Hidalgo, Esteve-Pvt. Landry's Company, Donaldsonville Artillery, LA
Hidalgo, Felix-Pvt. Company A, 26th LA Infantry
Hidalgo, Francisco-Pvt. Company A, 30th GA Infantry
Hidalgo, Francisco-Sgt. Company H, 28th Thomas' LA Infantry
Hidalgo, Joseph L.-Pvt. Company D, 1st LA Heavy Artillery
Hidalgo, Juan-Pvt. Company F, 3rd TX Infantry
Hidalgo, M.-Pvt. Co. 5, 5th (Spanish) Regiment, European Brigade, LA Militia
Hilario, Fernando-Pvt. Company 1, Cazadores Espanoles Regiment, LA Militia

Hinojas, Jose-Pvt. Company B, Baylor's Regiment, TX Cavalry
Hinojas, Jose-Pvt. Company B, 17th TX Field Battery
Hinojos, Thomas-Sgt. Davis' Company, Confederate Light Artillery
Hinojosa, Cortinas-Pvt. Cameron County Coast Guards, TX Militia
Hinojosa, Jesus-Pvt. Company I, 8th TX Infantry
Hinojosa, Juan Jose-Pvt. Company I, 8th TX Infantry
Hinojosa, Julian-Pvt. Jeff Davis Home Guards, Refugio County, TX Militia
Hinojosa, Julio-Pvt. Minute Men (Scouts), Starr County, TX Militia
Hinojosa, Lino-Pvt. Medina Guards, Bexar County, TX Militia
Hinojosa, Martin Garcia-Pvt. Trevinio's Squad, TX Partisan Mounted Rangers
Hinojosa, Mathias-Pvt. Cameron County Coast Guards, TX Militia
Hinojosa, Santiago-Pvt. Company F, 1st Yager's TX Cavalry
Hinojosa, Thomas-Pvt. Cameron County Coast Guard, TX Militia
Hoa, Alberto-Pvt. Company A, 1st Chauseurs a Pied, LA Militia
Holguin >> see Olgin and Olguin
Horta, Peter-2nd Lt. Company G, 21st ALA Infantry
Horta, Victoriano-Pvt. 1st Company C, 3rd TX Infantry
***Also found as Hoyos, Francisco
Hoya, Francisco-Sgt. Company G, 12th TX Infantry
Hoya, T.-Pvt. Company G, 12th TX Infantry
Hoyas, Jean-Pvt. Company A, Confederate States Zouave Battalion, LA
Hoz > see De La Hoz Garcia, Francisco
Huerta, Victoriano-Pvt. Company C, 3rd TX Infantry
Huertas, James-Pvt. Company E, 54th VIR Militia
Huisa, Juan-Pvt. Company B, Ragsdale's Battalion, TX Cavalry
Huisa, Vicente-Pvt. Company B, Ragsdale's Battalion, TX Cavalry

I

***See also Ybanes
Ibanes, J.M.-Pvt. Trevinio's Company, TX Cavalry
Ibara, John M.-Pvt. Company C, 1st LA Heavy Artillery
Ibarra, Leonardo-Pvt. Zapata's Company, Nueces County, TX State Troops
Ibarra, Juan-Pvt. Benavides' Regiment, TX Cavalry. He was one of the 2 heroes of the Battle of Laredo, TX (3/19/1864) who, along with Major Swope, single handedly charged an attacking Union force of 40 men (of the 200 engaged) and forced them to retreat; in the process he had 3 horses shot out from under him. This maneuver broke the overall Union attack on the small Confederate defensive force of 42 men and led to a Confederate victory.
***See also E'Barbo, Barbo, Ybarbo and Yebarbo
Ibarbo, L.F.-Cpl. Company B, Maddox's Regiment, LA Reserve Corps
Ibarbo, Martin-Pvt. Company B, Maddox's Regiment, LA Reserve Corps
***See also Yglesias
Iglesias, Antonio-Pvt. Company A, 3rd TX Infantry
Iglesias, Francisco-Pvt. Co. 10, 5th (Spanish) Regt., European Brig., LA Militia

Hispanic Confederates

***See also Ygnacio
Ignacio, Joachin-Pvt. Co. 8, 5th (Spanish) Regt., European Brigade, LA Militia
Ignacio, Manuel-Pvt. Company C, 2nd MO Cavalry
Indo, Miguel-Pvt. Gray's Company, Bexar County, TX Militia
Infante, J.-Pvt. Company C, Cater's Battalion, TX Cavalry
Infante, T.-Pvt. Company G, 8th TX Infantry
Ingles, M.-Pvt. Spanish Guards, Mobile Home Guard, ALA Militia
Irola, Emanuel-Pvt. Company C, 24th VIR Cavalry
Iturbide, Francisco-Pvt. 1st Company C, Ragsdale's Battalion, TX Cavalry

J

Jacquinet, D.-Pvt. Company A, Orleans Fire Regiment, LA Militia
Jaime, Jose-Pvt. Company H, 8th TX Infantry
Jara, Frank-Pvt. Co. 5, 5th (Spanish) Regiment, European Brigade, LA Militia
Jara, Jose-Pvt. Company I, Charleston Guard, S.C.
Jarnto, Jesus-Sgt. Company K, 3rd TX Infantry
Jasso, Casimiro-Pvt. Zapata's Company, Nueces County, TX State Troops
***The 2 men surnamed Jeanmard were the Grandsons of Cristoval Artacho, an early Spanish settler of Louisiana.
Jeanmard, Francois-Pvt. Company C, 8th LA Infantry
Jeanmard, J.-Pvt. Company A, 30th LA Infantry
***See also Gil
Jil, Francisco-Pvt. Company H, Benavides' Regiment, TX Cavalry
***See also Hemanus, Gimenez and Ximenez
Jimenes, Benito-Pvt. Company C, 8th TX Infantry
Jimenes, Monico-Pvt. Company F, 3rd TX Cavalry
Jimenez, Angel-Pvt. 1st Company I, 33rd TX Infantry
Jimenez, Antonio-Pvt. Gray's Company, Bexar County, TX Militia
Jimenez, Esteban-Pvt. Gray's Company, Bexar County, TX Militia
Jimenez, F.-Pvt. Co. 1, 5th (Spanish) Regiment, European Brigade, LA Militia
Jimenez, Francisco-Capt. Wilson County, TX Militia
Jimenez, Jesus-Pvt. Company F, 3rd TX Infantry
Jimenez, Simon-2nd Sgt. Company G, 21st ALA Infantry
Joachim, Albert-Pvt. Lafourche Militia, LA
Joachim, John-Pvt. Co. 8, 5th (Spanish) Regiment, European Brigade, LA Militia
Joachim, Manuel-Pvt. Company D, 30th LA Infantry
Jorda, Armand-Pvt. Company H, 7th LA Infantry
Jorda, Arthur-Pvt. Company F, 30th LA Infantry
Jorda, J.-Pvt. Pointe Coupee Artillery, LA
Jorda, Lawrence-Pvt. Company H, Orleans Guards Regiment, LA Militia
Jorda, Pierre-Pvt. Company F, Orleans Guards Regiment, LA Militia
Jorda, T.-Pvt. Co. 1, 5th (Spanish) Regiment, European Brigade, LA Militia
Jose, Maria-Pvt. 1st LA Infantry
Jose, Victor-Pvt. Co. A, 5th (Spanish) Regiment, European Brigade, LA Militia

Juan, Alfred-Pvt. Company E, 1st LA Heavy Artillery
Juan, Batires-Pvt. Company C, 3rd TX Infantry
Juan, Francisco-Pvt. Co. A, 5th (Spanish) Regiment, European Brigade, LA Mil.
Juan, Joe-Pvt. Company D, 30th LA Infantry
Juan, P.-Pvt. Brown's Company, VIR Horse Artillery
Juares, Antonio-Pvt. 1st Company I, 33rd TX Cavalry
Juares, C.-Pvt. Teel's Company, TX State Troops
Juares, Toribo-Pvt. Company 1, 33rd TX Cavalry
Juares, Yldefonso-Sgt. 1st Company I, 33rd TX Cavalry
Juarez, Juan-Pvt. Co. 10, 5th (Spanish) Regiment, European Brigade, LA Militia
Juarez, Juan-Pvt. 8th Field Battery, TX Artillery
Juarez, Lorenzo-Pvt. Bustillo's Company, Bexar County, TX Militia
Juaro, Antonio-Pvt. Co. 10, 5th (Spanish) Regiment, European Brigade, LA Mil.
Juncal > see surname Oncal / Oncale
Jurado, Demetrio-Pvt. Company G, 3rd TX Infantry
Jurado, Ramon-Pvt. Company 2, Cazadores Espanoles Regiment, LA Militia

K

No names found

L

Labea, Joseph-Pvt. Company I, 5th LA Infantry
La Flor, Antonio-Pvt. Company G, 12th TX Infantry
La Fuente, Juan-Pvt. Gray's Company, Bexar County, TX Militia
La Garca, Jose Antimide-Pvt. TX Militia
Lagos, Philma-Pvt. Company H, 19th LA Infantry
Lagos, Richard-Pvt. Company H, 19th LA Infantry
Lagos, Valco-Pvt. Company H, 19th LA Infantry
Lamas, T.J.-Pvt. Company F, 3rd TX Cavalry
Lambaras, Elocor-Pvt. Lamar Home Guard, Refugio County, TX Militia
Lamero, Joseph-Pvt. Company A, 38th ARK Infantry
Landa, Alejandro-Pvt. Company F, 3rd TX Infantry
Landa, Edward-Pvt. Company C, Benavides' Regiment, TX Cavalry
Landeburo, Jose-Pvt. Company A, 30th LA Infantry
Landeira, Juan-Cpl. Co. 10, 5th (Spanish) Regt., European Brigade, LA Militia
Landin, Felipe-Pvt. Company I, Benavides' Regiment, TX Cavalry
Laosa, Evaristo-Pvt. Company 5, Cazadores Espanoles Regiment, LA Militia
Lara, David-Pvt. 5th N.C. Infantry
Lara, G.-Pvt. Company 1, 1st Chasseurs a pied, LA Militia
Lara, Isaac-Pvt. Company C, 9th MO Infantry
Lara, James-Pvt. 2nd/6th Consolidated MO Infantry
Lara, Juan-Pvt. Company G, 3rd TX Infantry
La Rosa, F.-Pvt. Company 1, Cazadores Espanoles Regiment, LA Militia

***The Larramendi brothers of Oriente Province, Cuba, were Blockade Runners who aided the Confederacy and were said to have been part of both the FLA and LA Coast Guard Militia, while ashore. They ran the blockade both into New Orleans and St. Bernard Parish, LA until 1862 and coastal Florida until the end of the war. The Blockade Runner was said to have been named the SAN QUINTIN.
Larramendi, Jose Comas-Captain Blockade Runner SAN QUINTIN, Cuba
Larramendi, Manolito Comas-1st Lt. Blockade Runner SAN QUINTIN, Cuba
Lasso, Alvino-Pvt. Company D, 25th TX Cavalry
Lavante, Ynacio-Pvt. Co. A, 5th (Spanish) Regt., European Brigade, LA Militia
Lazara, Mariano-Pvt. Co. A, 5th (Spanish) Regt., European Brigade, LA Militia
Lazaro, M.-Pvt. Company D, Seige Train Battalion, LA
Lazarro, A.-Pvt. Bass' Company, 1st Regiment Mobile Volunteers, ALA
Lazarus, Benjamin Doris-Pvt. Company A, 2nd S.C. Cavalry
Lazarus, Edgar Marks-Pvt. Company A, Manigault's Battalion, S.C. Artillery
Lazarus, J.-Assistant Surgeon C.S.A.
Lazarus, Mark H.-Pvt. Walter's Company, S.C. Light Artillery
Lazarus, Solomon-Pvt. Walter's Company, S.C. Light Artillery
Leal, Alphonso-Pvt. Company B, 2nd TX Cavalry
Leal, Circaco-Pvt. Company C, 3rd TX Infantry
Leal, Cristoval-Pvt. Thomas' Company, TX Partisan Rangers
Leal, Esteban-Pvt. Gray's Company, Bexar County, TX Militia
Leal, Francisco-Sgt. Company F, 3rd TX Infantry
Leal, Joaquin-Pvt. Skidmore's Company, San Patricio County, TX Militia
Leal, Jose-2nd Lt. Bexar County, TX Militia
Leal, Juan-Pvt. Gray's Company, Bexar County, TX Militia
Leal, Macario-Pvt. Company H, 33rd TX Cavalry
Leal, Manuel-Pvt. Co. 6, 5th (Spanish) Regiment, European Brigade, LA Militia
Leal, Mareiso-Pvt. Company H, 8th Hobby's TX Infantry
Leal, Pedro-Pvt. Engledow's Company, Nueces County, TX Militia
Leal, Pilar-Pvt. Gray's Company, Bexar County, TX Militia
Leal, Raphael-Pvt. 24th TX Cavalry
Leal, Tiburcio-Sgt. Company F, 3rd TX Infantry
Leal, Yldefonso-Sgt. Company H, 8th Hobby's TX Infantry
Leano, Gabino-Cpl. Co. 4, 5th (Spanish) Regiment, European Brigade, LA Mil.
Lebo, Severio-Pvt. Company B, Cazadores Espanoles Regiment, LA Militia
Lechuga, F.-Pvt. Teel's Company, TX State Troops
Lechuga, Librado-Pvt. Company C, Ragsdale's Battalion, TX Cavalry
Lechunga, Luis-Pvt. Company C, Ragsdale's Battalion, TX Cavalry
Ledesma, Juan Antonio-Pvt. Lamar Home Guards, Refugio County, TX Militia
Ledesma, Manuel-Pvt. Lamar Home Guards, Refugio County, TX Militia
Leija, Clemente-Pvt. Company I, 33rd TX Cavalry
Leon, A.-Pvt. Company C, Chalmette Regiment, LA Militia
Leon, Bernardino-Pvt. Company I, Benavide's Regiment, TX Cavalry
Leon, Lewis-Pvt. Company B, 53rd N.C. Infantry
Leon, Martin-Pvt. 1st Company C, 3rd TX Infantry

Leon, Pablo-Pvt. Company F, 3rd TX Infantry
Leon, Rafael-Pvt. Company C, 3rd TX Infantry
Leon, Silvain-Cpl. Landry's Company, Donaldsonville Artillery, LA
Leonardy, Celestial John-Pvt. Company B, 3rd FLA Infantry
Leonardy, George-Pvt. Company D, 8th FLA Infantry
Leonardy, John-Pvt. Company B, 3rd FLA Infantry
Leonardy, Joseph-2nd Sgt. Company B, 3rd FLA Infantry
Leonardy, Phillip-2nd Lt. Company B, 3rd FLA Infantry
Leone, Jose-Pvt. Company C, 28th Gray's LA Infantry
Leone, Juan-Pvt. Sabine Reserves, LA Militia
Lerchundi, Emanuel-Pvt. Dunham's Company, Milton Light Artillery, FLA
Lerma, R.-Pvt. Trevinio's Company, TX Cavalry
Lerna, A.-Pvt. Spanish Guards, Mobile County, ALA Militia
Lerna, M.-Pvt. Spanish Guards, Mobile County, ALA Militia
Lerrin De Saucedo, Antonio-Pvt. TX Militia
Leos, Rafael-Pvt. Company C, 3rd TX Infantry
Levante, Ynacio-Pvt. Co. A, 5th (Spanish) Regt., European Brigade, LA Militia
*** See also the De Leon and Moses surnames
Levi, Tomaso-Pvt. Company F, Cazadores Espanoles Regiment, LA Militia
Levy, Eugene Henry-Pvt. Landry's Company, Donaldsonville Artillery, LA
Levy, Joseph Calhoun-Pvt. New Co. C, 1st Special Battalion, Rightor's LA Inf.
Levy, Julian Camden De Leon-Sgt. Co. E, 3rd ALA Infantry (son of Almeria De Leon).
Levy, Julian H.-Pvt. Landry's Company, Donaldsonville Artillery, LA
Levy, Saul Solomon De Leon-C.S.A. rank unknown (son of Almeria De Leon).
Leyva, Lazaro-Pvt. Company C, 8th TX Infantry
Lial, Fernando-Pvt. Company F, 1st Yager's TX Cavalry
Lial, Pedro-Pvt. Company F, Ist Yager's TX Cavalry
Liano, M.-3rd Lt. Company 2, 5th (Spanish) Regt., European Brig., LA Militia
Libano, J.J.-1st Sgt. Company 5, 5th (Spanish) Regt., European Brig., LA Militia
Licon, Pedro-Pvt. Company C, 8th TX Infantry
Lima, G.-Pvt. 1st Company A, Ragsdale's Battalion, TX Cavalry
Lima, Juan-Pvt. Company G, 10th LA Infantry
Lima, Tomas-Pvt. Company B, Ragsdale's Battalion, TX Cavalry
Linas, D.-Pvt. Company 1, 5th (Spanish) Regt., European Brigade, LA Militia
Lino, Manuel-Pvt. 1st Native Guards, LA Militia
Liscero, Florencio-2nd Lt. Trevinio's Company, TX Cavalry
Lizana, Ernest-Pvt. Company H, 3rd MISS Infantry
Lizana, John-Pvt. Company F, 3rd MISS Infantry
Lizana, Joseph-Pvt. Company E, 17th Battalion, MISS Cavalry
Lizana, Roselius-Pvt. Company H, 3rd MISS Infantry
Llado, Jamie-Pvt. Co. 9, 5th (Spanish) Regiment, European Brigade, LA Militia
Llado, Joachin-Pvt. Company 2, Cazadores Espanoles Regiment, LA Militia
Llado, Jose-Capt. Company 1, Cazadores Espanoles Regiment, LA Militia
Llado, Juan-Pvt. Company 2, Cazadores Espanoles Regiment, LA Militia
Llado, Pablo-Pvt. Company 2, Cazadores Espanoles Regiment, LA Militia

Llambias, Antonio-Pvt. Company B, 3rd FLA Infantry
Llambias, John-Pvt. Company B, 3rd FLA Infantry
Llambias, Joseph-Pvt. Company H, 2nd FLA Infantry
Llambias, M.G.-1st Sgt. Company H, 2nd FLA Infantry
Llambre, (no 1st name)-Pvt. Company C, Orleans Guard Regiment, LA Militia
Llaurador, Ramon-Capt. Company 4, Cazadores Espanoles Regiment, LA Mil.
Lleno, Thomas-Pvt. Company B, Ragsdale's Battalion, TX Cavalry
Lloret, Asencio-Pvt. Co. 10, 5th (Spanish) Regt., European Brigade, LA Militia
Loa, Antonio-Pvt. Company C, 8th TX Infantry
Lobel, Manuel-Pvt. Company A, 8th LA Infantry
Lobrano, Frank-Pvt. Company C, Washington Artillery Battalion, LA
Lombas, Agustin-Pvt. Company G, 18th LA Infantry
Londono, J.P.-Pvt. Company G, Waul's Legion, TX
Longa, John-Pvt. Company D, 25th Battalion, VIR Infantry
Longavilla, Francisco-Pvt. Company H, 8th TX Infantry
Longoria, Caribio-Pvt. Company G, 3rd LA Infantry
Longoria, Cedro-Pvt. Company D, Ragsdale's Battalion, TX Cavalry
Longoria, Francisco-Pvt. Company D, Ragsdale's Battalion, TX Cavalry
Longoria, Juan S.-Pvt. Minute Men (Scouts), Starr County, TX Militia
Longoria, Policarpio-Pvt. Company C, 5th TX Cavalry
Longoria, Senabio-Pvt. Minute Men (Scouts), Starr County, TX Militia
Longorio, Cipio-Pvt. 2nd Company F, 2nd TX Cavalry
Longorio, Eulopia-Pvt. Company I, Benavides' Regiment, TX Cavalry
Longorio, Fontorio-Pvt. Company I, Benavides' Regiment, TX Cavalry
Longorio, Nasario-Pvt. Thomas' Company, TX Partisan Rangers
Longorio, Pedro-Pvt. Trevinio's Squad, TX Mounted Partisan Volunteers
Longovia, Francisco-Pvt. Company D, 1st McCulloch's TX Cavalry
Lopes, Agapito-Pvt. Minute Men (Scouts), Starr County, TX Militia
Lopes, Alphonse-Pvt. 1st Native Guards, LA Militia
Lopes, Andres-Pvt. Company H, 3rd TX Infantry
Lopes, Gregory-Pvt. Company A, 11th TX Infantry
Lopes, H.-Pvt. Company 1, 1st Regiment, French Brigade, LA Militia
Lopes, Jacinto-Pvt. Minute Men (Scouts), Starr County, TX Militia
Lopes, Leonito-Pvt. Company B, 2nd TX Cavalry
Lopes, Manuel-Pvt. Company E, Benavides' Regiment, TX Cavalry
Lopes, Manuel-Pvt. Company H, 3rd TX Infantry
Lopes, Rafael G.-Pvt. Minute Men (Scouts), Starr County, TX Militia
Lopes, Seferino-Pvt. Minute Men (Scouts), Starr County, TX Militia
Lopez, A.-Pvt. Company F, 12th TX Cavalry
Lopez, Aaron-Surgeon 2nd ALA Militia Volunteers
Lopez, A.C.-Pvt. Gordon's Company, 1st Olmstead's GA Infantry
Lopez, Anthony N.-2nd Sgt. Gordon's Company, 1st Olmstead's GA Infantry
Lopez, Alonzo-Pvt. Company B, 3rd FLA Infantry
Lopez, Andreas-Pvt. Company F, 3rd TX Infantry
Lopez, Andrew-Pvt. Company D, 8th FLA Infantry

Lopez, Andrew A.-Pvt. Company A, 3rd FLA Infantry
Lopez, Andrew E.-Gunsmith 63rd GA Infantry, was detailed as Foreman of the Savannah, Georgia Armory Gunsmith Department.
Lopez, Andrew M. Sr.-2nd Sgt. Company D, 8th FLA Infantry
Lopez, Angel-Sgt. Company 2, Cazadores Espanoles Regiment, LA Militia
Lopez, Antonio-Sgt. Company K, 63rd GA Infantry
Lopez, Antonio-Pvt. Company G, 10th LA Infantry
Lopez, Antonio-Pvt. Company B, 8th TX Cavalry
Lopez, Antonio-Cpl. Trevinio's Company, TX Cavalry
Lopez, Augustin-Pvt. Company E, 18th Consolidated LA Infantry
Lopez, Augustine-Pvt. Company D, 8th FLA Infantry
Lopez, Benjamin-Pvt. Company H, 7th TX Cavalry
Lopez, Brigido-Pvt. 1st Company A, Ragsdale's Battalion, TX Cavalry
Lopez, Carlos-Pvt. Co. 7, 5th (Spanish) Regt., European Brigade, LA Militia
Lopez, Catarino-Pvt. Company B, Ragsdale's Battalion, TX Cavalry
Lopez, Charles P.-Pvt. Company B, Lewis' Regiment, LA Infantry
Lopez, Clemente-Pvt. Company I, 8th LA Infantry
Lopez, David-Contractor / Superintendent of South Carolina State Works
Lopez, D.-Pvt. Company K, 7th LA Cavalry
Lopez, D.-Cpl. Company 1, 3rd Regiment, European Brigade, LA Militia
Lopez, Darmancourt-Pvt. Company K, 3rd Harrison's LA Cavalry
Lopez, Donacio-Pvt. Company D, 3rd TX Infantry
Lopez, E.-Pvt. Company K, 3rd LA Cavalry
Lopez, E.M.-Pvt. Company K, 1st Fannin's GA Reserve
Lopez, Eduardo-Pvt. Co. 10, 5th (Spanish) Regt., European Brigade, LA Militia
Lopez, Elivodais-Pvt. Todd's Independent Company, Praire Rangers, LA Militia
Lopez, Emanuel M.-Cpl. Company B, 3rd FLA Infantry
Lopez, F.-Pvt. Co. 1, 5th (Spanish) Regiment, European Brigade, LA Militia
Lopez, Felix-Pvt. Company A, 35th Likens' TX Cavalry
Lopez, Felix-Pvt. Company D, 2nd TX Infantry
Lopez, Fernando-2nd Sgt. Engledow's Company, Nueces County, TX Militia
Lopez, Francisco-Pvt. Company A, 8th Battalion, LA Heavy Artillery
Lopez, Francisco-Pvt. Mobile Southern Guards, ALA Infantry
Lopez, Francisco-Pvt. Company D, 3rd TX Infantry
Lopez, Francois Drauzin-Pvt. Company D, 18th Consolidated LA Infantry
Lopez, Frank-Pvt. Company F, 25th LA Infantry
Lopez, Frederick-Pvt. LA Militia
Lopez, Gerardo-Sgt. Thomas' Company, TX Partisan Rangers
Lopez, Gustave-Pvt. Company C, 10th LA Infantry
Lopez, Gustavo-Cpl. 1st Company C, 34th TENN Infantry
Lopez, Henry C.-Pvt. Company C, 1st LA Cavalry
Lopez, Hilaire-Pvt. LA Militia
Lopez, I.-Pvt. Giddings' Battalion, TX Cavalry
Lopez, Ignatio-Sgt. Company D, 8th FLA Infantry
Lopez, Isaac-Pvt. Company E, 6th TX Infantry

Lopez, J.-Pvt. Company H, Chalmette Regiment, LA Militia
Lopez, J.-Pvt. Weisiger's Company, Giddings' Battalion, TX Cavalry
Lopez, J.C.-Exempt Men, ALA-MISS Railway, Marengo County, ALA
Lopez, J.H.-Pvt. 1st Company A, Manigault's Battalion, S.C. Artillery
Lopez, Joel-Pvt. Company H, 12th TX Infantry
Lopez, John-Pvt. Company K, 1st LA Infantry
Lopez, John-Pvt. Company H, 9th LA Infantry
Lopez, John-Pvt. Company A, 12th LA Infantry
Lopez, John-Pvt. 2nd Company A, 1st TENN Heavy Artillery
Lopez, John-Pvt. Palmetto Guards, 2nd S.C. Infantry
Lopez, John B.-Pvt. Belser's Company, ALA Militia Reserve
Lopez, John Justo-Capt. Company B, 63rd GA Infantry
Lopez, John P.-Pvt. Company D, 8th FLA Infantry
Lopez, Jose-Pvt. Co. 10, 5th (Spanish) Regiment, European Brigade, LA Militia
Lopez, Jose Maria-Pvt. Co. 7, 5th (Spanish) Regt., European Brigade, LA Militia
Lopez, Joseph-Pvt. Company A, 3rd FLA Infantry
Lopez, Joseph C.-Pvt. Mann's Regiment, TX Cavalry
Lopez, Joseph G.-Pvt. Burrough's Company, TENN Light Artillery
Lopez, Juan-Pvt. Co. 4, 5th (Spanish) Regiment, European Brigade, LA Militia
Lopez, Juan-Pvt. 8th Field Battery, TX Artillery
Lopez, Juan Manuel-Pvt. 1st Company A, 3rd TX Infantry
Lopez, Julian-Cpl. 1st Company C, Ragsdale's Battalion, TX Cavalry
Lopez, L.-Pvt. Company G, 12th Young's TX Infantry
Lopez, Laurence-Pvt. Company H, 28th Thomas' LA Infantry
Lopez, Lazaro-Pvt. Company 8, 2nd TX Cavalry
Lopez, Leonardo-Pvt. Bustillo's Company, Bexar County, TX Militia
Lopez, Mariano-Pvt. Tom's Company, Atascosa County, TX Troops
Lopez, M.-Pvt. Company G, Timmons' Regiment, TX Infantry
Lopez, Moses E.-Pvt. Company A, Manigault's Battalion, S.C. Artillery
Lopez, Manuel-Pvt. Company H, 3rd TX Infantry
Lopez, Manuel-Pvt. Co. 4, 5th (Spanish) Regt., European Brigade, LA Militia
Lopez, Manuel-Pvt. Company H, 8th TX Infantry
Lopez, Michael-Pvt. Company C, 9th Nichols' TX Infantry
Lopez, Miguel-Pvt. Company A, Waul's Legion, TX
Lopez, Ozime-Pvt. LA Militia
Lopez, Pauline A.-Pvt. Company A, 3rd FLA Infantry
Lopez, Pedro-Pvt. Company B, Ragsdale's Battalion, TX Cavalry
Lopez, Peter-Pvt. Company G, 12th TX Infantry
Lopez, Prudencio-Pvt. Company C, 8th TX Infantry
Lopez, Santiago-Pvt. Company F, Waul's Legion, TX
Lopez, Savior-Pvt. Company G, 12th TX Infantry
Lopez, Sylvia H.-Cpl. Company 1, 1st Regiment, French Brigade, LA Militia
Lopez, Tip-Pvt. Company C, 1st LA Cavalry
Lopez, Victorine-Pvt. Company 3, 3rd Harrison's LA Cavalry
Lopez, Viviano-Pvt. 1st Company I, 33rd TX Cavalry

Lopez, Xavier-Pvt. Company G, 12th TX Infantry
Lopez, Y.-Cpl. Co. 1, 5th (Spanish) Regiment, European Brigade, LA Militia
Lorano, S.-Pvt. Trevinio's Company, TX Cavalry
Lorenzo, J.-Pvt. 1st Native Guards, LA Militia
Lorenzo, Lorello-Pvt. Company B, 1st LA Cavalry
Lorenzo, M.-Pvt. Company G, 21st ALA Infantry
Lorenzo, Nicolas-Pvt. Company H, Benavides' Regiment, TX Cavalry
Lorenzo, P.-Pvt. Company K, Chalmette Regiment, LA Militia
Lores, Manuel-Pvt. Company I, 10th LA Infantry
Loris, Agustin-Pvt. Company E, 4th LA Cavalry
Losano, B.-Pvt. Company C, 4th TX Cavalry
Losano, Crisoforo-2nd Lt. Jeff Davis Home Guard, Refugio County, TX Mil.
Losano, Salvador-Pvt. Jeff Davis Home Guard, Refugio County, TX Militia
Losanto, Nasario-Pvt. 1st Company A, Ragsdale's Battalion, TX Cavalry
Losanto, Pedro-Pvt. 1st Company A, Ragsdale's Battalion, TX Cavalry
Losaya, Pedro-Pvt. TX (unknown unit or branch).
Losoyo, Leorro-Pvt. Company A, 33rd TX Cavalry
Losoyo, S.-Pvt. Company A, 33rd TX Cavalry
Loza, B.-Pvt. Company C, 5th LA Infantry
Loza, Blas-Pvt. Mitchell's Company, Bandera County, TX Militia
Lozano, Juan Elias-Pvt. Company C, 4th TX Cavalry
Lozano, Tomas-Pvt. Company H, 8th TX Infantry
Lozano, Tomas-Pvt. Company E, Benavides' Regiment, TX Cavalry
Lucas, Bartolo-Pvt. Company D, 8th FLA Infantry
Lucendo, Francis-Pvt. Company D, 95th ALA Militia
Luceriaga, M. Garcia-Pvt. Co. 2, 5th (Spanish) Regt., European Brigade, LA Mil.
Lucero, F.M.-Pvt. Company D, Benavides' Regiment, TX Cavalry
Lucero, Francisco-Pvt. Company F, 3rd TX Infantry
Lucero, S.-Pvt. Trevino's Company, TX Partisan Rangers
Luis, B.C.-Cpl. Company K, Crescent Regiment, LA Infantry
Luis, Francisco-Pvt. Co. 5, 5th (Spanish) Regiment, European Brigade, LA Mil.
Luis, Frank-1st Sgt. Co. 8, 5th (Spanish) Regiment, European Brigade, LA Militia
Luis, Tomas-Pvt. Co. 8, 5th (Spanish) Regiment, European Brigade, LA Militia
Lujal, J.M.-Pvt. Company 2, 4th Regiment, French Brigade, LA Militia
Lujan, Martin-Capt. Company A, Mexican Volunteers, C.S.A
Luna, A.-Cannoneer Company 6, Washington Artillery Battalion, LA
Luna, Guadalupe-Pvt. Company D, Benavides' Regiment, TX Cavalry
Luna, Huapa-Pvt. Benavides' Regiment, TX Cavalry
Luna, James-Pvt. Company D, 25th TX Cavalry
Luna, Jesus-Pvt. Ragsdale's Battalion, TX Cavalry
Luna, John-Pvt. Company E, 30th LA Infantry
Luna, Jose-Pvt. Company I, Benavides' Regiment, TX Cavalry
Luna, Jose Angel-Pvt. Bustillo's Company, Bexar County, TX Militia
Luna, Martin-Pvt. Company B, Consolidated Crescent Regiment, LA Infantry
Luna, Mathias-Pvt. Cameron County Coast Guard, TX Militia

Luria, Abe-Major Assistant Adjutant General, Staff of General Tracy, LA. He later served in the Conscript Bureau under Colonel Lockhart in Alabama.
Luria, Albert Moses-2nd Lt. Company I, 23rd N.C. Infantry
Luro, B.-Pvt. Company 3, 4th Regiment, European Brigade, LA Militia
Luvia, A.-Pvt. Company I, 3rd Harrison's LA Cavalry
Luvia, J.M.-Pvt. 3rd LA Cavalry
Luvia, Octave-Pvt. Company I, 3rd Harrison's LA Cavalry
Lux, Pedro-Capt. Co. 7, 5th (Spanish) Regiment, European Brigade, LA Militia
Luz, Fridolin-Pvt. Binsford's Company, VIR Volunteers
Luz, J.-Pvt. Company G, 4th LA Infantry

M

Macena, Frank-Pvt. Company A, 2nd FLA Cavalry
***See also Manuel Machado Fecundo
Machado, Guillermo-Pvt. Co. 5, 5th (Spanish) Regt., European Brigade, LA Mil.
Machado, Ines-Pvt. Company I, 8th TX Infantry
Machado, Juan-Pvt. Co. 8, 5th (Spanish) Regiment, European Brigade, LA Mil.
Machado, Pedro-Pvt. Co. 2, 5th (Spanish) Regt., European Brigade, LA Militia
Machado, William-Pvt. Co. 5, 5th (Spanish) Regt., European Brigade, LA Militia
Machildo, T.-Pvt. Company B, 2nd TX Mounted Rifles
Macias, Jose-Pvt. Company G, 3rd TX Infantry
Macias, Pablo-Pvt. Company F, 3rd TX Infantry
Macias, Salome-Pvt. Company F, 3rd TX Infantry
Maciel, Jose-Pvt. Company D, 30th LA Infantry
Maciel, Manuel-Pvt. Company D, 30th LA Infantry
Madariaga, V.-Pvt. Co. 1, 5th (Spanish) Regiment, European Brigade, LA Militia
Madera, Aaron-Pvt. Company D, 4th LA Infantry
Madera, F.F.-1st Lt. Company F, 1st ARK Mounted Rifles
Madera, George E.-Pvt. Company K, 34th MISS Infantry
Madera, Thomas F.-Pvt. Company 4, 4th ARK Infantry
Madera, Wager W.-Pvt. Pegram's Company, VIR Light Artillery
Madera, William E.-Pvt. Pegram's Company, VIR Light Artillery
Madero, M.-Pvt. Company B, 18th Consolidated LA Infantry
Madinas, J.-Pvt. Company K, 27th LA Infantry
Madinas, T.-Pvt. Company K, 27th LA Infantry
Madguer, Antonio-2nd Lt. Co. 4, 5th (Spanish) Regt., European Brig., LA Militia
Madrada, Manuel-Pvt. Co. 3, 5th (Spanish) Regt., European Brigade, LA Militia
Madregal, M.-Pvt. 15th Field Battery, TX Artillery
Madrigal, Maximo-Pvt. Company B, Ragsdale's Battalion, TX Cavalry
Madrigal, R.R.-Pvt. Company K, 27th LA Infantry
Madrigales, F.-Pvt. Company G, 8th TX Infantry
Maduell, Charles-1st Sgt. Co. 2, 5th (Spanish) Regt., European Brigade, LA Mil.
Maganos, J.L.-Cpl. Company D, 4th MISS Cavalry
Magi, Jayme-Capt. Co. 5/6, 5th (Spanish) Regt., European Brigade, LA Militia

Maimy, Esteban-Pvt. Cazadores Espanoles Regiment, LA Militia
Mainegra, J.-Pvt. Co. 1, 5th (Spanish) Regiment, European Brigade, LA Militia
Maldonado, Claudio-Pvt. Zapata's Company, Nueces County, TX State Troops
Maldonado, Sirido-Pvt. Duff's Regiment, TX Cavalry
Malia, Duke-Pvt. Company D, 22nd TENN Infantry
Malia, Edward-Pvt. Company F, 10th TENN Infantry
Malia, Martin-Cpl. Company I, 11th TENN Infantry
Malia, Pascual-Pvt. Co. 6, 5th (Spanish) Regiment, European Brigade, LA Militia
Mallory, Stephen Russell Jr.-Son of Stephen Russell Mallory Confederate Secretary of the Navy and Angela Sylvania Moreno. He served briefly in the Confederate Army as a Private in Virginia and later as a MidShipman on the Confederate Steamer PATRICK HENRY.
Mancha, Jesus-Pvt. Company G, 8th TX Infantry
***See also Menchaca
Manchaca, Bernavet-Pvt. Company B, 2nd TX Cavalry
Manchaca, Fabian-Pvt. Company G, 3rd TX Infantry
Manchaca, Fernando-Pvt. TX Militia
Manchaca, Jose A.-Pvt. Company H, 4th TX Cavalry
Manchaca, Manuel-Pvt. Company B, 33rd TX Cavalry
Mandoza, (no 1st name listed)-Pvt. Company G, 13th LA Infantry
Mandoza, L.A.-Pvt. 7th LA Infantry
Manent, Anthony-Pvt. Co. 5, 5th (Spanish) Regt., European Brigade, LA Militia
Manent, Domingo-Pvt. Co. 2, 5th (Spanish) Regt., European Brigade, LA Militia
Manent, Francisco-Pvt. Co. 3, 5th (Spanish) Regt., European Brigade, LA Militia
Manent, Joseph-Sgt. Co. 3, 5th (Spanish) Regt., European Brigade, LA Militia
Manent, Manuel-Pvt. Co. 8, 5th (Spanish) Regt., European Brigade, LA Militia
Manju, Anthony-Pvt. Co. 5, 5th (Spanish) Regt., European Brigade, LA Militia
Manos, A.L.-Pvt. 2nd LA Cavalry
Mans, Agustin-Cpl. Co. 10, 5th (Spanish) Regt., European Brigade, LA Militia
Mansola, Antonio-Pvt. Company G, 12th TX Infantry
Mansola, Lorenzo-Pvt. Company A, 17th TX Cavalry
Mansola, Mariano-Pvt. Company B, Ragsdale's Battalion, TX Cavalry
Mantes, Juan-Pvt. Benavides' Regiment, TX Cavalry
Mantez, Pablo-Pvt. Company C, Benavides' Regiment, TX Cavalry
Mantilo, John E.-Pvt. VIR Militia
Mantucu, Manuel-Pvt. Company G, 21st ALA Infantry
Manucy, Dominc-Catholic Priest, St. Mary's Hospital Montgomery, ALA Militia
Manucy, Felix-Pvt. Company K, 1st Nelligan's LA Infantry
Manucy, John-Pvt. Company B, 3rd FLA Infantry
Manucy, Mark-Pvt. Company A, 3rd FLA Infantry
Manucy, Phillip-Pvt. Company A, 3rd FLA Infantry
Manuel, Alphonse-Pvt. Company A, 1st LA Heavy Artillery
Manuel, Antonio-Pvt. LA Militia
Manuel, Raphael-Pvt. Company H, Miles' Legion, LA
Manuel, Satillo-Pvt. 8th Field Battery, TX Artillery

Marcadal, A.-Pvt. Orleans Guard Battery, LA Light Artillery
Marcadal, F.-Pvt. Orleans Guard Battery, LA Light Artillery
Marcadal, Juan-Sgt. Co. 7, 5th (Spanish) Regiment, European Brigade, LA Mil.
Marcadal, M.-Sgt. Co. 7, 5th (Spanish) Regiment, European Brigade, LA Militia
Marcial, Jose Tejera-Pvt. Co. 4, 5th (Spanish) Regt., European Brigade, LA Mil.
Marcial, Manuel Tejera-Pvt. Co. 4, 5th (Span.) Regt., European Brigade, LA Mil.
Marco, J.J.-Pvt. Company F, 22nd S.C.Infantry
Marco, John-Pvt. Company G, 3rd S.C. Infantry
Marco, Julian-Pvt. LA Militia
Marco, M.-Pvt. Company F, 8th S.C. Infantry
Marco, Samuel-Cpl. Company D, 2nd N.C. Infantry
Marcos, Anselmo-Pvt. 4th Field Battery, TX Artillery
Marcos, Claro-Pvt. Company B, Ragsdale's Battalion, TX Cavalry
Marcos, Juan M.-Pvt. Company B, Ragsdale's Battalion, TX Cavalry
Mareno, Luis-Pvt. 1st Company C, Ragsdale's Battalion, TX Cavalry
Mareno, Manuel-Pvt. 1st Company C, Ragsdale's Battalion, TX Cavalry
Mares, Francisco-1st Sgt. Co. 9, 5th (Span.) Regt., European Brigade, LA Militia
Mari, Joseph-Pvt. Co. 8, 5th (Spanish) Regiment, European Brigade, LA Militia
Maria, H.-Pvt. Company F, 2nd TX Infantry
Maria, Jose-Pvt. Company 1, Cazadores Espanoles Regiment, LA Militia
Maria, Jose-Pvt. Company I, Granbury's Consolidated Brigade, TX
Maria, Jose-Pvt. Company A, 1st TX State Troops
Mariadal, Antonio-2nd Lt. Co. 7, 5th (Spanish) Regt., European Brigade, LA Mil.
Mariano, Joseph-Pvt. Company I, 5th FLA Infantry
Mariano, Joseph C.-Cpl. Company K, 16th TX Cavalry
Mariano, Macedonia-Pvt. 1st Company C, 3rd TX Infantry
Mariano, Vicente-Pvt. Medina Guards, Bexar County, TX Militia
Mariano, Vicente-Pvt. Co. A, 5th (Spanish) Regt., European Brigade, LA Militia
Marin, A.-Pvt. Company 7, 4th Regiment, French Brigade, LA Militia
Marin, D.-Pvt. Company I, 12th ARK Infantry
Marin, Edgard-Pvt. Company F, Orleans Guard Regiment, LA Militia
Marin, J.-Pvt. Company 1, 5th (Spanish) Regiment, European Brigade, LA Mil.
Marin, J.S.-Pvt. Company I, 12th ARK Infantry
Marin, Manuel-Pvt. Company C/F, 3rd TX Infantry
Marin, W.N.-Pvt. Company D, 10th GA Cavalry
Marino, Vivian-Pvt. Medina Guards, Bexar County, TX Militia
Mario, Jose-Pvt. 4th Field Battery, TX Artillery
Marguez, E. Jr.-Pvt. Watson Battery, LA Artillery
Marguez, Louis-Pvt. Company D, 13th LA Infantry
Maristany, Jose-Pvt. Co. 7, 5th (Spanish) Regt., European Brigade, LA Militia
Marques, Nicolas-Pvt. Co. A, 5th (Spanish) Regt., European Brigade, LA Militia
Marquez, Antonio-Pvt. Co. 5, 5th (Spanish) Regt., European Brigade, LA Militia
Marquez, Antonio-Pvt. 1st Company C, 3rd TX Infantry
Marquez, Mateo-Pvt. Company 1, Cazadores Espanoles Regiment, LA Militia
Marrero, Antonio-Colonel Saint Bernard, LA Militia. He was also a Delegate to the

LA Secession Convention.
Marrero, B.-Pvt. Company H, Chalmette Regiment, LA Militia
Marrero, Jose-Pvt. Co. 6, 5th (Spanish) Regiment, European Brigade, LA Militia
Marrero, Louis H.-Pvt. Company C, 25th LA Infantry
Marrero, P.-2nd Lt. Company A, 22nd LA Infantry
Marsal, Marcelino-Pvt. Co. 5, 5th (Spanish) Regt., European Brigade, LA Militia
Martenin, Pedro-Pvt. Company I, Benavides' Regiment, TX Cavalry
***See also Marty
Marti, Alejandro-Pvt. Co. 10, 5th (Spanish) Regt., European Brigade, LA Militia
Marti, Pedro-Pvt. Co. 2, 5th (Spanish) Regiment, European Brigade, LA Militia
Martin, Amable-Pvt. Company D, 10th TENN Infantry
Martin, Antonio-Pvt. Company F, 1st Regiment, ALA Militia
Martin, Antonio-Pvt. Key West Avengers, Coast Guard, FLA Militia
Martin, Domingo-Pvt. Co. A, 5th (Spanish) Regt., European Brigade, LA Militia
Martin, Ferdinand-1st Sgt. Lartigue's Company, Bienville Guards, LA Militia
Martin, Fernando De F.-Pvt. Co. 5, 5th (Span.) Regt., European Brigade, LA Mil.
Martin, Francisco-Pvt. Co. 7, 5th (Spanish) Regt., European Brigade, LA Militia
Martin, Ignacio-Sgt. 1st Company C, Ragsdale's Battalion, TX Cavalry
Martin, Jose-Cpl. Company G, 21st ALA Infantry
Martin, Leonidas M.-1st Lt. Company K, 6th TX Cavalry
Martin, Lequilian-Pvt. Company E, 17th TX Cavalry
Martin, Manuel-Pvt. Company G, 1st LA Heavy Artillery
Martin, Orlando-2nd Lt. Company B, 1st Yager's TX Cavalry
Martin, P.A.-Cpl. Co. 1, 5th (Spanish) Regiment, European Brigade, LA Militia
Martin, Sebastian-Pvt. Company A, 6th TX Infantry
Martin, Valentin-Pvt. Company H, 15th LA Infantry
Martinas, Ugenes-Pvt. Company E, 8th TX Infantry
Martinay, Jules-Pvt. Company A, 12th ALA Infantry
Martines, A.-Pvt. LA Artillery
Martines, Antoine-Pvt. Lafourche Regiment, LA Militia
Martines, Benito-Pvt. Company E, 8th TX Infantry
Martines, Carlos-Cpl. 1st Company C, Ragsdale's Battalion, TX Cavalry
Martines, Casimero-Pvt. Company B, Ragsdale's Battalion, TX Cavalry
Martines, F.B.-Pvt. Co. A, 1st Regiment, 3rd Brigade, 1st Division, LA Militia
Martines, Felix-Pvt. Co. 7, 5th (Spanish) Regiment, European Brigade, LA Militia
Martines, John-Pvt. Company E, 5th ALA Cavalry
Martines, Jose M.-Pvt. Company B, Ragsdale's Battalion, TX Cavalry
Martines, Robert-Pvt. Company D, 16th LA Infantry
Martines, Sinforiano-Pvt. Company A, Benavides' Regiment, TX Cavalry
Martinette, Francisco-Pvt. 1st Company E, 41st VIR Infantry
Martiney, A.-Pvt. Company H, 2nd LA Cavalry
Martinez, Adrian-Pvt. Co. 7, 5th (Spanish) Regt., European Brigade, LA Militia
Martinez, Adrian-Cpl. Company C, 3rd TX Infantry
Martinez, Adrien-Pvt. Company C, 9th Battalion, LA Infantry
Martinez, Angel E.-Pvt. Co. 7, 5th (Spanish) Regt., European Brigade, LA Mil.

Martinez, Anselmo-Pvt. Company F, 3rd TX Infantry
Martinez, Antonio-Sgt. Co. 8, 5th (Spanish) Regt., European Brigade, LA Militia
Martinez, Antonio-Pvt. Rhodes' Company, 3rd Yager's TX Cavalry
Martinez, Antonio-Cpl. Co. 10, 5th (Spanish) Regt., European Brigade, LA Mil.
Martinez, Antonio-Pvt. Company G, 3rd TX Infantry
Martinez, Antonio-Pvt. Company C, 8th TX Infantry
Martinez, Bernard-Cpl. Co. E, 28th Thomas' LA Infantry, he also served on the CSS ARKANSAS where he was wounded.
Martinez, C.S.-Pvt. Company H, 2nd LA Cavalry
Martinez, Carlos-Pvt. Company 1, Cazadores Espanoles Regiment, LA Militia
Martinez, Carlos-Pvt. Company H, Baird's Regiment, TX Cavalry
Martinez, Carlos- Pvt. Benavides' Regiment, TX Cavalry
Martinez, Casimero-Pvt. Company E, Madison's Regiment, TX Cavalry
Martinez, Clemente-Pvt. Co. 4, 5th (Spanish) Regt., European Brigade, LA Mil.
Martinez, Domingo-Pvt. Co. 9, 5th (Spanish) Regt., European Brigade, LA Mil.
Martinez, E.-Pvt. Hall's Company, Orleans Guard Regiment, LA Militia
Martinez, E.H.-Pvt. Company D, 27th LA Infantry
Martinez, E.P.-Pvt. Company E, Orleans Guard Regiment, LA Militia
Martinez, Erineo-Pvt. Company D, 3rd TX Infantry
Martinez, Ernesto-Pvt. Company A, 9th Battalion, LA Infantry
Martinez, Esperidion-Pvt. 1st Company A, Ragsdale's Battalion, TX Cavalry
Martinez, F.P.-Pvt. Company E, Orleans Guard Regiment, LA Militia
Martinez, Fermin-1st Sgt. Bustillo's Company, Bexar County, TX Militia
Martinez, Fermin-Cpl. Company H, 36th TX Cavalry
Martinez, Fernando-Pvt. Company D, 3rd TX Infantry
Martinez, Francisco-Pvt. 1st Company H, 33rd TX Cavalry
Martinez, Francisco-Pvt. 1st Company A, Ragsdale's Battalion, TX Cavalry
Martinez, Francisco-Pvt. Company C, 8th TX Infantry
Martinez, Francisco-Pvt. Co. 4, 5th (Spanish) Regt., European Brigade, LA Mil.
Martinez, G.-Pvt. Company A, Crescent Regiment, LA Infantry
Martinez, Gabriel-Jr. 2nd Lt. Bexar County, TX Militia
Martinez, Hipolito-Pvt. Co. 5, 5th (Spanish) Regt., European Brigade, LA Mil.
Martinez, J.-Pvt. Trevinio's Company, TX Cavalry
Martinez, J.A.-Pvt. Co. 1, 5th (Spanish) Regiment, European Brigade, LA Militia
Martinez, Jesus-Pvt. Company B, 2nd TX Cavalry
Martinez, John-Pvt. Co. 5, 5th (Spanish) Regiment, European Brigade, LA Mil.
Martinez, John-Arsenal Department, LA (unknown rank or position).
Martinez, Jose-Pvt. Company G, 10th LA Infantry
Martinez, Jose-Pvt. Company D, Benavides' Regiment, TX Cavalry
Martinez, Jose-Pvt. 8th Field Battery, TX Artillery
Martinez, Jose A.-Pvt. Frontier Battalion, TX
Martinez, Jose Maria (1st)-Pvt. 1st Company A, 3rd TX Infantry
Martinez, Jose Maria (2nd)-Pvt. Bustillo's Company, Bexar County, TX Militia
Martinez, Jose Pedro-Pvt. Co. 5, Cazadores Espanoles Regiment, LA Militia
Martinez, Josiah-Pvt. 2nd LA Cavalry

Martinez, Josiah-Pvt. Company A, Miles' Legion, LA
Martinez, Josiah-Pvt. Company C, 9th LA Infantry
Martinez, Josiah- Pvt. Company E, 8th TX Infantry
Martinez, Juan-Pvt. Medina Guards, Bexar County, TX Militia
Martinez, Juan-Pvt. Engledow's Company, Nueces County, TX Militia
Martinez, Juan-Pvt. 1st Company I, 33rd TX Cavalry
Martinez, Loriano-Pvt. Company C, Ragsdales' Battalion, TX Cavalry
Martinez, M.E.-Pvt. Company A, Miles' Legion, LA
Martinez, Manuel-Pvt. Co. 3, 5th (Spanish) Regt., European Brigade, LA Militia
Martinez, Manuel-Sgt. Co. 10, 5th (Spanish) Regt., European Brigade, LA Militia
Martinez, Manuel-Pvt. Company H, 33rd TX Cavalry
Martinez, Marcos-Pvt. Company I, 33rd TX Cavalry
Martinez, Maximiano-3rd Sgt. Bustillo's Company, Bexar County, TX Militia
Martinez, Miguel-Pvt. Hardeman's Regiment, TX Cavalry
Martinez, Monseis-Pvt. Company D, Benavides' Regiment, TX Cavalry
Martinez, Pedro-Pvt. Company I, Benavides' Regiment, TX Cavalry
Martinez, Peter Amede-Pvt. Company B, Pelican Battery, LA
Martinez, Prudencia-Pvt. Company K, 24th TX Cavalry
Martinez, R.-2nd Lt. Co. 2, 5th (Spanish) Regt., European Brigade, LA Militia
Martinez, R.-Pvt. Company E, 2nd MO Infantry
Martinez, R.-1st Lt. Cater's Battalion, TX Cavalry
Martinez, Rafael-Pvt. Company H, 8th TX Infantry
Martinez, S.P.-Artificer Orleans Guard Battalion, LA Infantry
Martinez, Sinfariano-Pvt. TX Cavalry
Martinez, Sisto A.-Pvt. 1st Company H, 33rd TX Cavalry
Martinez, Stephan Sr.-Pvt. Stoker's Company, LA Militia
Martinez, Susino-Pvt. Company I, Benavides' Regiment, TX Cavalry
Martinez, Teodoro-Pvt. Rhodes' Company, 3rd Yager's Battalion, TX Cavalry
Martinez, Tranes-Pvt. Company 2, Cazadores Espanoles Regiment, LA Militia
Martinez, Valentin-Pvt. Company B, Benavides' Regiment, TX Cavalry
Martinez, Vicente-1st Lt. Company A, Ragsdale's Battalion, TX Cavalry
Martinez, William-Pvt. Nueces County Militia, TX
Martinez, Ygnacio-Pvt. 1st Company C, Ragsdale's Battalion, TX Cavalry
Martori, Fabiano-Pvt. Co. 9, 5th (Spanish) Regt., European Brigade, LA Militia
***See also Marti
Marty, Miguel-1st Sgt. Company A, Confederate States Zouave Battalion, LA
Martymus, Jose-Pvt. Company G, 12th TX Infantry
Marugo, Dunencio-Pvt. Company C, 8th TX Infantry
Mas, Lorenzo-Sgt. Co. 9, 5th (Spanish) Regiment, European Brigade, LA Militia
Masca, Salondino-Pvt. Company C, Benavides' Regiment, TX Cavalry
Mascaro, Antonio-Pvt. Co. 5, 5th (Spanish) Regt., European Brigade, LA Militia
Mascaro, Antonio-Pvt. Co. 4, 5th (Spanish) Regt., European Brigade, LA Militia
Mascaro, Juan-Pvt. Co. 4, 5th (Spanish) Regt., European Brigade, LA Militia
Mascaro, Magin-Pvt. Co. 5, 5th (Spanish) Regt., European Brigade, LA Militia
Mascaro, Pedro-Pvt Co. 5, 5th (Spanish) Regiment, European Brigade, LA Militia

Mascoso, Rafael-Pvt. Cameron County Coast Guard, TX Militia
Masden, Jose Garcia-Cpl. Co. 1, 5th (Spanish) Regt., European Brigade, LA Mil.
Masedo, R. Pereira-Pvt. Co. 4, 5th (Spanish) Regt., European Brigade, LA Militia
*** Masters is the FLA version of the surname Maestre / Mestre
Masters, Bartolo-Pvt. Company A, 2nd FLA Infantry Battalion
Masters, Benjamin J.-Pvt. Marion Artillery, FLA
Masters, Casimero-Pvt. Company A, 2nd FLA Infantry Battalion
Masters, Decidario-Pvt. / Blacksmith Company B, 3rd FLA Infantry
Masters, Edwin D.-Pvt. Company F, 7th FLA Infantry
Masters, Francis-Pvt. Company D, 8th FLA Infantry
Masters, Gabriel-4th Cpl. Company D, 8th FLA Infantry
Masters, Joseph Elias-2nd Cpl. Company B, 3rd FLA Infantry
Masters, Joseph P.-Pvt. Company B, 2nd FLA Cavalry
Masters, Lawrence Alexander-1st Cpl. Company B, 7th FLA Infantry
Masters, Paul Edward-Pvt. Company B, 3rd FLA Infantry
Masters, Peter Andreu-Pvt. Company G, 5th FLA Cavalry
Masters, Peter B.-Pvt. Company A, 2nd FLA Infantry
Masters, Peter Clarence-Pvt. Company B, 3rd FLA Infantry
Masters, R.J.-Bugler Company K, 2nd FLA Cavalry
Masters, Theodosia Benjamin-Pvt. Company A, 2nd FLA Infantry Battalion
Mata, Andreas-Pvt. Dunn's Company, Waller's Regiment, TX Cavalry
Mata, Deciderio-Pvt. Company A, Benavides' Regiment, TX Cavalry
Mata, Gregorio-Pvt. Gray's Company, Bexar County, TX Militia
Mata, Luerino-Pvt. Gray's Company, Bexar County, TX Militia
Mata, Pedro-Pvt. 1st Company C, 3rd TX Infantry
Mataro, Leon-Pvt. Co. A, 5th (Spanish) Regiment, European Brigade, LA Militia
Mateo, Domingo-Pvt. Co. A, 5th (Spanish) Regt., European Brigade, LA Militia
Matero, Alafita-Pvt. Company I, Benavides' Regiment, TX Cavalry
Maura, Frank Z.-Sgt. Company A, 2nd FLA Infantry
Maura, Joseph-Pvt. Company B, 3rd Battalion, FLA Cavalry
Mauricio, Eluterio-Pvt. Company B, Benavides' Regiment, TX Cavalry
Mauricio, Miguel-Cpl. Company D, 30th LA Infantry
Mayans, Diego-Pvt. Co. 3, 5th (Spanish) Regt., European Brigade, LA Militia
Mayans, George-Pvt. Co. 7, 5th (Spanish) Regt., European Brigade, LA Militia
Mayas, Joseph-Pvt. Company E, 20th LA Infantry
Maza, Mateo-Pvt. Co. 3, 5th (Spanish) Regiment, European Brigade, LA Militia
Mecindo, Lancedo-Pvt. Company C, Benavides' Regiment, TX Cavalry
***See also Garcia y Medina, Emilio and the surname Madinas
Medina, Benjamin M.-Pvt. Company I, 5th VIR Cavalry
Medina, G.E.-Pvt. Company E, Confederate Guards Regiment, LA Militia
Medina, Juan-Pvt. Co. 5, 5th (Spanish) Regiment, European Brigade, LA Militia
Medina, Lucio-Pvt. 1st Company H, 33rd TX Cavalry
Medina, Luis-Pvt. Cameron County Coast Guard, TX Militia
Medina, Manuel-Pvt. Gray's Company, Bexar County, TX Militia
Medrano, Antonio-Pvt. Thomas' Company, TX Partisan Rangers

Medrano, Bartolo-Pvt. 1st Company C, 3rd TX Infantry
Medrano, Juan-Pvt. Trevinio's Squad, TX Partisan Mounted Rangers
Medrano, Macedonio-Pvt. 3rd TX Infantry
Mejia, Simon-Pvt. Company C, 8th TX Infantry
Melgarejo, Cristoval-Sgt. Company C, 3rd TX Infantry
Melhado, Nathaniel-Cpl. Company C, 1st Rightor's LA Infantry
Melerine, Nicholas-Pvt. Company A, Lafourche Militia, LA
Mencal, W.-Pvt. Company E, 6th MO Cavalry
***See also Manchaca
Menchaca, Bernar-Pvt. Trevinio's Company, TX Cavalry
Menchaca, Francisco-Pvt. Company H, 8th TX Infantry
Menchaca, Javian-Pvt. Bustillo's Company, Bexar County, TX Militia
Menchaca, Jesus-Pvt. Company C, 8th TX Infantry
Menchaca, John-Pvt. Company D, 2nd TX Mounted Rifles
Menchaca, Jose M.-Capt. 6th TX Cavalry
Menchaca, Martin-Pvt. Company A, Ragsdale's Battalion, TX Cavalry
Menchaco, John-Pvt. Davis' Company, Confederate Light Artillery
Mendes, Gumasindoly-Pvt. Co. 1, Cazadores Espanoles Regiment, LA Militia
Mendes, L.-Pvt. Company C, 22nd LA Infantry
Mendes, Samuel L.-Pvt. Company D, 11th LA Infantry
Mendez, A.L.-Pvt. Company A, Dreux's LA Cavalry
Mendez, Antonio-Pvt. 1st TX Heavy Artillery
Mendez, Antonio-Pvt. Company C, Baird's Regiment, TX Cavalry
Mendez, Antonio-Pvt. Company C, Benavides' Regiment, TX Cavalry
Mendez, Doroteo-Pvt. Davis' Company, Confederate Light Artillery
Mendez, F.-Pvt. Company B, Orleans Guard Regiment, LA Militia
Mendez, F. Augustus-Musician Maxwell's Regiment, GA Light Artillery
Mendez, J.M.-4th Sgt. Company 1, Cazadores Espanoles Regiment, LA Militia
Mendez, Jesus-Pvt. Gray's Company, Bexar County, TX Militia
Mendez, Juan-Pvt. Company I, 33rd TX Cavalry
Mendez, Manuel-Pvt. Bustillo's Company, Bexar County, TX Militia
Mendez, Samuel P.-Pvt. Company D, 12th VIR Infantry
Mendez, T.-Pvt. Company B, Orleans Guard Regiment, LA Militia
Mendiola, Aniseto-Pvt. Company B, 33rd TX Cavalry
Mendiola, Antonio-Pvt. Company C, Baird's Regiment, ARIZ
Mendiola, Juan-Pvt. 1st Company I, 33rd TX Cavalry
Mendiola, Julian-Pvt. Company H, 33rd TX Cavalry
Mendiola, Pilar-Pvt. 1st Company H, 33rd TX Cavalry
Mendiola, Ramon-Pvt. 1st Company I, 33rd TX Cavalry
Mendiola, Santiago-Pvt. 1st Company H, 33rd TX Cavalry
Mendiola, Valentin-Pvt. 1st Company I, 33rd TX Cavalry
Mendizabal, Frank-Pvt. Company C, ALA State Artillery
Mendola, Antonio-Sgt. Co. 7, 5th (Spanish) Regt., European Brigade, LA Militia
***See also Mandoza
Mendosa, Florencio-Pvt. Company A, Benavides' Regiment, TX Cavalry

Mendosa, Matilda-Pvt. 1st Company A, 3rd TX Infantry
Mendoza, Antoine-Pvt. Company C, 2nd LA Cavalry
Mendoza, Cristobal-Pvt. Gray's Company, Bexar County, TX Militia
Mendoza, E.-Pvt. Company A, 7th LA Cavalry
Mendoza, F.-Pvt. Company E, 1st Regiment Mobile Volunteers, ALA
Mendoza, Florencio-Pvt. Company D, Ragsdale's Battalion, TX Cavalry
Mendoza, Freeman-Pvt. Company E, 24th TX Cavalry
Mendoza, Hosea-Pvt. Company B, Waul's Legion, TX
Mendoza, John-Pvt. Company C, 2nd LA Cavalry
Mendoza, Juan-Pvt. Company C, 2nd TX State Troops
Mendoza, Lucien-Pvt. 1st Field Battery, LA Artillery
Mendoza, Manuel-Pvt. Company G, 3rd TX Infantry
Mendoza, P.D.-Pvt. King's Battery, LA Artillery
Mendoza, Silvestre-Pvt. Davis' Company, Confederate Light Artillery
Mends, Antonio-Pvt. Company D, 1st TX Heavy Artillery
Menendez, A.-Pvt. Co. 2, 5th (Spanish) Regiment, European Brigade, LA Militia
Menendez, Carlos-Pvt. Co. 3, 5th (Spanish) Regt., European Brigade, LA Militia
Menendez, F.-Pvt. Co. 1, 5th (Spanish) Regiment, European Brigade, LA Militia
Menendez, Felipe-Pvt. Co. 3, 5th (Spanish) Regt., European Brigade, LA Militia
Menendez, J.M.-Sgt. Company 1, Cazadores Espanoles Regiment, LA Militia
Menendez, Jose-Pvt. Co. 5, 5th (Spanish) Regt., European Brigade, LA Militia
Menendez, Martin-Sgt. Company 1, Cazadores Espanoles Regiment, LA Militia
Menes, M.-Pvt. Co. 2, 5th (Spanish) Regiment, European Brigade, LA Militia
Menez, Romanis-Pvt. Company G, 28th Thomas' LA Infantry
Mercadal, A.-Pvt. Company K, Orleans Guard Regiment, LA Militia
Mercadal, Antonio-2nd Lt. Co. 7, 5th (Spanish) Regt., European Brigade, LA Mil.
Mercadal, Jaime-Pvt. Co. 9, 5th (Spanish) Regt., European Brigade, LA Militia
Mercado, Juan-Jr. 2nd Lt. Medina Guards, Bexar County, TX Militia
Mereadal, Pablo-Pvt. Co. 3, 5th (Spanish) Regt., European Brigade, LA Militia
Mereadal, Pedro-Pvt. Co. 3, 5th (Spanish) Regt., European Brigade, LA Militia
Merequer, Fernando-Pvt. Co. 2, 5th (Spanish) Regt., European Brigade, LA Mil.
Merelo, Manuel-Pvt. Co. 10, 5th (Spanish) Regt., European Brigade, LA Militia
Merene, J.-QMaster / Cpl. Co. 1, 5th (Spanish) Regt., European Brigade, LA Mil.
Merillo, Angelo-Pvt. Company D, 28th Thomas' LA Infantry
Merino, J.F.-Pvt. Company A, 6th LA Cavalry
Mesa, Andres-Pvt. Co. 4, 5th (Spanish) Regiment, European Brigade, LA Militia
Mesa, Antonio-Pvt. Company D, 30th LA Infantry
Mesa, Jose Maria-Pvt. 1st Company C, Ragsdale's Battalion, TX Cavalry
Mesa, Manuel-Pvt. Co. 4, 5th (Spanish) Regiment, European Brigade, LA Militia
Mesado, Pedro-Pvt. Co. 2, 5th (Spanish) Regiment, European Brigade, LA Militia
Mesquida, Mateo-Pvt. Co. 7, 5th (Spanish) Regt., European Brigade, LA Militia
Mestella, J.F.-Pvt. Company C, 33rd TX Cavalry
Mestas, Manuel-Pvt. Davis' Company, Confederate Light Artillery
Mestes, Lazaro-Pvt. 1st Company I, 33rd TX Cavalry
Mestre, John-Pvt. Co. F, 4th Regiment, 2nd Brigade, 1st Division, LA Militia

Miangolara, Juan-Colonel Cazadores Espanoles Regiment, LA Militia
Miguel, Barney-Pvt. Co. D, 4th Regiment, 1st Brigade, 1st Division, LA Militia
Miguel, J.-Pvt. Company 7, 3rd Regiment, French Brigade, LA Militia
Miguel, Mauricio-Pvt. Company 2, Cazadores Espanoles Regiment, LA Militia
Miguel, Patrick-Pvt. Company D, Benavides' Regiment, TX Cavalry
***Megues, Meguez, Miguey are all Louisiana versions of the surname Miguez
Megues, F.R.-Pvt. Company G, 7th LA Cavalry
Megues, N.-Pvt. Company K, 2nd LA Cavalry
Meguez, Clet-Pvt. Company G, 18th Consolidated LA Infantry
Meguez, Derozan-Pvt. Company E, 7th LA Cavalry
Miguey, Lucien-Pvt. Company E, 7th LA Cavalry
Miguez, Antoine Theomile-Pvt. LA (unknown branch).
Miguez, Balthazar-Pvt. Company I, 7th LA Cavalry
Miguez, Camile-Pvt. Company G, 7th LA Cavalry
Miguez, Clemente-Pvt. Company F, 10th Battalion, LA Infantry
Miquez, Daniel Drauzin-Pvt. LA (unknown branch)
Miguez, Derozan A.-Pvt. Company G, 7th LA Cavalry
Miguez, Despaliere-Pvt. Company F, 10th Battalion, LA Infantry
Miguez, Eloi-Pvt. Company E, 7th LA Cavalry
Miguez, Gustave-Pvt. Company E, 7th LA Cavalry
Miguez, Honore-Pvt. Company G, 7th LA Cavalry
Miguez, Ilet-Pvt. LA Militia
Miguez, Jules-Pvt. Company A, 7th LA Cavalry
Miguez, Numa-3rd Lt. Company F, 10th Battalion, LA Infantry
Miguez, O.-Sgt. Company G, 7th LA Cavalry
Miguez, Octave-Pvt. Company D, 18th LA Infantry
Miguez, Theome-Pvt. Company G, 7th LA Cavalry
Miguez, Ulysse-Pvt. Company G, 7th LA Cavalry
Miguez, Valise-Pvt. Company F, 33rd Battalion, LA Infantry
Mijares, B. Alvarez-Pvt. Co. 1, 5th (Spanish) Regt., European Brigade, LA Militia
Millan, Jose Maria-Pvt. Rhodes' Company, 1st Yager's TX Cavalry
Mirahildo, S.-Pvt. Teel's Company, TX State Troops
Miranda, Able-2nd Lt. Coast Guard, FLA Militia
Miranda, Frank-Sgt. Co. 5, 5th (Spanish) Regiment, European Brigade, LA Mil.
Miranda, Henry G.-Pvt. Company G, 6th LA Infantry
Miranda, L.-Pvt. Company H, 21st ALA Infantry
Miranda, Nicolas-Pvt. Co. 3, 5th (Spanish) Regt., European Brigade, LA Militia
Miranda, Thomas E.-Pvt. Pickett's Company, FLA Cavalry
Miranda, William-Pvt. Company B, 3rd FLA Cavalry
Moise, Albert Welborne-Lt. Company D, 24th GA Infantry
Moise, Charles Henry-Pvt. Walter's Company, 1st Regiment, S.C. Artillery Militia
Moise, Camillus T.-Pvt. Walter's Company, S.C. Light Artillery
Moise, David Calhoun-Pvt. Company A, 5th Battalion, S.C. Reserve
Moise, Domingo-Pvt. Company K, 13th S.C. Infantry
Moise, Edwin Henry-Pvt. 1st Company A, Manigault's Battalion, S.C. Artillery

Moise, Edwin Warren (1st)-Major Company A, 10th GA Infantry
Moise, Edwin Warren (2nd)-Circuit Judge, New Orleans, LA 1861-1862.
Moise, Gridon-Pvt. Company A, 16th MISS Infantry
Moise, H.-Pvt. 6th Field Battery, LA Artillery
Moise, Howard Cohen-Pvt. Company H, 25th S.C. Infantry
Moise, Isaac-Pvt. 1st Company A, Manigault's Battalion, S.C. Artillery
Moise, Isadore-Pvt. Company A, 16th MISS Infantry
Moise, Izene-Pvt. Company H, 2nd LA Cavalry
Moise, J.-Pvt. Buist's Company, 17th Regiment, S.C. Militia
Moise, J.-Pvt. Company A, 16th MISS Cavalry
Moise, John-Pvt. Company D, 3rd VIR Reserve
Moise, John L.-Pvt. Company H, 17th MISS Infantry
Moise, Phillip Augustus-Pvt. Company G, 4th State Troops S.C.
Moise, Theodore Sidney-Major / QMaster Staff of General Paul O. Herbert, LA
Molano, Jose Maria-Pvt. Thomas' Company, TX Partisan Rangers
Molano, Juan-Cpl. Thomas' Company, TX Partisan Rangers
Molero, Edward G.-Sgt. Company A, 1st ARK Mounted Rifles
Molero, William-Pvt. Company G, 23rd ARK Infantry
Molina, Antonio-Pvt. Company B, Benavides' Regiment, TX Cavalry
Molina, Antonio-Pvt. 1st Company C, Ragsdale's Battalion, TX Cavalry
Molina, Cayetano-Pvt. Company I, 8th TX Infantry
Molina, Eutimio-Pvt. 1st Company I, 33rd TX Cavalry
Molina, F.-Pvt. Trevinio's Company, TX Partisan Rangers
Molina, Juan G.-2nd Cpl. Company I, Benavides' Regiment, TX Cavalry
Molina, Juan R.-Pvt. Tom's Company, Atascosa County, TX Militia
Molina, Luis-Pvt. Cameron County Coast Guard, TX Militia
Molina, Manuel-2nd Lt. Company D, 1st Battalion, GA Sharpshooters
Molina, Miguel-Pvt. Co. 6, 5th (Spanish) Regt., European Brigade, LA Militia
Molina, Miguel S.-Pvt. Company 5, Cazadores Espanoles Regiment, LA Militia
Molina, R.-Pvt. Company H, 63rd GA Infantry
Molina, Regino-Pvt. Duran's Company, Atascosa County, TX State Troops
Molina, Secundino-Pvt. TX Militia
Molinari, Pablo-Pvt. Co. 10, 5th (Spanish) Regt., European Brigade, LA Militia
Molines, Gregorio-Pvt. Co. A, 5th (Spanish) Regt., European Brigade, LA Mil.
Molino, Antonio-Pvt. 1st Company I, 33rd TX Cavalry
Molja, Feliciano-Pvt. Co. 10, 5th (Spanish) Regt., European Brigade, LA Militia
Molla, Feliz-Pvt. Jeff Davis Home Guard, Refugio County, TX Militia
Mon, Edmond-Pvt. Company I, 21st ALA Infantry
Monares, Patrick-Pvt. Company D, 16th TX Cavalry
Monasteria, Ceferino-2nd Lt. Cazadores Espanoles Regiment, LA Militia
Monasterio, Jose Gonzalez-Pvt. Co. 3, 5th (Sp.) Regt., European Brigade, LA Mil.
Mondeiro, Joachin-Pvt. Co. 7, 5th (Spanish) Regt., European Brigade, LA Militia
Mondragon, E.-Pvt. Mitchell's Company, Bexar County, TX Militia
Mondragon, Francisco-2nd Lt. Company B, Benavides' Regiment, TX Cavalry
Mondragon, Francisco-Pvt. Company H, 8th TX Infantry

Monguya, Anastacio-Pvt. Company E, 1st McCulloch's TX Cavalry
Monillo, P.-Sgt. Company A, 2nd LA Reserve Corps
Monios, Antonio-Pvt. Company H, 1st S.C. Artillery
Monjaras, Benito-Pvt. Company H, 8th TX Infantry
Monju, Jose-Pvt. Company G, 21st ALA Infantry
Monju, Rafael-Pvt. Company G, 21st ALA Infantry
Monoso, Trinidad-Pvt. 8th Field Battery, TX Artillery
Monserrat, Juan-Cpl. Co. 6, 5th (Spanish) Regt., European Brigade, LA Militia
Montalbo, Antonio-Pvt. Company H, 8th TX Infantry
Montalbo, Blas-Pvt. Company H, 8th TX Infantry
Montalbo, Cresencio-Pvt. Company H, 8th TX Infantry
Montalbo, Elisio-Pvt. 1st Company C, Ragsdale's Battalion, TX Cavalry
Montales, Jean-Pvt. Company 4, 2nd Regiment, French Brigade, LA Militia
Montallia, M.-Pvt. Trevinio's Company, TX Cavalry.
Montane, J.R.-Pvt. Co. I, 5th (Spanish) Regiment, European Brigade, LA Militia
Montane, Miguel-Pvt. Company D, 30th LA Infantry
Monteguedo, James Albert-Pvt. Company B, 7th LA Infantry
Monteiro, Aristides-Surgeon 26th VIR Infantry
Monteiro, E.H.-Pvt. VIR Mounted Guard, 4th Congressional District
Monteiro, James M.-Pvt. VIR Mounted Guard, 4th Congressional District
Montenegro, Henry-Pvt. Brown's Company, VIR Horse Artillery
Monter, Salvador-Pvt. Co. 8, 5th (Spanish) Regt., European Brigade, LA Militia
Monteray, D.-Pvt. Company H, 2nd VIR Cavalry
Monterey, Andrew-Pvt. Company F, 1st MD Cavalry
Montero, Francis-Pvt. Landry's Company, Donaldsonville Artillery, LA
Montero, Jose-Pvt. Co. 4, 5th (Spanish) Regiment, European Brigade, LA Militia
Montero, Juan-Pvt. Co. 4, 5th (Spanish) Regiment, European Brigade, LA Militia
Montero, Walter-Sgt. Company H, 5th VIR Cavalry
Montes, Alejo-Pvt. Mitchell's Company, Bexar County, TX Militia
Montes, Anastacio-Pvt. Company B, 2nd TX Cavalry
Montes, Cresencio-Pvt. Company H, 8th TX Infantry
Montes, Felipe-Pvt. Company B, Ragsdale's Battalion, TX Cavalry
Montes, J.A.-Pvt. Co. 1, 5th (Spanish) Regiment, European Brigade, LA Militia
Montes, Jose M.-Pvt. Company A, 17th TX Consolidated Dismounted Cavalry
Montes, Joseph-Pvt. Company B, 2nd TX Infantry
Montes, Juan-Cpl. Company E, Benavides' Regiment, TX Cavalry
Montes, Juan-Pvt. Company H, 8th TX Infantry
Montes, Nicacio-Pvt. Company H, 8th TX Infantry
Montes, Pedro-Pvt. Company I, Benavides' Regiment, TX Cavalry
Montes De Oca > see De Oca
Montez, J.H.-Pvt. Company F, Benavides' Regiment, TX Cavalry
Montez, Pablo-Cpl. Company C, 8th TX Infantry
Montoja, Anastasio-Pvt. 8th Field Battery, TX Artillery
Montojo, Mariano-Pvt. Dunn's Company, Waller's Regiment, TX Cavalry
Montotto, Jose-Pvt. 1st Company C, Ragsdale's Battalion, TX Cavalry

Montoya, Anastacio-Pvt. Company G, 3rd TX Infantry
Mora, Emedia-Pvt. Company A, 11th TX Infantry
Mora, Hosa A.-Pvt. Company A, 11th TX Infantry
Mora, J.-Pvt. Company F, 18th Consolidated LA Infantry
Mora, Jim-Pvt. Company A, 11th TX Infantry
Mora, Jose-2nd Lt. Company 3, LA Defenders Battalion
Mora, Jose-Pvt. Company D, 30th LA Infantry
Mora, Jose-Pvt. Company G, 17th TX Dismounted Cavalry
Mora, Joseph-Pvt. Company F, 7th LA Cavalry
Mora, Joseph-Pvt. Company F, 8th FLA Infantry
Mora, Joseph-Pvt. Company A, 11th TX Infantry
Mora, Juan-Pvt. Company H, Baird's Regiment, TX Cavalry
Mora, Juan-Pvt. 1st Company C, Ragsdale's Battalion, TX Cavalry
Mora, Luis-Pvt. Company E, 19th TX Infantry
Mora, Robert-Pvt. Company A, 11th TX Infantry
Mora, Thomas-Pvt. Company I, 3rd Harrison's LA Cavalry
Morale, Thomas-Pvt. Company A, 37th ARK Infantry
Morales, Antonio-Pvt. 1st Company A, 3rd TX Infantry
Morales, Bentura-Pvt. Jeff Davis Home Guard, Refugio County, TX Militia
Morales, Felipe-Pvt. Company G, 21st ALA Infantry
Morales, Francisco-Pvt. Company C, 8th TX Infantry
Morales, Julian-Pvt. Company I, 2nd VIR Infantry
Morales, Olivario-Pvt. 8th Field Battery, TX Artillery
Morales, Polinario-Pvt. Bustillo's Company, Bexar County, TX Militia
Moralles, P.-Pvt. Company H, 18th LA Infantry
Morano, N.-Pvt. Company G, 8th TX Infantry
Morano, Theodore-1st Lt. Company 6, Orleans Artillery Battalion, LA
Moreira, Alexander-Pvt. Co. 5, 5th (Spanish) Regt., European Brigade, LA Militia
Morel, Jose-Pvt. 1st Company I, 33rd TX Cavalry
Morel, Victor-Pvt. 1st Company I, 33rd TX Cavalry
Morelas, Santa Ana-Pvt. Company H, Border's Regiment, TX Cavalry
***See also Morreno
Moreno, Antonio-Pvt. Company H, 3rd TX Infantry
Moreno, Bartolo-1st Sgt. 1st Company I, 33rd TX Cavalry
Moreno, Benito Julian-Clerk in Major T. J. Moreno's Office, Engineering Bureau
Moreno, Carlos-Pvt. 4th Field Battery, TX Artillery
Moreno, Celestino-2nd Lt. Company G, 60th N.C. Infantry
Moreno, Damacio-Pvt. 1st Company I, 33rd TX Cavalry
Moreno, Fernando Joaquin-Marshal of the Federal Court at Key West, FLA, March 16th, 1853, to April 3rd, 1861. He was threatened with banishment from Key West for his pro-Confederate sympathies.
Moreno, Francisco Jr.-2nd Lt. Company A, Orleans Guard Regiment, LA Militia
Moreno, Francisco Sr.-Spanish Consul in Pensacola, FLA. He spied on behalf of the Confederacy under cover of Spain's neutrality. His sons all served in the Confederate Military.

Moreno, Hilario-Pvt. TX Militia
Moreno, J.-Lt. Orleans Guard Regiment, LA Militia
Moreno, James Nicholas-Capt. QuarterMaster Department, C.S.A. He had also served as a Private, Mobile Cadets, 3rd ALA Infantry.
Moreno, John-Pvt. Co. 5, 5th (Spanish) Regiment, European Brigade, LA Militia
Moreno, Jose Maria-1st Sgt. 1st Company H, 33rd TX Cavalry
Moreno, Joseph F.-Pvt. Company A, 6th LA Cavalry
Moreno, L.H.-Pvt. Company C, 25th LA Infantry
Moreno, Leandro-Pvt. Company F, 3rd TX Infantry
Moreno, Manuel-Pvt. Company C, 3rd TX Infantry
Moreno, N.-Pvt. Company G, 8th TX Infantry
Moreno, Rafael-Pvt. Company C, 3rd TX Infantry
Moreno, Stephen Anastasium-Major 17th ALA Infantry. He also served as Assistant Adjutant General, Staff of General G.P. Harrison, GA and General J.K. Jackson.
Moreno, Segundo-Pvt. 1st Company I, 33rd TX Cavalry
Moreno, Theodore J.-Major / Engineering Officer, Staff of General Beauregard and General Cobb Gardner.
Moreno, Tomas-Pvt. Duff's Regiment, TX Cavalry
Moreno, Ylario-Pvt. 1st Company I, 33rd TX Cavalry
Moreno, Ynes-Pvt. Company I, 27th LA Infantry
Moret, Pedro-Pvt. Co. 6, 5th (Spanish) Regiment, European Brigade, LA Militia
Morillo, Ysidro-Pvt. Minute Men (Scouts), Starr County, TX Militia
Morin, J.M.-Pvt. Company D, 8th TX Infantry
Moris, Benito-Pvt. Co. 3, 5th (Spanish) Regiment, European Brigade, LA Militia
Morito, J.B.-Pvt. Company F, 3rd LA Infantry
Moro, E.-Pvt. Company I, 18th LA Infantry
Moro, Lewis-Pvt. Company E, 19th TX Infantry
Morreno, Julius-Musician Company E, 16th LA Infantry
*** See also the De Leon, Moise and Levy surnames
Moses, Andrew Jackson-Pvt. / Scout Company B, 5th Battalion, S.C. Reserve
Moses, David L. De Leon-Pvt. Company C, 3rd Palmetto Battn., S.C. Light Arty.
Moses, Henry Claremont-1st Lt. Company B, 15th Lucas' S.C. Light Artillery
Moses, Joshua Lazarus-1st Lt. Co. C, 3rd Palmetto Battalion, S.C. Light Artillery
Moses, M.-Pvt. Company A, Charleston Guard, S.C. Militia
Moses, Meyer B.-QuarterMaster Sgt. Company D, 2nd S.C. Infantry
Moses, Oliver Hazard Perry De Leon Jr.-2nd Lt. Company C, 3rd Palmetto Battn., S.C. Light Artillery
Moses, Rafael J. Sr.-Major / Chief of Commissary, General Longstreet. He was later Chief Commissary for Georgia.
Mosos, Andre-Pvt. 1st LA Heavy Artillery
Moya, Blas-Pvt. Company H, 8th TX Infantry
Muguerza, Pedro-Pvt. Company I, Benavides' Regiment, TX Cavalry
Munguia, Anastacio-Pvt. Company C, 8th TX Infantry
Munguia, Epifanio-Pvt. Thomas' Company, TX Partisan Rangers
Munguia, Francisco-Pvt. Thomas' Company, TX Partisan Rangers

Munguia, Jacinto-Pvt. Thomas' Company, TX Partisan Rangers
Munguia, Jesus-Pvt. Thomas' Company, TX Partisan Rangers
Munguia, Nepomenceno-Pvt. Thomas' Company, TX Partisan Rangers
Munguia, Pedro-Pvt. Thomas' Company, TX Partisan Rangers
Munguia, Ramon-Pvt. Thomas' Company, TX Partisan Rangers
Munes, F.-Pvt. Company A, 1st TX State Troops
Munez Polo, Bonifacio-Pvt. Co. 6, 5th (Span.) Regt., European Brigade, LA Mil.
Munis, S.-Pvt. Company K, 5th MO Cavalry
Munos, Florencio-Pvt. 1st Company C, 3rd TX Infantry
Munos, Isidoro-Pvt. Medina Guards, Bexar County, TX Militia
Munos, Jose Maria-Pvt. Company H, 3rd TX Infantry
Munos, Jose Maria-Pvt. Company C, 8th TX Infantry
Munoz, Joseph-Pvt. Co. 2, 5th (Spanish) Regt., European Brigade, LA Militia
Munoz, Juan-Pvt. Company F, 3rd TX Infantry
Munoz, Luis-Pvt. McNeel's Coast Guards, TX Local Defense
Munoz, Pifano-Pvt. Company C, 8th TX Infantry
Murillo, Alejandro-Pvt. Jeff Davis Home Guard, Refugio County, TX Militia
Murillo, S.-Pvt. Teel's Company, TX State Troops
Musquez, Secundino-Pvt. Company C, 8th TX Infantry
Musquita, Manuel-Pvt. Company D, 13th LA Infantry

N

Naba, Manuel-Pvt. Company 5, Cazadores Espanoles Regiment, LA Militia
Naibara, Rodriguez-Sgt. Company F, Benavides' Regiment, TX Cavalry
Nanez, J.M.-Major / Staff of General Longstreet
Nanez, Leandro-Pvt. Company F, 3rd TX Infantry
Nara, L.P.-Pvt. Co. D, 2nd Regiment, Confederate Engineer Troops
Nara, Martin-Pvt. LA Militia
Naras, J.-Pvt. Co. 1, 5th (Spanish) Regiment, European Brigade, LA Militia
Nardena, Raphael-Pvt. Consolidated Crescent Regiment, LA Infantry
Nardio, Antonio-Pvt. Co. 10, 5th (Spanish) Regt., European Brigade, LA Militia
Natan, Francisco-Pvt. Co. 6, 5th (Spanish) Regt., European Brigade, LA Militia
Navaro, Louis-Pvt. Mallory's Company, VIR Local Defense
Navaro, Peter-Pvt. Company B, 7th ARK Infantry
Navarra, Encarnacion-Pvt. Company D, 35th Brauns' TX Cavalry
Navarro, Alejandro-Pvt. 1st Company H, 33rd TX Cavalry
Navarro, Angel-Capt. Atascosa County, TX Militia
Navarro, Celso C.-Sgt. Company H, 8th TX Infantry
Navarro, Cresencio-Pvt. Company H, 36th TX Cavalry
Navarro, E.-Pvt. Duff's Company, Bexar County, TX Militia
Navarro, Eugenio-1st Lt. Company K, 6th/15th Consolidated TX Infantry
Navarro, Jesus-Pvt. Jeff Davis Home Guard, Refugio County, TX Militia
Navarro, Jose Angel-Capt. Company H, 8th TX Infantry
Navarro, Jose Antonio G.-1st Lt. Mitchell's Company, Bexar County, TX Mil.

Navarro, Juan-Pvt. 1st Company I, 33rd TX Cavalry
Navarro, Lino-Pvt. Jeff Davis Home Guard, Refugio County, TX Militia
Navarro, Mauricio-Pvt. Company C, Benavides' Regiment, TX Cavalry
Navarro, Rodrigo-Pvt. TX Militia
Navarro, Santiago-Pvt. Company G, 10th LA Infantry
Navarro, Sexto E.-Capt. Company H, 8th TX Infantry
Navarro, Valentin-Cpl. Company C, 8th TX Infantry
Navarro, Valentin-Pvt. Company G, 3rd TX Infantry
Navas, M.-Pvt. Co. 1, 5th (Spanish) Regiment, European Brigade, LA Militia
Navero, Rafael-Pvt. Company B, 1st LA Infantry
Naves, Robert A.-Pvt. Company E, 1st Orr's Rifles S.C. Infantry
Negroto, Domingo-Pvt. Co. 5, 5th (Spanish) Regt., European Brigade, LA Militia
Neira, Pedro Fernandez-Cpl. Co. 8, 5th (Span.) Regt., European Brigade, LA Mil.
Neto, Jose-Pvt. Co. 4, 5th (Spanish) Regiment, European Brigade, LA Militia
Netto, Francisco-Sgt. Company G, 21st ALA Infantry
***See also Nunes, Nunez
Newnez, J.M.-Pvt. Company K, 12th Robinson's Cavalry State Guards, GA
Newnis, Dean-Pvt. Company I, 41st GA Infantry
Newnis, James A.-Pvt. Company E, Cobb's Legion, GA
Newnos, George N.-Pvt. Company A, 2nd Battalion, GA Sharpshooters
Nicolan, Jose-Pvt. Company G, 21st ALA Infantry
Nicolas, Antonio-Pvt. Co. I, 3rd Regiment, 2nd Brigade, 1st Division, LA Militia
Nicolas, G.-Pvt. Company G, 21st ALA Infantry
Nicolas, Juan-Pvt. Co. 3, 5th (Spanish) Regiment, European Brigade, LA Militia
Nieto, Andres-Pvt. Company A, 3rd TX Infantry
Nieto, Andrew-Pvt. 1st Company A, 1st MD Cavalry
Nieto, Ilario-Pvt. Company D, 35th Brown's TX Cavalry
Nieves, Olivera-Pvt. Company F, 3rd TX Infantry
Noda, Joseph-Pvt. Company I, 10th FLA Infantry
Nodal, P.-Pvt. Co. 1, 5th (Spanish) Regiment, European Brigade, LA Militia
Noel, Evaristo-Pvt. Company H, 30th LA Infantry
Noel, Marcial-Pvt. Company A, 28th Thomas' LA Infantry
Nogueira, Adel Valle-Pvt. Co. 5, 5th (Spanish) Regt., European Brigade, LA Mil.
Nogues, A.-Pvt. Company 7, 3rd Regiment, French Brigade, LA Militia
Nogues, F.-Pvt. Company 4, 3rd Regiment, French Brigade, LA Militia
Nogues, James-Pvt. Company G, 21st TX Cavalry
Nogues, John-Pvt. Orange City Coast Guard, TX Militia
Noguis, Charles-Pvt. Company B, 14th LA Infantry
Noriega, Manuel-Pvt. Co. 2, 5th (Spanish) Regt., European Brigade, LA Militia
***See also Newnez, Newnis
Nunes, L.-Pvt. Pointe Coupee Artillery, LA
Nunes, R.-Pvt. Company B, Pointe Coupee Artillery, LA
Nunes, M.-Pvt. Trevinio's Company, TX Cavalry
Nunez, Adrien-State Legislator Vermillion Parish, LA elected in 1860 to 1862.
Nunez, Alexander-Pvt. Company A, 50th GA Infantry

Nunez, Cleofas-Pvt. Company H, 3rd TX Infantry
Nunez, Coleman M.-Pvt. Company K, 26th GA Infantry
Nunez, Daniel G.-Pvt. Company C, 50th GA Infantry
Nunez, Demosthene-Pvt. / Courier Company E, 33rd LA Infantry
Nunez, Domartin-Pvt. LA Reserve Corps
Nunez, Felix-2nd Lt. Company H, Crescent Regiment, LA Infantry
Nunez, Felix E.-Pvt. Company B, 18th Consolidated LA Infantry
Nunez, George W.-Pvt. Company B, 54th GA Infantry
Nunez, H.A.-Pvt. Baldwin County Home Guard, ALA Militia
Nunez, Jasper V.-Pvt. Company G, 1st Symons' GA Reserve
Nunez, Jose-2nd Lt. Company E, Yellow Jacket Battalion, LA Infantry
Nunez, Jose Maria-Cpl. 1st Company I, 33rd TX Cavalry
Nunez, Joseph-Lt. LA Artillery
Nunez, Joseph S.-Pvt. Company E, 33rd LA Infantry
Nunez, L.-Pvt. Company B, 22nd LA Infantry
Nunez, L.-Cpl. Company K, Orleans Guard Regiment, LA Militia
Nunez, Leandro-Pvt. Company F, 3rd TX Infantry
Nunez, M.-Pvt. Trevinio's Company, TX Partisan Rangers
Nunez, Manuel-Cpl. Co. 8, 5th (Spanish) Regiment, European Brigade, LA Militia
Nunez, Mauricio-Pvt. Co. 8, 5th (Spanish) Regt., European Brigade, LA Militia
Nunez, Israel Moses-Pvt. Parker's Company, VIR Light Artillery
Nunez, Phillip H.-Sgt. Company H, 48th GA Infantry
Nunez, Robert Flournoy-Capt. Company B, 7th FLA Infantry
Nunez, W.-Pvt. Trevinio's Company, TX Cavalry
Nunez, William P.-Pvt. Company K, 26th GA Infantry
Nunis, Benjamin W.-Musician Company E, 13th ALA Infantry
Nunis, Samuel-Musician Company E, 13th ALA Infantry
Nuno, J.-Pvt. Company C, 2nd Battalion, GA Infantry
Nuza, Francisco-Pvt. Co. 3, 5th (Spanish) Regt., European Brigade, LA Militia

O

Ochandiano, Hilario-Pvt. Company B, Confederate States Zouave Battalion, LA
*** See also Trevino De Ochoa
Ochoa, Andres-Pvt. TX Militia
Ochoa, Cornelio-Pvt. Thomas' Company, TX Partisan Rangers
Ochoa, Encarnacion-Pvt. TX Militia
Ochoa, Francisco-Pvt. 1st Company H, 33rd TX Cavalry
Ochoa, Huncancian-Pvt. Company I, Benavides' Regiment, TX Cavalry
Ochoa, Jacinto-Pvt. Company I, Benavides' Regiment, TX Cavalry
Ochoa, Nator-Pvt. Thomas' Company, TX Partisan Rangers
Ochoa, Nicolas-Pvt. Thomas' Company, TX Partisan Rangers
Ochoa, Pacifico-Pvt. Thomas' Company, TX Partisan Rangers
Ojca, Antonio-Pvt. Company 5, Cazadores Espanoles Regiment, LA Militia
Ojca, Hilario-Pvt. Company 5, Cazadores Espanoles Regiment, LA Militia

Ojos, Francisco-1st Cpl. Medina Guards, Bexar County, TX Militia
Olbera, Antonio-Pvt. Company I, 33rd TX Cavalry
Olbera, Jose Maria-Pvt. Company I, 33rd TX Cavalry
Olbera, Lorenzo-Pvt. Zapata's Company, Nueces County, TX State Troops
Olevari, Pablo-Cpl. Company H, 8th TX Infantry
Olevari, Trinidad-Pvt. Company H, 8th TX Infantry
Olgin, Esmerigildo-Cpl. Company C, Benavides' Regiment, TX Cavalry
Olguin, Pedro-Pvt. Company E, 8th Hobby's TX Infantry
Olias, Valentine-Pvt. Company G, 3rd S.C. Cavalry
*** See also Juan Auliva
Oliva, Antonio-Pvt. Company H, 3rd TX Infantry
Oliva, Carpio-Pvt. Co. A, 5th (Spanish) Regiment, European Brigade, LA Militia
Olivan, Lucas-Pvt. Company F, 13th LA Infantry
Olivares, Agapito-Pvt. Thomas' Company, TX Partisan Rangers
Olivares, Leonardo-Pvt. Minute Men (Scouts), Starr County, TX Militia
Olivares, Matias-Pvt. Medina Guards, Bexar County, TX Militia
Olivares, Narcisco-Pvt. Zapata's Company, Nueces County, TX State Troops
Olivares, Pablo-Pvt. Company B, 2nd TX Mounted Rifles
Olivares, Polinario-Pvt. Zapata's Company, Nueces County, TX State Troops
Olivares, Rafael-Bugler 1st Company H, 33rd TX Cavalry
Olivari, Bartol-Pvt. Company F, Cazadores Espanoles Regiment, LA Militia
Olivari, Paulo-Pvt. Company B, 2nd TX Cavalry
Oliveira, William D.-Pvt. Company F, 25th GA Infantry
Olivera, Nieves-Pvt. Company F, 3rd TX Infantry
Olivera, Pedro-Pvt. Company D, 30th LA Infantry
Olivera, W.P.-1st Sgt. Company B, 5th LA Cavalry
Oliveras, Celestin-Pvt. Company B, 8th LA Infantry
Oliveros, B.F.-Pvt. Company H, 2nd FLA Cavalry
Oliveros, Esidro J.-1st Lt. Company A, 57th GA Infantry
Oliveros, J.B.-Lt. Colonel 1st Battalion, GA State Guards
Ollos, Francisco-Pvt. Company B, 2nd TX Infantry
Olmos, Vincente-Pvt. Company I, 2nd TX Cavalry
Oluez, Pedro-Pvt. Company D, 30th LA Infantry
***The Surname Oncal / Oncale is the Louisiana French version of the surname Juncal
Oncal, Dosilien-Pvt. Company B, 1st LA Heavy Artillery
Oncale, Jean-Pvt. Company H, 2nd LA Cavalry
Orato, Estevan-Pvt. Co. 7, 5th (Spanish) Regt., European Brigade, LA Militia
***This is the Louisiana French version of the surname Ordonez
Ordenan, John-Pvt. Company H, 26th LA Infantry
Ordogne, Joseph-Pvt. Lafourche Regiment, LA Militia
Ordone, Emile-Pvt. Lafourche Regiment, LA Militia
Oreri, Manuel-Pvt. Company 2, Cazadores Espanoles Regiment, LA Militia
Oreste, D.-Pvt. LA Militia
Orfila, Francisco-Cpl. Co. 7, 5th (Spanish) Regt., European Brigade, LA Militia
Orfila, Juan-Sgt. Co. 5, 5th (Spanish) Regiment, European Brigade, LA Militia

Orfila > see also Pons Orfila, Jayme
***Also spelled Oriango
Oriego, Bruno-Pvt. Company B, Ragsdale's Battalion, TX Cavalry
Oriego, Juan-Pvt. Company B, Ragsdale's Battalion, TX Cavalry
Origuela, E.-Pvt. Co. 1, 5th (Spanish) Regiment, European Brigade, LA Militia
Oriol > See Puig y Oriol
Orosco, S.-Pvt. Trevinio's Company, TX Cavalry
Orosco, Y.-Pvt. Trevinio's Company, TX Cavalry
Ors, Manuel-Pvt. Co. 10, 5th (Spanish) Regiment, European Brigade, LA Militia
Ortago, A.J.-Pvt. Company G, 18th Consolidated LA Infantry
Ortagus, John-Pvt. Company A, 2nd FLA Infantry
Ortagus, Peter-Pvt. Pickett's Company, FLA Cavalry
Ortega, Narciso-Pvt. Company I, Benavides' Regiment, TX Cavalry
Ortegas, Ignedis-Pvt. Acosta's Milton Artillery, FLA
Ortegas, Prudencio-Pvt. Company A, 3rd FLA Infantry
Ortego, Alcide-Pvt. Company G, 18th Consolidated LA Infantry
Ortego, Alcide J.-Pvt. Company K, 28th Thomas' LA Infantry
Ortego, Aristide-Pvt. Company I, 2nd LA Reserve Corps
Ortego, Aristide J.-Pvt. Company B, 8th LA Cavalry
Ortego, Aristile-Pvt. Company K, 3rd Harrison's LA Cavalry
Ortego, Atanas-Pvt. Company I, 2nd LA Reserve Corps
Ortego, Dorcino-Pvt. Company K, 3rd Harrison's LA Cavalry
Ortego, Edmond-Pvt. Company H, Miles' Legion, LA
Ortego, Emile Augustin-Pvt. Company K, 16th LA Infantry
Ortego, Jean Baptiste-Pvt. Company K, 3rd Harrison's LA Cavalry
Ortego, Joachim-Sgt. Company I, 2nd LA Reserve Corps
Ortego, John B.-Pvt. Company I, 2nd LA Reserve Corps
Oretgo, Joseph Sosthene-Pvt. Company H, Miles' Legion, LA
Ortego, Valmon-Pvt. Company H, Miles' Legion, LA
Ortegon, Eduardo-Pvt. Bustillo's Company, Bexar County, TX Militia
Ortegus, Gregorie-Pvt. Locoul's Company, 30th LA Infantry
Ortejon, Jose-Pvt. Davis' Company, Confederate Light Artillery
Ortez, Antonio-Pvt. Company B, Waul's Legion, TX
Ortez, B.-Pvt. Trevinio's Company, TX Cavalry
Ortez, Jesus-Pvt. Company D, Benavides' Regiment, TX Cavalry
Ortez, Joachin A.-Pvt. Company C, 9th Battalion, GA Artillery
Ortez, Juan Jose-Pvt. Company B, Benavides' Regiment, TX Cavalry
Ortez, Luz-Pvt. Company D, Benavides' Regiment, TX Cavalry
Ortez, Manuel-Pvt. Co. 7, 5th (Spanish) Regt., European Brigade, LA Militia
Ortez, Martin-Pvt. Company C, Benavides' Regiment, TX Cavalry
Ortez, Miguel-Pvt. Company F, 16th TX Infantry
Ortez, Pedro-Pvt. Company D, Benavides' Regiment, TX Cavalry
Ortis, A.-Pvt. Company A, 2nd Battalion, LA Heavy Artillery
Ortis, Andre-Pvt. Company G, 28th Grays' LA Infantry
Ortis, Antonio-Pvt. Company I, 8th TX Infantry

Ortis, Emile-Pvt. Company H, 11th LA Infantry
Ortis, John-Pvt. Company D, 4th LA Infantry
Ortis, Juan Antonio-Pvt. Company I, 8th TX Infantry
Ortis, Juan Jose-Pvt. 1st Company I, 33rd TX Cavalry
Ortis, Jules-Pvt. Company D, 4th LA Infantry
Ortis, M.-Pvt. Company D, Benavides' Regiment, TX Cavalry
Ortis, Phillipe-Pvt. Company A, Mann's Battalion, TX Cavalry
Ortis, Selso-Pvt. Company A, Mann's Battalion, TX Cavalry
Ortis, Serpano-Pvt. Company D, 3rd TX Infantry
Ortis, Zaul-Pvt. Company K, 20th LA Infantry
Ortis, Zemon-Pvt. Company I, 11th LA Infantry
Ortiz, Esmergildo-Cpl. Rhodes' Company, 3rd Yager's TX Cavalry
Ortiz, Estanislaus-Pvt. 1st Company A, 3rd TX Infantry
Ortiz, Jesus-Pvt. 1st Company A, Ragsdale's Battalion, TX Cavalry
Ortiz, Jose-Pvt. Co. 2, 5th (Spanish) Regiment, European Brigade, LA Militia
Ortiz, Juan-Pvt. 1st Company C, Ragsdale's Battalion, TX Cavalry
Ortiz, Lujan-Pvt. Victoria County Militia, TX
Ortiz, Luz-Pvt. 1st Company A, Ragsdale's Battalion, TX Cavalry
Ortiz, Monico-Sgt. 1st Company A, Ragsdale's Battalion, TX Cavalry
Ortiz, P.-Pvt. Victoria County Militia, TX
Ortiz, Pedro-Pvt. 1st Company A, Ragsdale's Battalion, TX Cavalry
Ortiz, R.-Pvt. Victoria County Militia, TX
Ortiz, Rafael-Pvt. 1st Company C, Ragsdale's Battalion, TX Cavalry
Ortiz, S.-Pvt. Victoria County Militia, TX
Ortiz, Victor-Cpl. Rhodes' Company, 3rd Yager's TX Cavalry
Osuna, Guadalupe-Cpl. Company E, Ragsdale's Battalion, TX Cavalry
Osuna, Hilario-Sgt. Company F, 3rd TX Infantry
Osuna, Victor-Cpl. Rhodes' Company, 3rd Yager's TX Cavalry
Osuna, Viviano-Pvt. Bustillo's Company, Bexar County, TX Militia
Otera, Juaquin-Pvt. Company 1, Cazadores Espanoles Regiment, LA Militia
Otero, B.-Capt. Otero's Titterton's Guards, LA Militia
Otero, Jose-Cpl. Co. 4, 5th (Spanish) Regiment, European Brigade, LA Militia
Ottolengui, Daniel-Pvt. Company I, 1st Regiment, Charleston Guard, SC
Ottolengui, Israel-1st Lt. Company I, 1st Regiment, Charleston Guard, SC
Oyo, John-Pvt. Company F, 16th TX Infantry
Oyos, Francis-Pvt. Company B, 2nd TX Cavalry
Ozaga, Juan-Pvt. Co. A, 5th (Spanish) Regiment, European Brigade, LA Militia
Ozos, Simon-Pvt. 1st Company A, Ragsdale's Battalion, TX Cavalry

P

Pa, Anselmo-Pvt. Co. A, 5th (Spanish) Regiment, European Brigade, LA Militia
Pablo, Jose-Pvt. Co. 5, 5th (Spanish) Regiment, European Brigade, LA Militia
Pablo, Jose-Pvt. Company 6, 12th TX Infantry
Pablo, Pedro-Pvt. Co. 4, 5th (Spanish) Regiment, European Brigade, LA Militia

Hispanic Confederates 101

Pablo, Sebastian-Pvt. Co. 5, 5th (Spanish) Regt., European Brigade, LA Militia
Pacetti, Albert-Pvt. Company B, 3rd FLA Infantry
Pacetti, Alexander-Pvt. Company B, 54th GA Infantry
Pacetti, Andrew B.-Pvt. Company K, 63rd GA Infantry
Pacetti, B.A.-Pvt. Company H, 5th Battalion, FLA Cavalry
Pacetti, Bartolo-Pvt. Company D, 8th FLA Infantry
Pacetti, Bartolo J.-Pvt. Company B, 3rd FLA Infantry
Pacetti, D.B.-Pvt. Company C, 4th Clinch's GA Cavalry
Pacetti, Dennis-Pvt. Company D, 8th FLA Infantry
Pacetti, Dennis J.-Pvt. Company H, 3rd FLA Infantry
Pacetti, Dennis S.-Pvt. Company C, 18th Battalion, GA Infantry
Pacetti, Domingo Sr.-Pvt. Company H, 2nd FLA Cavalry
Pacetti, Edward-Pvt. Company D, 8th FLA Infantry
Pacetti, F.G.-Pvt. Company C, 18th Battalion, GA Infantry
Pacetti, Felix-Cpl. Company D, 8th FLA Infantry
Pacetti, G.-Pvt. Company K, 7th FLA Infantry. He escaped from Key West while it was in Union hands and made it to Confederate lines where he enlisted.
Pacetti, Hebert Albert-Pvt. Company B, 3rd FLA Infantry
Pacetti, John-Pvt. Company A, 26th GA Infantry
Pacetti, John N.-Pvt. Company C, 18th Battalion, GA Infantry
Pacetti, John T.-Pvt. Company C, 1st Olmstead's GA Infantry
Pacetti, Joseph A.-Pvt. Company B, 3rd FLA Infantry
Pacetti, Joseph Anthony-Capt. Company D, 8th FLA Infantry
Pacetti, Lewis N.-2nd Lt. Company K, 2nd FLA Infantry
Pacetti, Peter P.-Pvt. Company H, 2nd FLA Cavalry
Pacetti, Thomas-Confederate Spy in Baltimore, See also Naval Listing
Pacetti, Venancio-Pvt. Davis' Company, 1st Olmstead's GA Infantry
Pacheco, Alvino-Pvt. Company B, Ragsdale's Battalion, TX Cavalry
Pacheco, Fabian-Pvt. Company H, 8th TX Infantry
Pacheco, Felipe-Pvt. Rhodes' Company, 3rd Yager's TX Cavalry
Pacheco, Francisco-Pvt. Company B, Ragsdale's Battalion, TX Cavalry
Pacheco, Luciano-Pvt. Company F, 3rd TX Infantry
Pacheco, Martin-Musician Company F, 20th TX Infantry
Pachon, Jose Francisco-Pvt. Co. 8, 5th (Spanish) Regt., European Brigade, LA Mil.
Paderas, Theodore-Pvt. Company F, Orleans Fire Regiment, LA Militia
Padilla, Antonio-2nd Lt. Mexican Volunteers, C.S.A
Padilla, B.-Pvt. Company G, 3rd LA Infantry
Padilla, Jesus-1st Lt. Mexican Volunteers, C.S.A
Padilla, Juan Jose-Pvt. Company B, 28th LA Infantry
Padilla, Jose-Pvt. Medina Guards, Bexar County, TX Militia
Padron, Adolfo-Pvt. Co. 6, 5th (Spanish) Regt., European Brigade, LA Militia
Padron, Andre-Pvt. Company H, 15th Confederate Cavalry
Padron, David-Pvt. Company B, 17th TX Infantry
Padron, Felix-Pvt. Company B, 8th LA Infantry
Padron, Henry-1st Sgt. Saint Martin's Company, VIR Mounted Rifleman

Pagana, Sebastiano-Pvt. Company F, Cazadores Espanoles Regiment, LA Militia
Pagua, I.-Pvt. B.H. Smith's Company, VIR Artillery
Pajes, Jose-Pvt. Co. 2, 5th (Spanish) Regiment, European Brigade, LA Militia
Palacio, Diego-Pvt. 8th TX Field Battery
Palacio, Jesus-Pvt. TX Militia
Palacio, Leandro-Pvt. Ford's Regiment, TX Cavalry
Palacio, Necleto-Pvt. 8th Field Battery, TX Artillery
Palacios, Francisco-Pvt. Company G, 16th TX Infantry
Palau, Valentin-Pvt. Co. 3, 5th (Spanish) Regt., European Brigade, LA Militia
Pale, Jose-Cpl. Company F, 10th LA Infantry
Paliado, Ylario-Pvt. Company I, Benavides' Regiment, TX Cavalry
Palos, M.-Pvt. Co. 2, 5th (Spanish) Regiment, European Brigade, LA Militia
Palliser, Diego-Pvt. Company A, 2nd Regiment Volunteers, ALA Militia
Palliser, Gregorie-Sgt. Co. 7, 5th (Spanish) Regt., European Brigade, LA Militia
Pallisser, M.-Pvt. Company B, 1st Regiment, Charleston Reserve, S.C. Militia
Palmes, Manuel-Port Warden, Escambia County, FLA 1861.
Paluco, Juan-Pvt. Gray's Company, Bexar County, TX Militia
Pancho, Oyos-Pvt. Company B, 2nd TX Cavalry
Papy, Charles-Pvt. Company B, 7th FLA Infantry
Papy, Edward Ambrose-Pvt. Company B, 3rd FLA Infantry
Papy, Francisco Bartolo-Pvt. Co. M, 2nd FLA Inf. (there is also a F.B. Papy who is listed as a 1st Sgt. Leon Light Artillery, FLA, possibly same person).
Papy, Isadore B.-Musician Company B, 3rd FLA Infantry
Papy, John-Pvt. Company B, 3rd FLA Infantry
Papy, John C.-Pvt. Company K, 8th FLA Infantry
Papy, Joseph B.-Musician Company A, 3rd FLA Infantry
Papy, M.-Pvt. Company H, 2nd FLA Infantry
Papy, M.E.-Pvt. Company B, 17th SC Infantry
Papy, Mariano-State Attorney General, FLA 1861
Papy, Pablo Marin-Pvt. Company H, 2nd FLA Infantry
Parago, John-Bugler Company K, 24th TX Cavalry
Pardilla, B.-Pvt. Company G, 3rd LA Infantry
Pardo, Andre-Sgt. 1st Battery Regiment, Confederate Light Artillery
Pardo, A.J.-Pvt. Orleans Guard Battery, LA Light Artillery
Pardo, J.-Cpl. 1st Regiment Battery, Confederate Light Artillery
Pardo, James-Pvt. Company C, 1st Strawbridge's LA Infantry
Pardo, Joseph-2nd Lt. Company C, 15th LA Infantry
Parea, Herbaceo-Pvt. Company B, Ragsdale's Battalion, TX Cavalry
Paredes, Estevan-Pvt. Co. 5, 5th (Spanish) Regt., European Brigade, LA Militia
Paredes, Jesus-Pvt. 1st Company H, 33rd TX Cavalry
Paredes, Manuel-Pvt. 1st Company H, 33rd TX Cavalry
Pareno, Tamicus-Pvt. Company A, 3rd ALA Infantry
Paris, Anastacio-Pvt. Company I, 8th TX Infantry
Paris, Bernardo-Cpl. Co. 3, 5th (Spanish) Regt., European Brigade, LA Militia
Parodi, D.-Pvt. Company H, Orleans Fire Regiment, LA Militia

Parodi, Lorenzo-Cpl. Co. 5, 5th (Spanish) Regt., European Brigade, LA Militia
Parodi, Manuel-Musician Co. 5, Cazadores Espanoles Regiment, LA Militia
Parodi, Michael-Pvt. Company C, 1st Strawbridge's LA Infantry
Parpada, Antonio-Pvt. Company 2, Cazadores Espanoles Regiment, LA Militia
*** See also De Perez Parra
Parra, F.P.-Pvt. Company B, 22nd LA Infantry
Parra, Fernando-Pvt. Co. 9, 5th (Spanish) Regiment, European Brigade, LA Mil.
Parra, Joachin-1st Sgt. Co. 7, 5th (Spanish) Regt., European Brigade, LA Militia
Parra, Juan-2nd Lt. Co. 5, 5th (Spanish) Regiment, European Brigade, LA Militia
Parra, Michael-Sgt. Company F, 15th LA Infantry
Parras, Diego-Pvt. Co. 7, 5th (Spanish) Regiment, European Brigade, LA Militia
Parrera, J.-Pvt. 22nd Consolidated LA Infantry
Partella, Joachin-Pvt. Co. 8, 5th (Spanish) Regt., European Brigade, LA Militia
Partigas, Antonio-1st Lt. Co. 7, 5th (Spanish) Regt., European Brigade, LA Mil.
Pas, Cypriano-Pvt. Company K, 2nd TX Cavalry
Pasalagua, Henrico-Pvt. Company I, 10th LA Infantry
Pascual, Antonio-Pvt. Company D, 1st TX Heavy Artillery
Pascual, Cristobal-Pvt. Co. 9, 5th (Spanish) Regt., European Brigade, LA Militia
Pascual, Juan-Pvt. Co. 3, 5th (Spanish) Regiment, European Brigade, LA Militia
Pascual, Mariano-Pvt. Co. 9, 5th (Spanish) Regiment, European Brigade, LA Militia
Pascual, Pedro-Cpl. Co. A, 5th (Spanish) Regt., European Brigade, LA Militia
Pascual, S.-Pvt. Company G, 21st ALA Infantry
Pascual, Salvador-Pvt. Company D, 30th LA Infantry
Pastor, Millan-Pvt. Company 1, Cazadores Espanoles Regiment, LA Militia
Pastor, Roman-Pvt. Company E, 13th LA Infantry
Patria, J.-Pvt. Company 8, 1st Chasseurs a pied, LA Militia
Patriota, Pablo-Pvt. Co. 3, 5th (Spanish) Regiment, European Brigade, LA Mil.
Pattila, Jose G.-Pvt. Company G, 34th ALA Infantry
Payro, L.-Pvt. Co. 5, 5th (Spanish) Regiment, European Brigade, LA Militia
Pazo, F.-Cpl. / QMaster Co. 1, 5th (Spanish) Regt., European Brigade, LA Militia
Pederas, James-Pvt. Company F, Benavides' Regiment, TX Cavalry
***Also found as Pedrasa
Pedraso, Faustino-Pvt. Company C, 8th TX Infantry
Pedro, Jean-Pvt. Company I, 5th LA Infantry
Pedro, Joachin-Pvt. Company I, 10th LA Infantry
Pedro, Lewis-Pvt. Company C, Tucker's Regiment, Confederate Infantry
Pedro, Oliver-Pvt. Company D, 30th LA Infantry
Pedro, Samuel M.-2nd Lt. Morris' Company, Ferguson's Battalion, VIR Cavalry
Pedron, Andre-Pvt. Tobin's Company, TENN Light Artillery
***See also Puxotto
Peixotto, Sol. C.-Pvt. Company A, 15th S.C. Infantry
Pelayo, Mariano-Pvt. Co. 9, 5th (Spanish) Regt., European Brigade, LA Militia
Pellicer, Anthony D.-Catholic Priest St. Mary's Hospital, Montgomery, ALA Mil.
Pellicer, James G.-1st Lt. Company D, 8th FLA Infantry
Pellicer, Paul Francis-Pvt. Company A, 2nd FLA Infantry

Pellicer, Peter-Pvt. Company H, 2nd FLA Cavalry
Pellize, Antonio-Pvt. Co. 10, 5th (Spanish) Regt., European Brigade, LA Militia
Pellon, Pablo-Pvt. Company F, 8th FLA Infantry
Pelloquin, Cesar-Pvt. Company A, Ragsdale's Battalion, TX Cavalry
Pena, A.-Cpl. Company 3, 1st Chasseurs a pied, LA Militia
Pena, Cenobio-Pvt. 1st Company H, 33rd TX Cavalry
Pena, Liberto-Pvt. Gray's Company, Bexar County, TX Militia
Pena, Luis-Pvt. 1st Company A, 3rd TX Infantry
Pena, Manuel-Pvt. Zapata's Company, Nueces County, TX State Troops
Pena, Modesto-Pvt. Company I, 2nd TX Infantry
Pena, Ramon-Pvt. Benavides' Regiment, TX Cavalry
Penagas, Anselmo-Pvt. Co. 2, 5th (Spanish) Regt., European Brigade, LA Militia
Penal, Francisco-Pvt. Co. 4, 5th (Spanish) Regt., European Brigade, LA Militia
Penal, Joseph-Pvt. Company K, 9th Young's TX Cavalry
Penaloza, Joseph M.-Capt. Company C, 8th TX Infantry
Penas, Charles-Pvt. 1st Native Guards, LA Militia
Pera, Rafael-Sgt. Co. 8, 5th (Spanish) Regiment, European Brigade, LA Militia
Perales, J.F.-Pvt. Company F, 3rd TX Infantry
Peralta, Francis E.-Pvt. Pointe Coupee Artillery, LA
Peralta, John-Sgt. Company A, 7th Battalion, LA Infantry
Peralto, J.-1st Lt. Company E, Confederate States Zouave Battalion, LA
Perat, J.-Pvt. Company D, Cazadores Espanoles Regiment, LA Militia
Perea, Herbacio-Pvt. Company B, Ragsdale's Battalion, TX Cavalry
Peredas, Santiago-Pvt. Co. C, 5th (Spanish) Regt., European Brigade, LA Militia
Pereira, Andres-Pvt. Company E, 28th Thomas' LA Infantry
Pereira, Antonio-Pvt. Co. 8, 5th (Spanish) Regt., European Brigade, LA Militia
Pereira, Jose-Pvt. Co. 8, 5th (Spanish) Regiment, European Brigade, LA Militia
Pereira, Joseph-Pvt. Kellersberg's Corps, Sappers / Miners C.S.A
Pereira, Madero-Pvt. Company B, Ragsdale's Battalion, TX Cavalry
Pereira, Manuel-Pvt. Co. 8, 5th (Spanish) Regt., European Brigade, LA Militia
Pereira, Manuel Soza-Pvt. Co. 8, 5th (Spanish) Regt., European Brigade, LA Mil.
Perer, Cayetano-Cpl. Company 5, Cazadores Espanoles Regiment, LA Militia
Perera, Manuel-Pvt. Company G, 3rd LA Infantry
Peres, A.-Pvt. Teel's Company, TX State Troops
Peres, B.-Pvt. Teel's Company, TX State Troops
Peres, C.-Pvt. Company 4, 3rd Regiment, French Brigade, LA Militia
Peres, Francisco-Pvt. 2nd Field Battery, TX Artillery
Peres, J.M.-Pvt. Trevinio's Company, TX Cavalry
Peres, J.P.-Pvt. Company 4, 4th Regiment, French Brigade, LA Militia
Peres, Jean Marie-Pvt. 18th LA Infantry
Peres, Jesus-Pvt. Thomas' Company, TX Partisan Rangers
Peres, Jesus-Pvt. Trevinio's Company, TX Cavalry
Peres, Joseph-Pvt. Company 7, 1st Regiment, French Brigade, LA Militia
Peres, Robert-Pvt. Company C, Benavides' Regiment, TX Cavalry
Peres, Stephen-Pvt. Bass' Company, 1st Regiment Mobile Volunteers, ALA

Pereyeo, Juan-Pvt. Co. 3, 5th (Spanish) Regiment, European Brigade, LA Militia
Perez, A.-Pvt. Donaldsonville Artillery, LA
Perez, A.-Pvt. 1st Native Guards, LA Militia
Perez, A.-Pvt. Company E, 33rd TX Cavalry
Perez, A.-Pvt. Company C, 8th TX Infantry
Perez, Alejo-Cpl. Company B, 2nd TX Cavalry
Perez, Angel-Pvt. Tom's Company, Atascosa County, TX State Troops
Perez, Antonio-Pvt. Co. 7, 5th (Spanish) Regiment, European Brigade, LA Mil.
Perez, Antonio-Pvt. Company H, 3rd TX Infantry
Perez, Agustin-Cpl. Co. 3, 5th (Spanish) Regiment, European Brigade, LA Mil.
Perez, B.-Pvt. Company 7, 1st Chasseurs a pied, LA Militia
Perez, B.-Pvt. Company I, 3rd Regiment, French Brigade, LA Militia
Perez, Benito-1st Sgt. Company F, 3rd TX Infantry
Perez, Cayetano-Cpl. Co. 6, 5th (Spanish) Regt., European Brigade, LA Militia
Perez, Cerbuelo-Pvt. Company H, 8th TX Infantry
Perez, Cerbola-Pvt. Company D, Benavides' Regiment, TX Cavalry
Perez, Desiderio-Pvt. Company B, 2nd TX Cavalry
Perez, Eugenio-Pvt. Company F, 3rd TX Infantry
Perez, Eusebio-Pvt. Company H, 8th TX Infantry
Perez, Francisco-Musician 2nd TX Mounted Rifles
Perez, Francois-Pvt. / Cannoneer Donaldsonville Artillery, LA
Perez, Guillermo-Pvt. Co. 4, 5th (Spanish) Regiment, European Brigade, LA Mil.
Perez, Ignacio-Pvt. Company D, Benavides' Regiment, TX Cavalry
Perez, J.M.-Pvt. Lartigue's Company, Bienville Guards, LA Militia
Perez, J. Mazio-Pvt. Company C, Benavides' Regiment, TX Cavalry
Perez, Jesus-Pvt. Medina Guards, Bexar County, TX Militia
Perez, Joachin-Pvt. Co. 9, 5th (Spanish) Regiment, European Brigade, LA Militia
Perez, Johnson-Pvt. Lartigue's Company, Bienville Guards, LA Militia
Perez, Jomas-Pvt. Company E, Benavides' Regiment, TX Cavalry
Perez Piloto, Jose-Pvt. Co. 2, 5th (Spanish) Regt., European Brigade, LA Militia
Perez, Jose Antonio-Pvt. Duran's Company, Atascosa County, TX Troops
Perez, Jose Maria-Pvt. Company H, 8th TX Infantry
Perez, Juan-3rd Sgt. Trevinio's Company, TX Partisan Rangers
Perez, L.-Sgt. Company 2, 5th (Spanish) Regiment, European Brigade, LA Mil.
Perez, M.-Pvt. Co. 1, 5th (Spanish) Regiment, European Brigade, LA Militia
Perez, Maleno-Pvt. Company E, 8th TX Infantry
Perez, Manuel-Pvt. Co. 9, 5th (Spanish) Regiment, European Brigade, LA Mil.
Perez, Martin-Pvt. Co. 6, 5th (Spanish) Regiment, European Brigade, LA Militia
Perez, Narciso-Pvt. Zapata's Company, Nueces County, TX Troops
Perez, Norberto-Pvt. Company C, 8th TX Infantry
Perez, Novuto-Pvt. Company C, Benavides' Regiment, TX Cavalry
Perez, Octave-Sgt. Lartigue's Company, Bienville Guards, LA Militia
Perez, Pablo-Pvt. Zapata's Company, Nueces County, TX Troops
Perez, Pedro-Pvt. Co. 6, 5th (Spanish) Regiment, European Brigade, LA Militia
Perez, Roman-Assistant Surgeon 3rd Regiment, French Brigade, LA Militia

Perez, Rosario-Pvt. Bustillo's Company, Bexar County, TX Militia
Perez, Sedro-Pvt. 1st Native Guards, LA Militia
Perez, Sylvester-Teamster Company H, 6th LA Cavalry
Perez, T.M.-Pvt. 1st Native Guards, LA Militia
Perez, Theodoro-Pvt. 1st Company A, 3rd TX Infantry
Perez, Thomas-2nd Lt. Duran's Company, Atascosa County, TX Troops
Perez, Tomas-Pvt. Company H, 8th TX Infantry
Perez, Valente-Pvt. Zapata's Company, Nueces County, TX State Troops
Perez, Valentin-Pvt. Co. 4, 5th (Spanish) Regiment, European Brigade, LA Mil.
Perez, Vincent-Pvt. Company B, 22nd LA Infantry
Perez, Viviano-Pvt. Ford's Regiment, TX Cavalry
Perez, Ygnacio-Pvt. 1st Company A, Ragsdale's Battalion, TX Cavalry
Perico, John-Pvt. Company H, 1st LA Heavy Artillery
Perico, Louis-Pvt. Compny D, 30th LA Infantry
Perido, Clovin-Pvt. Company C, Benavides' Regiment, TX Cavalry
Perillos, Jose Manuel-Pvt. Co 1, Cazadores Espanoles Regiment, LA Militia
***Unknown if this surname is Fernando or Hernando
Pernando, Bernardo-Pvt. Company 2, 8th Battalion, LA Heavy Artillery
Perpal, Charles F.-Musician Company A, 3rd FLA Infantry
Perpal, William O.-Musician Company A, 3rd FLA Infantry
Pessana, Antonio-Pvt. Company 5, Cazadores Espanoles Regiment, LA Militia
Pessica, Ferdinando-Pvt. Company D, 30th LA Infantry
Pico, Bartolome-Pvt. Co. 9, 5th (Spanish) Regt., European Brigade, LA Militia
Pico, Joshua Jr.-3rd Lt. Company C, Confederate Guards Regiment, LA Militia
Pidal, Jose B.-Pvt. Co. 4, 5th (Spanish) Regiment, European Brigade, LA Militia
Piere, J. Perez-Pvt. Co. 1, 5th (Spanish) Regiment, European Brigade, LA Militia
Piernas, Antoine-Pvt. 1st Native Guards, LA Militia
Pierra, Adolph-Sgt. Company C, 28th Thomas' LA Infantry
Pierra, Ramon-Pvt. Co. 2, 5th (Spanish) Regiment, European Brigade, LA Militia
Piloto > see Perez Piloto, Jose
Pina, Ramon-Pvt. Company D, Benavides' Regiment, TX Cavalry
Pino, Anthony-Pvt. Company K, 3rd LA Infantry
Pino, J.-Pvt. Washington Artillery Battalion, LA
Pino, J.A.C.-Pvt. Company A, Miles' Legion, LA
Pino, Joseph Anthony-Pvt. Company A, 8th LA Infantry
Pino, Lawrence-Pvt. Company B, 7th LA Infantry
Pino, Thomas-Pvt. Company B, 7th LA Infantry
Pinta, Henry-Pvt. 1st Native Guards, LA Militia
Pinto, Augustin-Pvt. Co. 6, 5th (Spanish) Regiment, European Brigade, LA Mil.
Pinto, Cristoval-Pvt. Company C, 3rd TX Infantry
Pinto, Joachin-Pvt. Co. 6, 5th Spanish) Regiment, European Brigade, LA Militia
Piseros, Alcee Felix-Pvt. Orleans Guard Battery, LA Light Artillery
Piseros, Lawrence J.-Pvt. Company A, 30th LA Infantry, detached on duty at Engineer's Office.
***Plaisance/Pleasance is the Louisiana French version of the surname Plasencia

Hispanic Confederates 107

Placiencia, Arsene-Pvt. 1st Native Guards, LA Militia
Plaisance, Dupre-Pvt. Company E, Miles' Legion, LA
Plaisance, Emile-Pvt. Company E, 10th Battalion, LA Infantry
Plaisance, H.-Pvt. Company C, 2nd LA Cavalry
Plaisance, Joseph-Pvt. Company G, 18th LA Infantry
Plaisance, M.P.-Pvt. Company D, 7th LA Cavalry
Plaisance, P.-Pvt. French Company of Saint James Parish, LA Militia
Plaisance, Usebe-Teamster / Pvt. Company G, 18th LA Infantry
Plaisencia, Augustin-Pvt. Company H, 28th LA Infantry
Plasencia, Narcisse-Pvt. Landry's Company, Donaldsonville Artillery, LA
Pleasance, Philip-Pvt. Lafourche Regiment, LA Militia
Pleasance, Raymond-Pvt. Lafourche Regiment, LA Militia
Planas, Jose-Pvt. Co. 4, 5th (Spanish) Regiment, European Brigade, LA Militia
Planas, Manuel-Pvt. Co. 6, 5th (Spanish) Regiment, European Brigade, LA Mil.
Planella, Juan-1st Sgt. Company 1, Cazadores Espanoles Regiment, LA Militia
Planellas, Vicente-1st Lt. Company 1, Cazadores Espanoles Regiment, LA Mil.
Plaza, C.A.-Pvt. Company I, 30th ALA Infantry
Plaza, Bicente-Pvt. / Blacksmith Company A, Benavides' Regiment, TX Cavalry
Plaza, Emanuel-Pvt. ALA Militia
Polanco, Manuel-Pvt. Company H, 8th TX Infantry
Polinares, Victor-Pvt. Company C, 3rd TX Infantry
Pol > see Pol in Naval Section
Polo > see Munez Polo, Bonifacio
Pomar, Cristobal-Gun Smith, He assisted the Confederate Forces/Militia of Saint Augustine, FLA.
Pomar, Joseph-Pvt. Company G, 1st Olmstead's GA Infantry
Pomar, Peter-Pvt. Company I, 10th FLA Infantry
Pomar, William-Pvt. Company B, 3rd FLA Infantry
Ponce, Anthony-Pvt. Company B, 3rd FLA Infantry
Ponce, Antonio Jr.-Pvt. Company H, 1st Olmstead's GA Infantry
Ponce, Bartolo D.-Sgt. Company B, 3rd FLA Infantry
Ponce, Dimas R.-1st. Lt. Company I, 5th TX Infantry
Ponce, Isadora B.-Pvt. Company B, 3rd FLA Infantry
Ponce, Jacob-Pvt. / Teamster Company I, 6th KY Cavalry
Ponce, James-Pvt. Company B, 3rd FLA Infantry
Ponce, James B.-Sgt. Company D, 8th FLA Infantry
Ponce, John-Pvt. Company A, 3rd FLA Infantry
Ponce, Nicolas-Sgt. Company D, 12th TX Cavalry
Ponce, Paul-Pvt. Company D, 14th LA Infantry
Ponce, Thomas-Pvt. Company B, 3rd FLA Infantry
Ponce, Tolomy-Pvt. Company I, 10th FLA Infantry
Ponce, William G.-Cpl. Company I, 10th FLA Infantry
Ponciana, John-Pvt. Company D, 9th TX Cavalry
Ponjuan, M.-Pvt. Co. 1, 5th (Spanish) Regiment, European Brigade, LA Militia
Pons, A.-Pvt. Company I, Orleans Guard Regiment, LA Militia

Pons Valencia, A.-Capt. Co. 3, 5th (Spanish) Regt., European Brigade, LA Mil.
Pons, Antonio-Pvt. Company E, 3rd VIR Infantry
Pons, Antonio-Pvt. Co. 9, 5th (Spanish) Regiment, European Brigade, LA Militia
Pons, Bartolomew-Pvt. Company A, 3rd MISS Infantry
Pons, Benito-Pvt. Co. 4, 5th (Spanish) Regiment, European Brigade, LA Militia
Pons, E.-Pvt. Company G, 1st Junior Reserve N.C. Infantry
Pons, Estanislao-Cpl. Company 2, Cazadores Espanoles Regiment, LA Militia
Pons, H.-Pvt. Company 6, 3rd Regiment, French Brigade, LA Militia
Pons, J. Gomila-Pvt. Co. 1, 5th (Spanish) Regt., European Brigade, LA Militia
Pons Orfila, Jayme-Pvt. Co. 3, 5th (Spanish) Regt., European Brigade, LA Militia
Pons Valencia, Jayme-Cpl. Co. 3, 5th (Spanish) Regt., European Brigade, LA Mil.
Pons, James-Pvt. Company E, 7th LA Infantry
Pons, John M.-Lt. Colonel 8th FLA Infantry
Pons, Jose-Pvt. Company 3, 5th (Spanish) Regiment, European Brig., LA Militia
Pons, Joseph Francis-Capt. Company D, 1st FLA Cavalry
Pons, Juan-Pvt. Co. 4, 5th (Spanish) Regiment, European Brigade, LA Militia
Pons, Jules-Pvt. Company E, 1st Strawbridge's LA Infantry
Pons, Julius-Pvt. Company F, 21st Kennedy's LA Infantry
Pons, M.-Pvt. Co. 1, 5th (Spanish) Regiment, European Brigade, LA Militia
Pons, P.A.-Pvt. Company A, 3rd MISS Infantry
Pons, Pablo-Capt. Company G, Cazadores Espanoles Regiment, LA Militia
Pons, Pedro-Pvt. Co. 3, 5th (Spanish) Regiment, European Brigade, LA Militia
Pons, Richard-Pvt. Company D, 14th LA Infantry
Ponsel, John-Pvt. Company F, 2nd TX Infantry
Ponselin, Emilio-Pvt. Company 5, Cazadores Espanoles Regiment, LA Militia
Ponset, Paul-Pvt. Company E, 2nd Regiment, ALA Infantry
Ponsets, G.-Pvt. Co. 1, 5th (Spanish) Regiment, European Brigade, LA Militia
Pontero, Charles-Pvt. Company L, 44th MISS Infantry
Porras, Jesus-Cpl. Trevinio's Squad, TX Partisan Mounted Volunteers
Portal, A.J.-Pvt. Company B, 10th Battalion, LA Infantry
Porto, Frank-Pvt. Co. 5th (Spanish) Regiment, European Brigade, LA Militia
Postillo, Edwardo-Pvt. Company D, 3rd TX Infantry
Postillo, Leonardo-Pvt. Company D, 3rd TX Infantry
Pradas, V.-Sgt. Company A, Orleans Guard Regiment, LA Militia
Praderes, A.-Pvt. Jackson Rifle Battalion, LA Militia
Pradhos, John-Pvt. 18th LA Infantry
Prado, Locario-Pvt. Company A, 11th TX Infantry
Prados, A.-Pvt. Orleans Guard Battery, LA Light Artillery
Prados, A. Jr.-Sgt. Company A, Orleans Guard Regiment, LA Militia
Prados, Anthony J.-Capt. Co. C, 3rd Regt., 2nd Brigade, 1st Division, LA Militia
Prados, Arthur A.-Pvt. Company K, 21st ALA Infantry
Prados, C.-Pvt. 1st Native Guards, LA Militia
Prados, John B.-Major 8th LA Infantry
Prados, John S.-Major / QuarterMaster, C.S.A.
Prados, Joseph-Pvt. Green's Company, LA Guard Battery

Prados, Louis-Capt. Company B, 8th LA Infantry
Prados, Victor-4th Sgt. Orleans Guard Regiment, LA Militia
Prats, B.-Pvt. Company 2, 5th (Spanish) Regiment, European Brigade, LA Mil.
Prats, Gabriel-Pvt. Co. 4, 5th (Spanish) Regiment, European Brigade, LA Militia
Prats, Jayme-Pvt. Co. 4, 5th (Spanish) Regiment, European Brigade, LA Militia
Prats, John-Pvt. Co. 2, 5th (Spanish) Regiment, European Brigade, LA Militia
Prats, Leon-Pvt. Company D, Orleans Guard Regiment, LA Militia
Prats, Vicente-Pvt. Co. 5, 5th (Spanish) Regiment, European Brigade, LA Militia
Precilla, H.-Pvt. Company F, Waul's Legion, TX
Precilla, Lope-Pvt. Company B, Maddox's Regiment, LA Reserve Corps
Pretto, David-Sgt. Confederate States Guards Regiment, LA Militia
Pretto, Manuel-Pvt. Orleans Guard Battery, LA Light Artillery
Pretus, E.-Sgt. Company 2, 5th (Spanish) Regiment, European Brigade, LA Mil.
Pretus, Matias-Pvt. Co. 5, 5th (Spanish) Regiment, European Brigade, LA Mil.
Pretus, Pedro-Pvt. Co. 7, 5th (Spanish) Regiment, European Brigade, LA Militia
Pretus, Vicente-Pvt. Co. 7, 5th (Spanish) Regiment, European Brigade, LA Mil.
Primo, Manuel-Hospital Steward, C.S.A., LA
Prieto, Francisco-Sgt. Co. 10, 5th (Spanish) Regiment, European Brigade, LA Mil.
*** The surnames below are all variations of the surname Procela/Procella, as found in the Louisiana Adaeseno settlements (see also Precilla).
Procell, J.-Pvt. Company E, Pelican Regiment, LA Infantry
Procell, Phillip-Pvt. Company B, 28th LA Infantry
Procell, Philma-Pvt. Company H, 19th LA Infantry
Procell, Samuel (1st)-Pvt. Company H, 19th LA Infantry
Procell, Samuel (2nd)-Pvt. Company H, 19th LA Infantry
Procella, Narcisse-Pvt. Company D, 1st LA Heavy Artillery
Procile, Jackson-Pvt. Company B, 28th Thomas' LA Infantry
Procile, M.-Pvt. Company C, 18th LA Infantry
Procile, P.-Pvt. Company D, Consolidated Crescent Regiment, LA Infantry
Prosella, A.-Pvt. Company K, 4th Regiment, 2nd Brigade, 1st Division, LA Militia
Protim, Manuel Alfaro-2nd Lt. Gray's Company, Bexar County, TX Militia
Pruneda, Casildo-Pvt. Minute Men (Scouts), Starr County, TX Militia
Puentes, J.-Pvt. 1st Chasseurs a pied, LA Militia
Puig, Bentura-Pvt. Co. 2, 5th (Spanish) Regiment, European Brigade, LA Militia
Puig, Francisco-Pvt. Co. 9, 5th (Spanish) Regiment, European Brigade, LA Mil.
Puig, Jamie-Sgt. Co. 9, 5th (Spanish) Regiment, European Brigade, LA Militia
Puig, Jose-Pvt. Co. 2, 5th (Spanish) Regiment, European Brigade, LA Militia
Puig, Juan-Cpl. Co. 9, 5th (Spanish) Regiment, European Brigade, LA Militia
Puig, Magin-Capt. Co. 5, 5th (Spanish) Regiment, European Brigade, LA Militia
Puig, Miguel-Pvt. Co. 5, 5th (Spanish) Regiment, European Brigade, LA Militia
Puig, Valentin-Cpl. Co. 9, 5th (Spanish) Regiment, European Brigade, LA Militia
Puignau, Silvestre-Pvt. Co. 9, 5th (Spanish) Regt., European Brigade, LA Militia
Puigserver, Pedro-Cpl. Company 5, Cazadores Espanoles Regiment, LA Militia
Puig y Oriol, Gaspar-Cpl. Co. 8, 5th (Spanish) Regt., European Brigade, LA Mil.
Pujol, A.-Pvt. Company E, 22nd Consolidated LA Infantry

Pujol, Antonio-Pvt. Co. 9, 5th (Spanish) Regiment, European Brigade, LA Militia
Pujol, Dionesio-Pvt. Co. 6, 5th (Spanish) Regiment, European Brigade, LA Militia
Pujol, Jayme-Pvt. Company D, 30th LA Infantry
Pujol, Joachin J.-Pvt. Co. 6, 5th (Spanish) Regiment, European Brigade, LA Mil.
Pujol, John-Pvt. Company A/D, 30th LA Infantry
Pujol, Joseph-Pvt. Company A, 30th LA Infantry
Pujos, Antonio-Pvt. Company G, 10th LA Infantry
Pujos, Victor-Sgt. Company F, 30th LA Infantry
Pulido, Canuto-Pvt. Company F, 3rd TX Infantry
Pulido, Ylario-Pvt. Company I, Benavides' Regiment, TX Cavalry
***See also Peixotto
Puxotto, D.C.-Pvt. Company G, 4th S.C. State Troops

Q

Quadras, Geronino-Pvt. Co. 2, 5th (Spanish) Regt., European Brigade, LA Militia
***Quave is the Mississippi French version of the surname Cuevas,
Quave, Christopher L.-Sherrif Harrison County, MISS 1861-1862.
Quave, Lewis-Pvt. Company E, 3rd MISS Infantry
Quave, Peter Simon-MISS Militia (rank or unit unknown).
Quave, Usant-Pvt. Company A, 3rd MISS Infantry
***This is the French version of the surname Quevedo, which arrived in Louisiana via the French Illinois Colonial Settlements; see also Cavedo for the Floridian version of this surname.
Quebedeau, Andreal-Pvt. Company B, 7th LA Cavalry
Quebedeau, Desosthene-Pvt. Company B, 7th LA Cavalry
Quebedeau, Joseph-Pvt. Company B, 18th LA Infantry
Quebedeaux, Charles E.-Pvt. Spaight's Battalion, TX
Quebedeaux, Denis-Pvt. Company A, Miles' Legion, LA
Quebedeaux, J.-Pvt. Company A, 28th Thomas' LA Infantry
Quebedeaux, Joseph Neville-Pvt. Company C/D, Crescent Regiment, LA Infantry
Quebedeaux, Nicholas-Pvt. Company E, Spaight's Battalion, TX
Quibedeau, Aladin A.-Sgt. Company G, 18th Consolidated LA Infantry
Quibedeau, Joseph E.-1st Sgt. Company G, 18th Consolidated LA Infantry
Quilacio, Julian-Pvt. Co. A, 5th (Spanish) Regt., European Brigade, LA Militia
Quina, Arthur L.-Pvt. Company B, 62nd ALA Infantry
Quina, C.F.-Pvt. Company A, 1st Regiment Mobile Volunteers, ALA
Quina, N.C.-Pvt. Company G, 1st ALA Cavalry
Quinones, Candelario-Pvt. Bustillo's Company, Bexar County, TX Militia
Quinones, Francisco-Pvt. 8th TX Field Battery
Quintal, Antonio-Pvt. 1st Native Guards, LA Militia
Quintall, J.-Sgt. Company E, 1st LA Infantry
Quintan, Luis-Cpl. Company I, 7th LA Infantry
Quintana, Andres-Pvt. Co. 6, 5th (Spanish) Regt., European Brigade, LA Militia
Quintana, Jose-Capt. Co. 4, 5th (Spanish) Regt., European Brigade, LA Militia

Quintero, Camilo-Pvt. Co. 4, 5th (Spanish) Regt., European Brigade, LA Militia
Quintero, Fernandez-Pvt. Company G, 3rd TX Infantry
Quintero, Francisco-3rd Cpl. Company D, Benavides' Regiment, TX Cavalry
Quintero, Francisco-Pvt. 1st Company A, Ragsdale's Battalion, TX Cavalry
Quintero, Gabriel-Pvt. 1st Company C, 3rd TX Infantry
Quintero, Jesus-Pvt. 1st Company A, Ragsdale's Battalion, TX Cavalry
Quintero, Juan A.-Cpl. Company A, 3rd TX Infantry
Quintero, Jose Agustin-Pvt. Quitman Rifles, San Antonio, TX Militia. A native of Cuba, he was assigned by President Davis as Diplomatic Representative to Mexico from 1861 to 1865.
Quintero, Manuel-Pvt. Medina Guards, Bexar County, TX Militia
Quintero, Thomas-Sgt. 1st Company A, Ragsdale's Battalion, TX Cavalry
Quintero, Vidal-Pvt. Gray's Company, Bexar County, TX Militia
Quintes, Fernandez-Pvt. Company G, 3rd TX Infantry
***Also found as Quinto
Quito, Agustine-Pvt. Company B, Ragsdale's Battalion, TX Cavalry
Quiroga, Juan-Pvt. Company G, 3rd TX Infantry

R

Rabassa, A.D.-Sgt. Company 3, 1st Chasseurs a pied, LA Militia
Rabassa, Joseph Dervigne-Pvt. Company G, 15th Confederate Cavalry
Rabassa, N.-Pvt. Company 1, 1st Chasseurs a pied, LA Militia
Rabassa, Octave-Pvt. LA Militia
Rabell, Jose-Cpl. Co. 5, 5th (Spanish) Regiment, European Brigade, LA Militia
Rabell, M.-Pvt. Co. 5, 5th (Spanish) Regiment, European Brigade, LA Militia
Rafael, C.-Pvt. Company G, 21st ALA Infantry
Rafael, Joaquin-Pvt. Company A, 1st TX State Troops
Rafael, Jose-Pvt. Company A, 1st TX State Troops
Ramas, D.-Pvt. Bancroft Jrs. Co., 16th S.C Militia (possibly same as Ramos, D.)
Ramas, Henry-Pvt. Leeds' Guards Regiment, 16th S.C. Militia
Ramas, Serafin-Cpl. Co. A, 5th (Spanish) Regt., European Brigade, LA Militia
***See also Remerez and Remerz
Ramires, Enemecio-Pvt. Lamar Home Guards, Refugio County, TX Militia
Ramires, Frank-Pvt. Company B, 9th Battalion, LA Infantry
Ramires, Jenaro-Pvt. 1st Company I, 33rd TX Infantry
Ramires, Juan-Pvt. Thomas' Company, TX Partisan Rangers
Ramires, Roberto-Pvt. Company G, 3rd TX Infantry
Ramires, Ynosente-Pvt. Minute Men (Scouts), Starr County, TX Militia
Ramirez, Antonio-Pvt. Company C, 8th TX Infantry
Ramirez, Antonio-Pvt. Company H, 3rd TX Infantry
Ramirez, Eulogio-Cpl. 1st Company C, 3rd TX Infantry
Ramirez, Jesus-Pvt. TX Militia
Ramirez, Julian-Pvt. Zapata's Company, Nueces County, TX State Troops
Ramirez, Leonides-Pvt. Company C, 8th TX Infantry

Ramirez, Matias-Sgt. Landry's Company, Donaldsonville Artillery, LA
Ramirez, Miguel-Sgt. Co. 3, 5th (Spanish) Regt., European Brigade, LA Militia
Ramirez, Nicolas-Pvt. Company E, 8th TX Infantry
Ramirez, Pedro-Pvt. Gray's Company, Bexar County, TX Militia
Ramirez, Peter-Pvt. Co. 5, 5th (Spanish) Regiment, European Brigade, LA Mil.
Ramirez, Pierre-1st Sgt. Landry's Company, Donaldsonville Artillery, LA
Ramirez, Ynacio-Pvt. Company 1, Cazadores Espanoles Regiment, LA Militia
Ramon, A.-Pvt. Teel's Company, TX State Troops
Ramon, Genza-Pvt. Company I, Benavides' Regiment, TX Cavalry
Ramon, Geraldo-Musician Company C, 8th TX Infantry
Ramon, Juan-Pvt. Co. 4, 5th (Spanish) Regiment, European Brigade, LA Militia
Ramon, Juan-Pvt. Company D, Benavides' Regiment, TX Cavalry
Ramon, Martin-Sgt. 1st Company I, 33rd TX Cavalry
Ramon, Zeferino-Pvt. Company F, 3rd TX Infantry
Ramos, A.-Pvt. 1st Native Guards, LA Militia
Ramos, A.-Pvt. 15th Field Battery, TX Artillery
Ramos, Angel-Pvt. Company B, Ragsdale's Battalion, TX Cavalry
Ramos, Antonio-Pvt. / Musician Company F, 3rd TX Infantry
Ramos, Charles R.-Pvt. Company A, 30th LA Infantry
Ramos, D.-Pvt. 1st Charleston Battalion, S.C. Infantry
Ramos, Emanuel-Pvt. Company L, 44th MISS Infantry
Ramos, H.-Pvt. Company B, Crump's TX Cavalry
Ramos, J.-Pvt. Company C, Benavides' Regiment, TX Cavalry
Ramos, Juan-Pvt. Company C, 8th TX Infantry
Ramos, Julian-Pvt. Zapata's Company, Nueces County, TX Militia
Ramos, Luciano-Pvt. 4th Field Battery, TX Artillery
Ramos, Manuel-Pvt. Company F, 3rd TX Infantry
Ramos, Narcissius-Pvt. Company B, Ragsdale's Battalion, TX Cavalry
Ramos, Pascual-Pvt. Company C, 8th TX Infantry
Ramos, Pedro-Pvt. 1st Company I, 33rd TX Cavalry
Ramos, Serafin-Cpl. Co. A, 5th (Spanish) Regt., European Brigade, LA Militia
Ramos, T.-Pvt. Company A, 30th LA Infantry
Ramos, Thomas-Pvt. Company B, Ragsdale's Battalion, TX Cavalry
Rangel, Antonio-Pvt. Zapata's Company, Nueces County, TX State Troops
Rangel, Gabriel-Pvt. Zapata's Company, Nueces County, TX State Troops
Rangel, H.-Pvt. Crump's Regiment, TX Cavalry
Rangel, Jesus-Pvt. Zapata's Company, Nueces County, TX State Troops
Rangel, Luciano-Pvt. 4th Field Battery, TX Artillery
Rangel, Macedonio-Pvt. Zapata's Company, Nueces County, TX State Troops
Rangel, Manuel-Pvt. Company F, 3rd TX Infantry
Rangel, Natividad-Pvt. Company F, 3rd TX Infantry
Rangel, Pascual-Pvt. Company C, 8th TX Infantry
Rangel, Rosales-Pvt. Engledow's Company, Nueces County, TX Militia
Rangel, Tomas-Pvt. Company B, Ragsdale's Battalion, TX Cavalry
Rangel, Ursino-Pvt. Zapata's Company, Nueces County, TX State Troops

Ranguel, Francisco-Pvt. Company G, 3rd TX Infantry
Rano, Angel-Pvt. Company B, Ragsdale's Battalion, TX Cavalry
Rante, Felix-Cpl. Company D, 8th FLA Infantry
Rantero, Victor-Pvt. Company F, 18th Consolidated LA Infantry
Rapanie, Matias-Pvt. Co. 10, 5th (Spanish) Regt., European Brigade, LA Militia
Rayes, Julius-Pvt. Company D, Benavides' Regiment, TX Cavalry
***See also Resendes
Recendes, Cevero-Pvt. Company A, 3rd Yager's TX Cavalry
Recendes, Pedro-Pvt. Company A, 3rd Yager's TX Cavalry
Reeyes, Pedro-Pvt. Company F, 3rd TX Infantry
Refino, Aeissia-Pvt. Company B, Pointe Coupee Artillery, LA
Regalado, Francisco-Pvt. Company D, Ragsdale's Battalion, TX Cavalry
Regalia, Antonio-Pvt. Company A, 32nd VIR Cavalry Battalion
***See also Reyna
Reina, Frank-Pvt. Company C, 6th LA Infantry
Reina, Ventura-Pvt. Co. 9, 5th (Spanish) Regiment, European Brigade, LA Militia
Relimpio, Frank-Pvt. Company G, 7th LA Infantry
Reller, Eulogio-Bugler 1st Company C, Ragsdale's Battalion, TX Cavalry
***See also Reyes
Relles, Andres-Pvt. Company B, Benavides' Regiment, TX Cavalry
Relles, Juardelos-Pvt. Company E, Benavides' Regiment, TX Cavalry
Relles, Polinario-Pvt. Company C, 8th TX Infantry
Relles, Richardo-Pvt. Company E, Madison's Regiment, TX Cavalry
Remendo, Jose-Pvt. Co. 5, 5th (Spanish) Regiment, European Brigade, LA Mil.
Remerez, Juan-Pvt. Company E, 8th TX Infantry
Remerz, Domingo-Pvt. Company A, 17th Consolidated Dismounted, TX Cav.
Rendon, Andre-Sgt. Company B, 2nd LA Infantry
Rendon, Dionicio-Pvt. 1st Company H, 33rd TX Cavalry
Rendon, J.-Pvt. Company G, 19th GA Infantry
Rendon, Theofilo-Musician Company I, 8th TX Infantry
Rendon, Ygnacio-Pvt. Company A, 3rd Yager's TX Cavalry
Renteria, Juan Bautista-Pvt. Co. 2, 5th (Spanish) Regt., European Brig., LA Mil.
Repete, Antonio-Pvt. Co. 8, 5th (Spanish) Regt., European Brigade, LA Militia
***See also Recendes
Resendes, G.-Pvt. Company C, 8th TX Infantry
Resendez, Severo-Pvt. Company A, 3rd TX Cavalry
Revas, L.-Pvt. Company F, 18th LA Infantry
***See also Relles
Rey, Juan-Pvt. Davidson's Company, TX
Reyes, Balvino-Pvt. Bustillo's Company, Bexar County, TX Militia
Reyes, Catarino-Pvt. Medina Guards, Bexar County, TX Militia
Reyes, F.-2nd Lt. 1st Native Guards, LA Militia
Reyes, Francisco-Pvt. Company C, 8th TX Infantry
Reyes, Francisco-Pvt. Company C, Benavides' Regiment, TX Cavalry
Reyes, Juan-Pvt. Teel's Company, TX State Troops

Reyes, Juan-Pvt. Co. 4, 5th (Spanish) Regiment, European Brigade, LA Militia
Reyes, Lewis-Pvt. Trevinio's Squad, TX Partisan Mounted Volunteers
Reyes, Mathilde-Pvt. Jeff Davis Home Guard, Refugio County, TX Militia
Reyes, Manuel-Pvt. 8th Field Battery, TX Artillery
Reyes, Miguel-Pvt. Co. 8, 5th (Spanish) Regiment, European Brigade, LA Mil.
Reyes, Pacifico-Pvt. TX Militia
Reyes, Pedro-Pvt. Company G, 8th TX Infantry
Reyes, Peter-Pvt. Company I, 2nd TX Cavalry
Reyes, Prejedes-Pvt. 1st Company A, Ragsdale's Battalion, TX Cavalry
Reyes, Refugio-Pvt. Company C, Benavides' Regiment, TX Cavalry
Reyes, S.-Pvt. Company K, Crescent Regiment, LA Infantry
Reyes, Thomas C.-Cpl. Company K, 1st Olmstead's GA Infantry
Reyes, Victor-Pvt. 8th Field Battery, TX Artillery
Reyna, Angel-Pvt. TX Militia
Reynaldos, Enrique-Pvt. Co. 3, 5th (Spanish) Regt., European Brigade, LA Mil.
Riancho, Francisco-Pvt. Co. 4, 5th (Spanish) Regt., European Brigade, LA Militia
Rias, Francisco-Pvt. 4th Field Battery, TX Artillery
Ribas y Castanos, Jose-Pvt. Co. 6, 5th (Span.) Regt., European Brigade, LA Mil.
Ribera, Jose M.-Sgt. Company 1, Cazadores Espanoles Regiment, LA Militia
Ribera, Juan-Pvt. 1st Company A, Ragsdale's Battalion, TX Cavalry
Ribera, Mauricis-Pvt. 1st Company A, Ragsdale's Battalion, TX Cavalry
Ribero, Antonio-Pvt. Co. 2, 5th (Spanish) Regiment, European Brigade, LA Mil.
Ribero, D.-Pvt. Company C, 8th TX Infantry
Ribero, Manuel-Pvt. Co. 4, 5th (Spanish) Regiment, European Brigade, LA Mil.
Ribero, Thomas L.-2nd Lt. Company F, 28th Battalion, GA Siege Artillery
Riberon, A.-Pvt. Company G, 21st ALA Infantry
Riberon, David Manuel-Pvt. Company H, 26th GA Infantry
Riberon, Frank-Pvt. Floyd's Legion, GA
Ribes, Bernardo-Pvt. Co. 7, 5th (Spanish) Regiment, European Brigade, LA Mil.
Ribes, Eduardo-Pvt. Company E, Benavides' Regiment, TX Cavalry
Ribot, Francisco-Surgeon Cazadores Espanoles Regiment, LA Militia
Rica, Francois-Pvt. 3rd Regiment, 2nd Brigade, 1st Division, LA Militia
Ricardo, (unknown if 1st or last name)-Pvt. Co. A, Baylor's Regiment, ARIZ
Ricardo, Benjamin-Pvt. Co. L, Consolidated Crescent Regiment, LA Infantry
Riera, Albert-Pvt. Company B, 3rd Battalion, FLA Cavalry
Riera, Anthony-Pvt. Company B, 3rd Battalion, FLA Cavalry
Riera, Ramon-Pvt. Co. 4, 5th (Spanish) Regiment, European Brigade, LA Militia
Riffe, Fernandez-Pvt. 1st Company B, 36th VIR Infantry
Rincon, Jose-Pvt. Company A, Ragsdale's Battalion, TX Cavalry
Riojas, Jesus-Pvt. Company I, Benavides' Regiment, TX Cavalry
Riola, Antonio-Pvt. Company G, 10th LA Infantry
Rios, C.-Pvt. Company C, 4th TX Mounted Volunteers
Rios, Cayetano-Pvt. Zapata's Company, Nueces County, TX State Troops
Rios, Demas-Pvt. Company F, 3rd TX Infantry
Rios, Fermin-Pvt. Company H, 3rd TX Infantry

Hispanic Confederates 115

Rios, Manuel-Pvt. Watkin's Company, Uvalde County Troops, TX
Rios, Nabor-Pvt. Zapata's Company, Nueces County, TX State Troops
Rios, Rafael-Pvt. Minute Men (Scouts), Starr County, TX Militia
Rios > see also Barrera, Jose Rios
Ripoll, Francisco-Cpl. Co. 5, 5th (Spanish) Regt., European Brigade, LA Militia
Riquer, Francisco-Pvt. Co. 2, 5th (Spanish) Regt., European Brigade, LA Militia
***See also Reves and Ribas y Castano
Rivas, Andrew-Pvt. Company B, 2nd TX Cavalry
Rivas, Augustine-Pvt. 1st Company A, 3rd TX Infantry
Rivas, Edwardo-Pvt. Company H, 8th TX Infantry
Rivas, Frank-Sgt. Company A, 9th Battalion, LA Infantry
Rivas, Frank-Pvt. Co. 5, 5th (Spanish) Regiment, European Brigade, LA Militia
Rivas, Federico-Pvt. Company B, 2nd TX Cavalry
Rivas, George-Pvt. Company B, 2nd TX Cavalry
Rivas, Hilaire-2nd Lt. Company B, 8th LA Infantry
Rivas, Idalecio-Pvt. Company F, Benavides' Regiment, TX Cavalry
Rivas, Jesus-Pvt. TX Militia
Rivas, Jose-Cpl. 1st Company C, Ragsdale's Battalion, TX Cavalry
Rivas, Jose Manuel-Pvt. Company A, 3rd TX Infantry
Rivas Roig, Jose-Pvt. Co. 4, 5th (Spanish) Regt., European Brigade, LA Militia
Rivas, Juan Miguel-Pvt. 1st Company C, 3rd TX Infantry
Rivas, Manuel-Sgt. Company D, 30th LA Infantry
Rivas, Mauricio-Pvt. Company A, Ragsdale's Battalion, TX Cavalry
Rivas, Serafin S.-Capt. Company G, 10th LA Infantry
Rivas y Chincho, J.-Sgt. Co. 1, 5th (Spanish) Regt., European Brigade, LA Mil.
Rivas y Rivas, J.-Sgt. Co. 1, 5th (Spanish) Regt., European Brigade, LA Militia
Rivegio, Jose-Pvt. Co. 3, 5th (Spanish) Regiment, European Brigade, LA Militia
***See also Ribera and Rivers
Rivera, Diego-Pvt. Zapata's Company, Nueces County, TX State Troops
Rivera, Elijio-Pvt. Bustillo's Company, Bexar County, TX Militia
Rivera, Eugenio-Pvt. Zapata's Company, Nueces County, TX State Troops
Rivera, Francisco-Pvt. Bustillo's Company, Bexar County, TX Militia
Rivera, John J.-Major 6th LA Infantry
Rivera, M.-Pvt. / Scout San Elizario Spy Company, 2nd TX Mounted Rifles
Rivera, M.-Pvt. Company G, 3rd LA Infantry
Rivera, N.- Jr. 1st Lt. Orleans Artillery Battalion, LA
Rivera, Rodrigo-Pvt. Company I, 8th TX Infantry
Rivera, Tito P.-Sgt. Company E, 33rd TX Cavalry
***See also Ribero
Rivero, Juan-Pvt. Orleans Guard Battery, LA Light Artillery
Rivero, M.-Pvt. Company A, 22nd TENN Infantry
Rivero, M.-Pvt. Coopwoods' Spy Company, TX Cavalry
Rivero, Maruerti-Pvt. Company G, 13th LA Infantry
*** Rivers is the Louisiana Adaeseno version of the surname Rivera
Rivers, Jose-Pvt. Company H, 19th LA Infantry

Rivers, Leon-Pvt. Company F, 18th LA Infantry
Rivers, Robert-Pvt. Company B, 28th LA Infantry
Robasto, Tomas-Pvt. Dunn's Company, Waller's Regiment, TX Cavalry
Robera, Antonio-1st Lt. 15th Field Battery, TX Artillery
Robes > see Garcia Robes, M.
Robira, Antonio-1st Lt. Co. 4, 5th (Spanish) Regt., European Brigade, LA Militia
Robira, Isidore-Pvt. Company 5, 1st Chasseurs a pied, LA Militia
Robira, J.-Pvt. Jackson Rifle Battalion, LA Militia
Robiso, T.-Pvt. Company G, 18th LA Infantry
***Also listed as Robledo
Roblero, Fusto-Pvt. Company I, Benavides' Regiment, TX Cavalry
Robles, Dolores-Pvt. 1st Company A, Ragsdale's Battalion, TX Cavalry
Robles, John Godeff-Pvt. Company C, 9th FLA Infantry
Robles, Joseph Paul-Home Guard / Commissary Department, FLA, also Pvt. Company C, FLA Cow Cavalry. He single handedly captured a Union raiding party of 8 men at the Salt works at Rocky Point, FLA in 1864.
Robles, Juan-Pvt. Company B, Benavides' Regiment, TX Cavalry
Robles, Michael F.-Pvt. Company K, 4th FLA Infantry
Robles, Punciano-Pvt. 1st Company A, Ragsdale's Battalion, TX Cavalry
Roca, Augustin-Pvt. Co. 3, 5th (Spanish) Regt., European Brigade, LA Militia
Roca, Federico-Pvt. Co. 3, 5th (Spanish) Regiment, European Brigade, LA Mil.
Roca, John-Pvt. Co. 5, 5th (Spanish) Regiment, European Brigade, LA Militia
Roca, Juan-Pvt. Co. 6, 5th (Spanish) Regiment, European Brigade, LA Militia
Roca, Lazaro-Capt. Company 3, Cazadores Espanoles Regiment, LA Militia
Roca, Mateo-Pvt. Co. 3, 5th (Spanish) Regiment, European Brigade, LA Militia
Roca, P.-Pvt. Company E, 4th Regiment, 2nd Brigade, 1st Division, LA Militia
Rocca, Francisco-Pvt. Company G, 12th MISS Infantry
Rocha, Julian-Pvt. Company I, 33rd TX Cavalry
***There were 2 families in Louisiana surnamed Rodrigues/z; one was of Portuguese descent via Quebec, Canada, and the other was Spanish. In many cases the Spanish surname was spelled exactly as the Portuguese surname in its Louisiana French version of Rodrigue, which is also found as Rodrigues and Rodriguez or spelled with a Q, as in Rodriques/z. Uuse caution when citing who was who, as I listed only those men I felt were of the Spanish lines, but I am sure that many Spanish men are not listed and that a few of Portuguese descent might be listed in error.
Roderigo, G.-Pvt. Pulaski Lancers Company, Borland's Regiment, ARK
Roderigues, C.-Pvt. 1st Regiment Battery, Confederate Light Artillery
Roderigues, M.-Pvt. Company A, 3rd Yager's Battalion, TX Cavalry
Roderiguez, Joseph-Pvt. Company B, 2nd Regiment Volunteers, ALA Militia
Rodiregres, Antonio-Pvt. Company D, 35th Brown's TX Cavalry
Rodiricus, Jose M.-Pvt. Company D, 18th TX Cavalry
Rodriges, E.-Pvt. Company G, Benavides' Regiment, TX Cavalry
Rodriges, Jose M.-Cpl. Company E, Benavides' Regiment, TX Cavalry
Rodriges, Mariano-Sgt. Company E, Benavides' Regiment, TX Cavalry
Rodriges, Rafael-Pvt. Company A, Benavides' Regiment, TX Cavalry

Rodrigez, F.-Pvt. Ritter's Company, GA Light Artillery
Rodriguas, E.-Pvt. 24th Battalion, State Troops, TX Infantry
Rodrigued, O.-Lt. 12th LA Artillery
Rodrigues, A.B.-Pvt. 15th Field Battery, TX Artillery
Rodrigues, Antonio-Musician Co. 4, 5th (Sp.) Regt., European Brigade, LA Mil.
Rodrigues, Benjamin A.-Pvt. Company E, S.C. Militia
Rodrigues, C.-Pvt. Squire's Battalion, LA
Rodrigues, Checacio-Pvt. Company B, 2nd TX Cavalry
Rodrigues, D.-Pvt. Company K, Chalmette Regiment, LA Militia
Rodrigues, Damacio-Pvt. Company B, Ragsdale's Battalion, TX Cavalry
Rodrigues, Doroteo-Pvt. Jeff Davis Home Guard, Refugio County, TX Militia
Rodrigues, Eugene-Pvt. Company F, Saint James Regiment, LA Militia
Rodrigues, Felipe-Pvt. 18th LA Infantry
Rodrigues, Francisco-Pvt. Company B, Ragsdale's Battalion, TX Cavalry
Rodrigues, Frank-Bugler Company A, 26th TX Cavalry
Rodrigues, J.-Pvt. Continental Cadets, LA Militia
Rodrigues, John-Pvt. Lafourche Regiment, LA Militia
Rodrigues, Jose-Pvt. Oury's Company, Hebert's Battalion, ARIZ Cavalry
Rodrigues, Jose-Pvt. Co. 10, 5th (Spanish) Regt., European Brigade, LA Militia
Rodrigues, Joseph-Pvt. Company E, 10th Battalion, LA Infantry
Rodrigues, Juan-Pvt. 1st Company C, 3rd TX Infantry
Rodrigues, Juan Felix-Pvt. Company A, 3rd MISS Infantry
Rodrigues, Manuel-Pvt. Company C, 8th TX Infantry
Rodrigues, Miguel-Pvt. Company B, 2nd TX Cavalry
Rodrigues, Narcisso-Cpl. Company H, 18th TX Cavalry
Rodrigues, Oscar-Lt. Castellanos' Battery, LA Artillery
Rodrigues, Philip-Cpl. Company E, 8th ALA Infantry
Rodrigues, R.-Pvt. Company H, Pelican Regiment, LA Infantry
Rodrigues, Rafael-Pvt. Company D, 3rd TX Infantry
Rodrigues, Raphael-Pvt. Lafourche Regiment, LA Militia
Rodrigues, Remond-Pvt. LA Reserve Corps
Rodrigues, Revara-Pvt. Company I, 8th TX Infantry
Rodrigues, Rigardo-Pvt. Company E, 8th TX Infantry
Rodrigues, Ventura-Pvt. Company B, Ragsdale's Battalion, TX Cavalry
Rodrigues, Victoriano-Pvt. Co. A, 5th (Spanish) Regt., European Brig., LA Mil.
Rodriguez, Adam-Pvt. Landry's Company, Donaldsonville Artillery, LA
Rodriguez, Agustin-Pvt. Bustillo's Company, Bexar County, TX Militia
Rodriguez, Alario-Pvt. Company C, 8th TX Infantry
Rodriguez, Anastacio-Pvt. Company C, 8th TX Infantry
Rodriguez, Andreas-Pvt. Company C, 8th TX Infantry
Rodriguez, Antonio-Pvt. 1st Company C, 3rd TX Infantry
Rodriguez, Auguste-Pvt. Company D, 30th LA Infantry
Rodriguez, Benito-Pvt. 8th Field Battery, TX Artillery
Rodriguez, Bernardo-3rd Lt. Co. 8, 5th (Spanish) Regt., European Brig., LA Mil.
Rodriguez, Cayetano-Pvt. 1st Company C, 3rd TX Infantry

Rodriguez, Celso-Pvt. Gray's Company, Bexar County, TX Militia
Rodriguez, Cesario-Pvt. Company I, 33rd TX Cavalry
Rodriguez, Desire-Pvt. Company K, 27th LA Infantry
Rodriguez, Emanuel-Pvt. Company H, 3rd LA Infantry
Rodriguez, Enemesio-Pvt. Lamar County Home Guard, Refugio County, TX Mil.
Rodriguez, Esperion-Pvt. Company C, 8th TX Infantry
Rodriguez, Espinoza-Pvt. Company C, Benavides' Regiment, TX Cavalry
Rodriguez, Evaristo-Pvt. 1st Company I, 33rd TX Cavalry
Rodriguez, Francisco-Pvt. Medina Guards, Bexar County, TX Militia
Rodriguez, Francisco-Pvt. Company G, 3rd TX Infantry
Rodriguez, Francisco-Pvt. Company 2, Cazadores Espanoles Regiment, LA Mil.
Rodriguez, Guadalupe-Pvt. 1st Company C, 3rd TX Infantry
Rodriguez, Gumecindo-Cpl. Company H, 8th TX Infantry
Rodriguez, Hilario-Pvt. Tom's Company, Atascosa County, TX State Troops
Rodriguez, Hipolyte-Treasurer Town of Port Barrow, LA
Rodriguez, Isidro-Pvt. Company F, 3rd TX Infantry
Rodriguez, J.C.-Pvt. Company C, 1st LA Cavalry
Rodriguez, J.P.-Pvt. Mitchell's Company, Bandera County, TX Militia
Rodriguez, James-Pvt. Company D, 30th LA Infantry
Rodriguez, Jazar-Pvt. LA Militia
Rodriguez, Jesus-Pvt. 1st Company I, 33rd TX Infantry
Rodriguez, Jesus-1st Sgt. Trevinio's Company, TX Partisan Rangers
Rodriguez, Jesus-Pvt. 1st Company C, 3rd TX Infantry
Rodriguez, Jesus-Pvt. Company F, 3rd TX Infantry
Rodriguez, Jesus-Musician Company H, 3rd TX Infantry
Rodriguez, Jesus-Cpl. Company C, 8th TX Infantry
Rodriquez, Jesus-2nd Sgt. Bustillo's Company, Bexar County, TX Militia
Rodriguez, Jesus Manuel-Pvt. Gray's Company, Bexar County, TX Militia
Rodriguez, Jose-Pvt. Company B, 2nd TX Cavalry
Rodriguez, Jose-Pvt. Company D, 30th LA Infantry
Rodriguez, Jose-Pvt. Jeff Davis Home Guard, Refugio County, TX Militia
Rodriguez, Jose M.-Cpl. Company C, 8th TX Infantry
Rodriguez, Jose Maria-1st Sgt. Company F, 3rd TX Infantry
Rodriguez, Joseph C.-Pvt. Company B, 7th LA Infantry
Rodriguez, Juan-Sgt. Rhodes' Company, 3rd Yager's Battalion, TX Cavalry
Rodriguez, Juan-Pvt. Company C, 8th TX Infantry
Rodriguez, Juan Antoine-Pvt. Company D, 30th LA Infantry
Rodriguez, Juan Jose-Pvt. Medina Guards, Bexar County, TX Militia
Rodriguez, Juan M.-1st Lt. Gray Town Pioneers, Bexar County, TX Militia
Rodriguez, Lafoinesino-2nd Lt. Gray Town Pioneers, Bexar County, TX Militia
Rodriguez, M.-Lt. Southern Star Guards Mobile, ALA Infantry
Rodriguez, Maesi Malino-2nd Lt. Gray Town Pioneers, TX Militia
Rodriguez, Manuel-Pvt. Tom's Company, Atascosa County, TX Troops
Rodriguez, Manuel-Pvt. Co. 6, 5th (Spanish) Regt., European Brigade, LA Mil.
Rodriguez, Marcel-Pvt. Company A, Ogden's LA Cavalry

Rodriguez, Marcello-Pvt. Medina Guards, Bexar County, TX Militia
Rodriguez, Mariano-Pvt. Company H, 8th TX Infantry
Rodriguez, Martiniano-Lt. Company F, 3rd TX Infantry
Rodriguez, Mateo-Pvt. Company 1, Cazadores Espanoles Regiment, LA Militia
Rodriguez, Macsimiliano-2nd Lt. Gray's Company, Bexar County, TX Militia
Rodriguez, Nepomuceno-2nd Lt. Gray's Company, Bexar County, TX Militia
Rodriguez, Oscar-Lt. Castellano's Battery, LA Artillery
Rodriguez, P.-Pvt. Trevinio's Company, TX Cavalry
Rodriguez, Papinesino-Lt. Gray Town Pioneers, TX Militia
Rodriguez, Pedro-Pvt. Duran's Company, Atascosa County, TX Troops
Rodriguez, Pedro-Pvt. 1st Company C, 3rd TX Infantry
Rodriguez, Prudencio-Pvt. Gray's Company, Bexar County, TX Militia
Rodriguez, R.-2nd Cpl. Company C/F, Ogden's LA Cavalry
Rodriguez, R.-Pvt. Company H, Pelican Regiment, LA Infantry
Rodriguez, Rafael-Pvt. Victoria County Militia, TX
Rodriguez, Rafael-Pvt. 1st Company H, 33rd TX Cavalry
Rodriguez, Ramon-Pvt. Co. 6, 5th (Spanish) Regt., European Brigade, LA Mil.
Rodriguez, Raymond-Pvt. Company H, 11th LA Infantry
Rodriguez, Roque-Pvt. Company I, 33rd TX Cavalry
Rodriguez, Rosalle-Pvt. Company D, 3rd LA Infantry
Rodriguez, S.-Pvt. Teel's Company, TX State Troops
Rodriguez, Salvador-Pvt. Company C, 8th TX Infantry
Rodriguez, Serapio-Pvt. Gray's Company, Bexar County, TX Militia
Rodriguez, Simon (1st)-Pvt. Tom's Company, Atascosa County, TX Militia
Rodriguez, Simon (2nd)-Pvt. Tom's Company, Atascosa County, TX Militia
Rodriguez, Theodore-Pvt. Company H, 2nd LA Cavalry
Rodriguez, Thomas-Pvt. Company D, 30th LA Infantry
Rodriguez, Thomas A.-Capt. Benavides' Regiment, TX Cavalry
Rodriguez, Tomas-2nd Lt. Company H, 8th TX Infantry
Rodriguez, Timoteo-Pvt. Company B, Benavides' Regiment, TX Cavalry
Rodriguez, Trinidad-Pvt. Company I, 33rd TX Cavalry
Rodriguez, William-Pvt. Company B, 63rd GA Infantry
Rodriguez, Ysabel-Pvt. Company H, 8th TX Infantry
Rodriguez, Ysidro-Pvt. Bustillo's Company, Bexar County, TX Militia
Rodrigus, Frank-Pvt. Company E, 1st TX Heavy Artillery
Rodrigus, Rogue-Pvt. 1st Company I, 33rd TX Cavalry
Rodriques, Ignace A.-Cpl. Company C, Ogden's LA Cavalry
Rodriques, John-Pvt. Lafourche Regiment, LA Militia
Rodriquez, Andrew-Pvt. Company D, 1st LA Heavy Artillery
Rodriquez, J.-Pvt. Trevinio's Company, TX Cavalry
Rodriquez, Juan-Pvt. Company C, Benavides' Regiment, TX Cavalry
Rodriquez, P.-Pvt. Company A, Crescent Regiment, LA Militia
Rodriquez, Prudencio-Sgt. Co. 3, 5th (Spanish) Regt., European Brigade, LA Mil.
Rodriquez, R.-Pvt. Company A, Crescent Regiment, LA Militia
Rodriquez, S.-Pvt. Trevinio's Company, TX Partisan Rangers

Rodriquez, Tomas-Pvt. Company D, Benavides' Regiment, TX Cavalry
Regalado, Francisco-Pvt. Company D, Ragsdales' Battalion, TX Cavalry
Rogero, Alberto D.-Sheriff of St. Johns County, FLA 1861-1862.
Rogero, John C.-Pvt. Company A, 2nd Battalion, TX Cavalry
Rogero, Manuel H.-2nd Lt. Company F, 9th FLA Infantry
Rogero, Nicholas-Pvt. Hopkins's Company, FLA Artillery
Roget, Avelino-Cpl. Co. 9, 5th (Spanish) Regt., European Brigade, LA Militia
Roget, Joachin-Pvt. Company 5, Cazadores Espanoles Regiment, LA Militia
Rogiero, R.-Pvt. Company D, 1st Regiment, Charleston Guard S.C.
Rogillio, Benjamin F.-3rd Sgt. Company G, 16th MISS Infantry
Rogillio, C.B.-Cpl. New Company G, 4th LA Infantry
Rogillio, C.E.-Pvt. Company C, Hughes' Battalion, MISS Cavalry
Rogillio, Elias-Pvt. Darden's Company, Jefferson Artillery, MISS
Rogillio, E.R.-Pvt. Company F, 48th MISS Infantry
Rogillio, George W.-Pvt. Company K, 4th LA Infantry
Rogillio, Guy-Pvt. Company E, 1st LA Cavalry
Rogillio, H.S.-Cpl. New Company G, 4th LA Infantry
Rogillio, John- Sgt. Company D, 20th Confederate Cavalry
Rogillio, John G.-Pvt. Company K, 4th LA Infantry
Rogillio, John W.-Pvt. Company B, 38th MISS Cavalry
Rogillio, Joseph-Pvt. Company C/H, 3rd LA Cavalry
Rogillio, Julian Robert-Pvt. Company E, 1st LA Cavalry
Rogillio, Martin-Pvt. Company E, 1st LA Cavalry
Rogillio, Scott-Pvt. Company E, 1st LA Cavalry
Rogillio, William H.-Pvt. Company K, 4th LA Infantry
Rogillio, William F.-Sgt. Company F, 48th MISS Infantry
Roig, J.-Pvt. Company 1, 5th (Spanish) Regiment, European Brigade, LA Militia
Roig, Juan-Pvt. Co. 4, 5th (Spanish) Regiment, European Brigade, LA Militia
Rojas, Joseph-Pvt. Co. 5, 5th (Spanish) Regiment, European Brigade, LA Militia
Romagosa, Louis F.-Pvt. Company F, 18th Consolidated LA Infantry
Romaguera, Frank-Pvt. Co. 5, 5th (Spanish) Regt., European Brigade, LA Militia
Romaguera, J.-Pvt. Co. 5, 5th (Spanish) Regiment, European Brigade, LA Militia
Romaguera, S.-Pvt. Co. 2, 5th (Spanish) Regiment, European Brigade, LA Militia
Roman, Francisco-Bugler Company I, 33rd TX Cavalry
Roman, Jose Maria-Pvt. Company E, 8th TX Infantry
Romano, Augustus B.-Pvt. Company F, 38th N.C. Infantry
Romano, Jose-Pvt. Co. 10, 5th (Spanish) Regiment, European Brigade, LA Militia
Romano, Rovusto-Pvt. Company B, Ford's TX Cavalry
Romero, Adolphe-Pvt. Pvt. Company G, 7th LA Cavalry
Romero, Aladin-Pvt. Company C, 10th Battalion, LA Infantry
Romero, Alcide-Pvt. Company K, 18th Consolidated LA Infantry
Romero, Alexander-Pvt. Company A, 18th Consolidated LA Infantry
Romero, Antoine Duplessis-Pvt. Company A, 18th Consolidated LA Infantry
Romero, Aristide-Pvt. LA Reserve Corps
Romero, Aurelian-Pvt. Saint Martin Parish, LA Militia

Romero, Charles-Sgt. Company E, 7th LA Infantry
Romero, Cleveland-Pvt. Company A, 18th Consolidated LA Infantry
Romero, Domingue-Pvt. LA Militia
Romero, Dorsele-Pvt. LA Militia
Romero, Duplexis-Pvt. LA Militia
Romero, Dupre-Pvt. LA Militia
Romero, E. Ferdinand-Pvt. Company A, 18th Consolidated LA Infantry
Romero, Emile-Pvt. LA Militia
Romero, Emile Laclair-Pvt. Company A, 18th Consolidated LA Infantry
Romero, Eutimo-Pvt. Davis' Company, Confederate Light Artillery
Romero, Ferdinand-Pvt. Company F, 7th LA Cavalry
Romero, Felipe-Pvt. Company B, Ragsdale's Battalion, TX Cavalry
Romero, Francisco-Pvt. Company B, Ragsdale's Battalion, TX Cavalry
Romero, G.V.-Pvt. LA Militia
Romero, Gerard-Pvt. Company C, 10th LA Infantry
Romero, J. Desire-Pvt. Company I, 7th LA Cavalry
Romero, J.S.-Pvt. LA Militia
Romero, Jose-Pvt. Co. 9, 5th (Spanish) Regiment, European Brigade, LA Militia
Romero, Joseph-Pvt. Company A, 18th Consolidated LA Infantry
Romero, Joseph D.-Pvt. Company C, 10th LA Infantry
Romero, L.F.-Pvt. LA Militia
Romero, Leon-Pvt. Company C, 10th LA Infantry
Romero, Lewis-Pvt. Company A, Granbury's Consolidated Brigade, TX
Romero, Louis-Pvt. Company I, 7th LA Cavalry
Romero, Louis-Pvt. Company H, 6th TX Infantry
Romero, Moleon-Pvt. LA Militia
Romero, Osmar-Pvt. Company F, 2nd LA Infantry
Romero, Ozeme-Pvt. Company C, 10th LA Infantry
Romero, P.-Pvt. 3rd Regiment, 2nd Brigade, 1st Division, LA Militia
Romero, Presentario-Pvt. Company I, Benavides' Regiment, TX Cavalry
Romero, Prosper-Pvt. Company G, 7th LA Cavalry
Romero, Pedro-Pvt. Co. 6, 5th (Spanish) Regiment, European Brigade, LA Militia
Romero, Pedro-Pvt. Davis' Company, Confederate Light Artillery
Romero, Severicus-Pvt. Company G, 7th LA Cavalry
Romero, Theogene-Pvt. LA Militia
Romero, Valcourt-Pvt. Company C, 18th Consolidated LA Infantry
Romero, Venence-Pvt. Company I, 7th LA Cavalry
Romero, Vilmont-Pvt. Company A, 18th LA Infantry
Romgel, Presentario-Pvt. Company I, Benavides' Regiment, TX Cavalry
Romo, Nicolas-Pvt. Company C, 3rd Yager's Battalion, TX Cavalry
Rondal, Marco-Pvt. Co. A, 5th (Spanish) Regt., European Brigade, LA Militia
***This surname also was found in the Louisiana French version of Ronquille
Ronquillo, Anselme Eugene-Cpl. Company G, 28th Thomas' LA Infantry
Ronquillo, Emerend-Pvt. 7th LA Cavalry
Roque, Francisco-Pvt. Co. 4, 5th (Spanish) Regt., European Brigade, LA Militia

Roques, F.-Pvt. Company 7, 3rd Regiment, European Brigade, LA Militia
Roques, P.-Cpl. Company 5, 3rd Regiment, European Brigade, LA Militia
Rosa, Alceste-Pvt. Company G, 1st LA Heavy Artillery
Rosa, Antonio-Pvt. Co. 4, 5th (Spanish) Regiment, European Brigade, LA Militia
Rosa, Lastin-Pvt. Company B, 1st LA Heavy Artillery
Rosada, Jose-Pvt. Co. 6, 5th (Spanish) Regiment, European Brigade, LA Militia
Rosado, Antonio-Sgt. Co. 10, 5th (Spanish) Regt., European Brigade, LA Militia
***See also Rangel, Rosales
Rosales, Andres-Pvt. Company I, 8th TX Infantry
Rosales, Carlin-Pvt. LA Militia
Rosales, F.-Pvt. Company E, Border's Regiment, TX Cavalry
Rosales, Pedro-Pvt. Company C, 8th TX Infantry
Rosales, Vidal-Pvt. 1st Company C, Ragsdale's Battalion, TX Cavalry
Rosas, Eugene-Musician Company E, 18th LA Infantry
Rosas, Santos-Pvt. Company F, 5th TX Infantry
Rosco, Desiderio-Pvt. Medina Guards, Bexar County, TX Militia
Rosello, Jose-Pvt. Co. 9, 5th (Spanish) Regiment, European Brigade, LA Militia
Rosello, Miguel-Pvt. Co. 9, 5th (Spanish) Regt., European Brigade, LA Militia
Rosello, Pedro-Pvt. Co. 3, 5th (Spanish) Regiment, European Brigade, LA Militia
Rosendez, Faustino-Pvt. Co. 7, 5th (Spanish) Regt., European Brigade, LA Militia
Rosis, Joseph-Pvt. Company C, 25th S.C. Infantry
Rosis, Juan-Pvt. Co. 9, 5th (Spanish) Regiment, European Brigade, LA Militia
Rossas, Santos-Pvt. Company F, 5th TX Infantry
Rouis, Rofine-Pvt. Company G, 7th LA Infantry
***Roure is also listed as Roura
Roure, Juan-Pvt. Co. 3, 5th (Spanish) Regiment, European Brigade, LA Militia
Rovello, Candelario-Pvt. Company F, Cazadores Espanoles Regiment, LA Militia
Roxo, Jose Maria-Pvt. Trevinio's Company, TX Cavalry
Royes, M.-Pvt. Continental Cadets, LA Militia
Royes, Manuel C.-Capt. Company A, Meyer's Regiment, TX Infantry
***Also listed as Rubalcaba
Rualcada, Antonio-Pvt. 1st Company A, 3rd TX Infantry
Rubio, Adriano-Pvt. Company C, 8th TX Infantry
Rubio, Francisco-Pvt. Company B, 2nd TX Cavalry
Rubio, Francisco-Pvt. Company F, Benavides' Regiment, TX Cavalry
Rubio, Juan-Pvt. Company E, 8th TX Infantry
Rubio, Manuel-Sgt. Co. 3, 5th (Spanish) Regiment, European Brigade, LA Militia
Rubio, Miguel-Pvt. Company H, Miles' Legion, LA
Rubio, Salama-Pvt. 1st Company H, 33rd TX Cavalry
Rubira, P.-Pvt. Co. 1, 5th (Spanish) Regiment, European Brigade, LA Militia
***Also listed as Ruelas
Ruedas, Claudio-Pvt. 1st Company C, 3rd TX Infantry
***See also Rouis
Rues, Jales-Pvt. Company G, 26th LA Infantry
Rues, Jose-Pvt. Trevinio's Company, TX Cavalry

Ruess, Jean-Pvt. Co. G, 4th Regiment, 2nd Brigade, 1st Division, LA Militia
Ruez, Thomas-Pvt. 21st ALA Infantry
Ruis, Alfred-Pvt. 1st Symons' GA Reserve
Ruis, Andrew J.-Musician Company I, 3rd FLA Infantry
Ruis, Calvin-Pvt. Company C, 50th GA Infantry
Ruis, Carpio-Pvt. 1st Company C, 3rd TX Infantry
Ruis, Eugene-Pvt. Company B, 2nd TX Cavalry
Ruis, General E.-Pvt. Company B, 61st GA Infantry
Ruis, Graviel-Pvt. Company B, Ragsdale's Battalion, TX Cavalry
Ruis, Jackson J.-Pvt. Company C, 50th GA Infantry
Ruis, James J.-Pvt. Company C, 50th GA Infantry
Ruis, James M.-Pvt. Company B, 61st GA Infantry
Ruis, John-Pvt. Company C, 50th GA Infantry
Ruis, Juan Antonio-Pvt. Duran's Company, Atascosa County, TX State Troops
Ruis, Madison-Pvt. Company B, 61st GA Infantry
Ruis, Malakiah-Pvt. Company B, 50th GA Infantry
Ruis, Manning-Pvt. Company B, 50th GA Infantry
Ruis, Obediah-Pvt. Company I, 3rd FLA Infantry
Ruis, Randal-Musician Company E, 9th FLA Infantry
Ruis, Robert R.-Pvt. Company B, 1st Local Troops Augusta, GA Militia
Ruis, Solomon-Pvt. Company G, 47th GA Infantry
Ruis, William-Pvt. Company F, 1st Symons' GA Reserve
Ruiz, A.-Pvt. Company H, Orleans Fire Regiment, LA Militia
Ruiz, A.J.-Pvt. Company A, 30th LA Infantry
Ruiz, Alejo-Pvt. Company H, 8th TX Infantry
Ruiz, Alex M.-Capt. 1st Company A, 3rd TX Infantry
Ruiz, Antonio-Pvt. Company F, 10th LA Infantry
Ruiz, Brade-Pvt. Company D, 2nd TX Mounted Rifles
Ruiz, Emile-Capt. Company I, 4th Regiment, 1st Brigade, 1st Division, LA Militia
Ruiz, Eugene-Pvt. Company F, Benavides' Regiment, TX Cavalry
Ruiz, F.-1st Sgt. Company D, 30th LA Infantry
Ruiz, Frank Adam-Sgt. Company D, 22nd LA Infantry
Ruiz, Fausto-Sgt. Company F, Confederate States Zouave Battalion, LA
Ruiz, Francisco-Cpl. Rhodes' Company, 3rd Yager's Battalion, TX Cavalry
Ruiz, Gines-Pvt. 28th LA Infantry
Ruiz, Inez-Pvt. Company G, 28th Thomas' LA Infantry
Ruiz, Jesus-Pvt. Company F, 2nd TX Mounted Rifles
Ruiz, Jose Antonio-Pvt. Duran's Company, Atascosa County, TX Troops
Ruiz, Jose Maria-Pvt. 1st Company A, 3rd TX Infantry
Ruiz, Joseph Armand-2nd Lt. Company A, 30th LA Infantry
Ruiz, Leopold-Pvt. Company D, 21st Patton's LA Infantry
Ruiz, Manuel-Pvt. Company H, 28th Thomas' LA Infantry
Ruiz, Marcelino-Pvt. Company C, 8th TX Infantry
Ruiz, Matias-Pvt. Company D, 2nd TX Mounted Rifles
Ruiz, P.-Pvt. Company D, 21st Patton's LA Infantry

Ruiz, Paul-Pvt. Company H, Chalmette Regiment, LA Militia
Ruiz, Pedro-Pvt. 1st Company A, 3rd TX Infantry
Ruiz, R.-Pvt. Company H, Orleans Fire Regiment, LA Militia
Ruiz, Thomas Adelaide-Pvt. Company A, 30th LA Infantry
Ruize, Jessus-Pvt. Company F, 2nd TX Cavalry

S

Saba, Mateo-Pvt. Co. 8, 5th (Spanish) Regiment, European Brigade, LA Militia
Sabado, Rafael-Pvt. Victoria County Militia, TX
Sabal, Adolphus M.-Surgeon C.S.A., FLA
Sabal, Emile Talvande-Surgeon / Medical Director under General Grayson, FLA
Sabal, Francis H.-1st Lt. Company A, 3rd FLA Infantry
Saballo, S.-Pvt. Company 5, 5th LA Infantry
Saballos, Auguste-Pvt. Company 2, 2nd French Brigade, LA Militia
Sabate, Paul E.-Pvt. Company H, 2nd FLA Cavalry
Sabate, Robert P.-Pvt. Company B/D, 63rd GA Infantry
Sabates, Jose-Pvt. Co. 4, 5th (Spanish) Regiment, European Brigade, LA Militia
Sabedra, Rafael-Pvt. Company A, Mann's Regiment, TX Cavalry
Sabio, Jose-Pvt. Company B, 1st LA Cavalry
Saenz, Juan-Pvt. Zapata's Company, Nueces County, TX State Troops
***See also Zagarra
Sagarras, Antoine-Pvt. Company D, 13th LA Infantry
Sais, Basilio-Pvt. Medina Guards, Bexar County, TX Militia
Sais, Colpia-Pvt. Skidmore's Company, San Patricio County, TX Militia
Sais, Guadalupe-Pvt. 1st Company C, 3rd TX Infantry
Sais, Jose-Pvt. Company I, 8th TX Infantry
Sais, M.-Pvt. Company A, 1st TX Cavalry
Sais, Manuel-Drummer Company E, 8th TX Infantry
Sais, Martin-Pvt. Company A, 3rd Yager's Battalion, TX Cavalry
Sais, Sisto-Pvt. Cameron County Coast Guard, TX Militia
Sais, Ylanio-Pvt. Company I, 33rd TX Cavalry
Saiz, Albino-Pvt. Thomas' Company, TX Partisan Rangers
Saiz, Guadalupe-Pvt. Company B, TX Reserve Corps
Sala, Pueblo-Pvt. Co. 2, 5th (Spanish) Regiment, European Brigade, LA Militia
Sala, Ramon-Pvt. Co. 9, 5th (Spanish) Regiment, European Brigade, LA Militia
Salado, Marcello-Pvt. Medina Guards, Bexar County, TX Militia
Salas, Agustin-Pvt. Company D, 30th LA Infantry
Salas, Jose M.-Pvt. Zapata's Company, Nueces County, TX State Troops
Salasar, Crecencio-Pvt. 1st Company C, 3rd TX Infantry
Salasar, Santiago-Pvt. Company E, 8th TX Infantry
Salatan, Casimiro-Pvt. 2nd Field Battery, TX Artillery
Salazar, Candelario-Pvt. Victoria County, TX Militia
Salazar, Casimiro-Musician 2nd TX Mounted Rifles
Salazar, Diego-Pvt. Co. A, 5th (Spanish) Regiment, European Brigade, LA Mil.

Salazar, Fernando-Pvt. Rhodes' Company, 3rd Yager's Battalion, TX Cavalry
Salazar, Griserto-Pvt. Rhodes' Company, 3rd Yager's Battalion, TX Cavalry
Salazar, Jose-Pvt. 1st Company C, Ragsdale's Battalion, TX Cavalry
Salazar, Juan-Pvt. 1st Company C, Ragsdale's Battalion, TX Cavalry
Salazar, Margarito-Pvt. Company F, 1st Yager's TX Cavalry
Salazar, Narcisso-Pvt. Company D, Benavides' Regiment, TX Cavalry
Salazar, Natividad-Pvt. Company F, 3rd TX Infantry
Salazar, Patricio-Pvt. Company E, 8th TX Infantry
Salazar, T.-Pvt. Company D, 5th TX Cavalry
Salazar, Tomas-Pvt. Company C, 36th TX Cavalry
Salazar, Vicente-Pvt. Company I, 8th TX Infantry
***See also Salzedo
Salcedo, D.-Pvt. LA Militia
Salcedo, Mariano-Pvt. Company E, Madison's Regiment, TX Cavalry
Saldania, Antoine-Pvt. Pointe Coupee Artillery, LA
Saldiva, Vicente-Pvt. Company I, 8th TX Infantry
Salina, Rafael-Pvt. Company D, Benavides' Regiment, TX Cavalry
Salinas, A.J.-Prominent Confederate supporter in South Carolina
Salinas, Andres-1st Sgt. Thomas' Company, TX Partisan Rangers
Salinas, Augustino-Pvt. Minute Men (Scouts), Starr County, TX Militia
Salinas, Carlos-Pvt. Company B, Benavides' Regiment, TX Cavalry
Salinas, Celestino-Pvt. Company C, 3rd TX Infantry
Salinas, Damacio-Pvt. Zapata's Company, Nueces County, TX State Troops
Salinas, Desiderio-Pvt. Zapata's Company, Nueces County, TX State Troops
Salinas, F.E.-Sgt. Company A, 23rd S.C. Infantry
Salinas, Francisco-Pvt. Thomas' Company, TX Partisan Rangers
Salinas, Jacobo-2nd Lt. 1st Company I, 33rd TX Cavalry
Salinas, Jose-Pvt. Company B, Baylor's Regiment, TX Cavalry
Salinas, Jose-Pvt. 17th Field Battery, TX Artillery
Salinas, Jose M.-Pvt. Zapata's Company, Nueces County, TX State Troops
Salinas, Juan-3rd Sgt. Minute Men (Scouts), Starr County, TX Militia
Salinas, M.-Pvt. Company B, Benavides' Regiment, TX Cavalry
Salinas, Manuel-Pvt. 1st Company C, Ragsdale's Battalion, TX Cavalry
Salinas, Martin-Pvt. 1st Company C, 3rd TX Infantry
Salinas, Mauricio-Pvt. Zapata's Company, Nueces County, TX State Troops
Salinas, Monico-Pvt. Company H, 33rd TX Cavalry
Salinas, Pablo-Pvt. 2nd Field Battery, TX Artillery
Salinas, Rafael-Pvt. Company D, Ragsdale's Battalion, TX Cavalry
Salinas, Ramon-Cpl. Thomas' Company, TX Partisan Rangers
Salinas, Refugio-Pvt. Engledow's Company, Nueces County, TX Militia
Salinas, Vicente-Cpl. Company F, 3rd TX Infantry
Salinas, Ynes-Pvt. 1st Company C, Ragsdale's Battalion, TX Cavalry
Salis, Seferino-Pvt. TX Militia
Salisair, Thomas-Pvt. Company C, 36th TX Cavalry
Salisar, N.-Pvt. 1st Company C, Ragsdale's Battalion, TX Cavalry

Sallas, Fabian-2nd Cpl. Company A, 3rd FLA Infantry
Sallas, Gomocindo-Cpl. Company D, 1st FLA Cavalry
Salles, Joseph-Pvt. Company 1, Rabby's Coast Guard Volunteers, ALA
Sallus, Damacio-Pvt. Company A, 3rd FLA Infantry
Salome, Bacilio-Pvt. 1st Company H, 33rd TX Cavalry
Salome, Thomas-Pvt. Company K, 37th TX Cavalry
Salor, Jose-3rd Lt. Co. 10, 5th (Spanish) Regiment, European Brigade, LA Militia
Saltillo, Manuel-Pvt. 8th Field Battery, TX Artillery
Salvador, F.-Pvt. Company A, 12th ALA Infantry
Salvador, Gaspard-Pvt. 1st Native Guards, LA Militia
Salvador, J. Ferro-Pvt. Co. 1, 5th (Spanish) Regt., European Brigade, LA Militia
Salvador, Juan-Pvt. Co. 3, 5th (Spanish) Regiment, European Brigade, LA Mil.
Salvador, Manuel-Sgt. Co. A, 5th (Spanish) Regt., European Brigade, LA Militia
Salvador, Pedro-Pvt. Co. A, 5th (Spanish) Regt., European Brigade, LA Militia
***See also Salcedo
Salzedo, Benjamin L.-Pvt. Company C, 18th MISS Infantry
Samaniego, Manuel Guadalupe-Interpreter TX State Troops
Sambola, Anthony-Capt. Company 5, Washington Artillery Battn., LA. He was also Clerk of the Militiary Court under General Hardee and J.B. Hood's Corps.
Sambola, Francisco-Lt. Company 2, Cazadores Espanoles Regiment, LA Militia
San, Domingo-Pvt. Company H, 17th TX Cavalry
Sanceda, Albino-Pvt. Company G, 3rd TX Infantry
Sanceda, Juan-2nd Lt. Company C, 8th TX Infantry
Sancedo, Severiano-Pvt. Company H, 8th TX Infantry
Sancedo, Umecindo-Sgt. Company C, 8th TX Infantry
Sanche, Joseph-Pvt. Company A, 29th TX Cavalry
Sanche, Raymond-Sgt. Company E, 1st LA Infantry
Sancher, Brigido-Pvt. Company I, Benavides' Regiment, TX Cavalry
Sancher, Dionino-Cpl. Co. 4, 5th (Spanish) Regt., European Brigade, LA Militia
Sanches, Antonio-Pvt. 1st Company H, 33rd TX Cavalry
Sanches, Carlos-Pvt. Company 1, Cazadores Espanoles Regiment, LA Militia
Sanches, Cimon-Pvt. Company I, 8th TX Infantry
Sanches, Clemente-Pvt. 1st Company H, 33rd TX Infantry
Sanches, D.-Pvt. Teels Company, TX State Troops
Sanches, Demetris-Pvt. Trevinio's Squad, TX Partisan Mounted Volunteers
Sanches, Felix-Pvt. Trevinio's Squad, TX Partisan Mounted Volunteers
Sanches, Francisco-Pvt. 1st Company H, 33rd TX Cavalry
Sanches, George-Pvt. Company A, 9th FLA Infantry
Sanches, Hijinio-Sgt. 1st Company H, 33rd TX Cavalry
Sanches, John-Musician Company D, 2nd Battalion, FLA Infantry
Sanches, Justo-Pvt. 1st Company C, Ragsdale's Battalion, TX Cavalry
Sanches, Leon-Pvt. 1st Company H, 33rd TX Cavalry
Sanches, M.-Pvt. Whiteheads' Company, 1st TX State Troops
Sanches, Manuel-Pvt. Duran's Company, Atascosa County, TX Troops
Sanches, Mathias-Pvt. Company H, 18th Consolidated LA Infantry

Sanches, Mariano-Pvt. 1st Company C, 3rd TX Infantry
Sanches, State-Pvt. Company G, Charleston Guards, 1st S.C. Infantry
Sanches, U.-Pvt. Company K, 5th LA Infantry
Sanchez, A.-Pvt. Company B, Richardson's Battalion, Confederate Light Artillery
Sanchez, A.-Pvt. Company D, 9th LA Cavalry
Sanchez, A.-Pvt. Company A, Miles' Legion, LA
Sanchez, A.-Pvt. Bancroft Jr's Company, 16th Regiment, S.C. Militia
Sanchez, Abner-Pvt. Company I, Ogden's LA Cavalry
Sanchez, Agapito-Pvt. Company D, 2nd TX Mounted Rifles
Sanchez, Anselmo-Pvt. Bustillo's Company, Bexar County, TX Militia
Sanchez, Anthony-Pvt. Company B, 9th Battalion, LA Infantry
Sanchez, Anthony R.-2nd Lt. Landry's Company, Donaldsonville Artillery, LA
Sanchez, Antonio-Pvt. Co. 7, 5th (Spanish) Regt., European Brigade, LA Militia
Sanchez, Antonio-Pvt. Company D, 6th Battalion, TX Cavalry
Sanchez, Antonio-Pvt. 8th Field Battery, TX Artillery
Sanchez, B.-Cpl. Ritter's Company, GA Light Artillery
Sanchez, B.-Cpl. 3rd Battery, MD Artillery
Sanchez, Bernardio S.-1st Lt. Claghorn's Company, 1st Olmstead's GA Infantry
Sanchez, Bernardo-Pvt. Company B, 28th Thomas' LA Infantry
Sanchez, Cayetano-Pvt. Co. 5, Cazadores Espanoles Regiment, LA Militia
Sanchez, Daniel-Drummer Company F, 3rd FLA Infantry
Sanchez, Desidera-Pvt. Company I, 8th TX Infantry
Sanchez, E.-Pvt. Company H, 2nd FLA Infantry
Sanchez, E.-Pvt. / Scout 2nd LA Cavalry
Sanchez, E.-Pvt. Orleans Fire Regiment, LA Militia
Sanchez, E.-Pvt. Company I, Orleans Guard Regiment, LA Militia
Sanchez, Edward Carrington-Pvt. FLA Militia
Sanchez, Epifanio-Pvt. Bustillo's Company, Bexar County, TX Militia
Sanchez, Eugene Joseph-Pvt. Company K, 8th LA Infantry
Sanchez, Evariste-Pvt. Company F, 4th LA Infantry
Sanchez, F.-Pvt. Company D, 22nd Consolidated LA Infantry
Sanchez, F.-Pvt. Company H, Orleans Guard Regiment, LA Militia
Sanchez, F.N.-Sgt. Company G, 3rd LA Infantry
Sanchez, Francis P.-Pvt. Company H, 1st Infantry Reserve, FLA
Sanchez, Francis Roman-Pvt. Company F, 10th FLA Infantry
Sanchez, Francis X.-Pvt. Company G, 1st FLA Cavalry
Sanchez, Francisco-Pvt. Co. 8, 5th (Spanish) Regt., European Brigade, LA Mil.
Sanchez, Francisco-Pvt. 1st Company C, 3rd TX Infantry
Sanchez, Francisco P.-Pvt. Company C, 2nd Battalion, ALA Light Artillery
Sanchez, Frank-Pvt. Company H, 2nd LA Cavalry
Sanchez, Gadsen Humphreys-Cpl. New Company K, 1st FLA Infantry
Sanchez, George Washington-Cpl. New Company K, 1st FLA Infantry
Sanchez, Henry C.-Pvt. Company F, 10th FLA Infantry
Sanchez, Herman-Pvt. Company I, 8th LA Infantry
***The Sanchez Sisters- Lola, a young Cuban woman with her sisters Panchita and

Eulogia spied, on behalf of the Confederacy. They had a brother who was in the Confederate Army; when their aged father Mauritia Sanchez was arrested for his support of the Confederate Government, they planned their revenge. They relayed information which led to the ambush of a Union Gunboat, and the Battle of Braddock's Farm, Florida. This was a Confederate victory due to the intelligence supplied by the Sanchez sister's and resulted in the destruction and capture of part of the 17th Connecticut Infantry, on February 5th, 1865.

Sanchez, J.-Pvt. Company K, 3rd LA Infantry
Sanchez, J.-Pvt. Company A, Miles' Legion, LA
Sanchez, James-Pvt. Company A, 1st LA Cavalry
Sanchez, James P.-Pvt. Company B, 3rd FLA Infantry
Sanchez, Jesus-Pvt. 1st Company A, 3rd TX Infantry
Sanchez, John-Pvt. Company B, 22nd Consolidated LA Infantry
Sanchez, John-Pvt. Company H, 8th LA Infantry
Sanchez, John-Pvt. 18th LA Infantry
Sanchez, John Y.-Pvt. Company F, 10th FLA Infantry
Sanchez, Jose-Pvt. Company K, 2nd TX Infantry
Sanchez, Jose-Pvt. Co. 2, 5th (Spanish) Regiment, European Brigade, LA Militia
Sanchez, Joseph-Pvt. Company E, 4th LA Infantry
Sanchez, Joseph-Pvt. Company I, Ogden's LA Cavalry
Sanchez, Juan-Pvt. Tom's Company, Atascosa County, TX Militia
Sanchez, Juan-Pvt. Company G, 2nd TX Infantry
Sanchez, Juan Esteban-Pvt. Company F, 3rd TX Infantry
Sanchez, Julian-Pvt. Company H, 8th TX Infantry
Sanchez, M.-Sgt. Company E, 22nd LA Infantry
Sanchez, M.-Pvt. 6th Field Battery, LA Light Artillery
Sanchez, Manuel-Pvt. Medina Guards, Bexar County, TX Militia
Sanchez, Manuel-Pvt. Duran's Company, Atascosa County, TX State Troops
Sanchez, Manuel-Pvt. Company B, 7th LA Infantry
Sanchez, Manuel R.-Pvt. Company H, 2nd FLA Infantry
Sanchez, Marcos-Pvt. Co. 2, 5th (Spanish) Regt., European Brigade, LA Militia
Sanchez, Marion-Pvt. Company H, 6th TX Infantry
Sanchez, Martin-Pvt. Company B, Maddox's LA Reserve Corps
Sanchez, Massaline-Pvt. Company H, 17th TX Cavalry
Sanchez, Miguel-Pvt. Medina Guards, Bexar County, TX Militia
Sanchez, Morris Mrs.-Civilian, had her home near Palatka, FLA looted by Union Troops for her support of the Confederacy on March 23rd, 1863.
Sanchez, N.-Pvt. 2nd LA Cavalry
Sanchez, Nestor-Pvt. Company C, 8th TX Infantry
Sanchez, Nicolas-Courier 33rd TX Cavalry
Sanchez, Pancho-Pvt. Coast Guard, FLA Militia
Sanchez, Pedro-Pvt. Company F, 1st Yager's TX Cavalry
Sanchez, Placido-Pvt. Company G, 2nd TX Infantry
Sanchez, Rafael-Pvt. Company I, Ogden's LA Cavalry
Sanchez, Raphael P.-Pvt. Company A, Miles' Legion, LA

Sanchez, Ricardo-Pvt. Co. 7, 5th (Spanish) Regt., European Brigade, LA Militia
Sanchez, Roman-Pvt. Company F, 10th FLA Infantry
Sanchez, Rufino-Pvt. Company H, 8th TX Infantry
Sanchez, Simeon J.-3rd Sgt. Company B, 2nd FLA Infantry
Sanchez, Stephen-Pvt. Company H, 17th TX Cavalry
Sanchez, W.-Pvt. Stockton Cavalry, Johnson County, TX Militia
Sanchez, W.J.-Pvt. FLA Militia
Sanchez, William-Capt. Company A, 18th Consolidated LA Infantry
Sanchis, Manuel-Pvt. Company H, 4th TX Cavalry
Sancho, Francisco-QuarterMaster Cazadores Espanoles Regiment, LA Militia
Sancho, Thomas-Pvt. Company B, Ragsdale's Battalion, TX Cavalry
Sancius, Manuel-Pvt. Company A, 11th TX Infantry
Sanchoz, A.-Pvt. 2nd LA Cavalry
Sandaval, Tomas-Pvt. Trevinio's Company, TX Cavalry
Sandoval, Carlos-Cpl. Trevinio's Company, TX Cavalry
Sandoval, Crisanto-Pvt. Bustillo's Company, Bexar County, TX Militia
Sandoval, Fernando-1st Sgt. Tom's Company, Atascosa County, TX State Tr.
Sandoval, Gregario-Pvt. 1st Company C, 3rd TX Infantry
Sandoval, Ignacio-5th Sgt. Bustillo's Company, Bexar County, TX Militia
Sandoval, Jesus-Pvt. Company C, Benavides' Regiment, TX Cavalry
Sandoval, Jesus-Sgt. 1st Company C, Ragsdale's Battalion, TX Cavalry
Sandoval, Pilar-Pvt. 1st Company A, Ragsdale's Battalion, TX Cavalry
Sandoval, Vemgio-Pvt. Bustillo's Company, Bexar County, TX Militia
Sandoval, Vivan-Pvt. Company A, 3rd Yager's Battalion, TX Cavalry
Sandz, Ferdinando-Pvt. Company F, 28th Thomas' LA Infantry
San Miguel, Alejandro-Pvt. Company I, 33rd TX Cavalry
San Miguel, Andrew-Pvt. Company K, 6th TX Infantry
San Miguel, Blas-Pvt. Company D, Benavides' Regiment, TX Cavalry
San Miguel, Domingo-Pvt. 1st Company H, 33rd TX Cavalry
San Miguel, Felipe-Pvt. Company H, 33rd TX Cavalry
San Miguel, George-Pvt. 1st Company A, 3rd TX Infantry
San Miguel, Jacinto-Pvt. 17th Field Battery, TX Artillery
San Miguel, Nabor-Pvt. 1st Company H, 33rd TX Cavalry
San Miguel, Rafael-Pvt. 1st Company A, Ragsdale's Battalion, TX Cavalry
Sans, Diego-Pvt. Co. 5, 5th (Spanish) Regiment, European Brigade, LA Militia
Sansero, Germasinto-Sgt. Company C, Benavides' Regiment, TX Cavalry
Santa, Jose M.-Pvt. Company I, Benavides' Regiment, TX Cavalry
Santa Anna, Benito-Pvt. Trevinio's Company, TX Partisan Rangers
Santa Anna, Francisco-Pvt. Thomas' Company, TX Partisan Rangers
Santa Bella, Manuel-Pvt. Company 2, Cazadores Espanoles Regiment, LA Mil.
Santana, Charles-Pvt. Company A, Miles' Legion, LA
Santana, Juan-Pvt. Company B, 33rd TX Cavalry
Santano, Emile-Pvt. Company C, 25th LA Infantry
Santano, Santiago-Pvt. Davis' Company, Confederate Light Artillery
Santiago, Aneseto-Pvt. Co. A, 5th (Spanish) Regt., European Brigade, LA Militia

Santiago, Cacais-Pvt. Company B, 2nd TX Cavalry
Santiago, Carpio-Cpl. Co. A, 5th (Spanish) Regt., European Brigade, LA Militia
Santiago, D.-Pvt. Company 7, 1st Chasseurs a pied, LA Militia
Santillana, Benito-Pvt. Trevinio's Squad, TX Partisan Mounted Cavalry
Santina, J.A.-Pvt. Company G, 1st Olmstead's GA Infantry
Santina, John Francis-Pvt. Company G, 1st Olmstead's GA Infantry
Santina, William H.-Sgt. Company G, 1st Olmstead's GA Infantry
Santochie, Pedro-Pvt. Company F, 22nd TX Cavalry
Santos, Alexander F.-1st Lt. Company H, 12th VIR Infantry
Santos, C.-Pvt. Company G, 17th TX Infantry
Santos, Charles A.-Pvt. Company A, 54th VIR Militia
Santos, Joel-Pvt. Company E, 2nd LA Cavalry
Santos, John-Pvt. Company E, 2nd LA Cavalry
Santos, Jose M.-Pvt. Company I, 33rd TX Cavalry
Santos, Leonard-Pvt. 1st Native Guards, LA Militia
Santos, M.-Pvt. Co. 1, 5th (Spanish) Regiment, European Brigade, LA Militia
Santos, Natano-Pvt. Company H, Bairds' Regiment, TX Cavalry
Santos, R.W.-Pvt. Company B, 54th VIR Militia
Santos, T.-Pvt. Company H, 15th Confederate Cavalry
Santos, T.-Pvt. Company E, Orleans Guard Regiment, LA Militia
Santos, Tigerino-Pvt. Company C, 3rd TX Infantry
Santos, V.-Pvt. Company E, 2nd LA Cavalry
Santos, Zeferino-Pvt. 1st Company C, 3rd TX Infantry
Santus, Cornelio-Pvt. Company B, 2nd LA Cavalry
Sapera, Joseph-Pvt. Co. 2, 5th (Spanish) Regiment, European Brigade, LA Militia
Sar, Pablo-Pvt. Company G, 4th Regiment, 1st Brigade, 1st Division, LA Militia
Sarate, Vicente-Pvt. Company F, 3rd TX Infantry
Sarda, Pedro-Pvt. Co. 4, 5th (Spanish) Regiment, European Brigade, LA Militia
Sarrano, A.-Pvt. Company 3, 4th Regiment, French Brigade, LA Militia
Sarrasqueta, Jose-Pvt. Co. 5, 5th (Spanish) Regt., European Brigade, LA Militia
***See also Zarza
Sarsa, Evaristo-Pvt. Co. 3, 5th (Spanish) Regiment, European Brigade, LA Mil.
Saso, Luis-Pvt. Co. 7, 5th (Spanish) Regiment, European Brigade, LA Militia
Sasportas, J.-Pvt. Co. B, 1st Regiment Charleston Reserve, SC Militia
Sastre, Jayme-Pvt. Co. 2, 5th (Spanish) Regiment, European Brigade, LA Militia
Sastre, Juan-Pvt. Co. 2, 5th (Spanish) Regiment, European Brigade, LA Militia
Sauceda, Albino-Pvt. Company G, 3rd TX Infantry
Sauceda, Juan-2nd Lt. Company H, 8th TX Infantry
Savario, John-Pvt. Company E, 28th Thomas' LA Infantry
Sayavedra, Manuel-Pvt. Company H, 8th TX Infantry
Sayes, Abraham-Pvt. Company K, 3rd LA Cavalry
Sebastian, John B.-Pvt. Company 5, Washington Artillery Battalion, LA
Sebastian, P.-Pvt. Co. A, 4th Regiment, 2nd Brigade, 1st Division, LA Militia
Sedocha, Pedro-Pvt. Webb's Lamar Mounted Volunteers, TX State Troops
***See also Ceferia

Seferia, Talario-Pvt. Co. A, 5th (Spanish) Regt., European Brigade, LA Militia
Segui, Bartolo-2nd Cpl. Company D, 8th FLA Infantry
Segui, Celestin H.-Pvt. Company B, 3rd FLA Infantry
Segui, Charles Downing-1st Lt. Company B, 3rd FLA Infantry
Segui, J.-3rd Lt. Company G, 21st ALA Infantry
Segui, John-Pvt. Company D, 8th FLA Infantry
Segui, Thomas-Musician Company E, 3rd FLA Infantry
Segui y Gahona, Gabriel-1st Lt. / Adjutant Cazadores Espanoles Regt., LA Militia
Seguin, J. Antonio-Pvt. Gray's Company, Bexar County, TX Militia
Seguin, James-Pvt. Company H, Chalmette Regiment, LA Militia
Seguin, R.-Pvt. Company 4, 1st Regiment, French Brigade, LA Militia
Seguin, Valmon-Pvt. Company F, 4th LA Infantry
***The following are Louisiana French versions of the surname Segura
Sagure, G.D.-Pvt. Company I, 7th LA Cavalry
Segoura, Gerald-Pvt. LA Militia
Segoura, Joseph-Pvt. LA Militia
Segura, A.-Pvt. 1st Native Guards, LA Militia
Segura, Alcibiade-Pvt. Company I, 7th LA Cavalry
Segura, Hervillien-Pvt. Company C, 10th Battalion, LA Infantry
Segura, Jesus-Pvt. Dunn's Company, Waller's Regiment, TX Cavalry
Segura, Juan-Pvt. Company C, 8th TX Infantry
Segura, J. Ozeme-Pvt. Company D/I, 7th LA Cavalry
Segura, Ovide-Pvt. Company I, 7th LA Cavalry
Segura, Ulysse-Pvt. Company I, 7th LA Cavalry
Segurado, Joachin-Pvt. Company G, 21st ALA Infantry
Seguro, Teodoro-Pvt. Rhodes' Company, 3rd Yager's Battalion, TX Cavalry
Seguro, Tomas-Pvt. 1st Company A, 3rd TX Infantry
Sigur, Frederic-Pvt. Company I, 3rd Harrison's LA Cavalry
Sigura, A.N.-Sgt. Company H, 10th Battalion, LA Infantry
Seixas, Benjamin Mendes-Pvt. Company G, 20th S.C. Infantry
Seixas, C.L.-Pvt. Company D, 3rd VIR Local Defense
Seixas, Henry C.-Pvt. Company B, 1st Nelligan's LA Infantry
Seixas, Henry O.-Pvt. Greens' Company, LA Guard Battery
Seixas, J. Madison-Major C.S.A., LA
Seis, Basilio-Pvt. Medina Guards, Bexar County, TX Militia
Seiz, Antonis-Pvt. Company B, Ragsdale's Battalion, TX Cavalry
Sel, Frank-Pvt. Pointe Coupee Artillery, LA
Selero, Neil-Pvt. Company H, 3rd Battalion, ALA Reserve
Selles, Antonio-Pvt. Co. 8, 5th (Spanish) Regt., European Brigade, LA Militia
Selles, F.-Sgt. Company E, 22nd Consolidated LA Infantry
Selles, Miguel-Pvt. Co. 6, 5th (Spanish) Regiment, European Brigade, LA Militia
Selles, Stephen R.-Pvt. Company F, 8th MISS Infantry
Selvera, Juan-Pvt. Jeff Davis Home Guard, Refugio County, TX Militia
Selvera, Manuel-Pvt. Company H, 8th TX Infantry
***See also Zamora

Semorah, Holcan-Pvt. Company I, 2nd TX Infantry
Sena, Francisco A.-Pvt. Co. I, 2nd Regiment, 2nd Brigade, 1st Division, LA Mil.
Senat, Antonio-Pvt. Co. 6, 5th (Spanish) Regiment, European Brigade, LA Militia
Senson, Eduardo-Cpl. Co. A, 5th (Spanish) Regt., European Brigade, LA Militia
***See also Zepeda
Sepeda, Teodosa-Pvt. Company F, 3rd TX Infantry
Sepulvado, Hulan-Pvt. 8th LA Infantry
Sepulvado, Vivian-Pvt. Company B, 28th LA Infantry
Sepulvera, Antonio-Pvt. Company F, 3rd TX Infantry
Sequi, G.-2nd Lt. Company G, 21st ALA Infantry
Sera, Tomas-Pvt. Co. A, 5th (Spanish) Regiment, European Brigade, LA Militia
Serafin, Marselina-Pvt. Co. A, 5th (Spanish) Regt., European Brigade, LA Militia
***See also Cerda
Serda, Pedro-Pvt. Company D, 30th LA Infantry
Serinano, B.B.-Pvt. Co. 1, 5th (Spanish) Regiment, European Brigade, LA Militia
Serna, Antonio-Pvt. Rhodes' Company, 3rd Yager's Battalion, TX Cavalry
Serna, Blas-Pvt. Company B, 33rd TX Cavalry
Serna, Ignacio F.-Pvt. Company B, 1st McCulloch's TX Cavalry
Serpas, Antonio-Pvt. Company K, Chalmette Regiment, LA Militia
Serpas, Francisco-Pvt. Company I, Chalmette Regiment, LA Militia
Serpas, J.-Pvt. Company K, Chalmette Regiment, LA Militia
Serpas, John-Pvt. Company G, 28th Thomas' LA Infantry
Serpas, Raphael Leon-Cpl. Company G, 28th Thomas' LA Infantry
Serra, Adolph-Pvt. Company A, Arrington's Mobile City Troop, ALA
Serra, Ansiguel-Pvt. Company G, 22nd Consolidated LA Infantry
Serra, Charles P.-Pvt. New Company G, 1st FLA Infantry
Serra, John Baptiste-Catholic Priest who assited in the production of salt, at the Salt works, on Mon Louis Island, ALA for the Confederate war effort; he also assisted in the procuring of oxen and sheep from his Mission in Bayou La Batre, ALA to help feed the civilians and military in Mobile, ALA
***See also Cevallos
Sevallos, Antonio-Pvt. Davis' Company, Confederate Light Artillery
Sevanino, Castella-Pvt. Company C, Benavides' Regiment, TX Cavalry
***See also Cervantes
Servantez, Casdnia-Pvt. Company I, 8th TX Infantry
Servia, Valentin-Pvt. Co. 4, 5th (Spanish) Regiment, European Brigade, LA Mil.
Severio, William-Pvt. Company A, Ogden's LA Cavalry
Sevilla, Valentin-Pvt. Co. A, 5th (Spanish) Regiment, European Brigade, LA Mil.
*** The surname Seymour was originally Zamora; its originator was Jose Zamora who settled in Mississippi during the Spanish colonial period.
Seymour, Henry-Pvt. Company A, 3rd MISS Infantry
Seymour, Jean Baptiste-Pvt. Company A, 3rd MISS Infantry
Seymour, Lazarus-Pvt. Company H, 15th Confederate Cavalry, ALA
Seymour, Raymour-Pvt. Company A, 17th Battalion, MISS Cavalry
Sibargas, Antonio-Pvt. Company D, 11th LA Infantry

***See also Zierra
Sierra, Antonio-Capt. Bexar County, TX Militia
Sierra, Bicente-Pvt. Company B, Baylor's Regiment, TX Cavalry
Sierra, G.-Pvt. Company 2, 5th (Spanish) Regiment, European Brigade, LA Militia
Sierra, Jose-Pvt. Company 2, Cazadores Espanoles Regiment, LA Militia
Sierra, Joseph-Alderman of the Exiled Conf. Municipal Govt. of Pensacola, FLA
Sierra, Joseph E.-Pvt. Company B, 3rd Battalion, FLA Cavalry
Sierra, Juan-Pvt. Company B, 2nd TX Cavalry
Sierra, Manuel-Sgt. Co. 2, 5th (Spanish) Regiment, European Brigade, LA Militia
Sierra, Norberto-1st Lt. Mission Guards, Bexar County, TX Militia
Sierra, Vicente-Pvt. Company B, Baylor's Regiment, TX
Sifuentes, Bartolo-Pvt. Bustillo's Company, Bexar County, TX Militia
Sigues, Joshua P.-Pvt. 36th Broyles' GA Infantry
Silba, Manuel-Pvt. Co. 10, 5th (Spanish) Regiment, European Brigade, LA Militia
Silbeira, Francisco-Pvt. Co. 4, 5th (Spanish) Regt., European Brigade, LA Militia
***See also Silba and Sylva
Silva, Emanuel-Pvt. Noyes's Coast Guard, FLA Militia
Silva, Emiliano A.-3rd Sgt. Company C, 1st Olmstead's GA Infantry
Silva, F.-Pvt. Company D, Charleston Guard, 1st S.C. Regiment
Silva, Francisco-Pvt. Co. 8, 5th (Spanish) Regiment, European Brigade, LA Mil.
Silva, Francisco Jr.-Pvt. Co. 8, 5th (Spanish) Regt., European Brigade, LA Mil.
Silva, J.B.-Pvt. Company F, 2nd Regiment Volunteers, ALA Militia
Silva, Jose-Pvt. Company G, 21st ALA Infantry
Silva, Jose Maria-Pvt. Company A, Confederate States Zouave Battalion, LA
Silva, Juan-Pvt. Co. 8, 5th (Spanish) Regiment, European Brigade, LA Militia
Silva, Manuel-Pvt. Co. 3, 5th (Spanish) Regiment, European Brigade, LA Mil.
Silva, Manuel Sr.-Pvt. Co. 8, 5th (Spanish) Regiment, European Brigade, LA Mil.
Silveira y Caldeira, I.-Pvt. Co. 8, 5th (Spanish) Regt., European Brigade, LA Mil.
Simon, Antonio-Pvt. Co. 7, 5th (Spanish) Regiment, European Brigade, LA Mil.
Simon, Ferdinand-Pvt. Company A, Comal Reserve, TX Militia
Simon, Geronimo-Pvt. Co. 8, 5th (Spanish) Regt., European Brigade, LA Militia
Simon, Gimenez-Pvt. Company C, 1st Strawbridge's LA Infantry
Simon, Jose-Pvt. Co. 4, 5th (Spanish) Regiment, European Brigade, LA Militia
Simon, Juan-Pvt. Company 1, Cazadores Espanoles Regiment, LA Militia
*** See also Cintes
Sintes, Francisco-Pvt. Co. 9, 5th (Spanish) Regt., European Brigade, LA Militia
Sintes, Gabriel-Pvt. Co. 9, 5th (Spanish) Regiment, European Brigade, LA Militia
Sintes, Miguel-Pvt. Co. 9, 5th (Spanish) Regiment, European Brigade, LA Militia
Sintes, Pedro Fridy-Sgt. Co. 2, 5th (Spanish) Regt., European Brigade, LA Militia
Sisa, Lorenzo-Pvt. Co. 9, 5th (Spanish) Regiment, European Brigade, LA Militia
Sisa, Pablo-Pvt. Co. 2, 5th (Spanish) Regiment, European Brigade, LA Militia
Sisa, Salvador-Pvt. Co. 2, 5th (Spanish) Regiment, European Brigade, LA Militia
Sitges, F.-Pvt. Company 5, 5th (Spanish) Regiment, European Brigade, LA Mil.
Sitges, Marcos-Sgt. Co. 5, 5th (Spanish) Regiment, European Brigade, LA Militia
Slado, Ramon-Pvt. Co. 9, 5th (Span.) Regt., Euro., Brigade, LA Mil. (see Ramon

Slado listed under Hispanic Naval section at begining of book)
***This is the Louisiana French version of the surname Suarez
Soires, Augustin-Pvt. Company D, 27th LA Infantry
Soirez, Hypolite-Pvt. Company H, 28th Thomas' LA Infantry
Soiris, J.-Pvt. Company H, 18th LA Infantry
Sola, William-Musisian Company E, 3rd FLA Infantry
Sola > see also De Cruz Sola, Manuel
Solana, Mathew- He was a Delegate to the FLA Secession Convention from the St. Augustine area. He might be the same individual listed as Mathew Solano and / or M. Solano below.
Solana, Phillip M.-Pvt. Company D, 8th FLA Infantry
Solano, Joseph M.-Pvt. Company B, 3rd FLA Infantry
Solano, M.-County Commissioner, St. Johns County, FLA 1861
Solano, Mathew-Pvt. 2nd FLA Cavalry
Solar, Michel-Pvt. Company B, Confederate States Zouave Battalion, LA
Solayre, Antonio-Pvt. Company G, 2nd FLA Infantry
Soler, Gayetano-Pvt. Co. 5, 5th (Spanish) Regt., European Brigade, LA Militia
Soler, Miguel-Pvt. Co. 7, 5th (Spanish) Regiment, European Brigade, LA Militia
Solez, Jesus-Cpl. Co. 8, 5th (Spanish) Regiment, European Brigade, LA Militia
Solice, Ygnacio-Pvt. Company C, 8th TX Infantry
Solis, Adolphe-Sgt. Company G, 28th Thomas' LA Infantry
Solis, Alfred-Pvt. Lartigue's Company, Bienville Guards, LA Militia
Solis, Antonio-Pvt. Minute Men (Scouts), Starr County, TX Militia
Solis, Benjamin-Pvt. Company G, 1st Field's TENN Infantry
Solis, Ceferino-Pvt. Company A, Benavides' Regiment, TX Cavalry
Solis, Eugenio-Pvt. Company H, 33rd TX Infantry
Solis, Felix-Pvt. Company G, 3rd LA Infantry
Solis, Isidore Narcisse-Pvt. Lartigue's Company, Bienville Guards, LA Militia
Solis, Jesus-Sgt. Trevinio's Squad, TX Partisan Mounted Rangers
Solis, John-Pvt. 19th ALA Cavalry
Solis, Jose Manuel-Pvt. Trevinio's Squad, TX Partisan Mounted Rangers
Solis, Juan-Pvt. 1st Company I, 33rd TX Cavalry
Solis, Leander Manuel-Pvt. Lartigues' Company, Bienville Guards, LA Militia
Solis, Leon Manuel-Pvt. / Scout Lartigue's Company, Bienville Guards, LA Mil.
Solis, Lucien-Pvt. Lartigue's Company, Bienville Guards, LA Militia
Solis, R.-Pvt. Company G, 4th Regiment, 1st Brigade, 1st Division, LA Militia
Solis, Richard-Pvt. Company B, 3rd Battalion, FLA Cavalry
Solis, Santiago-Pvt. Trevinio's Squad, TX Partisan Mounted Rangers
Solis, Ysedre-Pvt. Trevinio's Squad, TX Partisan Mounted Rangers
Solomon, Solomon-Sutler 14th LA Infantry and the 18th MISS Infantry. He participated in many battles, as a volunteer soldier, when he wasn't selling his goods.
Sombra, Lewis-Pvt. Company C, 11th LA Infantry
Sonora, Antonio-Pvt. Company F, 3rd TX Infantry
Soria, Henry N.-Capt. Company B, 21st Kennedy's LA Infantry
Sosa, F.-Pvt. Teel's Company, TX State Troops

Sosa, Guilermo-Cpl. Company D, Benavides' Regiment, TX Cavalry
Sosa, John D.-2nd Cpl. Company C, Benavides' Regiment, TX Cavalry
Sosa, M.-Pvt. Company 5, 5th (Spanish) Regiment, European Brigade, LA Mil.
Sosa, Raul-Pvt. Ferguson's Company, Victoria County, TX Militia
Sosa, Vicente-Pvt. Gray's Company, Bexar County, TX Militia
Sotello > see Zotello
***See also Garcia Soto, M.
Soto, Antonio-Pvt. Company C, Benavides' Regiment, TX Cavalry
Soto, Antonio-Pvt. 2nd Field Battery, TX Artillery
Soto, Augustin-Cpl. Company C, 3rd TX Infantry
Soto, Esper J.-Pvt. Creole Fire Company, Mobile, ALA Militia
Soto, John A.-Cpl. Company A, 3rd ALA Infantry
Soto, Juan Garcia-Lt. Benavides' Regiment, TX Cavalry
Soto, Juan J.-Pvt. Company B, Ragsdale's Battalion, TX Cavalry
Soto, Juan Manuel-Pvt. Company C, 8th TX Infantry
Soto, Lino-Pvt. 1st Company C, 3rd TX Infantry
Soto, Martin-Pvt. Company C, Benavides' Regiment, TX Cavalry
Soto, Vicente-Pvt. Company G, 3rd TX Infantry
Soto, Ysidero-Pvt. Company C, Benavides' Regiment, TX Cavalry
Sotres, Santos-Pvt. Co. 9, 5th (Spanish) Regiment, European Brigade, LA Militia
Soza, Briles-Pvt. Company C, 5th LA Infantry
Spazas, Guadalupe-Pvt. Company B, Ragsdale's Battalion, TX Cavalry
***See also Soires, Soirez, Soiris
Suares, Aubrey-Pvt. Company D, 3rd ALA Cavalry
Suares, B.M.-Cpl. Company A, 1st Charleston Battalion, S.C. Infantry
Suares, Frank-Pvt. Company A, Arrington's Mobile City Troop, ALA
Suares, Jacob Edgar-Pvt. Company I, 27th S.C. Infantry
Suares, Thomas F.-Pvt. Company A, Arrington's Mobile City Troop, ALA
Suares, Ysabel-Pvt. Company C, Benavides' Regiment, TX Cavalry
Suarez, Andre-Pvt. Landry's Company, Donaldsonville Artillery, LA
Suarez, Antoine-Pvt. Donaldsonville Artillery, LA
Suarez, Antoine Andre-Pvt. Company H, 8th LA Infantry
Suarez, F.-3rd Lt. Co. 1, 5th (Spanish) Regiment, European Brigade, LA Militia
Suarez, Francisco-Pvt. Co. 5, 5th (Spanish) Regt., European Brigade, LA Militia
Suarez, John-Pvt. Landry's Company, Donaldsonville Artillery, LA
Suarez, Manuel-Pvt. Co. 3, 5th (Spanish) Regt., European Brigade, LA Militia
Suarez, Rafael-Pvt. Landry's Company, Donaldsonville Artillery, LA
Suarez, Raphael-Pvt. Company F, 3rd FLA Infantry
Suarez, Thomas-County Commissioner, Duval County, FLA 1863
Suarez, Vicente-Pvt. Co. 3, 5th (Spanish) Regt., European Brigade, LA Militia
Suarez, Ysabel-Pvt. Company C, 8th Hobby's TX Infantry
Sulado, Peter-Pvt. 24th Battalion, TX State Troops
***See also Zuniga
Suniga, Alejandro-Pvt. 1st Company H, 33rd TX Cavalry
Suniga, Antonio-Pvt. Company K, 6th TX Infantry

Swares, E.-Pvt. 25th TX Cavalry
***See also Silba and Silva
Sylva, G.-Pvt. Landry's Company, Donaldsonville Artillery, LA
Sylva, Joseph-Pvt. Company F, 1st FLA Cavalry

T

***See also Tobar, Tober
Tabor, Calixto-Pvt. Medina Guards, Bexar County, TX Militia
Tabor, D.-Pvt. Company C, Benavides' Regiment, TX Cavalry
Tabor, Enriques-Pvt. Company D, Benavides' Regiment, TX Cavalry
Tacon, H.-Pvt. Company I, 3rd Regiment, European Brigade, LA Militia
Tacon, Juan-Pvt. Company G, 10th LA Infantry
Tafolla, James-Musician Company B, 33rd TX Cavalry
Talamante, Eulajio-Pvt. 1st Company C, Ragsdale's Battalion, TX Cavalry
Talamente, Ucebio-Cpl. 1st Company A, Ragsdale's Battalion, TX Cavalry
Talamantes, Jose Maria-Pvt. Company F, 3rd TX Infantry
Talamantes, Mariano-Pvt. Grays' Company, Bexar County, TX Militia
Talamas, Leon-Pvt. Company 1, 3rd Regiment, French Brigade, LA Militia
Tapia, Antonia-Pvt. Company I, Benavides' Regiment, TX Cavalry
Tapia, Leon-Cpl. Thomas' Company, TX Partisan Rangers
Tapia, P.-Pvt. Company G, 8th TX Infantry
Tapiano, Joseph-2nd Cpl. Duran's Company, Atascosa County, TX Troops
Tapis, B.-Pvt. Company 5, 4th Regiment, French Brigade, LA Militia
Taquino, Anthony Alexander-Pvt. Company D, 60th ALA Infantry
Taquino, Augustus-Pvt. Company A, 27th LA Infantry
Taquino, Francis-Pvt. Company K, 3rd LA Infantry
Taquino, T.-3rd Lt. Company 3, 1st Chasseurs a pied, LA Militia
Taquino, Thomas-Pvt. Pointe Coupee Artillery, LA
Tarango, Julio-Pvt. Company C, Benavides' Regiment, TX Cavalry
Targarona, P.-Pvt. Company A, Red River Sharpshooters, LA
Tarrara, Bernardo-Pvt. Co. 4, 5th (Spanish) Regt., European Brigade, LA Militia
Tartavull, Antonio-Pvt. Co. 9, 5th (Spanish) Regt., European Brigade, LA Mil.
Tavares, Benjamin-Pvt. Hall's Company, Orleans Fire Regiment, LA Militia
Tavares, W.-Pvt. Company K, Confederate Guards Regiment, LA Militia
Taverra, (unknown)-Pvt. 2nd Regiment, French Brigade, LA Militia
Tebuche, Hernando-Pvt. Company K, 12th TX Infantry
Teclas, Bartolome-Pvt. Co. 2, 5th (Spanish) Regt., European Brigade, LA Militia
Telles, H.-Pvt. Company B, 3rd TX Infantry
Telles, Luis-Pvt. Medina Guards, Bexar County, TX Militia
Telles, Jose Maria-Pvt. Company E, 24th TX Infantry
Tejada, Emeterio-Pvt. Company F, 3rd TX Infantry
Tejada, Severiano-Pvt. Trevinio's Company, TX Cavalry
Tejeda, Jesus-Pvt. Company H, 8th Hobby's TX Infantry
Tejeda, Rafael-Pvt. Trevinio's Company, TX Cavalry

Hispanic Confederates 137

Tejera > see Jose Tejera Marcial, Manuel Tejera Marcial and Jose Tejera Aranter
Tejida, G.-Pvt. Company H, 8th TX Infantry
Tejida, Ignacio-Pvt. Company B, 33rd TX Cavalry
Tenio, H.-Sgt. Company A, 21st MISS Infantry
*** This is the Louisiana version of the surname Tejada
Texada, James-Pvt. Company A, 1st LA Cavalry
Texada, Jerome-Pvt. Consolidated Crescent Regiment, LA Infantry
Texada, Jerome-Pvt. Company A, 1st LA Cavalry
Texada, Joseph Welsh-Capt. Company A, 8th LA Cavalry
Texada, Lewis-Capt. Company D, 1st Regiment, LA Reserve Corps
Texada, Theodore J.-Pvt. Company G, 2nd LA Cavalry
Texas, W.-Musician 2nd Battery, MD Artillery
***See also Tisero
Ticero, Theodore-Pvt. GA Militia
Tiern, Pedro-Cpl. Co. 4, 5th (Spanish) Regiment, European Brigade, LA Militia
Tigirina, Juan-Sgt. Thomas' Company, TX Partisan Rangers
Tijerina, Francisco-Pvt. Company H, 8th Hobby's TX Infantry
Tijerina, Gregorio-Pvt. Company H, 8th Hobby's TX Infantry
Tilano, Hampton-Pvt. Company B, 7th LA Infantry
Tilano, Michael-Pvt. Company H, 11th LA Infantry
Tirado, J.H.-Pvt. Orleans Guard Battery, LA Artillery
Tirroa, Juan-Pvt. Company G, 3rd TX Infantry
***See also Ticero
Tisero, Berto-Pvt. Company D, 10th Battalion, GA Infantry
To, Rosendo-Pvt. Co. 4, 5th (Spanish) Regiment, European Brigade, LA Militia
Tobal, M.-Pvt. Company K, 27th LA Infantry
***See also Tabor
Tobar, Sabas-Pvt. 1st Company C, 3rd TX Infantry
Tober, Dario-Pvt. Medina Guards, Bexar County, TX Militia
Tober, Esechio-Pvt. Medina Guards, Bexar County, TX Militia
Tobias, A.L.-QuarterMaster 1st Regiment, S.C. Artillery Militia
Tobias, C.H.-Cpl. Company C, 9th S.C. Infantry
Tobias, F.W.-Pvt. Company C, 21st S.C. Infantry
Tobias, I.H.-Pvt. Company I, 25th S.C. Infantry
Tobias, James-Pvt. 3rd Regiment, S.C. Reserve
Tobias, J.B.-Pvt. Company C, 9th S.C. Infantry
Tobias, J.H.-Pvt. Company C, 21st S.C. Infantry
Tobias, J.L.-Pvt. Walter's Company, 1st Regiment, S.C. Artillery Militia
Tobias, J.N.-Pvt. Company I, 23rd S.C. Infantry
Tobias, J.W.-Pvt. Company I, 25th S.C. Infantry
Tobias, S.R.-Sgt. 2nd Company K, 6th S.C. Infantry
Tobias, T.E.-Cpl. Company I, 25th S.C. Infantry
Tobias, T.J.-Pvt. Company I, 25th S.C. Infantry
Tobias, T.N.-Pvt. Company I, 25th S.C. Infantry
Tobias, William M.-Pvt. Company I, 25th S.C. Infantry

Toca, A.-Pvt. Company B, 22nd Consolidated LA Infantry
Toca, Octave-Pvt. Company A, Manigault's Battalion, S.C. Artillery
Toca, Septime-Pvt. Orleans Guard Battery, LA Light Artillery
Toca, Telesphore-2nd Lt. 2nd Field Battery, LA Light Artillery
Toledano, Benjamin-Lt. Company B, Jefferson Mounted Guards, LA Infantry
Toledano, Edmund Arthur-Capt. Watson Battery, LA Artillery
Toledano, Ernest-Pvt. Company 3, Washington Artillery Battalion, LA
Toledano, J.P.-Pvt. Company K, Chalmette Regiment, LA Militia
Toledano, Jules Raphael-1st Lt. Co. E, Orleans Guard Regiment, LA Militia
Toledano, Oswald J.-Pvt. Company 3, Washington Artillery Battalion, LA
Toledano, William S.-Pvt. Company 3, Washington Artillery Battalion, LA
Toledano, W.Y.-Pvt. Company D, 3rd Infantry Local Defense, VIR
Toledo, Pablo-Pvt. 1st Company H, Baird's Regiment, TX Cavalry
Tomas, Francisco-Pvt. Co. 8, 5th (Spanish) Regt., European Brigade, LA Militia
Topiano, Joseph-Pvt. Tom's Company, Atascosa County, TX Militia
Toras, John-Sgt. LA Defenders Battalion
Tores, A.-Pvt. Company G, Saint James Regiment, LA Militia
Tores, Jose-Pvt. Company A, 11th TX Infantry
Torigano, Colastus-Pvt. 1st Native Guards, LA Militia
Toro, Franco-Pvt. Co. 4, 5th (Spanish) Regiment, European Brigade, LA Militia
Torras, Jose-Capt. Planters Guards, LA Mil. He also served in the Commissary Department of the C.S.A. in charge of cotton transports from Alexandria, LA to Niblos Bluff, TX.
Torres, Angel C.-Pvt. Company D, 1st McCulloch's TX Cavalry
Torres, Antonio-Pvt. Company I, Benavides' Regiment, TX Cavalry
Torres, Antonio-Pvt. Co. 9, 5th (Spanish) Regt., European Brigade, LA Militia
Torres, Cisario-1st Lt. Bexar County, TX Militia
Torres, Enriques-Pvt. Medina Guards, Bexar County, TX Militia
Torres, Epemenio-Pvt. 1st Company C, 3rd TX Infantry
Torres, Francisco-Pvt. Company F, 3rd TX Infantry
Torres, G.-Pvt. Company 8, 1st Chasseurs a pied, LA Militia
Torres, J.B.-Pvt. Company 1, 1st LA Heavy Artillery
Torres, Jacinto-Sgt. 1st Company C, 3rd TX Infantry
Torres, Jose-Cpl. Co. 9, 5th (Spanish) Regiment, European Brigade, LA Militia
Torres, Joseph-Pvt. Company I, 8th LA Infantry
Torres, Julius-Pvt. Mark's Company, 22nd LA Infantry
Torres, Manana-Pvt. Company I, Benavides' Regiment, TX Cavalry
Torres, Mariano-Pvt. Medina Guards, Bexar County, TX Militia
Torres, Merriday-Pvt. Company I, 8th LA Infantry
Torres, Modesto-Pvt. Company B, 33rd TX Cavalry
Torres, Ramon-Pvt. Co. 2, 5th (Spanish) Regiment, European Brigade, LA Mil.
Torres, Secundino-Pvt. Gray's Company, Bexar County, TX Militia
Torres, Severiano-Pvt. Company E, Madison's Regiment, TX Cavalry
Torres, Trinidad-Pvt. 1st Company I, 33rd TX Cavalry
Torres, Trinidad-Pvt. 8th Field Battery, TX Artillery

Torress, Justave-Pvt. 1st Native Guards, LA Militia
Torrez, Sebero-Pvt. 1st Company C, Ragsdale's Battalion, TX Cavalry
Torriss, J.G.-Pvt. LA Militia
Torro Ramon, Jose-Pvt. Company D, 30th LA Infantry
Traisurra, Manuel-Pvt. Co. 7, 5th (Spanish) Regt., European Brigade, LA Militia
Trasantas, Ramon-Pvt. Co. 9, 5th (Spanish) Regt., European Brigade, LA Militia
Travinio, Gragario-Pvt. Company B, Baylor's Regiment, TX Cavalry
Trecho, Cazalario-Pvt. Company E, 8th TX Infantry
***See also Trijo
Trejo, Cristoval-Pvt. 1st Company C, 3rd TX Infantry
Trejo, Tircio-Pvt. 1st Company C, Ragsdale's Battalion, TX Cavalry
Trescasas, James-Pvt. Co. 5, 5th (Spanish) Regt., European Brigade, LA Militia
Trevinia, Lorenzo-Sgt. Company B, 2nd TX Cavalry
Trevenio, Carlos-Pvt. Company I, 8th TX Infantry
Trevenio, Jesus-Pvt. Company E, 36th TX Cavalry
Trevinio, Julian-Pvt. Minute Men (Scouts), Starr County, TX Militia
Trevenio, Leonardo-Pvt. TX Militia
Trevenio, Tomas-Pvt. Company I, 8th TX Infantry
Trevinio, Clemento-Pvt. Company E, 8th TX Infantry
Trevinio, Lorenzo-Capt. Trevinio's Company, TX Cavalry
Trevino De Ochoa, Antonio-Pvt. TX Militia
Trevino, Anastacio-Pvt. Thomas' Company, TX Partisan Rangers
Trevino, Andreas-Pvt. Company D, 3rd TX Infantry
Trevino, Bonifacio-Pvt. Rhodes' Company, 3rd Yager's Battalion, TX Cavalry
Trevino, Cesario-Pvt. 1st Company H, 33rd TX Cavalry
Trevino, Demasio-Pvt. 1st Company C, 3rd TX Infantry
Trevino, Eujenio-Pvt. 1st Company H, 33rd TX Cavalry
Trevino, Francisco-Pvt. Company G, 3rd TX Infantry
Trevino, Jesus-Pvt. Company H, 3rd TX Infantry
Trevino, Jorge-1st Lt. Minute Men (Scouts), Starr County, TX Militia
Trevino, Jose-Pvt. 1st Company H, 33rd TX Cavalry
Trevino, Jose-Pvt. Trevinio's Squad, TX Partisan Mounted Volunteers
Trevino, Juan-Pvt. Company D, 30th LA Infantry
Trevino, Justo-Capt. Trevinio's Squad, TX Partisan Mounted Volunteers
Trevino, L.-Capt. Cater's Battalion, TX Cavalry
Trevino, Longino-Pvt. 1st Company I, 33rd TX Cavalry
Trevino, Manuel-Pvt. 1st Company H, 33rd TX Cavalry
Trevino, Martin-Pvt. Trevinio's Squad, TX Partisan Mounted Volunteers
Trevino, Oliverio-Pvt. Company I, 8th TX Infantry
Trevino, Pedro-2nd Lt. 1st Company I, 33rd TX Cavalry
Trevino, Polonario-Pvt. 1st Company H, 33rd TX Cavalry
Trevino, Rafael-Pvt. Company G, 3rd TX Infantry
Trevino, Sesario-Pvt. Company A, Benavides' Regiment, TX Cavalry
Trevino, Ygnacio-Pvt. Trevinio's Squad, TX Partisan Mounted Volunteers
Trevino, Ydalecio-2nd Lt. Rhodes' Company, 3rd Yager's Battalion, TX Cavalry

Triay, Francis-Pvt. Company G, 1st GA Infantry
Triay, Guillermo-Cpl. Co. 7, 5th (Spanish) Regt., European Brigade, LA Militia
Triay, Henry-Pvt. Company I, 1st GA Infantry
Triay, J.-Pvt. Company E, Orleans Guard Regiment, LA Militia
Triay, John-Pvt. Company D, 1st Olmstead's GA Infantry
Triay, Jose-Pvt. Co. 1, 5th (Spanish) Regiment, European Brigade, LA Militia
Triay, Lorenzo-Pvt. Co. 3, 5th (Spanish) Regiment, European Brigade, LA Mil.
Triay, Peter-Pvt. Company D, 8th FLA Infantry
Triay, Rafael-Pvt. Co. 5, 5th (Spanish) Regiment, European Brigade, LA Militia
Triay, Victorino-Pvt. Company D, 8th FLA Infantry
Trijo, Catalino-Pvt. Company E, Madison's Regiment, TX Cavalry
Trinidad, Domingo-Pvt. Company B, Ragsdale's Battalion, TX Cavalry
Trinidad, E.B.-Capt. Company E, 7th LA Cavalry
Truch, Manuel-Capt. Co. 10, 5th (Spanish) Regt., European Brigade, LA Militia
Trujillo, Jesus-Pvt. 1st Company A, 3rd TX Infantry
Truot, Sebastian-Pvt. Co. 3, 5th (Spanish) Regiment, European Brigade, LA Mil.
***This is the Louisiana version of the surname Trujillo
Truxillo, A.-2nd Lt. Company F, Jeff Davis Regiment, LA Militia
Truxillo, Andre-Pvt. Company C, 26th LA Infantry
Truxillo, Antoine-Pvt. Company H, 28th Thomas' LA Infantry
Truxillo, Denis-Cpl. Company H, 28th Thomas' LA Infantry
Truxillo, E.A. Jr.-Pvt. Company G, 26th LA Infantry
Truxillo, E.H.-Sgt. 28th Gray's LA Infantry
Truxillo, F.-Cpl. Hutton's Company, Crescent Artillery, LA
Truxillo, Florentin A.-Pvt. Company H, Thomas' LA Infantry
Truxillo, John-Pvt. Company B, 1st LA Heavy Artillery
Truxillo, Lucien-Cpl. Company H, 2nd LA Cavalry
Truxillo, Manuel-Pvt. Company H, 2nd LA Cavalry
Truxillo, Phillip H.-Sgt. Company H, 28th Thomas' LA Infantry
Truxillo, Sosthene-Pvt. Company H, 2nd LA Cavalry
Tudury, Anthony-Pvt. Co. 5, 5th (Spanish) Regt., European Brigade, LA Militia
Tudury, R.-Pvt. Co. 1, 5th (Spanish) Regiment, European Brigade, LA Militia
Tumi, Juan-Pvt. Co. 9, 5th (Spanish) Regiment, European Brigade, LA Militia
Tur, A.-Pvt. Company 1, 5th (Spanish) Regiment, European Brigade, LA Militia
Tur, Bartolome-Pvt. Co. 6, 5th (Spanish) Regiment, European Brigade, LA Mil.
Turla, Manuel-Sgt. Company B, 8th LA Infantry
Turro, Pablo-Pvt. Company 1, Cazadores Espanoles Regiment, LA Militia
Tuscand, Santiago-Pvt. Company A, 1st Battalion State Troops, TX Cavalry

U

Ubera, Francisco-Pvt. Company 1, Cazadores Espanoles Regiment, LA Militia
Ugarte, B.-Pvt. Co. 5, 5th (Spanish) Regiment, European Brigade, LA Militia
Uguet, Jayme-Pvt. Co. 3, 5th (Spanish) Regiment, European Brigade, LA Militia
Ulibarri, Pablo-Cpl. Company H, 8th TX Infantry

Ulibarri, Trinidad-Pvt. Company H, 8th TX Infantry
Umaran, Joseph-Pvt. Company H, Chalmette Regiment, LA Militia
Urbessa, Jose R.-Pvt. Co. 4, 5th (Spanish) Regt., European Brigade, LA Militia
Urbizu, C.-Pvt. Company 8, 1st Chasseurs a pied, LA Militia
Urbizu, P.-Pvt. Company 8, 1st Chasseurs a pied, LA Militia
Uriegies, Bruno-Pvt. Davidson's Company, TX
Urista, Julian-Pvt. Company E, 8th TX Infantry
Urista, Manuel-Pvt. Company C, 16th TX Infantry
Ursuelos, Sostenes-Pvt. Company D, 2nd TX Mounted Rifles
Usina, Domingo B.-Pvt. Company B, 3rd FLA Infantry
Usina, J.-County Commissioner, St. Johns County, FLA 1861.
Usina, John-Sgt. Company B, 2nd Battalion, FLA Infantry
Usina, Michael-Pvt. Company B, 3rd FLA Infantry
Usina, Michael Sanchez-Pvt. Company B, 3rd FLA Infantry
Uvano, J.M.-Pvt. Trevinio's Company, TX Cavalry

V

Valader, Juan Antonio-Pvt. TX Militia
Valdes, Antonio-Pvt. Trevinio's Squad, TX Partisan Mounted Rangers
Valdes, C.L.-Pvt. Company A, 1st Battalion, ALA Cadets
Valdez, Ambrosia-Pvt. Company D, 1st McCulloch's TX Cavalry
Valdez, D.-Pvt. Teel's Company, TX State Troops
Valdez, Emiterio-Pvt. Benavides' Regiment, TX Cavalry
Valdez, Eugenio-Pvt. Company G, 3rd TX Infantry
Valdez, Eulogio-Pvt. Company I, Benavides' Regiment, TX Cavalry
Valdez, Francisco-Pvt. Company C, Benavides' Regiment, TX Cavalry
Valdez, Ignacio-Pvt. Company C, 8th TX Infantry
Valdez, Jose D.-Pvt. Co. 1, 5th (Spanish) Regiment, European Brigade, LA Mil.
Valdez, Jose M.-Pvt. 2nd Company F, 2nd TX Cavalry
Valdez, Jose Maria-Pvt. Company D, 1st McCulloch's TX Cavalry
Valdez, Jose Maria-Pvt. Company H, 8th TX Infantry
Valdez, Juan-Pvt. Company E, 8th TX Infantry
Valdez, Manuel-Pvt. Bustillo's Company, Bexar County, TX Militia
Valdez, Nicanor-Pvt. Company B, 33rd TX Cavalry
Valdez, Santos-Pvt. Company E, 8th TX Infantry
Valencia > see Pons Valencia, A.
Valent, Juan-Pvt. Co. 3, 5th (Spanish) Regiment, European Brigade, LA Militia
Valentin, Oscar-Pvt. 1st Native Guards, LA Militia
Valenzuela, Incarnacion-Pvt. Company G, 3rd TX Infantry
Valiente, Antonio-Pvt. Company 2, Cazadores Espanoles Regiment, LA Militia
***Also listed as Valenciano, Florencio
Valincio, Florencio-Pvt. Oury's Company, Hebert's Battalion, ARIZ Cavalry
Vallasana, Refugio-Cpl. Company F, 3rd TX Infantry
Valle, Alejo-Pvt. Zapata's Company, Nueces County, TX State Troops

Valle, Jorge-Pvt. Co. 8, 5th (Spanish) Regiment, European Brigade, LA Militia
Valle, Silvestre-Pvt. Rhodes' Company, 3rd Battalion, TX Cavalry
Vallejo, Trinidad-Pvt. Bustillo's Company, Bexar County, TX Militia
Valles, Locario-Pvt. Company H, 33rd TX Cavalry
Vallie, Joseph-Pvt. Co. 5, 5th (Spanish) Regiment, European Brigade, LA Militia
Valls, A.R.-Pvt. Company H, 7th LA Infantry
Valls, Bartolome-Pvt. Co. 2, 5th (Spanish) Regt., European Brigade, LA Militia
Valls, G.-Pvt. Co. 1, 5th (Spanish) Regiment, European Brigade, LA Militia
Valores, Joseph-Pvt. Company D, 95th ALA Militia
***See also Balverde
Valverde, John-Pvt. Company E, 1st Yager's TX Cavalry
Valverde, William-Pvt. Company B, Murphy's Battalion, ALA Cavalry
Valverthe, Francisco-Pvt. Company K, 2nd TX Cavalry
Varela > see Barela
Varga, Alexander-Pvt. Company I, 3rd TX Infantry
Varga, Alexander D.-Pvt. 8th Field Battery, TX Artillery
Varga, John-Pvt. Company H, 3rd TX Infantry
Varga, Joseph H.-Sgt. 8th Field Battery, TX Artillery
Varga, Paul-Pvt. Company D, 5th TX Cavalry
***See also Bargus
Vargas, Antonio-Pvt. Medina Guards, Bexar County, TX Militia
Vargas, Benito-Cpl. 1st Company A, Ragsdale's Battalion, TX Cavalry
Vargas, Cristobal-Pvt. Company H, 8th TX Infantry
Vargas, Felipe-Sgt. Company C, 8th TX Infantry
Vargas, Florencio-Pvt. 1st Company A, Ragsdale's Battn., TX Cavalry
Vargas, Geronimo-Pvt. Company B, Ragsdale's Battalion, TX Cavalry
Vargas, Manuel-Pvt. Co. 8, 5th (Spanish) Regiment European Brigade, LA Mil.
Varrera, Jesus-Pvt. Company C, 8th TX Infantry
Varrnea, Victoriano-Pvt. 1st Company A, Ragsdale's Battalion, TX Cavalry
***See also Bascus, Basque, Basques
Vasque, Charles A.F.-Pvt. Paris' Company, VIR Artillery
Vasques, Celso-Pvt. Duran's Company, Atascosa County, TX Troops
Vasquez, Antonio-Pvt. Dunn's Company, Waller's Regiment, TX Cavalry
Vasquez, Cristobal-Pvt. Company H, 8th TX Infantry
Vasquez, Francisco-Pvt. Zapata's Company, Nueces County, TX State Troops
Vasquez, Jose-Pvt. Company C, 8th TX Infantry
Vasquez, Juan-Pvt. Company F, 3rd TX Infantry
Vasquez, Pamfilio-Pvt. Company F, 3rd TX Infantry
Vasquez, Policarpio-Pvt. Company F, 3rd TX Infantry
Vasquez, Saturnino-Pvt. Company H, 33rd TX Cavalry
Vasquez, Serano-Pvt. Company H, 33rd TX Cavalry
Vasquez, Tomas-Pvt. Company D, 3rd TX Infantry
Vasquez, Zacarias-Pvt. Company F, 3rd TX Infantry
Vega, Antoine D. Sr.-Pvt. Barnes' Battery, LA Artillery
Vegas, Agustin-Pvt. LA Militia

Hispanic Confederates 143

Vegas, Alexander B.-Pvt. Squires' Battalion, LA Artillery
Vegas, Antonio-Pvt. Squire's Battalion, LA Artillery
Vegas, Hypolite C.-Pvt. Company H, 28th Grays' LA Infantry
Vegas, James-Pvt. LA Militia
Vegas, John-Pvt. Co. 5, 5th (Spanish) Regiment, European Brigade, LA Militia
Vegas, P.A.-Pvt. Company H, 28th Grays' LA Infantry
Vegas, Paul-Ordnance Department C.S.A. (unknown rank or position).
Vegas, Salvador-Pvt. Co. 6, 5th (Spanish) Regiment, European Brigade, LA Militia
Vego, J.-Pvt. Company B, Chalmette Regiment, LA Militia
Vegua, C.-Pvt. 1st Native Guards, LA Militia
Veigas, Juan-Pvt. Company D, Ragsdale's Battalion, TX Cavalry
Vela, Calisto-Pvt. Zapata's Company, Nueces County, TX State Troops
Vela, Cesilio-2nd Sgt. Minute Men (Scouts), Starr County, TX Militia
Vela, Cristiano-Pvt. Co. 3, 5th (Spanish) Regiment, European Brigade, LA Mil.
Vela, Domingo-Pvt. 1st Company H, 33rd TX Cavalry
Vela, Jesus-Pvt. Company B, 33rd TX Cavalry
Vela, Juan-Pvt. Company A, 3rd Yager's Battalion, TX Cavalry
Vela, Juan-Sgt. Company 5, Cazadores Espanoles Regiment, LA Militia
Vela, Nuncio-Cpl. Company D, Ragsdales' Battalion, TX Cavalry
Vela, Santos-Pvt. Minute Men (Scouts), Starr County, TX Militia
Vela, Severo-Pvt. Company G, Benavides' Regiment, TX Cavalry
Vela, Victor-Pvt. Medina Guards, Bexar County, TX Militia
Vela, Ysidro-Pro Confederate Judge of Zapata County, Texas, who was hung by Pro-Union Mexican Guerillas in December 1862.
Veland, Antonio-Pvt. Company G, Chalmette Regiment, LA Militia
***See also Belasco and Velazco
Velasco, F.-Sgt. Company 1, 5th (Spanish) Regt., European Brigade, LA Militia
Velasco, Faustino-Pvt. Co. 10, 5th (Spanish) Regt., European Brigade, LA Militia
Velasquez, Antonio-Pvt. Company F, 3rd TX Infantry
Velasquez, Jose (1st)-Pvt. Company C, 3rd TX Infantry
Velasquez, Jose Maria (2nd)-Pvt. Company C, 3rd TX Infantry
Velasquez, Loretta Janeta- Disguised as a man, this Cuban woman fought in the Confederate Army at the Battles of Bull Run, Ball's Bluff, and Fort Donelson under the name of Lt. Harry T. Buford. She was wounded, discovered, and discharged; later she worked as a spy and courier for the Confederate Government.
Velasquez, P.-Pvt. Company 7, 1st Chasseurs a pied, LA Militia
Velazco, Tomas-Pvt. Co. 2, 5th (Spanish) Regt., European Brigade, LA Militia
Vella, Eduardo-Pvt. Co. 5, 5th (Spanish) Regiment, European Brigade, LA Militia
Vella, Jose-Pvt. Co. 5, 5th (Spanish) Regiment, European Brigade, LA Militia
Vellarial, Recente-Pvt. Company I, 8th TX Infantry
Vellastrigo, Tomas-Pvt. Company A, Benavides' Regiment, TX Cavalry
Ventura, J.-Pvt. 1st Native Guards, LA Militia
Veque, I.-Pvt. Company 5, Washington Artillery Battalion, LA
Vera, Angelo-Pvt. Company H, 16th TX Infantry
Vera, Eugenio-Pvt. Thomas' Company, TX Partisan Rangers

Vera, Harry-Pvt. Company C, 30th LA Infantry
Vera, Juan-Pvt. Cameron County Coast Guard, TX Militia
Veras, Felipe-Pvt. 4th Field Battery, TX Artillery
Verdella, Charles-Pvt. Company I, 5th LA Infantry
Verdella, L.-Pvt. Gomez's Company, 22nd Consolidated LA Infantry
Verial, Clemento-Pvt. Company E, 8th TX Infantry
Verial, Ecleto-Pvt. Company E, 8th TX Infantry
Verva, Angelo-Pvt. Company H, 16th TX Infantry
Vector, Joseph-Pvt. Company E, 7th LA Cavalry
Viade, Juan-Pvt. Co. 5, 5th (Spanish) Regiment, European Brigade, LA Militia
Viade, R.-Cpl. Company 1, Cazadores Espanoles Regiment, LA Militia
Viade, Tomas-Cpl. Company 2, Cazadores Espanoles Regiment, LA Militia
Vial, Felix-Pvt. LA Militia
Vial, Francisco-Pvt. Medina Guards, Bexar County, TX Militia
Viale, H.-Pvt. Terrebonne Regiment, LA Militia
Viasca, J.-Pvt. Company B, Orleans Guard Regiment, LA Militia
***The surname Viator is the Louisiana French version of the surname Villa Toro.
Viator, Alcide-Pvt. Company F, 7th LA Cavalry
Viator, Alphonse-Pvt. Company G, 7th LA Cavalry
Viator, Andre-Pvt. Saint Martin Parish, LA Militia
Viator, Antoine-Pvt. Company K, 7th LA Cavalry
Viator, Antoine-Pvt. Company C, 10th Battalion, LA Infantry
Viator, Arvillien-Pvt. Company F, 33rd LA Infantry
Viator, Baptiste-Pvt. Company H, 7th LA Cavalry
Viator, Edouard-Pvt. Saint Martin Parish, LA Militia
Viator, Emanuel-Pvt. Company C, 10th Battalion, LA Infantry
Viator, F.-Pvt. Company F, Yellow Jacket Battalion, LA Infantry
Viator, Hervillien-Pvt. Saint Martin Parish, LA Militia
Viator, Joseph-Pvt. Company F, Yellow Jacket Battalion, LA Infantry
Viator, Lasaline-Pvt. Company B, 7th LA Cavalry
Viator, Lasiter-Pvt. Company C, 10th Battalion, LA Infantry
Viator, Louis D.-Pvt. Company C, 10th Battalion, LA Infantry
Viator, Manuel-Pvt. Company C, 10th Battalion, LA Infantry
Viator, Nicholas-Pvt. Company C, 10th Battalion, LA Infantry
Viator, Ozine-Pvt. Company F, 33rd LA Infantry
Viator, Simecourt-Pvt. Company G, 7th LA Cavalry
Viator, Theogene-Pvt. Saint Martin Parish, LA Militia
Viator, Trinecourt-Pvt. Company G, 7th LA Cavalry
Viator, Vileor-Pvt. Company C, 33rd LA Infantry
Viator, William-Pvt. Company C, 10th Battalion, LA Infantry
Vicario, Diego-Cpl. Company D/G, 30th LA Infantry
Vicens, Guillermo-Pvt. Co. 2, 5th (Spanish) Regt., European Brigade, LA Militia
Vicente, John H.-Sgt. Company G, 1st Butler's S.C. Infantry
Vicentine, Felipe-Pvt. Co. 9, 5th (Spanish) Regt., European Brigade, LA Militia
Victori, Martin-Pvt. Co. 10, 5th (Spanish) Regt., European Brigade, LA Militia

Vidal, Adrian J.-Capt. Vidal's Company, TX Cavalry
Vidal, E.-Sgt. Company K, Orleans Guard Regiment, LA Militia
Vidal, F.-Pvt. 1st Native Guards, LA Militia
Vidal, J.F.-Pvt. 1st Native Guards, LA Militia
Vidal, Juan-Pvt. Co. 2, 5th (Spanish) Regiment, European Brigade, LA Militia
Vidal, Juan M.-Pvt. Co. 4, 5th (Spanish) Regiment, European Brigade, LA Militia
Vidal, S.-Pvt. Company 2, 5th (Spanish) Regiment, European Brigade, LA Militia
Vidaurri, Atanacio-2nd Lt. Company I, Benavides' Regiment, TX Cavalry
Vidaurri, Villegas-Pvt. 3rd TX Infantry
Viera, Antonio-Pvt. Company B, 21st ALA Infantry
Vierra, Louis-Pvt. 1st Native Guards, LA Militia
Vienuava, Santiago-Pvt. Company D, Benavides' Regiment, TX Cavalry
Vigil, Antonio Gonzales-Capt. Cuban Rifles, Jackson Rifle Battalion, LA Militia
Vigo, Domingo-1st Sgt. Company B, 24th ALA Infantry
Vigo, Joseph-Pvt. Bridge's Battery, LA Light Artillery
Vigo, Paul Joseph-Pvt. Company F, 1st Special Battalion, Rightor's LA Infantry
Vigo, Paul-Pvt. Fenner's Battery, LA Light Artillery
Vila, Joel-Pvt. 5th (Spanish) Regiment, European Brigade, LA Militia
Vila, Jose-Pvt. Co. 7, 5th (Spanish) Regiment, European Brigade, LA Militia
Vila, M.-Pvt. Company 1, 5th (Spanish) Regiment, European Brigade, LA Mil.
Vila, Santiago-Pvt. Co. 3, 5th (Spanish) Regiment, European Brigade, LA Militia
Villa, Eduardo-1st Lt. Co. 6, 5th (Spanish) Regt., European Brigade, LA Militia
Villa, George-Pvt. Company H, 22nd Consolidated LA Infantry
Villa, J.-Pvt. Company 3, 3rd Regiment, French Brigade, LA Militia
Villa, J.-Pvt. Company E, 22nd Consolidated LA Infantry
Villa, J.L.-Pvt. Company H, Chalmette Regiment, LA Militia
Villa, Jesus-Pvt. 8th TX Field Battery
Villa, Jose-Sgt. Co. 6, 5th (Spanish) Regiment, European Brigade, LA Militia
Villa, Joseph-Pvt. Company I, 1st LA Heavy Artillery
Villa, T.-Pvt. Company A, 1st LA Cavalry
Villa, Thomas-Pvt. Company E, 22nd Consolidated LA Infantry
Villa, V.-Pvt. Baas' Company, 1st Regiment Mobile Volunteers, ALA Militia
Villalobos, Julio-Pvt. Zapata's Company, Nueces County, TX State Troops
Villalonga, John L.-Major / Commissary Department, C.S.A
Villalonga, Julius A.-Pvt. Company F, 7th GA Infantry
Villannes, Jose-Pvt. Co. A, 5th (Spanish) Regiment, European Brigade, LA Mil.
Villanueva, Antonio-Pvt. Company D, 30th LA Infantry
Villanueva, Anastacio-Pvt. Bustillo's Company, Bexar County, TX Militia
Villanueva, Andres-Pvt. Trevino's Company, TX Partisan Rangers
Villanueva, Candelario-Pvt. Company F, 3rd TX Infantry
Villanueva, Felix-Pvt. Skidmore's Company, San Patricio County, TX Militia
Villanueva, Flario-Pvt. Co. A, 5th (Spanish) Regt., European Brigade, LA Militia
Villanueva, Santiago-Pvt. Company F, 3rd TX Infantry
Villar, Augustus-Pvt. Company A, 2nd FLA Infantry
Villar, Jose-Cpl. Co. 3, 5th (Spanish) Regiment, European Brigade, LA Militia

Villar, Martin-Pvt. Company C, 40th TENN Infantry
Villarana, Felipe P.-Bugler Company F, 5th LA Infantry
Villareal, Andres-Pvt. Trevinio's Squad, TX Partisan Mounted Volunteers
Villareal, Antonio(1st)-Pvt. Company F, 3rd TX Infantry
Villareal, Antonio(2nd)-Pvt. Company C, 8th TX Infantry
Villareal, Cesilio-Cpl. 1st Company 1, 33rd TX Cavalry
Villareal, Clemente-Pvt. Company E, 8th TX Infantry
Villareal, Cleofas-Pvt. Company C, 8th TX Infantry
Villareal, Cresencio-Pvt. Bustillo's Company, Bexar County, TX Militia
Villareal, Feliciana-5th Sgt. Company I, Benavides' Regiment, TX Cavalry
Villareal, Gregorio-Pvt. Minute Men (Scouts), Starr County, TX Militia
Villareal, Indelacio-Pvt. 1st Company H, 33rd TX Cavalry
Villareal, Martin-Pvt. Company F, 3rd TX Infantry
Villareal, Manuel-Pvt. Cameron County Coast Guard, TX Militia
Villareal, Onesimo-Pvt. Company I, 8th TX Infantry
Villareal, Ventura-Pvt. Company A, 3rd TX Infantry
Villareal, Vicente-Pvt. Company I, 8th TX Infantry
Villarial, Nasario-Pvt. Company I, 8th TX Infantry
Villarubia, E.-1st Sgt. Guyol's Company, Orleans Artillery, LA
Villarubia, J.-Ordnance Sgt. Guyol's Company, Orleans Artillery, LA
Villasana, Frank P.-Bugler Company 1, Washington Artillery Battalion, LA
Villasana, Refugio-Cpl. Company F, 3rd TX Infantry
Villastrigo, Tomas-Pvt. 1st Company H, 33rd TX Cavalry
Villato, J.-Pvt. Company A, Miles' Legion, LA
Villavaro, E.-Pvt. Company B/F, Orleans Guard Regiment, LA Militia
Villavaro, J.E.-4th Cpl. Company B, Orleans Guard Regiment, LA Militia
Villavaro, L.-Pvt. Company B, Orleans Guard Regiment, LA Militia
Villavaso, A.E.-Pvt. 5th Field Battery, LA Artillery
Villavaso, Alfred-Pvt. Company E, Saint James Regiment, LA Militia
Villavaso, Augustin-Pvt. Company K, Saint James Regiment, LA Militia
Villavaso, Emile-Pvt. Company A/D, Manigault's Battalion, S.C. Artillery
Villavaso, Joseph Martin-Cpl. Company A/D, Manigault's Battn., S.C. Artillery
Villavaso, Martin-Pvt. Delery's Co., Saint Bernard Horse Rifles, LA Militia
Villavaso, N.-Pvt. 6th Field Battery, LA Light Artillery
Villavaso, Paul-Pvt. 5th Field Battery, LA Artillery
Villa y Alvarez, J.-Pvt. Co. 1, 5th (Spanish) Regt., European Brigade, LA Militia
Villa y Columbo, J.-Pvt. Co. 1, 5th (Spanish) Regt., European Brigade, LA Mil.
Villegas, Fernando-Pvt. Co. 4, 5th (Spanish) Regt., European Brigade, LA Militia
Villegas, Jose-Pvt. Co. 3, 5th (Spanish) Regiment, European Brigade, LA Militia
Villegas, R.-Pvt. 1st Company A, Ragsdale's Battalion, TX Cavalry
Villero, Federico-Pvt. Co. 4, 5th (Spanish) Regiment, European Brigade, LA Mil.
Vines, Louis-Pvt. Company 5, Cazadores Espanoles Regiment, LA Militia
Vinet, Antonio-Pvt. Co. 4, 5th (Spanish) Regiment, European Brigade, LA Mil.
Viosca, Joachin Jr.-Capt. Company H, Orleans Guard Regiment, LA Militia
Viosca, Joachin-Pvt. Co. 5, 5th (Spanish) Regiment, European Brigade, LA Mil.

Viosca, Ramon-Pvt. Co. 2, 5th (Spanish) Regiment, European Brigade, LA Militia
Vitela, Feliz-Pvt. Company C, 8th TX Infantry
Vitela, Severo-Pvt. Company C, 8th TX Infantry
Vives, Damian-Pvt. Co. 2, 5th (Spanish) Regiment, European Brigade, LA Militia
Vives, Edouard-1st Lt. Company H, 28th Thomas' LA Infantry
Vives, Geronimo-Pvt. Co. 2, 5th (Spanish) Regt., European Brigade, LA Militia
Vives, Hypolite-Pvt. Company H, 2nd LA Cavalry
Vives, Joseph-Pvt. Company I, 2nd LA Cavalry
Vives, Juan M.-Pvt. Company 2, Cazadores Espanoles Regiment, LA Militia

W

*** The 2 brothers listed below were the natural children of Santiago Arevallo and Antoinette Toures Wallet
Wallet, Jean Baptiste-Pvt. Company K, 16th LA Infantry
Wallet, Silvere-Pvt. Company D, 1st LA Heavy Artillery

X

***See also Hemanus, Gimenez and Jimenez
Xamenes, Antonio L.-Pvt. Company D, 8th FLA Infantry
Xemenes, (no 1st name)-Pvt. Company 1, 1st Chasseurs a pied, LA Militia
Ximenes, I.-Pvt. 2nd Field Battery, LA Light Artillery
Ximenes, Juan-Pvt. Trevinio's Company, TX Cavalry
Ximenes, Jesus-Pvt. Company F, 3rd TX Infantry
Ximenes, Jose-Cpl. Co. 9, 5th (Spanish) Regiment, European Brigade, LA Militia
Ximenes, Monico-Pvt. Company F, 3rd TX Infantry
Ximenes, Rafael-Pvt. Rhodes' Company, 3rd Yager's Battalion, TX Cavalry
Ximenes, Raphael F.-Pvt. 3rd FLA Infantry
Ximenes, Ramon-Sgt. Company G, 10th LA Infantry
Ximenes, Trinidad-Pvt. TX Militia
Ximenes, Wennseslao-Cpl. Company F, 3rd TX Infantry
Ximenez, Francisco-Pvt. Company D, 30th LA Infantry
Ximenez, Mariana-Pvt. Company D, Ragsdale's Battalion, TX Cavalry

Y

Yaguina, Jose-Pvt. Company I, Benavides' TX Cavalry
Yarrito, Jesus-Sgt. 1st Company C, 3rd TX Infantry
***See also Ibanes
Ybanes, Angel G.-Pvt. Company B, 63rd GA Infantry
Ybanes, Francisco-Pvt. Co. 3, 5th (Spanish) Regt., European Brigade, LA Militia
Ybanes, Jose Maria-Pvt. Zapata's Company, Nueces County, TX State Troops
*** See also Barbo, E'Barbo, Yebarbo / Many of the Louisiana men were from the Adaeseno settlements.

Ybarbo, Hose-Pvt. Company A, 11th TX Infantry
Ybarbo, J.F.-Pvt. Company A, 2nd LA Infantry
Ybarbo, John-Pvt. Company A, 11th TX Infantry
Ybarbo, Jose-Pvt. Company A, 11th TX Infantry
Ybarbo, Jose-Pvt. 4th Field Battery, TX Artillery
Ybarbo, L.-Pvt. Maddox's Regiment, LA Reserve Corps
Ybarbo, Leon-Sgt. Company E, 8th TX Infantry
Ybarbo, Martin-Pvt. Maddox's Regiment, LA Reserve Corps
Ybarbo, Navele-Pvt. Company A, 11th TX Infantry
Ybarbo, Patricio-Pvt. Company A, 11th TX Infantry
Ybarbo, Pierre-Pvt. Company A, 3rd LA Infantry
Ybarbo, Richard-Pvt. Company A, 11th TX Infantry
Ybarbo, Vital-Pvt. Company A, 11th TX Infantry
Ybarbo, Votal-Pvt. Company G, 37th TX Infantry
***See also Ibara, Ibarra, Yvarra
Ybarra, J.-Pvt. Company 7, 1st Chasseurs a pied, LA Militia
Ybarra, Jose Maria-Pvt. Company D, 30th LA Infantry
Ybarra, Pedro-Pvt. Company B, 3rd Wingfield's LA Cavalry
Ybarra, T.M.-Pvt. Company D, 30th LA Infantry
Yebarbo, Cevero-Pvt. Company B, 2nd LA Cavalry
Yerto, Jesus-Sgt. Company C, 3rd TX Infantry
Ybarzabal, Miguel-2nd Lt. Co. 10, 5th (Spanish) Regt., European Brig., LA Mil.
***See also Iglesias
Yglesias, Francisco-Pvt. Co. 3, 5th (Spanish) Regt., European Brigade, LA Mil.
Yglessias, Crisanto-Pvt. Co. 2, 5th (Spanish) Regt., European Brigade, LA Mil.
***See also Ignacio
Ygnasio, Cesar-Pvt. Co. 4, 5th (Spanish) Regiment, European Brigade, LA Mil.
Ygues, Carlos-Pvt. Co. 6, 5th (Spanish) Regiment, European Brigade, LA Militia
Ylanio, Zais-Pvt. Company I, Benavides' Regiment, TX Cavalry
Ynacio, Gregorio-Pvt. Co. A, 5th (Spanish) Regt., European Brigade, LA Militia
Yniestra, A.T.-Pvt. Company D, 2nd Regiment Volunteers, ALA Militia
Yniestra, Bruno F.-Lt. Colonel Company B, 62nd ALA Infantry
Yniestra, Gregory D.-1st Lt. New Company A, 1st FLA Infantry. He was also Assistant
    Adjutant and Inspector General to General B.M. Thomas.
Yniestra, John M.-Pvt. Company B, 3rd Battalion, FLA Cavalry
Yniestra, Moses G.-1st Lt. Company B, 62nd ALA Infantry
Ynsua, Luis-Pvt. Co. 2, 5th (Spanish) Regiment, European Brigade, LA Militia
Yrguiano, J.-Cpl. Co. 1, 5th (Spanish) Regiment, European Brigade, LA Militia
Yturri, Manuel-Capt. Company F, 3rd TX Infantry
Yufante, D. Manuel-Capt. Co. 2, Cazadores Espanoles Regiment, LA Militia
Yulee, Elias Levy-Capt. / Assistant Commissary, Staff of General J.H. Trapier
Yvarra, Santos-Pvt. Minute Men (Scouts), Starr County, TX Militia
Yvarro, Matias-Pvt. Company B, Ragsdale's Battalion, TX Cavalry
Yzanaga, J.M.-Pvt. Red River Sharpshooters, LA Militia

Z

Zacarias, S.-Pvt. Company G, Charleston Guards, 1st S.C. Infantry
***See also Sagarras
Zagarra, Ramon-Pvt. Co. 9, 5th (Spanish) Regt., European Brigade, LA Militia
Zambrano, Jose-Pvt. Gray's Company, Bexar County, TX Militia
***See also Semorah and Seymour
Zamora, Antonio-Pvt. Company F, 3rd TX Infantry
Zamora, Antonio-Pvt. Company K, 6th TX Infantry
Zamora, Deciderio-Pvt. Company G, 3rd TX Infantry
Zamora, Eltameriado-Pvt. Rhodes' Company, 3rd Yager's Battalion, TX Cavalry
Zamora, Francisco-Pvt. Rhodes' Company, 3rd Yager's Battalion, TX Cavalry
Zamora, Gregorio-Pvt. Company C, 8th TX Infantry
Zamora, Joaquin-Pvt. Cameron County Coast Guard, TX Militia
Zamora, John-Pvt. 1st Native Guards, LA Militia
Zapata, Charles-Pvt. Guyol's Company, Orleans Artillery, LA
Zapata, Clemente-Capt. Zapata's Company, Nueces County, TX State Troops
Zapata, Jesus-Pvt. Gray's Company, Bexar County, TX Militia
Zapata, Marcial-Pvt. TX Militia
Zarate, Vicente-Pvt. Company F, 3rd TX Infantry
***See also Sarsa
Zarza, J. Fernandez-Cpl. Co. 1, 5th (Spanish) Regt., European Brigade, LA Mil.
Zataran, Jules-Pvt. Beauregard Battalion, LA Militia
Zavala, Ricardo-Pvt. Company K, 26th TX Cavalry
Zedelas, H.-Cpl. Company H, 7th LA Infantry
***See also Sepeda
Zepeda, Antonio-Pvt. 1st Company C, Ragsdale's Battalion, TX Cavalry
Zepeda, Gabino-Pvt. Gray's Company, Bexar County, TX Militia
Zepeda, Manuel-Pvt. Gray's Company, Bexar County, TX Militia
Zepeda, Remigio-Pvt. Company B, Benavides' Regiment, TX Cavalry
Zepeda, Romelo-Sgt. 1st Company C, Ragsdale's Battalion, TX Cavalry
Zertuche, Hernando-Pvt. Company K, 12th TX Infantry
Zertuche, Miguel-Sgt. Benavides' Regiment, TX Cavalry
Zevallos > see Cevallos, Sevallos, De Zevallos
***See also Sierra
Zierra, Juas-Pvt. Company E, Benavides' Regiment, TX Cavalry
Zotello, Antonio-Pvt. 1st Company H, 33rd TX Cavalry
Zotello, Ignacio-Pvt. Tom's Company, Atascosa County, TX Militia
***See also Suniga
Zuniga, Santiago-Pvt. 1st Company C, 3rd TX Infantry

BIBLIOGRAPHY OF PRIMARY AND SECONDARY SOURCES

Armistead, Samuel G. *The Spanish Tradition in Louisiana*. Newark, Delaware: Juan de la Cuesta, Hispanic Monographs.

Arthur, Stanley Clisby, and George Cambell Huchet De Kernion. *Old Families of Louisiana*. Reprint. Baltimore, Maryland: Clearfield Company, 1997.

Bartlett, Napier. *Military Record of Louisiana 1875*. Reprint. Louisiana: L.S.U. Press., 1964.

Bergeron, Arthur W., Jr. *Confederate Mobile*. Jackson, Mississippi: Univ. Press of Mississippi, 1991.

_____. *Guide to Louisiana Confederate Military Units 1861–1865*. Baton Rouge Louisiana: L.S.U. Press, 1989.

Birmingham, Stephen. *The Grandees: America's Sephardic Elite*. New York, New York: Harper and Row, 1971.

Boatner, Mark M. *Civil War Dictionary*. Rev. ed. David McKay and Co., 1987.

Booth, Andrew B. *Records of Louisiana Confederate Soldiers and Louisiana. Confederate Commands*. 3 Vols. New Orleans, Louisiana: 1920.

Brock, R. A. *The Appomattox Roster*. Reprint. New York, New York: Antiquarian Press, 1962.

Church of Jesus Christ of Latter-Day Saints Family History Center, Mobile, Alabama.

Coker, William S. *The Mobile Cadets 1845–1945*. Bagdad, Florida: Patagonia Press, 1993.

Crute, Joseph H., Jr. *Units of the Confederate States Army*. Midlothian, Virginia: Derwent Books, 1987.

Dauzat, A. *Dictionnaire Des Noms de Famille et Prenoms de France*. Paris: Librarie LaRousse, 1951.

DeVarona, Frank. *Hispanic Presence in the United States*. Mnemosyne Publishing, 1993.

Din, Gilbert C., and John E. Harkins. *The New Orleans Cabildo, Colonial Louisiana's First City Government 1769–1803*. Baton Rouge, Louisiana: L.S.U. Press, 1996.

Donnelly, Ralph W. *The Confederate States Marine Corps*. White Mane Publishing, 1989.

Dorman, Beth, and Emily Dorman. *Taxpayers of the Republic of Texas*. Beth and Emily Dorman, 1988

Dormon, James H., ed. *Creoles of Color of the Gulf South*. University of Tennessee Press, 1996.

Elzas, Barnett A. *The Jews of South Carolina*. Philadelphia, Pennsylvania: J. B. Lippincott, 1905.

Florida State Archives. All Confederate Pension Records and Applications.

Gayarre, Charles. *History of Louisiana: The Spanish Dominion*. Vol. 3. New Orleans, Louisiana: F. F. Hansell and Bro., 1903.

Gilbert, Charles E. *A Concise History of Early Texas*. Houston, Texas: 1964.

Griffm, Patricia C. *Mullet on the Beach: The Minorcans of Florida 1768–1788*. Jacksonville, Florida: St. Augustine Historical Society University of North Florida Press, 1991.

Hamilton, Peter J. *Colonial Mobile*. Boston and New York: Houghton Mifllin, 1898.

Hewet, Janet B. *The Roster of Confederate Soldiers 1861–1 865*. 16 Vols. Wilmington, North Carolina: Broadfoot Pub., 1995.

Holcornb, Brent H. *South Carolina Naturalizations 1783–1850*. Baltimore, Maryland: Genealogical Publishing Co. Inc., 1985.

Hollandhvorth James G., Jr. *The Louisiana Native Guards*. L.S.U. Press, 1995.

Holmes, Jack D. L. *Honor and Fidelity: The Louisiana Infantry Regiment and the Louisiana Militia Companies 1766–1821*. Birmingham, Alabama: 1965.

Ingmire, Frances and Carolyn Ericson. *Confederate P.O.W.'s*. Nacodoches, Texas: Ericson Books, 1984.. St. Louis, Missouri: Ingmire Pub., 1984.

Isern, Jose. *Pioneros Cubanos en U.S.A. 1575–1898*. Miami, Florida: Cenit Printing, 1971.

Kein, Sybil. *Creole: The History and Legacy of Louisiana Free People of Color*. Baton Rouge, Louisiana: L.S.U. Press, 2000.

Kom, Bertram Wallace. *The Early Jews of New Orleans*. The American Jewish Historical Society, 1969.

_____. *The Jews of Mobile Alabama 1763–1841*. Cincinnati, Ohio: Hebrew Union College Press, 1970.

Lipski, John M. *The Language of the Islenos: Vestigial Spanish in Louisiana*. Baton Rouge, Louisiana: L.S.U. Press., 1990.

Lonn, Ella. *Foreigners in the Confederacy*. Chapel Hill: University of North Carolina Press, 1940.

Louisiana State Archives. All Confederate Pension Records.

MacCurdy, Raymond R. *The Spanish Dialect in St. Bernard Parish, Louisiana*. Alburquerque, New Mexico: University of New Mexico Press, 1950.

Marchand, Sidney A. *Forgotten Fighters 1861–1865*. Donaldsonville, LA: 1966.

Martin, Fountaine. *A History of the Bouligny Family and Allied Families*. The Center for Louisiana Studies, University of Southwestern Louisiana, 1990.

McConnell, Roland C. Free Negro Troops of Antebellum Louisiana. Baton Rouge, Louisiana: L.S.U. Press, 1968.

Mills, Donna Rachal. *Florida's First Families*. Tuscaloosa, Alabama, and Naples, Florida: Mills Historical Press.

Mobile Public Library, Local History and Genealogy Section, Mobile, Alabama.

"Confederate Soldiers" Microfilm: Alabama, Mississippi, and Georgia (all Rolls).

'Mobile Companies in the Civil War" Compendium.

U.S. War Department. (1880–1901) *War of the Rebellion*. "Official Records of Union and Confederate Armies. (128 parts in 70 vols). U.S. Government Printing Office.

Fort Gaines and Fort Morgan Collections.

U.S. War Department. (1894) Official Records of the Union and Confederate Navies. Series I, 27 Vols. Series II, 3 Vols.

Mobile City Directories, 1861 and 1866.

Naturalization in the Courts of Mobile County, Alabama, 1833–1907.

Municipal and Court Records, Project of the W.P.A., undated.

Montero De Pedro, Jose. *The Spanish in New Orleans and Louisiana*. Gretna, Louisiana: Pelican Publishing Company, 2000.

National Park Service. *Confederate Soldier Rosters and Unit Rosters for all Confederate States,* found in Civil War Soldiers and Sailors System.

Neagles, James C. *U.S. Military Records*. Salt L,ake City, Utah: Ancestry, 1994.

Oakley, Peggy. *Index to Applications for Texas Confederate Pensions*. Rev. Ed. Austin, Texas: Archives Division, Texas State Library, 1997.

Pearce, George F. *Pensacola During the Civil War*. Gainsville, Florida: University of Florida Press, 2000.

Platt, Lyman D. *Hispanic Surnames and Family History*. Baltimore, Maryland: Genealogical Publishing, 1996.

Quinn, Jane. *Minorcans in Florida: Their History and Heritage*. St. Augustine, Florida: Mission Press, 1975.

Register of Officers of the Confederate States Navy 1861–1 865. Washington D.C.: United States Printing Office, 1931.

Reinders, Robert C. *Militia in New Orleans 1853–1861*. Vol. 3, No. 1 of *Louisiana History* (33–42): 1962.

Rietti, J.C. *Military Annals of Mississippi*. Jackson, Mississippi: 1895.

Robertson, Frederick L. *Soldiers of Florida in the Seminole Indian, Civil and Spanish American Wars*. Live Oak, Florida: Democrat Book and Job Print., 1909

Rosen, Robert N. *The Jewish Confederates*. Columbia, South Carolina: University of South Carolina Press, 2000.

Sally, Alexander Samuel. *South Carolina Troops in Confederate Service*. 3 Vols. Columbia, South Carolina: The State Company, 1913–1930.

Sistler, Byron. *1890 Civil War Veterans Census: Tennessee*. Evaston, Illinois: 1978.

Texas State Archives: Medina Guards, Jeff Davis Home Guard, Grey Town Pioneers Rosters. Also all other Texas Militia Rosters, as per those mentioned in the book. When contacting them, refer to the Unit name for the specific roster or for the specific name of the individual for his particular record. Some of the muster rolls used are numbered as follows and correspond to specific counties and units: #6, #157, #249, #259, #279, #626, #631, #649, #796, #966, #967, #1486, #1556.

Thompson, Jeny Don. *Vaqueros in Blue and Gray*. Austin, Texas: Presidial Press, 1976.

Villere, Sidney Louis. *The Canary Islands Migration to Louisiana 1778–1783*. New Orleans, Louisiana: 1971.

White, Virgil D. *Register of Florida C.S.A. Pension Applications*. Waynesboro, Tennessee: The National Historical Publishing Company, 1989.

Wittshire, Betty C. *Mississippi Confederate Pension Applications A to Z*. 3 Vols. Corrolton, Mississippi: Pioneer Publishing Co., n.d.

Wolf, Simon. *The American Jew as Patriot Soldier and Citizen*. Philadelphia, Pennsylvania: The Levytype Company Publishers, 1895.

www.ingramcontent.com/pod-product-compliance
Lightning Source LLC
Chambersburg PA
CBHW070944230426
43666CB00011B/2555